# GREAT MEN OF THE BIBLE

# GREAT MEN OF THE BIBLE

### F.B. MEYER

Marshall
Pickering

William Collins Sons & Co. Ltd
London · Glasgow · Sydney · Auckland
Toronto · Johannesburg

First published in Great Britain in 1990 by Marshall Pickering

Marshall Pickering is an imprint of the Collins Religious Division, part of the Collins Publishing Group, 8 Grafton Street, London W1X 3LA

Copyright © 1990 Marshall Pickering

Printed and bound in Great Britain by William Collins Sons & Co. Ltd, Glasgow

# Contents

# ABRAHAM

# 1

# The Hole of the Pit

*Acts 7:2–3 and Isaiah 51:1–2*

In the grey dawn of history the first great character that arrests our attention at any length is that of Abraham, if for nothing else than that he is spoken of as the 'Friend of God'.

Our story takes us back two thousand years before the birth of Christ, and to the ancient city of Ur. We must look for Ur not in Upper Mesopotamia, where a mistaken tradition has fixed it, but in the ruins of Mugheir, in the near vicinity of the Persian Gulf. Forty centuries, slowly silting up the shore, have driven the sea back about a hundred miles. But at the time of which we speak it is probable that Abraham's natal city stood on the coast near the spot where the Euphrates poured the volume of its waters into the ocean waves.

Chaldaea was a long green strip of garden land, sufficient to attract and maintain vast populations of men, and specially suitable for the settlement of those shepherd tribes that required extensive pasture lands for their herds and flocks.

These sons of Ham were grossly *idolatrous*. In that clear atmosphere, the heavenly bodies blazed with extraordinary effulgence, beguiling the early Chaldaeans into a system of nature-worship, which speedily became identified with rites of gross indulgence and impurity, and it was evident that some expedient must be speedily adopted to arrest the progress of moral defilement and to save mankind. This enterprise was undertaken by him who later could say, with majestic emphasis, 'Before Abraham was, I AM.' And he accomplished his purpose then, as so often since, by *separating* to himself one man, so that through him and his descendants, when they had been thoroughly purified and

9

prepared, he might operate on the fallen race of man, recalling it to himself and elevating it by a moral lever, working on a pivot outside itself.

Terah had settled down on the rich pasture lands outside Ur. The walled cities, civilized arts, and merchant traffic had little attraction for them; for they were a race of shepherds, living in tents, or in villages of slightly-constructed huts.

Amid such scenes Abraham was born and when he was grown up the God of glory appeared to him. In what form of glory Jehovah revealed himself we cannot guess, but we must believe that there was some outward manifestation that dated an epoch in Abraham's life, and gave him unmistakable basis of belief for all his future. The celestial vision was accompanied by a call, like that which in all ages of the world has come to loyal hearts, summoning them to awake to their true destiny, and take their place in the regeneration of the world: 'Get thee out of thy country, and from thy kindred, and from thy father's house, unto the land that I will show thee' (Gen. 12:1).

Despair not for the future of the world. Out of its heart will yet come those who shall lift it up to a new level. Sauls are being trained in the bosom of the Sanhedrin; Luthers in the cloisters of the church; Abrahams under the shadows of great heathen temples. God knows where to find them. And, when the times are darkest, they shall lead forth a host of pilgrim spirits, numberless as the sand on the seashore; or as the stardust, lying thick through the illimitable expanse of space.

# 2

# The Divine Summons

## Genesis 12:1–2

While Abraham was living quietly in Ur, 'The God of glory appeared unto him, and said, Get thee out of thy country, and from thy kindred, and come into the land which I shall show thee' (Acts 7:2–3).

When this divine appearance came we do not know; but suddenly there shone from heaven a great light round about Abraham, and a visible form appeared in the heart of the glory, and a voice spoke the message of heaven in his ear. God doesn't speak to us in that way now, and yet it is certain that he still speaks in the silence of the waiting spirit, impressing his will, and saying, 'Get thee out.' Listen for that voice in the inner shrine of your heart.

### 1 This call involved hardship

It was no small matter for Abraham to break up his camp, to tear himself from his nearest and dearest, and to start for a land which, as yet, he did not know.

And so must it always be. We must be prepared to take up our cross daily if we would follow where he points the way. Each step of real advance in the divine life will involve an altar on which some dear fragment of the self-life has been offered.

Nothing is more clear than that, in these critical days, God is summoning the whole church to a great advance.

### 2 But this call was eminently wise

It was wise for *Abraham himself*. Nothing strengthens us so much as isolation and transplantation. Let a young man emigrate, or be put into a responsible position; let him be thrown on his own resources, and he will develop powers of which there would have been no trace, if he had always lived at home, dependent on others. Under the wholesome demand his soul will put forth all her native vigour.

But what is true of the natural qualities of the soul is pre-eminently true of faith. So long as we are quietly at rest amid favourable and undisturbed surroundings, faith sleeps as an undeveloped sinew within us. But when we are pushed out from all these surroundings, with nothing but God to look to, then faith grows suddenly into a giant oak, a master principle of life.

As long as the bird lingers by the nest, it will not know the luxury of flight. As long as the trembling boy holds to the bank, or toes the bottom, he will not learn the ecstasy of battling with the ocean wave. Abram could never have become Abraham, the father of the faithful, the mighty exemplar of faith, if he had always lived in Ur. No; he had to journey forth into the untried and unknown, so that faith could rise up to all its glorious proportions in his soul.

It may not be necessary for us to withdraw from home and friends; but we shall have to withdraw our heart's deepest dependence from all earthly props and supports, if we are ever to learn what it is to trust simply and absolutely on the eternal God.

## 3   This call was accompanied by a promise

God's commands are not always accompanied by reasons, but always by promises, expressed or understood.

It may seem that the hardships involved in the summons to exile are too great to be borne; yet study well the promise that is attached. And as the 'City which hath foundations' looms on the view, it will dwarf the proportions of the Ur in which you have been content to spend your days.

St Francis de Sales used to say, 'When the house is on fire, men are ready to throw everything out of the window; and when the heart is full of God's true love, men are sure to count all else but worthless.'

## 4   This call teaches us the meaning of election

Everywhere we find beings and things more loftily endowed than others of the same kind. There is at first a jarring wonder at the apparent inequality of the divine arrangements; until we understand that the superior endowment of the few is intended to enable them the better to help and bless the rest. 'I will bless thee, and thou shalt be a blessing.' Is this not a glimpse into the intention of God in selecting Abraham, and in him the whole family of Israel? It was not so much with a view to their personal salvation, though that was included; but that they might pass on the holy teachings and oracles with which they were entrusted. It was needful that definitions and methods of expression should be first well learned by the people, who, when they had learned them, might become the teachers of mankind. There is no need to envy God's elect ones.

## 5   This call gives the key to Abraham's life

It rang a clarion note at the very outset, which continued to vibrate through all his history. The key to Abraham's life is the word 'separation.' He was from first to last a separated man. Separated from his fatherland and kinsfolk; separated from Lot; separated, as a pilgrim and stranger, from the people of the land; separated from the rest of mankind by special sorrows, which brought him into closer fellowship with God than has ever been reached by man; separated to high and lofty fellowship in thoughts and plans, which God could not hide from him.

3

# The First of the Pilgrim Fathers

## *Genesis 12:4–9*

All through the history of mankind there has been a little band of men, in a sacred and unbroken succession, who have confessed that they were pilgrims and strangers upon earth. Sometimes they are found afar from the haunts of men, wandering in deserts and in mountains, dwelling in the dens and caves of the earth. But often they are to be found in the market places and homes of the men, distinguished only by their simpler dress, their girded loins, their restrained and abstemious appetite, their loose hold on gold, their independence of the maxims and opinions and applause of the world around, and the faraway look that now and again gleams in their eyes, the certain evidence of affections centred, not on the transitory things of time and earth, but on those eternal realities which, lying beneath the veil of the visible, are revealed only to faith.

These are the pilgrims. For them the annoyances and trials of life are not so crushing or so difficult to bear, because such things as these cannot touch their true treasure, or affect their real interest. They are children of a sublimer realm. The pilgrim has no other desire than to pass quickly over the appointed route to his home, fulfilling the duties, meeting the claims, and discharging faithfully the responsibilities devolving on him, but ever remembering that here he has no continuing city, and seeks one which is to come.

The Apostle Peter wrote to scattered strangers (1 Peter 1:1), and reminded them *as strangers and pilgrims* to abstain from fleshly lusts. And long before that day, in the sunniest period of Jewish prosperity, David, in the name of his people, confessed that they were *strangers and sojourners as were all their fathers.*

We left the patriarch moving leisurely southward, and thus he continued to journey through the land of promise, making no permanent halt, until he reached the place of Sichem, or Schechem, in the very heart of the land where our Lord years later sat and rested by the well. There was no city or settlement there then. The country was sparsely populated. The only thing that marked the site was a venerable oak. Beneath this oak on the plain of Sichem, the camp was pitched; and there, at last, the long silence was broken, the silence which had lasted since the first summons was spoken in Chaldaea, 'And the Lord appeared unto Abram, and said, Unto thy seed will I give this land: and there builded he an altar unto the Lord, who appeared unto him' (Gen. 12:7).

He did not stay there permanently, however, but moved a little to the south, to a place between Bethel and Ai, where there is now a high and beautiful plain, presenting one of the finest tracts of pasturage in the whole country.

Three things can engage our thought here: the Tent, the Altar, and the Promise.

## 1   The tents

When Abraham left Haran his age was seventy-five. When he died he was one hundred and seventy-five years old. And he spent that intervening century moving to and fro, dwelling in a frail and flimsy tent, probably of dark camel's hair. And that tent was only a befitting symbol of the spirit of his life.

He held himself aloof from the people of the land. He did not stay in any permanent location, but was ever on the move. The tent which had no foundations, which could be erected and struck in half-an-hour, was the apt symbol of his life.

To the end he dwelt in a tent. It was from a tent that he was carried to lie beside Sarah in Machpelah's rocky cave. 'Abraham dwelt in tents, because he looked for the city which hath the foundations' (Heb. 11:9–10, ASV). The tent life is the natural one for those who feel that their fatherland lies beyond the stars.

It is of the utmost importance that the children of God should live this detached life as a testimony to the world. How will people believe us, when we talk about our hope, if our hope does not pull us from excessive devotion to the things around us?

We must not go on as we are. Professing Christians are too much taken up in business cares, in pleasure seeking, in luxury, and self-indulgence. There is little difference between the children of the kingdom and the children of this generation.

Yet how is it to be altered? Shall we denounce the present practice? Shall we inveigh against the reckless worldliness of the times? This will not affect a permanent cure. Let us rather paint with glowing colours that city that John saw. Let us unfold the glories of that world to which we are bound, and surely there will come into many a life a separateness of heart and walk that will impress men with the reality of the unseen, as no sermon could no, however learned or eloquent.

## 2  The Altar

Wherever Abraham pitched his tent, he built an altar. And long after the tent was shifted, the altar stood to show where the man of God had been.

Let us also remember that the altar means sacrifice, whole burnt offering, self-denial, and self-surrender. In this sense the altar and the tent must ever go together. We cannot live the detached tent-life without some amount of pain and suffering, such as the altar bespeaks. But it is out of such a life that there spring the most intense devotion, the deepest fellowship, the happiest communion.

If your private prayer has been lately hindered, it may be that you have not been living enough in the tent. Confess that you are a stranger and a pilgrim on the earth; and you will find it pleasant and natural to call on the name of the Lord. We do not read of Abraham building an altar so long as he dwelt in Charran; he could not have fellowship with God while living in open disobedience to him.

But Abraham's altar was not for himself alone. At certain periods the whole clan gathered there for common worship. 'I know Abraham', said God, 'that he will command his children and his household after him' (Gen. 18:19). He, in whom all families of the earth were to be blessed, practiced family religion; and in this he sets a striking example to many Christians whose homes are altarless.

## 3    The Promise

'Unto thy seed will I give this land' (Gen. 12:7). As soon as Abraham had fully obeyed, this new promise broke upon his ear. And it is ever thus. Disobey – and you tread a path unlit by a single star. Obey, live up to the claims of God – and successive promises beam out from heaven to light your steps, each one richer and fuller than the one before. The separated pilgrim life always acquires promises.

There was no natural probability of that promise being fulfilled because 'the Canaanite was then in the land'. Powerful chieftains like Mamre and Eschol; flourishing towns like Sodom, Salem, and Hebron; the elements of civilization – all were there. The Canaanites were not wandering tribes. They had settled and taken root. Every day built up their power, and made it more unlikely that they could ever be dispossessed by the descendants of a childless shepherd.

But God had said it; and so it came to pass. I do not know what promise may be overarching your life with its bow of hope; but this is certain, that if you fulfill its conditions, and live up to its demands, it will be literally and gloriously fulfilled. Do not look at the difficulties and improbabilities of the Promiser. Promise after promise will light your life.

*But God had said it: and so it came to pass.*

# 4

# Separated from Lot

## *Genesis 13:9*

## 1    Who was Lot?

He was the son of Abraham's dead brother, Haran. He had probably succeeded to his father's inheritance. He seems to have been one of those men who take right steps, not because they are prompted by obedience to God, but because their friends are taking them. Around him was the inspiration of an heroic faith, the fascination of the untried and unknown, the stir of a great religious movement; and Lot was swept into the current, and resolved to go too. He was the Pliable of the earliest Pilgrim's Progress. He may have thought that he was as much in earnest as Abraham but it was a great mistake. He was simply an echo.

In every great religious movement there always has been, and always will be a number of individuals who cast in their lot with it, without knowing the power that inspires it. Beware of them! They cannot stand the stress of the life of separation to God. The mere excitement will soon die away from them, and, having no principle to take its place, they will become hindrances and disturbers of the peace. As certainly as they are harboured in the camp, or their principles are allowed within the heart, they will lower the spiritual tone. They will allure to worldly policy, suggest methods which would not otherwise occur to us, and draw us toward the Egypt-world.

Nothing but supreme principle can carry anyone through the real, separated, and surrendered life of the child of God. If you are prompted by anything less, you will first be a hindrance, and end by being a failure. Examine yourselves, whether you are in the faith. Prove your own selves. And, if you are consciously acting from a low and selfish motive, ask God to breathe into you his own pure love. Better act from an inferior motive, if only it be in the right direction, but covet earnestly the best.

## 2    The necessity of separation

Had Abraham been left to himself, he might never have thought of going down to Egypt: and, in that case, there would have been another paragraph or passage in the Bible describing the exploits of faith that dared to stand to God's promise, though threatened by disaster, and hemmed in by famine; waiting until God should bid it move, or make it possible to stay. There is something about that visit to Egypt that savours of the spirit of Lot's afterlife.

The outward separation of the body from the world of the ungodly in incomplete, unless accompanied and supplemented by the inner separation of the spirit. It is not enough to leave Ur,

Haran, and Egypt. We must be rid of Lot also. Though we lived in a monastery, yet so long as there was an alien principle in our breast, a Lot in our heart-life, there could not be that separation to God which is the condition of the growth of faith, and of all those higher forms of the true life which make earth most like heaven. Lot must go. 'Know that the Lord hath set apart him that is godly for himself' (Ps. 4:3). No other foot then must intrude within the enclosure of the divine proprietorship.

O souls that sigh for saintliness as harts pant for waterbrooks, have you counted the cost? Can you bear the fiery ordeal? The manufacture of saints is no child's play. The block has to be entirely separated from the mountain bed before the divine chisel can begin to fashion it. The gold must be plunged into the cleansing fire before it can be moulded or hammered into an ornament of beauty for the King.

We must be prepared to die to the world with its censure or praise; to the flesh, with its ambitions and schemes; to the delights of a friendship that is insidiously lowering the temperature of the spirit; to the self-life, in all its myriad subtle and overt manifestations; and even, if it be God's will, to the joys and consolations of religion.

All this is impossible of ourselves. But if we will surrender ourselves to God, we shall find that he will gradually and effectually, and as tenderly as possible, disentwine the clinging tendrils of the poisoning weed, and bring us into heart-union with himself.

It may be that Abraham had already felt for himself the ill effect of association with Lot, and may have longed to be free from him, without knowing how the emancipation could be effected. In any case, somewhat akin to this may be the condition of some who will read these words. Entangled in an alliance which you seem powerless to break off, your only hope is to bear it quietly until God sets you at liberty. That time will come at length; for God has a destiny in store for you, so great that neither he nor you can allow it to be forfeited for any light or trivial obstacle.

## 3   How the separation was brought about

The valleys around Bethel, which had been quite adequate for their needs when first they came to Canaan, were now altogether insufficient. The herdsmen were always wrangling for the first use of the wells, and the first crop of the pastures. The cattle were continually getting mixed. 'The land was not able to bear them, that they might dwell together.'

Abraham saw at once that such a state of things must not be allowed to go on: especially as 'the Canaanite and the Perizzite dwelled then in the land.' For if those war-like neighbours heard of the dissensions in the camp, they would take an early opportunity of falling on it. United they stood; divided, they must fall. Would that the near presence of the world might have the same wholesome effect of checking dissension and dispute among the children of the same Father!

And so Abraham called Lot to him, and said, 'Let there be no strife ... between me and thee, and between my herdmen and thy herdmen; for we be brethren. Is not the whole land before thee? separate thyself, I pray thee, from me: if thou wilt take the left hand, then I will go to the right; or if thou depart to the right hand, then I will go to the left' (Gen. 13:8–9).

The proposal was very *wise.* Abraham saw that there was a cause for the disturbance, which could lead to similar troubles continually. So he went to the root of the matter, and proposed their separation.

His line of action was very *magnanimous.* He had undoubted right to the first choice, but he waived his right in the interests of reconciliation.

But, above all, it was *based on faith.* Had not God pledged himself to take care of him, and to give him an inheritance?

The man who is sure of God can afford to hold very lightly the things of this world. God himself is his inalienable heritage, and, in having God, he has all. The man who 'hedges' for himself does not do as well in the long run as the man who, having the right of choice, hands it back to God, saying: 'Let others choose for themselves, if they please; but for myself, you shall choose my inheritance for me.'

# 5

# The Two Paths

## *Genesis 13:9*

Abraham and Lot stood together on the heights of Bethel. The Land of Promise spread out before them as a map. On three sides at least there was not much to attract a shepherd's gaze. The eye wandered over the outlines of the hills which hid from view the fertile valleys nestling within their embrace. There was, however, an exception in this monotony of hill, toward the southeast, where the waters of the Jordan spread out in a broad valley, before they entered the Sea of the Plain.

Even from the distance the two men could discern the rich luxuriance. This specially struck the eye of Lot; he was eager to do the best for himself, and determined to make the fullest use of the opportunity which the unexpected magnanimity of his uncle had thrown in his way.

But the time would come when he would bitterly rue his choice, and owe everything to the man of whom he was now prepared to take advantage.

Lot chose all the plain. He did not ask what God had chosen for him. His choice was entirely determined by the lust of the flesh, the lust of the eyes, and the pride of life.

Let us not condemn Lot too much because he chose without reference to the moral and religious conditions of the case, lest, in judging him, we pronounce sentence on ourselves. Lot did nothing more than is done by scores of professing Christians every day.

If Abraham had remonstrated with Lot, do you not suppose that he would have answered petulantly: 'Do you not think that we are as eager as you are to serve the Lord? Sodom needs just that witness we will be able to give. Is it not befitting that the light should shine in the darkness; and that the salt should be scattered where there is rot?' Abraham might not be able to contest these assertions, and yet he would have an inner conviction that these were not the considerations that were determining his nephew's choice. Of course, if God sends a man to Sodom, he will keep him there, as Daniel was kept in Babylon, and nothing shall by any means hurt him. But if God does not clearly send him to Sodom, it is a blunder, a crime, a peril to go.

Mark how Lot was swiftly swept into the centre, first he saw, then he chose, then he separated himself from Abraham, then he journeyed east, then he pitched his tent toward Sodom, then he dwelt there, then he became an alderman of the place, and sat in the gate. But his power of witness-bearing was gone. Or if he lifted up his voice in protest against deeds of shameless vice, he was laughed at for his pains, or threatened with violence. He was carried captive by Chedorlaomer. His property was destroyed in the overthrow of the cities. His wife was turned into a pillar of salt. And the blight of Sodom left but too evident a brand on his daughters. Wretched, indeed, must have been the last days of that hapless man, cowering in a cave, stripped of everything, face to face with the results of his own shameful sin.

Now, let us turn to a more inviting theme, and further consider the dealings of the Almighty God with Abraham, the one man who was being educated to hold fellowship with Jehovah as a friend.

## 1   God always comes near to his separated ones

'And the LORD said unto Abram, *after that Lot was separated from him.*' It may be that Abraham was feeling very lonely. We all dread being separated from companions and friends. It is hard to see them drop away one by one; and to be compelled to take a course alone. And yet, if we really wish to be only for God, it is inevitable that there should be many a link snapped, many a companionship forsaken, many a habit and conventionalism dropped.

But let us not stand looking on this aspect of it – the dark side of the cloud. Let us rather catch a glimpse of the other side, illuminated by the rainbow promise of God. And let this be understood that, when once the spirit has dared to take up that life of consecration to the will of God to which we are called, there break upon it visions, voices, comfortable words, of which the heart could have formed no previous idea.

## 2   God will do better for those who trust him than they could do for themselves

Twice here in the context we meet the phrase – 'lifted up his eyes.' But how great the contrast! Lot lifted up his eyes, at the dictate of worldly prudence, to spy out his own advantage. Abraham lifted up his eyes, not to discern what would best make for his material interests, but to behold what God had prepared for him. How much better it is to keep the eye steadfastly fastened on God until he says to us, 'Lift up now thine eyes, and look from the place where thou art northward, and southward, and eastward, and westward: For all the land which thou seest, to thee will I give it, and to thy seed for ever' (Gen. 13:14–15).

God honours those who honour him. He withholds 'no good thing from them that walk uprightly.' If only we will go on doing what is right, giving up the best to our neighbour to avoid dispute, considering God's interests first, and our own last, expending ourselves for the coming and glory of the kingdom of heaven, we shall find that God will charge himself with our interests. And he will do infinitely better for us than we could.

It is difficult to read these glowing words, '*northward, and southward, and eastward, and westward,*' without being reminded of 'the length, and breadth, and depth, and height, of the love of Christ, that passeth knowledge.' God's promises are ever on the ascending scale. One leads up to another, fuller and more blessed than itself. It is thus that God allures us to saintliness. Not giving anything until we have dared to act – that he may test us. Not giving everything at first – that he may not overwhelm us. And always keeping in hand an infinite reserve of blessing.

## 3   God bids us appropriate his gifts

'Arise, walk through the land in the length of it and in the breadth of it.' This surely means that God wished Abraham to feel as free in the land as if the title-deeds were actually in his hands. He was

to enjoy it; to travel through it; to look on it as his. By faith
Abraham was about to act toward it as if he were already in absolute possession.

There is a deep lesson here, as to the appropriation of faith. 'Be
strong and very courageous' was addressed six separate times to
Joshua. 'Be strong' refers to the strength of the wrists to grasp. 'Be
very courageous' refers to the tenacity of the ankle joints to hold
their ground. May our faith be strong in each of these particulars.
Strong to lay hold, and strong to keep.

We need not be surprised to learn that Abraham moved to Heb-
ron (which signifies fellowship), and built there an altar to the
Lord. New mercies call us to deeper fellowship with our Almighty
Friend, who never leaves or forsakes his own.

# Melchizedec

## *Hebrews 7:1*

There is a sense in which Christ was made *after the order of Melchizedec*; but there is a deeper sense in which Melchizedec was
made *after the order of the Son of God*. The writer to the Hebrews
tells us that Melchizedec was 'made like unto the Son of God'
(Heb. 7:3) that there might be given among men some premonition, some anticipation, of that glorious life that was already
being lived in heaven on man's behalf, and which, in due course,
would be manifested on our world, and at that very spot where
Melchizedec lived his Christlike life.

## 1   Melchizedec was a priest

He seems to have had that quick sympathy with the needs of his
times which is the true mark of the priestly heart (Heb. 4:15). And

he had acquired thereby so great an influence over his neighbours that they spontaneously acknowledged the claims of his special and unique position. Man must have a priest. And in all ages, men have selected from among their fellows one who should represent them to God, and God to them. It is a natural instinct. And it has been met in our glorious Lord, who, while he stands for us in the presence of God, face to face, ever making intercessions, at the same time is touched with the feeling of our infirmities, succours us in our temptations, and has compassion on our ignorance. Why need we travel farther afield?

## 2 This priesthood was also catholic

Abraham was not yet circumcised. He was not a Jew, but a Gentile still. It was as the father of many nations that he stood and worshipped and received the benediction from Melchizedec's saintly hands. It was not this way with the priesthood of Aaron's line. To share its benefit a man had to become a Jew, submitting to the initial rite of Judaism. None but Jewish names shone in his breastplate. Only Jewish wants or sins were borne on his consecrated lips. But Christ is the priest of man. He draws *all men* to himself. The one sufficient claim upon him is that we bear the nature that he has taken into irreversible union with his own – that we are sinners and penitents pressed by conscious need. Then have we a right to him, which cannot be disallowed. He is our Priest – our own; as if none other had claim on him. All kindreds, and people, and nations, and tongues, converge in him, and are welcome; and all their myriad needs are satisfactorily met.

## 3 This priesthood was superior to all human orders of priests

If there ever was a priesthood that held undisputed supremacy among the priesthoods of the world, it was that of Aaron's line. Yet even the Aaronic must yield obeisance to the Melchizedec priesthood. And it did. For Levi was yet in the loins of Abraham when Melchizedec met him; and he paid tithes in Abraham, and knelt in token of submission, in the person of the patriarch, beneath the blessing of this greater than himself (Heb. 7:4–10).

## 4   This priesthood partook of the mystery of eternity

We need not suppose that this mystic being had literally no father or mother, beginning of days, or end of life. No information is afforded us on any of these points. And these details were doubtless shrouded in obscurity, that there might be a still clearer approximation of the type to the glory of the Antitype, who abides continually. He is the Ancient of Days; the King of the Ages; the I AM. 'He is made after the power of an endless life.' 'He ever liveth to make intercession.' If, in the vision of Patmos, the hair of his head was white as snow, it was not the white of decay, but of incandescent fire. 'He continueth ever, and hath an unchangeable priesthood.' 'He is the same yesterday, today, and for ever.' He does for us now what he did for the world's grey fathers, and what he will do for the last sinner who shall claim his aid.

## 5   This priesthood was royal

'Melchizedec, king of Salem, priest.' Here again there is no analogy in the Levitical priesthood.

The royal and priestly offices were carefully kept apart. Uzziah was struck with the white brand of leprosy when he tried to unite them. But how marvellously they blended in the earthly life of Jesus! As Priest, he pitied, and helped, and fed men: as King, he ruled the waves. As Priest, he uttered his sublime intercessory prayer: as King, he spoke the 'I will' of royal prerogative. As Priest, he touched the ear of Malchus; as the disowned King, to whom even Caesar was preferred, he was hounded to the death. As Priest, he pleaded for his murderers, and spoke of Paradise to the dying thief, while his kingship was attested by the proclamation affixed to his cross. As Priest, he breathed peace on his disciples; as King, he ascended to sit on his throne.

Ah, souls, what is your attitude toward him? There are plenty who are willing enough to have him as Priest, who refuse to accept him as King. But it will not do. He must be King, or he will not be Priest. And he must be King in this order, first making you right, then giving you his peace that passes all understanding. Waste not your precious time in paltering, or arguing with him;

accept the situation as it is, and let your heart be the Salem, the city of peace, where he, the Priest-King, shall reign forever.

## 6   This priesthood receives tithes of all

'The patriarch Abraham gave the tenth of the spoils' (Heb. 7:4). This ancient custom shames us Christians. The patriach gave more to the representative of Christ than many of us give to Christ himself. Come, if you have never done so before, resolve to give your Lord a tithe of your time, your income, your all. 'Bring all the tithes into his storehouse.' Nay, glorious one, we will not rest content with this; take all, for all is yours.

# 7

# The Firmness of Abraham's Faith

## *Genesis 15*

In this chapter, for the first time in Scripture, four striking phrases occur, but each of them is destined to be frequently repeated with many charming variations. First, we meet the phrase, 'the word of the Lord came.' Here, first, we are told that 'the Lord God is a shield.' For the first time there rings out the silver chime of that divine assurance, 'Fear not!' And now we first meet in human history that great, that mighty word, 'believed'.

The 'word of the Lord' came to Abraham about two distinct matters.

## 1   God spoke to Abraham about his fear

Abraham had just returned from the rout of Cherdorlaomer and there was a natural reaction from the long and unwonted strain as he settled down again into the placid and uneventful course of a shepherd's life. In this state of mind he was most susceptible to fear; and there was good reason for fear. He had defeated Chedorlaomer, it is true; but in doing so he had made him his bitter foe. The arm of the warrior-king had been long enough to reach to Sodom; why should it not be long enough and strong enough to avenge his defeat on that one lonely man?

Besides all this, as a night wind in a desert land, there swept now and again over the heart of Abraham a feeling of lonely desolation, of disappointment, of hope deferred. More than ten years had passed since he had entered Canaan. Three successive promises had kindled his hopes, but they seemed as far from realisation as ever. Not one inch of territory! Not a sign of a child! Nothing of all that God had foretold!

It was under such circumstances that the word of the Lord came unto him, saying, 'Fear not, Abram: I am thy shield, and they exceeding great reward.' But God does not content himself with vague assurances. He gives us solid ground for comfort in some fresh revelation of himself. What could have been more reassuring at this moment to the defenceless pilgrim, with no stockade or walled city in which to shelter, but whose flocks were scattered far and wide, than to hear that God himself was around him and his, as a vast, impenetrable, though invisible shield. 'I am thy shield.'

Nor does God defend us only from without. He is the *reward* and satisfaction of the lonely heart. It was as if he asked Abraham to consider how much he had in having himself. 'Come now, my child, and think; even if you were never to have one foot of soil, and your tent were to stand silent, amid the merry laughter of childish voices all around – yet you would not have left your land in vain, for you have me. Am I not enough? I fill heaven and earth; cannot I fill one lonely soul? Am not I 'thy exceeding great reward'; about to compensate you by my friendship, to which you art called, for any sacrifice that you may have made?'

## 2   God spoke to Abraham about his childlessness

The patriarch was sleeping in his tent, when God came near him in a vision; and it was under the shadow of that vision that Abraham, was able to tell God all that was in his heart. And in that quiet watch of the night, Abraham poured out into the ear of

God the bitter agony of his heart's life. 'Behold, to me thou hast given no seed; and, lo, one born in my house is mine heir.' It was as if he said, 'I promised for myself something more than this; I have conned thy promises, and felt that they surely prognosticated a child of my own flesh and blood; but the slowly moving years have brought me no fulfillment of my hopes; and I suppose that I mistook thee. Thou never intendest more than that my steward should inherit my name and goods. Ah, me! it is a bitter disappointment, but thou hast done it, and it is well.'

So we often mistake God, and interpret his delays as denials. But such delays are not God's final answer to the soul that trusts him. They are but the winter before the burst of spring. 'And, behold, the word of the Lord came unto him, saying, This shall not be thine heir; but he that shall come forth out of thine own bowels shall be thine heir. Look now toward heaven, and tell the stars, if thou be able to number them . . . So shall thy seed be' (Gen. 15:4–5). And from that moment the stars shone with new meaning for him, as the sacraments of divine promise.

## 3 'And he believed in the Lord'

What wonder that those words are so often quoted by inspired men in after ages.

*a. He believed before he underwent the Jewish rite of circumcision.* The apostle Paul lays special emphasis on this, as showing that they who were not Jews might equally have faith, and be numbered among the spiritual children of the great father of the faithful (Rom. 4:9–21; Gal. 3:7–29). The promise that he should be the heir of the world was made to Abraham, when as yet he was only the far-travelled pilgrim; and so it is sure to all the seed, not to that only which is of the law, but to that also which is of the faith of Abraham, who is the father of us all.

*b. He believed in face of strong natural improbabilities.* Appearances were dead against such a thing as the birth of a child to that aged pair. The experience of many years said, 'It cannot be.' The nature and reason of the case said, 'It cannot be.' Any council of human friends and advisers would have instantly said, 'It cannot be!' And Abraham quietly considered and weighed them all 'without being weakened in faith' (Rom. 4:19 ASV). Then he as carefully looked into the promise of God. He reckoned on the faithfulness of God. He relied implicitly on the utter trustworthiness of the divine veracity. He was 'fully assured that what he had promised he was able also to perform.' Ah, child of God, for every look at the unlikelihood of the promise, take ten looks at the promise: this is the way in which faith waxes strong. 'Looking unto the promise of God, he wavered not through unbelief, but waxed strong' (Rom. 4:20 ASV).

*c. His faith was counted to him for righteousness.*        The righteousness of Abraham resulted not from his works, but from his faith. 'He believed God; and it was reckoned unto him for righteousness' (Gal. 3:6 ASV). Oh, miracle of grace! If we trust ever so simply in Jesus Christ our Lord, we shall be reckoned as righteous in the eye of the eternal God. We cannot realise all that is included in those marvellous words. This only is evident, that faith unites with him so absolutely to the Son of God that we are *one* with him forevermore.

Some teach imputed righteousness as if it were something apart from Christ, flung over the rags of the sinner. But it is truer and better to consider it as a matter of blessed identification with him through faith; so that as he was one with us in being made sin, we are one with him in being made the righteousness of God. Jesus Christ is made unto us righteousness, and we are accepted in the beloved. There is nothing in faith, considered in itself, which can account for this marvellous fact of imputation. Faith is only the link of union, but inasmuch as it unites us to the Son of God, it brings us into the enjoyment of all that he is as the Alpha and Omega, the Beginning and the End, the First and the Last.

# 8

# Hagar, the Slave Girl

## Genesis 16:1

None of us knows all that is involved when we tear ourselves from the familiar scenes of our Harans to follow God into the lands of separation that lie beyond the river.

There is here a very startling manifestation of the tenacity with which Abraham's self-life still survived. The long waiting of ten slow-moving years, the repeated promises of God, the habit of contact with God himself – all this had surely been enough to eradicate and burn out all desire to help himself to the realization of the promises of God. Surely, now, this much-tried man will wait until, in his own time and way, God shall do as he has said. We might have expected that he would have strenuously resisted every endeavour to induce him to realize for himself God's promise about his seed. Surely he will wait meekly and quietly for God to fulfill his own word, by means best known to himself.

Instead of this he listened to *the reasoning of expediency.* Simple-hearted faith waits for God to unfold his purpose, sure that he will not fail. But mistrust, reacting on the self-life, leads us to take matters into our own hands.

### 1   The quarter from where these reasonings came

'Sarai said unto Abram.' Poor Sarah! She had not had her husband's advantages. When he had been standing in fellowship with God, she had been quietly pursuing the routine of household duty, pondering many things.

It was clear that Abraham should have a son; but it was not definitely said by God that the child would be hers. Abraham was a strict monogamist; but the more lax notions of those days warranted the filling of the harem with others, who occupied an inferior rank to that of the principal wife, and whose children according to common practice were reckoned as if they were her own. Why should not her husband fall in with those notions of the marriage vow? Why should he now marry the slave girl? It was a heroic sacrifice for her to make. But her love to Abraham, her despair of having a child of her own, and her inability to conceive of God fulfilling his word by other than natural means – all these things combined to make the proposal.

No one else could have approached Abraham with such a proposition, with the slightest hope of success. But when Sarah made it, the case was altered. It seemed to be a likely expedient for realising God's promise, and 'Abram hearkened to the voice of Sarai.'

## 2   The sorrows to which they led

As soon as the end was obtained, the results, like a crop of nettles, began to appear in that home, which had been the abode of purity and bliss but which was now destined to be the scene of discord. Raised into a position of rivalry with Sarah, and expectant of giving the long-desired son to Abraham, and a young master to the camp, Hagar despised her childless mistress, and took no pains to conceal her contempt.

This was more than Sarah could endure. It was easier to make one heroic act of self-sacrifice, than to bear each day the insolent carriage of the maid whom she had herself exalted to this position. Nor was she reasonable in her irritation; instead of assuming the responsibility of having brought about the untoward event, so fraught with misery to herself, she passionately upbraided her husband, saying: 'My wrong be upon thee: the Lord judge between me and thee' (Gen. 16:5).

Out of this fleshly expedient sprang many sorrows. Sorrow to Sarah, who on this occasion as afterward must have drunk to the dregs the cup of bitter gall, of jealousy and wounded pride, of hate and malice. Sorrow to Hagar, driven forth as an exile from the home of which she had dreamed to become the mistress, and to which she had thought herself essential. Sorrow to Abraham, loath to part with one who, to all human appearance, would now become the mother of the child who should bless his life: stung, moreover, as he was, by the unwonted bitterness of his wife's reproaches.

## 3   The victim whose life course was so largely involved

Abraham, for the sake of the peace of his home, dared not interpose between his wife and her slave. 'Behold', he said, 'thy maid is in thy hand; do to her as it pleaseth thee.' Not slow to act upon this implied consent, the irate mistress dealt so bitterly with the girl that she fled from her face, and took the road, trodden by the caravans, toward her native land.

'The angel of the Lord' (and here, for the first time, that significant expression is used, which is held by many to express some evident manifestation of the Son of God in angel form) 'found her by a fountain of water' which was familiarly known in the days of Moses. There, worn and weary and lonely, she sat down to rest. How often does the angel of the Lord still find us in our extremity! And what questions could be more pertinent, whether to Hagar or to us: 'Whence camest thou? and whither wilt thou go?' Reader, answer those two questions, before you read further. What is your origin and destiny?

Then there followed the distinct command, which applies to us evermore, 'Return . . . and submit.' The day would come when God himself would open the door, and send Hagar out of that house (21:12–14). But until that moment should come, after thirteen years had rolled away, she must return to the place she had left, bearing her burden and fulfilling her duty as best she might. 'Return . . . and submit.'

We are all prone to act as Hagar did. If our lot is hard, and our cross is heavy, we start off in a fit of impatience and wounded pride. We make our own way out of the difficulty. But we shall never get right this way. Never! We must retrace our steps; we must meekly bend our necks under the yoke. We must accept the lot that God has ordained for us, even though it be the result of the cruelty and sin of others. We shall conquer by yielding. We shall escape by returning. By and by, when the lesson is perfectly learned, the prison door will open of its own accord.

Meanwhile the heart of the prodigal is cheered by promise (Gen. 16:10). The angel of the Lord unfolds all the blessed results of obedience. And as the spirit considers these, it finds the homeward way no longer lined by flints, but soft with flowers.

# 9

# 'Be thou perfect!'

## *Genesis 17:1*

Thirteen long years passed slowly after the return of Hagar to Abraham's camp. The child Ishmael was born and grew up in the patriarch's house – the acknowledged heir of the camp, and yet showing symptoms of the wild nature of which the angel had spoken (16:12). Abraham must have been perplexed with those strange manifestations, and yet the heart of the old man warmed to the lad, and clung to him, often asking that Ishmael might live before God.

And throughout that long period there was no fresh appearance, no new announcement. Not since God had spoken to him in Charran had there been so long a pause. And it must have been a terrible ordeal, driving him back on the promise that had been given, and searching his heart to ascertain if the cause lay within himself.

At last, 'when Abram was ninety years old and nine', the Lord appeared to him again, and gave him a new revelation of himself. He unfolded the terms of his covenant, and addressed to him that memorable charge that rings its summons in the ear and heart of every believer still: 'Walk before me, and be thou perfect.'

## 1   The divine summons

'Walk before me, and be thou perfect.' Men have sadly stumbled over that word 'perfect'. They have not erred when they have taught that there is an experience, denoted by the phrase, which is possible to men. But they have sadly erred in pressing their own significance into the word, and in then asserting that men are expected to fulfil it, or that they have themselves attained it.

'Perfection' is often supposed to denote sinlessness of moral character, which at the best is only a negative conception, and fails to bring out the positive force of this mighty word. Surely perfection means more than sinlessness. And if this is admitted, and the further admission is made that it contains the thought of moral completeness, then it becomes yet more absurd for any mortal to assert it of himself. The very assertion shows the lack of any perfection, and reveals little knowledge of the inner life and of the nature of sin. *Absolute sinlessness* is surely impossible for us so long as we do not have perfect knowledge; for as our light is growing constantly, so are we constantly discovering evil in things we once allowed without uneasiness. Surely the language of the apostle Paul should be on our lips as he cried, 'Not as though I had already attained, or were already perfect; but I follow after.'

Besides all this, the word 'perfect' bears different renderings from those often given to it. For instance, when we are told that the man of God must be *perfect* (2 Tim. 3:17), the underlying thought is that of a workman being 'thoroughly equipped for his work'. Again, when we join the prayer that the God of peace would make us *perfect* in every good work to do his will, we are, in fact, asking that we may be 'put in joint' with the blessed Lord; so that the glorious Head may freely secure through us the doing of his will (Heb. 13:20–21).

What, then, is the true force and significance of this word, 'Walk before me, and be thou perfect'? A comparison of the various passages where it occurs establishes its meaning beyond a doubt, and compels us to think the conception of 'wholeheartedness'. It denotes the entire surrender of the being.

This quality of wholehearted devotion has always been dear to God. It is for this that he pleads with Abraham; and it was because he met with it to so large an extent in his character and obedience that he entered into eternal covenant bond with him and his.

Here let each reader ask, Is my heart perfect with God? Am I wholehearted toward him? Is he first in my plans, pleasures, friendships, thoughts, and actions? Is his will my law, his love my light, his business my aim, his 'well done!' my exceeding great reward? Do others share me with him?

And such an attitude can be *maintained* only by a very careful walk. 'Walk before me, and be thou perfect.' We must seek to realize constantly the presence of God, becoming instantly aware when the fleeciest cloud draws its veil for a moment over his face, and asking whether the cause may not lie in some scarcely-noticed sin. We must cultivate the habit of feeling him near, as the friend from whom we would never be separated, in work, in prayer, in recreation, in rest. And yet we shall not live forced or unnatural lives. None so blithe or light-hearted as we. Would you walk before God? Then let there be nothing in heart or life that you would not open to the inspection of his holy and pitiful eye.

## 2   The revelation on which this summons was based

'I am the Almighty God' (*El-shaddai*). What a name is this! And what emotions it must have excited in the rapt heart of the listener! God had been known to him by other names, but not by this. And this was the first of a series of revelations of those depths of meaning that lay in the fathomless abyss of the divine name, each disclosure marking an epoch in the history of the race.

In God's dealings with men you will invariably find that some transcendent revelation precedes the divine summons to new and difficult duty; promise opens the door to precept; he gives what he commands, therefore he commands what he wills. And on this principle God acted here. It was no child's play to which he called his servant. To walk always before him – when heart is weak, and strength is frail, and the temptation strong to swerve to right or left. To be perfect in devotion and obedience, when so many crosslights distract, and perplex, and fascinate the soul. To forgo all methods of self-help, however tempting. To be separated from all alliances that others permit or follow. This is possible only through the might of the Almighty. And, therefore, there broke on him the assurance: 'I am the Almighty God'.

All this is as true today as ever. And if you will dare venture forth on the path of separation, cutting yourself aloof from all creature aid, and from all self-originated effort; content to walk alone with God, with no help from any but him – you will find that all the resources of the divine almightiness will be placed at your disposal, and that the resources of Omnipotence must be exhausted before their cause can fail for want of help.

### 3  The Covenant that was divinely proposed

'I will make my covenant between me and thee'. A covenant is a promise made under the most solemn sanctions, and binding the consenting parties in a definite and impressive way. We can't help but consent to the fact that the Almighty God proposed to enter into an everlasting covenant with his creature, a covenant that was ordered in all things and sure, and more stable than the everlasting hills!

*a. It referred to the seed.*   And there was a marked advance. In Haran it was, 'I will make of thee a great nation'. At Bethel, 'Thy seed shall be as the dust of the earth'. At Mamre, 'Tell the stars; so shall thy seed be'. But now, three times over, the patriarch is told that he would be the father of many nations, a phrase explained by the apostle as including all, of every land, who share Abraham's faith, though not sprung from him in the line of natural descent (Gal. 3:7–29). In memory of that promise his name was slightly altered, so that it signified the 'father of a great multitude'.

*b. It referred to the land.*   'I will give unto thee, and to thy seed after thee, the land wherein thou art a stranger, all the land of Canaan, for an everlasting possession.' This promise waits for fulfilment. The word 'everlasting' must mean something more than those few centuries of broken fitful rule. But there will be a time, when our covenant-keeping God will build again the tabernacle of David, which is fallen down, and will repair its ruins, and the land will be again inhabited by the seed of Abraham his friend.

*c. It referred to the coming child.*   Until then Abraham had no other thought than that Ishmael should be his heir. God said, Sarah thy wife shall bear thee a son indeed and thou shalt call his name Isaac' (v.19).

God pledges himself to be the God of our seed. And it is for us to claim the fulfilment of his pledge – not in heart-rending cries, but in quiet, determined faith, let us ask him to do as he has said.

# 10

# The Divine Guest

## *Genesis 18:1*

When, in the course of some royal progress, a sovereign decides to stay in the home of one of the subjects of his realm, the event becomes at once the theme of chroniclers, and the family selected for so high an honour is held in deepened respect. But what shall we say in the presence of such an episode as this – in which the God of heaven became the guest of his servant Abraham!

There is no doubt as to the august character of one of the three who visited the tent of the patriarch. In verse 1 we are expressly told that Jehovah appeared to him in the plains of Mamre, as he sat in the tent door in the heat of the day. And in verse 10 there is the accent of deity, in the words of promise that tell how certainly Sarah would have a son. Besides that, we are told that two angels came to Sodom in the evening. Evidently they were two of the three who had sat as Abraham's guests beneath the tree that sheltered his tent in the blazing noon. But as for the other, who throughout the wondrous hours had been the only spokesman, his dignity is disclosed in the amazing discussion that took place on the heights of Mamre, when Abraham stood yet before the Lord, and pleaded with him as the Judge of all the earth. Abraham, at the outset, evidently did not realize the full meaning of the episode in which he was taking part. So too we often fail to value aright characters with whom we come in contact. It is only as they pass away from us forever, and we look on them, that we realize that we have been entertaining angels unawares. Let us so act always and everywhere, that as we review the past we may have nothing to regret; and may not have to reproach ourselves because we omitted to do something or other, which we would have done had we only realised our opportunities.

### 1   Abraham treated his visitors with true eastern hospitality

He *ran* to meet them, and bowed himself toward the ground. He proposed water for their feet, and rest for their tired frames, beneath the spreading shadow of the tent. He started his wife kneading the meal for baking the bread on the scorching stones. He ran to choose his tenderest calf, refusing to delegate the work to another's hand. He served his visitors himself, and stood as a servant by their side, under the tree, while they ate. Christians do not have much to boast of – and a good deal to learn – as they consider the action of this old-time saint, and his dealings with the three strangers who came to his tent.

### 2   May it not be that Christ comes to us often in the guise of a stranger?

Does he not test us this way? Of course if he were to come in his manifested splendour as the Son of the highest, everyone would receive him, and provide him with sumptuous hospitality. But this would not reveal our true character. So he comes to us as a wayfaring man, hungry and thirsty; or as a stranger, naked and sick. Those who are his will show him mercy, in whatsoever disguise he comes, though they do not recognise him, and will be surprised to learn that they ministered to him. Those, on the other hand, who are not really his, will fail to discern him, will let him go away unhelped, and will wake up to find that 'inasmuch as ye did it not to one of the least of these, ye did it not to me' (Matt. 25:45).

### 3   But God never leaves us in his debt

He is careful to pay for his entertainment, royally and divinely. He uses Peter's fishing vessel, and gives it back, nearly submerged by the weight of the fish he has driven into the nets. He sits down with his friends to a country marriage feast, and pays for their simple fare by jars brimming with water turned to wine. He uses the five barley loaves and two small fishes; but the lad has an ample meal. He sends his prophet to lodge with a widow, and provides meal and oil for him and her for many days. And Abraham was no loser by his ready hospitality, for as they sat at meat the Lord foretold the birth of Sarah's child: 'I will certainly return unto thee . . . and, lo, Sarah thy wife shall have a son.'

Sarah was sitting behind the flimsy curtain of camel's hair, and as she heard the words, she laughed the laugh of incredulity. That laugh was at once noticed by him from whom nothing can be hid, and whose eyes are as a flame of fire. 'And the LORD said unto Abraham, Wherefore did Sarah laugh, saying, Shall I of a surety bear a child, which am old? Is anything too hard for the LORD?' (Gen. 18:13–14).

With strange simplicity she answered through the curtain, denying that she had laughed, for she was afraid. But her reply was met by the stern and uncompromising affirmation, 'Nay; but thou didst laugh.' These were the only audible words that we know to have passed between God and Abraham's wife. However, she seems to have been led by these words into a true faith; for it is said, 'Through faith also Sarah herself received strength to conceive seed, and was delivered of a child when she was past age, because she judged him faithful who had promised' (Heb. 11:11).

### 4   This is the true law of faith

Do not look at your faith or at your feelings, but look away to the word of promise, and, above all, to the Promiser. His power is omnipotent and would he ever have pledged himself to do what he could not effect? 'He is faithful who promised.' Look from faith to the promise, and from the promise to the Promiser.

### 5   'Is anything too hard for the Lord?'

That is one of God's unanswered questions. It may seem to you hard, almost impossible, that God should keep his word, in the conversion of that friend for whom you have prayed, according to 1 John 5:16. It may seem hard to vindicate your character from the aspersions with which it is being befouled; hard to keep your evil nature under control, and to cast down your evil thoughts, bringing every thought into captivity to the obedience of Christ; hard to make you sweet and gentle, forgiving and loving, hard to produce from you the fruits of a lovely and holy nature. It may be hard, but it is not too hard for the Lord. 'With God all things are possible.' And, as Sarah found, all things are possible to those who believe.

The one thing that hinders God is our unbelief. Sarah and Abraham had to believe before the child of promise could be born. And so must it be with us. As soon as we believe, then, according to our faith it is done to us; yes, exceedingly abundantly beyond all we had asked or thought.

You ask how to obtain this faith. Remember that faith is the receptive attitude of the soul, begotten and maintained by the grace of God. Christ is the Author and Finisher of faith; not only in the abstract, but also in the personal experience of the soul. Faith is the gift of God. If, then, you would receive it, put your will on the side of Christ. May it not be a passing wish, but the whole will of your being: will to believe patiently, persistently, yearningly; let your eyes be ever toward the Lord; study the promises of God; consider the nature of God; be prepared to be rid of everything that grieves his Holy Spirit; and it is as certain as the truth of Christ, that you will have begotten and maintained in you the faith that can move mountains and laugh at impossibilities.


# 11

# Pleading for Sodom

### *Genesis 18:22–23*


As the day wore on, Abraham's mysterious guests went off across the hills toward Sodom, and Abraham went with them to bring them on their way. But all three did not reach the guilty city over which the thunder clouds had already begun to gather. That evening two angels entered it alone. And where was their companion? He had stayed behind to talk yet further with his friend. Tradition still points out the spot on the hills at the head of a long steep ravine leading down to the sullen waters of the Dead Sea where the Lord tarried behind to tell Abraham all that was in his heart.

Abraham was the 'friend of God', and friendship constitutes a claim to be entrusted with secrets hidden from everyone else. The Septuagint version has well brought out the spirit of the divine discussion, when it puts the question this way: 'Shall I hide from Abraham, *my servant,* that thing which I do?' The Lord does nothing that he does not first reveal to his holy servants and prophets.

But the words that follow point to a further reason for the full disclosures that were made: 'For I know him, that he will command his children and his household after him, and they shall keep the way of the Lord to do justice and judgment' (Gen. 18:19). Was there a fear lest Abraham and his children might doubt the justice of the judgment of God if the righteous were summarily cut off with the wicked; and if the cities of the plain were destroyed without a revelation of their sin on the one hand, and the display of the divine mercy on the other?

## 1   The burden of the divine announcement

'The cry of Sodom and Gomorrah is great.' No sound travelled to the patriarch's ear. Quiet though Sodom seemed, yet to God there was a cry – the cry of the earth compelled to carry such a scar; the cry of inanimate creation, groaning and travailing in pain; the cry of the oppressed, the down-trodden, the victims of human violence and lust. These were the cries that had entered into the ears of the Lord God of Sabaoth.

'I will go down now, and see.' God always carefully investigates the true condition of the case before he executes his sentences. He is prepared, no, eager to give us the benefit of any excuse. But flagrant sin, like that which broke out in Sodom that night, is enough to settle forever the fate of a godless community when standing at the bar of him who is Judge and Witness both.

'And if not, I will know.' There was something very ominous in these words that Abraham clearly understood to indicate the approaching destruction of the place; for in his prayer he again and again alludes to the imminence of its doom. But what is there that God does not know? Yes, ungodly soul, who may read this page: remember that no secrets can be hid from God. He will search out the most hidden ramifications of your sins, bringing them out before the gaze of the universe, and justifying his righteous judgments which he will not spare.

## 2 The impression that this announcement made on Abraham's mind

As soon as the angels had left, leaving Abraham alone with the Lord, his mind was filled with a tumult of emotion. He hardly dared reason with God: what was he, but 'dust and ashes'? And yet he was impelled to make some attempt to avert the doom that threatened the cities of the plain.

The motives that prompted him were twofold: There was a natural anxiety about his kinsman, Lot. Twenty years had passed since Lot had left him; but he had never ceased to follow him with the most tender affection. The strong impulse of natural affection stirred him to make one strenuous effort to save Sodom, lest his nephew might be overwhelmed in its overthrow. Real religion tends not to destroy, but to fulfil all the impulses of true natural love.

There was also a fear lest the total destruction of the cities of the plain might prejudice the character of God in the minds of the neighbouring peoples. Abraham did not deny that the fate which was about to overtake the cities was deserved by many of the people of that enervating and luxuriant valley: but he could not bring his mind to suppose that the whole of the population was equally debased. He feared that if all were summarily swept away, the surrounding nations would have a handle of reproach against the justice of his God, and would accuse him of unrighteousness, inasmuch as he destroyed the righteous with the wicked.

The passion for glory of God burned with a clear, strong flame in Abraham's heart, and it was out of this that there arose his wondrous intercession. And when he became as closely identified with the interests of God as he was, we shall come to feel as he did. We will be eager that the divine character should be vindicated among the children of men; content, if need be, to lie dying in the ditch, so long as we can hear the shouts of triumph amid which our King rides over us to victory.

### 3 The elements in Abraham's intercession

*a. It was lonely prayer.* He waited until there was no living man to overhear this marvellous outpouring of a soul: 'He stood before the Lord.' It is fatal to all the strongest devotion to pray always in the presence of another, even the dearest. Every saint must have a closet of which he can shut the door, and in which he can pray to the Father who is in secret.

*b. It was prolonged prayer.* 'Abraham stood yet before the Lord.' The story takes but a few moments to read, but the scene may have lasted for the space of hours. We cannot climb the more elevated pinnacles of prayer in a hasty rush. Of course, our God is ever on the alert to hear and answer those prayers which we fire through the day, but we cannot maintain this posture of ejaculatory prayer unless we cultivate the prolonged occasions. How much we miss because we do not wait before God!

*c. It was very humble prayer.* 'Behold, now, I have taken upon me to speak unto the Lord, which am but dust and ashes.' 'Oh, let not the Lord be angry, and I will speak.' 'Behold now, I have taken upon me to speak unto the Lord.' 'Oh, let not the Lord be angry, and I will speak yet but this once.' The nearer we get to God, the more conscious are we of our own unworthiness; before him angels veil their faces, and the heavens are not clean in his sight.

*d. This prayer was based on a belief that God possessed the same moral institutions as himself.* 'Wilt thou also destroy the righteous with the wicked . . . that be far from thee. Shall not the Judge of all the earth do right?' There is an infinite interest in this. It was as if Abraham had said: 'Almighty God, I could not think it right to destroy the righteous with the wicked; and I am sure that any number of righteous men would shrink from doing so. And if this is binding on man, of course it must be much more binding on Thee, because Thou art the Judge of the earth.' And God was not angry; indeed, he assented to Abraham's plea. And, therefore, we may say that though God may act in ways above our reason, yet he will not contradict those instincts of the moral sense which he has placed within our hearts.

*e. This prayer was persevering.* Six times Abraham returned to the charge, and as each petition was granted his faith and courage grew; and, finding he had struck a right vein, he worked it again, and yet again. It looks at first sight as if he forced God back from point to point and wrung his petitions from an unwilling hand. But this is a mistake. In point of fact, *God was drawing him on*; and if he had dared to ask at first what he asked at the last, he would have got more than all that he asked or thought at the beginning of his intercession. What a pity that he stopped at ten! There is no knowing what he might have reached, had he gone on. As it was, the Almighty was obliged, by the demands of his own nature, to exceed the limits placed by Abraham, in bringing out of Sodom the only persons that could, by any possibility, be accounted 'righteous'.

There were not ten righteous men in Sodom; but Lot, and his wife, and his two daughters were saved, though three of them were deeply infected with the moral contagion of the place. And God's righteousness was clearly established and vindicated in the eyes of the surrounding peoples.

We note one of the great principles in the divine government of the world. A whole city would have been spared, if ten righteous men could have been found within its walls. Ungodly men little realise how much they owe to the presence of the children of God in their midst. How little the world realises the debt it owes to its saints, the salt to stay its corruption, the light to arrest the reinstitution of the reign of chaos and night! We cannot but yearn over the world as it rolls on its way toward its sad, dark doom. Let us plead for it from the heights above Mamre. And may we and our beloved ones be led out from it into safety, before the last plagues break full upon it in inevitable destruction!

# 12

# A Bit of the Old Nature

## Genesis 20:9

For many years an evil may lurk in our hearts, permitted and unjudged, breed failure and sorrow in our lives. But that which escapes our knowledge is patent in all its naked deformity to the eye of God. When he has laid bare the cancerous growth, he may bring us to long for and invite the knife that shall set us free from it forever.

These words have been suggested by the thirteenth verse of this chapter, which indicates an evil compact, into which Abraham had entered with Sarah some thirty years earlier. Addressing the king of the Philistines, the patriarch let fall a hint that sheds a startling light on his failure, when he first entered the Land of Promise and, under stress of famine, went down into Egypt; and upon that repetition of his failure which we must now consider. Here is what he said: 'And it came to pass, when God caused me to wander from my father's house, that I said unto [my wife], This is thy kindness which thou shalt shew unto me; at every place whither we shall come, say of me, he is my brother.'

This secret compact between Abraham and his wife, in the earliest days of his exodus, was due to his weak faith in God's power to take care of them, which again sprang from his limited experience of his Almighty Friend.

But the existence of this hidden understanding was inconsistent with the relation into which he had now entered with God. It was a secret flaw in his faith that would destroy its effectiveness in the dark trials that were approaching. God could afford to pass it over in those early days, when faith itself was yet young, but it could not be permitted when that faith was reaching to a maturity in which any flaw would be instantly detected.

The judgment and eradication of this lurking evil were brought about in this way. The day before Sodom's fall, the Almighty told Abraham that, at a set time in the following year, he would have a son and heir. And we would expect that he would have spent the slow-moving months beneath the oak of Mamre, already hallowed by so many associations. But he 'journeyed from thence toward the south country, and dwelled between Kadesh and Shur, and sojourned in Gerar' (Gen. 20:1).

Gerar was the capital of a race of men who had dispossessed the original inhabitants of the land, and were gradually passing from the condition of wandering shepherd life into that of a settled and warlike nation. Their chieftain bore the official title of Abimelech, 'My Father the King'.

Here, the almost forgotten agreement between Sarah and himself offered itself as a ready expedient, behind which Abraham's unbelief took shelter. He knew the ungoverned license of his time. He dreaded, lest the heathen monarch, enamoured with Sarah's beauty, might slay him for his wife's sake. So he again resorted to lying by calling her his sister. He acted as if God could not have defended him and her, screening them from all evil; as he had done so often in days gone by.

## 1  His conduct was very dishonouring to God

Among those untutored tribes Abraham was well known as the servant of Jehovah, and they could judge the character of him whom they could not see only by the traits they discerned in his servant. How sad that Abraham's standard was lower than their own! So much so that Abimelech was able to rebuke him.

It is heartbreaking when the heathen rebukes a professor of superior godliness for speaking lies. And it is lamentable to confess that such men often have higher standards of morality than those who profess godliness. The temperate Hindu is scandalised by the drunkenness of the American whose religion he is invited to embrace. The employee abhors a creed that is professed by his employer for one day of the week, but is disowned on the other six. Let us walk circumspectly toward those who are without.

## 2   It also stood out in poor relief against the behaviour of Abimelech

Abimelech commends himself to us as the nobler of the two. He rises early in the morning, prompt to set the great wrong right. He warns his people. He restores Sarah with munificent presents. His reproach and rebuke are spoken in the gentlest, kindest tones. He simply tells Sarah that her position as the wife of a prophet would be a sufficient security and veil (v.16). There is the air of high-minded nobility in his behaviour that is exceedingly winsome.

Let us ponder, as we close, some practical lessons:

*a.  We are never safe as long as we are in this world.*    Abraham was an old man. Thirty years had passed since that sin had last shown itself. Never boast against once-cherished sins: only by God's grace are they kept in check; and if you cease to abide in Christ, they will revive and revisit you.

*b.  We have no right to throw ourselves into the way of the temptation that has often mastered us.*    Those who daily cry, 'Lead us not into temptation', should see to it that they do not court the temptation against which they pray. We must not expect angels to catch us every time we choose to cast ourselves from the mountain brow.

*c.  We may be encouraged by God's treatment of Abraham's sin.*
Although God had a secret controversy with his child, he did not put him away. He told Abimelech that he was a dead man; he stopped him by the ministry of an ominous disease; and bade him apply to the intercession of the very man by whom he had been so grievously misled, and who, in spite of all his failures, was a prophet still, having power with God.

Have you sinned, bringing disrepute on the name of God? Do not despair. Go alone, as Abraham must have done, and confess your sin with tears and childlike trust. Trust then in the patience and forgiveness of God, and let his love, as consuming fire, rid you of concealed and hidden sin.

# 13

# Hagar and Ishmael Cast Out

## Genesis 21:10

The Almighty lover of souls knew the trial that awaited his child, and he set himself to prepare him for it by ridding him of certain clinging inconsistencies that would have paralysed the action of his faith in the hour of trial. We have already seen how one of these – the secret compact between Abraham and Sarah – was exposed to the light and judged. We have now to see how another matter, the patriarch's connection with Hagar and her child, was also dealt with by him.

In what way the presence of Hagar and Ishmael hindered the development of Abraham's noblest life of faith, we cannot entirely understand. Did his heart still cling to the girl who had given him his first born son? Was there any secret satisfaction in the arrangement, which had at least achieved one cherished purpose, though it had been unblessed by God? Was there any fear that if he were summoned to surrender Isaac, he would find it easier to do so, because he could fall back on Ishmael, as both son and heir? One darling idol after another was rent away that he himself might be cast naked and helpless on the omnipotence of the Eternal God. 'The thing was very grievous in Abraham's sight' (v.11).

The final separation from Abraham of ingredients that would have been prejudicial to the exercise of a supreme faith was brought about by the birth of the long-promised child, which is alluded to at the beginning of this chapter (Gen. 21), and which led up to the crisis with which we are now dealing.

'The Lord visited Sarah as he had said, and the Lord did unto Sarah as he had spoken' (Gen. 21:1). It is impossible to trust God too absolutely.

### 1   But we must be prepared to wait God's time

'Sarah bare Abraham a son in his old age, *at the set time* of which
God had spoken to him.' The set time came at last; and then the
laughter that filled the patriarch's home made the aged pair forget
the long and weary vigil. 'And Abraham called the name of his
son that was born unto him, whom Sarah bare unto him, Isaac'
(that is 'Laughter'). Take heart, waiting one, who waits for One
who cannot disappoint you; and who will not be five minutes
behind the appointed moment: before long 'your sorrow shall be
turned into joy.'

The laughter of incredulity, with which Sarah received the first
intimation of her approaching motherhood (18:12), was now
exchanged for the laughter of fulfilled hope.

Ah, happy soul, when God makes you laugh! Then sorrow and
crying shall flee away forever, as darkness before the dawn.

The peace of Abraham's house remained at first unbroken,
though there may have been some slight symptoms of the rupture
that was at hand. The dislike that Sarah had manifested to Hagar,
long years before, had never been extinguished: it had only
smouldered in her heart, waiting for some slight incident to stir it
again into a blaze. Nor had the warm passionate nature of Hagar
ever forgotten those hard dealings that had driven her away, to
far as best she might in the inhospitable desert. Abraham must
often have been sorely put to it to keep the peace between them.
At last the women's quarters could conceal the quarrel no longer,
and the scandal broke out into the open.

### 2   The immediate occasion of this open rupture

was the weaning of the young Isaac. 'The child grew, and was
weaned: and Abraham made a great feast the same day that Isaac
was weaned.' But amid all the bright joy of that happy occasion,
one shadow suddenly stole over the scene,and brooded on the
mother's soul. Sarah's jealous eye saw Ishmael mocking. And that
should be no surprise. This awoke all Sarah's slumbering
jealousy, which may often have been severely tested during the
last few years by Ishmael's assumption and independent bearing.
She would stand it no longer. Why should she, the chieftain's

wife, and mother of his heir, brook the insolence of a slave? And so she said to Abraham with a sneer and the sting of the old jealousy, 'Cast out this bondwoman and her son: for the son of this bondwoman shall not be heir with my son, even with Isaac.'

### 3   We cannot but recall the use that the apostle Paul makes of this incident

In his days the Jews, priding themselves on being the lineal descendents of Abraham, refused to consider it possible that any but themselves could be children of God, and the heirs of promise. They arrogated to themselves exclusive privileges and position. And when large numbers of Gentiles were born into the Christian church under the first preaching of the gospel, and claimed to be the spiritual seed with all the rights pertaining thereto; they who, like Ishmael, were simply born after the flesh, persecuted them who, like Isaac, were born after the Spirit. The Jews everywhere set themselves to resist the preaching of the gospel, which denied to them their exclusive privileges; and to harry those who would not enter the church through the rites of Judaism. And before long the Jewish nation was rejected, put aside, cast out. Succeeding ages have seen the building up of the church from among the once-persecuted ones, while the children of Abraham have wandered in the wilderness fainting for the true water of life (Gal. 4:29).

### 4   But there is still deeper reference

Hagar, the slave, who may even have been born in the Sinaitic Desert, with which she seems to have been so familiar, is a fitting representative of the spirit of legalism and bondage, seeking to win life by the observance of the law, which was given from those hoary cliffs. Hagar is the covenant of Mount Sinai in Arabia, 'which gendereth to bondage,' and 'is in bondage with her children' (Gal. 4:24–25). Sarah, the free woman, on the other hand, represents the covenant of free grace. Her children are love, and faith, and hope; they are not bound by the spirit of 'must', but by the promptings of spontaneous gratitude; their home is not in the frowning clefts of Sinai, but in Jerusalem above, which is free, and is the mother of us all. Now, argues the apostle, there was no room for Hagar and Sarah, with their respective children, in Abraham's tent. If Ishmael was there, it was because Isaac was not born. But as soon as Isaac came in, Ishmael must go out. So the two principles – of legalism, which insists on the performance of the outward rite of circumcision; and of faith, which accepts the finished work of the Saviour – cannot co-exist in one heart. It is a moral impossibility. So, addressing the Galatian converts, who were being tempted by Judaising teachers to mix legalism and faith, the apostle bade them follow the example of Abraham, and cast out the spirit of bondage that keeps the soul in one perpetual agony of unrest.

## 5.   The remaining history is briefly told

With many a pang Abraham sent Hagar and her child from his home, bidding them a last, sad farewell. In the dim twilight they left, before the camp was astir. Abraham must have suffered keenly as he put the bread into her hand, and with his own fingers bound the bottle of water on her shoulder, and kissed Ishmael once more.

It was better so. And God provided for them both. When the mother's hopes were on the point of expiring, and her son lay dying of thirst in the scorching noon, under the slender shade of a desert shrub, the Angel of God stayed her sobs, pointed out the well of water to which her tears had made her blind, and promised that her child would become a great nation. 'And God said unto Abraham, Let it not be grievous in thy sight . . . in all that Sarah hath said unto thee, hearken unto her voice' (21:12).

One more weight was laid aside, and one more step taken in the preparation of God's 'friend' for the supreme victory of his faith; for which his whole life had been a preparation, and which was now at hand.

# 14

# A Quiet Resting Place

### *Genesis 21:33–34*

We have already seen how wisely and tenderly Abraham's Almighty Friend had been preparing him for his approaching trial; first, in searching out his hidden compact with Sarah; and then in ridding him of the presence of Hagar and her son. And now some further preparation was to be wrought in his spirit, through this period of peaceful rest beside the well of the oath. Leaving Gerar, the patriarch travelled with his slow-moving flocks along the fertile valley, which extends from the sea into the country. Having reached a suitable camping ground, Abraham dug a well, which is probably one of those that remain to this day; and of which the water lying some forty feet below the surface is pure and sweet. Drinking troughs for the use of cattle are scattered around in close proximity to the mouth of the well, the curbstones of which are deeply worn by the friction of the ropes used in drawing up the water by hand. It is not improbable that these very stones were originally hewn under the patriarch's direction, even though their position may have been somewhat altered by the Arab workmen of a later date.

Shortly after Abraham had settled there, Abimelech the king, accompanied by Phicol, the chief captain of his host, came to his encampment, intent on entering into a treaty that would be binding, not only on themselves, but on their children: 'Swear unto me here by God, that thou wilt not deal falsely with me, nor with my son, nor with my son's son' (v.23). Before formally binding himself under these solemn sanctions, Abraham brought up a matter that is still a subject of dispute in Eastern lands. The herdsman of Abimelech had violently taken away the well of water that the servants of Abraham had dug. But the king immediately repudiated all knowledge of their action. It had been done without his knowledge and sanction. And in the treaty into which the two chieftains entered, there was, so to speak, a special clause inserted with reference to this well, destined later to be so famous. It was called 'Beer-sheba', the well of the oath, or 'the well of the seven', with reference to the seven gifts, or victims, on which the oath was taken.

In further commemoration of this treaty, Abraham planted a tamarisk tree which, as a hardy evergreen, would long perpetuate the memory of the transaction in those lands where the mind of man eagerly catches at anything that will break the monotony of the landscape. There also he erected an altar, or shrine, and called on the name of the Lord, the Everlasting God. 'And Abraham sojourned in the land of the Philistines many days'. Ah! those long, happy days! Who could have foretold that the greatest trial of all his life was yet to come, and that from a clear sky a thunderbolt was about to fall, threatening to destroy all his happiness at a single stroke?

# 15

# The Greatest Trial of All

## Genesis 22:2

As long as men live in the world, they will turn to this story with unwaning interest.

### 1   'God did tempt Abraham'

A better rendering might be 'God did put Abraham to the test'. Satan tempts us that he may bring out the evil that is in our hearts; God tries or tests us that he may bring out all the good.

The common incidents of daily life, as well as the rare incessant opportunities of exercising, and so strengthening, and exceptional crises, are so contrived as to give us the graces of Christian living.

## 2   God sends us no trial, whether great or small, without first preparing us

He 'will with the temptation also make a way to escape, that ye may be able to bear it' (1 Cor. 10:13). Trials are therefore God's vote of confidence in us. Many a trifling event is sent to test us before a greater trial is permitted to break on our heads. 'It came to pass *after these things,* that God did tempt Abraham.'

## 3   God often prepares us for coming trial by giving us some new and blessed revelation of himself

I notice that at the close of the preceding chapter we are told that 'Abraham called on the name of the Lord, the everlasting God'. We do not learn that he had never looked on God in this light before. He had known him as God, the Almighty (17:1), but not as God, the Everlasting. The unchangeableness, the eternity, the independence of change, and time, and tense,which mark the being of Jehovah – all these broke suddenly on his soul about that time in a fresh and more vivid manner. The new name was to enable him to better withstand the shock of coming sorrow.

## 4   The trial touched Abraham at his tenderest point

It concerned his Isaac. Nothing else in the circumference of his life could have been such a test as something connected with their heir of promise, the child of his old age, the laughter of his life. *His love was tested.* For love of God, he had done much. But at whatever cost, he had always put God first, glad to sacrifice all, for very love of him. For this he had torn himself from Charran; for this he had been willing to become a homeless wanderer; for this he had renounced the hopes he had built on Ishmael, driving him, as a scapegoat, into the wilderness to return no more. But if he had been asked if he felt that he loved God most of all, he perhaps would not have dared to say that he did. We can never gauge our love by feeling. The only true test of love is how much we are prepared to do for the one to whom we profess it. But God knew how true and strong his child's love was, that he loved him best. So he put him to a supreme test, that all men might hereafter know that a mortal man can love God so much as to put him first, though his dearest lay in the opposite scale of the balance of the heart. Would you not like to love God like this? Then tell him you are willing to pay the cost, if only he will create that love within you.

## 5   It was also a great test of his faith

Isaac was the child of promise. 'In Isaac shall thy seed be called.' With reiterated emphasis this boy had been indicated as the one essential link between the aged pair and the vast posterity that was promised them. And now the father was asked to sacrifice his son's life. It was a trememdous test to his faith. How could God keep his word, and let Isaac die? It was utterly inexplicable to human thought. If Isaac had been old enough to have a son who could perpetuate the seed to future generations, the difficulty would have been removed. But how could the childless Isaac die, and still the promise stand of a posterity through him, innumerable as stars and sand? As the Epistle to the Hebrews tells us, one thought filled the old man's mind, *God is able*. He 'accounted that God was able to raise him up, even from the dead' (Heb. 11:19). He felt sure that somehow God would keep his word. It was not for him to reason how, but simply to obey. He had already seen divine power giving life where all was as good as dead; why should it not do it again? In any case he must go on doing as he was told, and calculating on the inexhaustable stores in the secret hand of God. Oh, for faith like this! To simply believe what God says; to be assured that God will do just what he has promised; looking without alarm, from circumstances that threaten to make the fulfilment impossible, to the bare word of God's unswerving truthfulness.

## 6   It was a test of Abraham's obedience

It was in the visions of the night that the word of the Lord must have come to him, and early the next morning the patriarch was on his way. The night before, as he lay down, he did not have the least idea of the mission on which he would be started at the early beams of dawn. But he acted immediately. 'And Abraham rose up early in the morning' (v.3). No other hand was permitted to saddle the ass, or cleave the wood, or interfere with the promptness of his action. He 'saddled his ass . . . and clave the wood for the burnt offering, and rose up, and went unto the place of which God had told him.'

## 7 The influence of Abraham's behaviour was felt by his son

He caught his father's spirit. We do not know how old he was; he was at least old enough to sustain the toil of a long march on foot, and strong enough to carry uphill the wood, laid on his shoulders by his father. But he gladly bent his youthful strength under the weight of the wood, just as through the *Via Dolorosa* a greater than he carried his cross. It is beautiful to see the evident interest the boy took in the proceedings as they went 'both of them together.'

At all previous sacrifices Abraham had taken a lamb with him, but on this occasion Isaac's wondering attention was drawn to the fact there was no lamb to offer, and with simplicity that must have touched Abraham to the quick, he said, 'My father . . . behold the fire and the wood: but where is the lamb for a burnt offering?' What a stab this was to Abraham's sorely tried heart. With a gleam of prophetic insight, mingled with unwavering faith in him for whose sake he was suffering, the father answered, 'My son, God will provide himself a lamb for a burnt offering; so they went both of them together.'

## 8 At last the discovery could no longer be withheld

'They came to the place which God had told him of; and Abraham built an altar there, and laid the wood in order.' Can you not see the old man slowly gathering the stones, bringing them from the furthest distance possible, placing them with a reverent and judicious precision, and binding the wood with as much deliberation as possible? But at last everything is complete, and Abraham turns to break the fatal secret to his young son who has stood wonderingly by. Inspiration draws a veil over that last tender scene – the father's announcement of his mission, the broken sobs, the kisses wet with tears, the instant submission of the son who was old enough and strong enough to rebel if he had had the mind. Then the binding of that tender frame which, indeed, needed no compulsion because the young heart had learned the secret of obedience and resignation. Finally the lifting him to lie upon the altar, on the wood. Here was a spectacle that must have arrested the attention of heaven. Here was a proof of how much mortal man will do for the love of God. Here was an evidence of childlike faith that must have thrilled the heart of the eternal God, and moved him in the very depths of his being. Do you and I love God like this? Is he more to us than our nearest and dearest? Suppose they stood on this side, and he on that side: would we go with him, though it cost us the loss of all? You think you would. It is a great thing to say.

The blade was raised high, flashing in the rays of the morning sun, but it was not permitted to fall. With the temptation God also made a way of escape. 'And the angel of the Lord called upon him out of heaven, and said, Abraham!' Abraham would surely seize at anything that offered the chance of respite or of pause! and he said, his uplifted hand returning gladly to his side, 'Here am I!' Then followed words that spoke release and deliverance: 'Lay not thine hand upon the lad, neither do thou anything upon him: for now I know that thou fearest God, seeing thou hast not withheld thy son, thine only son, from me' (v.12).

'Abraham called the name of that place Jehovah-jireh' (The Lord will provide). So it passed into a proverb, and men said one to another, 'In the mount of the Lord deliverance shall be seen.' It is a true word. Deliverance is not seen till we come to the mount of sacrifice. God does not provide deliverance until we have reached the point of our extremest need. It is when our Isaac is on the altar, and the knife is about to descend on him, that God's angel interposes to deliver.

Near the altar was a thicket, and, as Abraham lifted up his eyes and looked around, he beheld a ram caught there by its horns. Nothing could be more opportune. He had wanted to show his gratitude and the fullness of his heart's devotion, and he gladly went and took the ram, and offered him up for a burnt offering in place of his son. Here, surely, is the great doctrine of substitution; and we are taught how life can be preserved only at the cost of life given.

Abraham's act enables us better to understand the sacrifice that God made to save us. The gentle submission of Isaac, laid on the altar with throat bare to the knife, gives us a better insight into Christ's obedience to death. Isaac's restoration to life, as from the dead, and after having been three days dead in his father's purpose, suggests the resurrection from Joseph's tomb.

Before they left the mountain brow, God said: 'By myself have I sworn . . . because thou hast done this thing, and hast not withheld thy son, thine only son: that in blessing I will bless thee; and in multiplying I will multiply thy seed as the stars of heaven, and as the sand which is upon the sea shore; and thy seed shall possess the gate of his enemies; and in thy seed shall all the nations of the earth be blessed; because thou hast obeyed my voice' (vv. 16–17). Do not think, O soul of man, that this is a unique and solitary experience. There is nothing that God will not do for a man who dares to step out upon what seems to be the mist; who then finds rock beneath him as he puts his foot down.

## 9   All who believe are the children of faithful Abraham

We then, Gentiles though we are, divided from Abraham by the lapse of centuries, may inherit the blessing that he won; and the more so as we follow closely in his steps. That blessing is for us if we will claim it. With a new light in his heart, with a new composure on his face, Abraham returned to his young men. 'And they rose up and went together to Beersheba; and Abraham dwelt at Beersheba', but the halo of the vision lit up the common places of his life, as it shall do for us, when from the mounts of sacrifice we turn back to the lowlands of daily duty.

# 16

# Machpelah, and its First Tenant

*Genesis 23:4, 19*

When Abraham came down the slopes of Mount Moriah, hand in hand with Isaac, fifty years of his long life still lay before him. Of those fifty years, twenty-five passed away before the event recorded in this chapter. In all likelihood one year was as much as possible like another. Few events broke their monotony.

Perhaps we can never realise how much the members of such a household as Abraham's would be to one another. Through long, unbroken periods they lived together, finding all their society in one another. Thus it must have happened that the loss through death of one loved and familiar face would leave a blank never to be filled, and scarcely ever to be forgotten. We need no wonder, therefore, that so much stress is laid on the death of Sarah, the chief event of those fifty years of Abraham's life.

## 1   We are first arrested by Abraham's tears

'And Sarah died in Kirjath-arba; the same is Hebron in the land of Canaan'. Abraham seems to have been away from home, perhaps at Beersheba, when Sarah breathed her last; but he came at once 'to mourn for Sarah, and to weep for her.' This is the first time we read of Abraham weeping. But now that Sarah is lying dead before him, the fountains of his grief are broken up.

Sarah had been the partner of his life for seventy or eighty years. She was the only link to the home of his childhood. She alone could sympathise with him when he talked of Terah and Nahor, or of Haran and Ur of the Chaldees. She alone was left of all who thirty years before had shared the hardships of his pilgrimage. As he knelt by her side, what a tide of memories must have rushed over him of their common plans, and hopes, and fears, and joys! He remembered her as the bright young wife, as his pilgrim, as the childless persecutor of Hagar, as the prisoner of Pharaoh and Abimelech, as the loving mother of Isaac, and every memory would bring a fresh rush of tears.

There are some who chide tears as unmanly, unsubmissive, unchristian. They would comfort us with a chill and pious stoicism, bidding us meet the most agitating passages of our history with rigid and tearless countenance. With such the spirit of the gospel and of the Bible, has little sympathy. Religion does not come to make us unnatural and inhuman, but to purify and ennoble all those natural emotions with which our complex nature is endowed. Jesus wept. Peter wept. The Ephesian converts wept on the neck of the apostle whose face they thought they were never to see again. Christ still stands by each mourner, saying, 'Weep, my child; weep, for I have wept.'

## 2   Notice Abraham's confession

'Abraham stood up from before his dead, and spake unto the sons of Heth, saying, I am a stranger and a sojourner with you: give me a possession of a burying place with you' (vv.3–4). See how sorrow reveals the heart. To look at Abraham as the great and wealthy patriarch, the emir, the chieftain of a mighty clan, we cannot guess his secret thoughts. He has been in the land for sixty-two years; and he is probably as settled and naturalised as any of the princes around. So you might think, until he is widowed of his beloved Sarah! Then, amidst his grief, you hear the real man speaking his most secret thought: 'I am a stranger and a sojourner with you.'

These are remarkable words, and they were never forgotten by his children. So deeply had those words of Abraham sunk in the national mind, that the apostle inscribes them over the cemetery where the great and the good of the Jewish nation lie entombed: 'These all died in faith, not having received the promises, but having seen them afar off, and were persuaded of them, and embraced them, and confessed that they were strangers and pilgrims on the earth' (Heb. 11:13).

We may ask what it was that maintained this spirit in Abraham for so many years. There is but one answer: 'They that say such things declare plainly that they seek a country' (Heb. 11:14). Uprooted from the land of his birth, the patriarch could never take root again in any earthly country, and his spirit was always on the alert, eagerly reaching out toward the city of God. He refused to be contented with anything short of this, and therefore God was not ashamed to be called his God, because he had prepared for him a city. How this elevation of soul shames some of us! We profess to look for a city, but we take good care to make for ourselves an assured position among the citizens of this world. We profess to count all things as dross, but the eagerness with which, muckrake in hand, we strive to heap together the treasures of earth is a startling commentary on our words.

### 3   Notice Abraham's faith

Men are wont to bury their dead alongside their ancestors. The graves of past generations are the heritage of their posterity. The American loves to visit the quiet English churchyard where his fathers lie. The Jew elects in old age to journey to Palestine, that dying he may be buried in soil consecrated by the remains of his race. And it may be that Abraham first thought of that far distant grave in Charran, where Terah and Haran lay buried. Should he take Sarah there? He decided against it, saying, 'that country, has no claim on me now. The only land on which I have a claim is this wherein I have been a stranger. Here in years to come shall my children live. Here the generations that bear my name shall spread themselves out as the sands on the seashore, and as the stars in the midnight sky. It is therefore necessary that I should place our grave, in which Sarah their mother, and I their father, shall lie, in the heart of the land – to be a nucleus around which our descendants shall gather in years to come.'

When the chieftains to whom he made his appeal heard it, they instantly offered him the choice of their sepulchre affirming that none of them could withhold his sepulchre from so mighty a prince. And afterward, when he sought their intercession with Ephron the son of Zohar, for the obtaining of the cave of Machpelah, which was at the end of his field, and Ephron proposed to give it him in the presence of the sons of his people, Abraham steadfastly refused. So, after many courteous speeches, in the dignified manner that still prevails amongst Orientals, 'the field, and the cave . . . and all the trees . . . were made sure unto Abraham for a possession in their presence of the children of Heth, before all that went in at the gate of his city' (vv.17–18). Their witness had the same binding effect in those rude days as legal documents have in our own.

There Abraham buried Sarah; there Isaac and Ishmael buried Abraham; there Isaac was buried, and Rebecca his wife; there Jacob buried Leah; and there Joseph buried Jacob his father; and there in all likelihood, guarded by the jealous Moslem, untouched by the changes and storms that have swept around their quiet resting place, those remains are sleeping still, holding that land in fee, and anticipating the time when on a larger and more prominent scale the promise of God to Abraham will be accomplished.

# 17

# Gathered to His People

## *Genesis 25:8*

No human name can vie with Abraham's for the widespread reverence it has evoked among all races throughout all time. What was the secret of this widespread renown? It is not because he headed one of the greatest movements of the human family; nor yet because he evinced manly and intellectual vigour; nor because he possessed vast wealth. It was rather the remarkable nobility and grandeur of his religious life that has made him the object of veneration to all generations of mankind.

### 1 At the basis of his character was a mighty faith

'Abraham believed God.' In that faith he left his native land and travelled to one that was promised, but not clearly indicated. In that faith he waited through long years, sure that God would give him the promised child. In that faith he lived a nomad life, dwelling in tents, and making no attempt to return to the settled country from which he had come out. In that faith he was prepared to offer Isaac, and buried Sarah.

## 2   To faith he added virtue, or manly courage

What could have been more manly than the speed with which he armed his trained servants; or than the heroism with which he, with a train of undisciplined shepherds, attacked the disciplined bands of Assyria, returning victorious down the long valley of the Jordan?

## 3   And to manly courage he added knowledge

All his life he was a student in God's college of divinity. He grew in the knowledge of God and the divine nature, which at the first had been to him a *terra incognita*. An unknown country grew beneath his gaze.

## 4   And to knowledge he added temperance, or self-control

That he was master of himself is evident from the way in which he repelled the offer of the king of Sodom; and curbed his spirit amid the irritations caused by Lot's herdsmen. There is no type of character more attractive than that of the man who is master of himself, because he is the servant of God; and who can rule others rightly because he can rule himself well.

## 5   And to temperance, patience

Speaking of him, the voice of New Testament inspiration affirms that he 'patiently endured' (Heb. 6:15). It was no ordinary patience that waited through the long years, not murmuring or complaining, but prepared to abide God's time (Ps. 131:2–3).

## 6   And to his patience he added godliness

One of Abraham's chief characteristics was his piety – a constant sense of the presence of God in his life, and a love and devotion to him. Wherever he pitched his tent, there his first care was to erect an altar. Shechem, Hebron, Beersheba – alike saw these tokens of his reverence and love. In every time of trouble he turned as naturally to God as a child to its father; and there was such holy intercourse between his spirit and that of God that the name by which he is now best known throughout the East is *The Friend*.

## 7   And to godliness he added brotherly kindness

Some men who are devoted toward God are lacking in the more tender qualities toward those most closely knit with them in family bonds. It was not so with Abraham. He was full of affection. Beneath the calm exterior and the erect bearing of the mighty chieftain there beat a warm and affectionate heart. Listen to that passionate cry, 'Oh that Ishmael might live before thee!'

## 8   And to brotherly kindness he added charity, or love

In his dealings with men he could afford to be generous, openhearted, openhanded; willing to pay the large price demanded for Machpelah's cave without haggling or complaint; destitute of petty pride; right with God, and therefore able to shed on men the rays of a genial, restful noble heart.

## 9   All these things were in him and abounded

and they made him neither barren nor unfruitful; they made his calling and election sure; they prepared for him an abundant entrance into the everlasting kingdom of God our Saviour.

## 10   'Abraham gave up the ghost'

There was no reluctance in his death; he did not cling to life – he was glad to be gone; and when the angel-messenger summoned him, without a struggle, and with the readiness of glad consent his spirit returned to God who gave it.

## 11   He was gathered to his people

This cannot refer to his body, for that did not sleep beside his ancestors, but side by side with Sarah's. Surely then it must refer to his spirit.

What a lovely synonym for death! To die is to rejoin our people; to pass into a world where the great clan is gathering, welcoming with shouts each newcomer through the shadows. Where are your people? I trust they are God's people; and if so, those who bear your name, standing on the other shore, are more numerous than the handful gathered around you here; many whom you have never known, but who know you; many whom you have loved and lost awhile; many who without you cannot be made perfect in their happiness. There they are, rank on rank, company on company, regiment on regiment, watching for your coming. Be sure you do not disappoint them!

## 12  'And his sons, Isaac and Ishmael, buried him in the cave of Machpelah'

There were great differences between these two. Ishmael, the child of his slave: Isaac, of the wedded wife. Ishmael, the offspring of expediency: Isaac, of promise. Ishmael, wild and masterful, 'the wild ass'; strongly marked in his individuality; proud, independent, swift to take an insult, swift to avenge it: Isaac, quiet and retiring, submissive and meek, willing to carry wood, to be kept in the dark, to be bound, to yield up his wells, and to let his wife govern his house. And yet all differences were wiped out in that moment of supreme sorrow; and coming from his desert fastnesses, surrounded by his wild and ruffian freebooters, Ishmael united with the other son of their common father, who had displaced him in his inheritance, and who was so great a contrast to himself; but all differences were smoothed out in that hour.

The remains of the man who had dared to trust God at all costs, and who with pilgrim steps had traversed so many weary miles, were solemnly laid beside the dust of Sarah, his faithful wife. There, in all probability, they rest even to this day, and thence they will be raised at the coming of the King.

Out of materials which were by no means extraordinary, God built up a character with which he could hold fellowship as friend with friend; and a life that has exerted a profound influence on all people since.

# JACOB

# 1

# First Impressions

## Genesis 25

There are many reasons why the story of Jacob is such an interesting account of a Bible 'great'.

## 1  Jacob was the father of the Jewish race, and a typical Jew

The Jews called themselves by the name of Jacob; and surnamed themselves by the name of Israel (Isa. 44:5). We speak of Jacob, rather than Abraham, as the founder of the people to which he gave his name because, though Abraham was their ancestor, he was not so exclusively. The wild son of the desert claims him as Father as does the industrious Jew. Nor is that all. We Gentiles have reason to be proud that we can trace back our lineage to the first great Hebrew, the man who *crossed over*, and whom God designated as his friend.

No thoughtful person can ignore this wonderful people. Their history is, without doubt, the key to the complications of modern politics; and it may be that their redemption is to be the fruit of that mighty travail that is beginning to convulse all peoples, announced as it is by all the national calamities we are seeing today.

If we can understand the life of Jacob, we can understand the history of his people. The extremes which startle us in them are all in him. Like them, he is the most successful schemer of his times; and, like them, he has that deep spirituality, that far-seeing faith, which are the grandest of all qualities, and make a man capable of the highest culture that a human spirit can receive. Like them, he spends the greatest part of his life in exile, and amid trying

69

conditions of toil and sorrow; and, like them, he is inalienably attached to that dear land, his only hold on which was by the promise of God and the graves of the heroic dead.

But Jacob's character was purified by tremendous discipline. Through such discipline his people have been passing for centuries; and surely, before its searching fires, the baser elements of their natures will be expelled, until they recognize the true Joseph of their seed.

## 2   Jacob also has so many points of contact with ourselves

His *failings* speak to us. He takes advantage of his brother when hard pressed with hunger. He deceives his father. He meets Laban's guile with guile. He thinks to buy himself out of his trouble with Esau. Mean, crafty and weak, are terms we can apply to him, but who is there who does not feel the germs of this harvest to be within his own breast. 'There, but for the grace of God, go I.'

His *aspirations* speak to us. We too have our angel-haunted dreams and make our vows when we leave home. We too count hard work a trifle, when inspired by all-mastering love. We too cling in a paroxysm of yearning to the departing angels, that they should bless us before they go. We too get back to our Bethels and bury our idols. We too confess ourselves pilgrims and strangers on the earth. We too recognize the shepherd care of God (Gen. 48:15). We too wait for God's salvation (Gen. 49:18).

# 2

# The Sale of the Birthright

## *Genesis 25*

## 1   The Birthright

What was it? It was not worldly prosperity, for of this, Esau, who lost it, probably had more than Jacob, who won it.

The birthright was a spiritual heritage. It gave the right to become the priest of the family or clan. It constituted a link in the line of descent by which the Messiah was to be born in the world.

## 2 The barter

One day Jacob was standing over a caldron of savoury pottage, made of those red lentils which to the present day form a dish highly relished in Syria and in Egypt. At that moment, who should come in but Esau, faint with hunger. 'Give me some of that,' he cried impatiently.

Now Jacob was not wholly a selfish man, but it suddenly occurred to him that this would be a good opportunity to win the right to be the spiritual leader of the clan. So knowing well how little his brother counted on his rights, he made the extraordinary proposal to exchange the mess of pottage for the birthright.

And as for Esau, we can never forget the beacon words of Scripture: 'Look diligently . . . lest there be any fornicator, or profane person, as Esau, who for one morsel of meat sold his birthright' (Heb. 12:16). How many are there among us, born into the world with wonderful talents, who yet fling away all these possiblities of blessing and blessedness, for one brief plunge into the Stygian pool of selfish and sensual indulgence!

# 3

# The Stolen Blessing

## *Genesis 27*

We need not be astonished to learn that temptation was allowed to come to Jacob from an unexpected source, taking him unawares.

**1   This temptation was greedily responded to by the weak and crafty nature of Jacob**

So long as we take our stand on what is lawful we are impregnable. But when once we argue with the tempter on the lower grounds of possible discovery and failure, we shall find ourselves outmatched by his arithmetic, and led as garlanded oxen to the slaughterhouse. Into this fault, to which all weak men are so liable, Jacob fell; and so, when his mother commanded him a second time to obey her voice (v.13), and go to the flock for two good kids of the goats, 'he went, and fetched, and brought them to his mother.'

When once the first step had been taken, it was quickly followed by others which it seemed to render needful.

He simulated his brother's dress and skin. While the meat was cooking, Rebekah was engaged in turning over Esau's wardrobe, to find some suitable garments, highly perfumed. This done, she prepared the delicate skins of the kids for his hands and neck. All was done with haste, lest Esau might come in. And when all was ready, Jacob arrayed himself to play his part.

He deceived his father with a direct falsehood. 'I am Esau thy firstborn; I have done according as thou badest me . . . eat of my venison, that thy soul may bless me.'

He made an impious use of the name of God. In answer to Isaac's question as to how he found it so quickly, he dared to say, 'The Lord thy God brought it to me.'

Yet what horror must have thrilled him as he found himself forced to take step after step, aware that he was being carried out by a rushing stream, yet not daring to stop. How his heart must have stood still when the old man became suspicious, and doubted his voice, and insisted on feeling, smelling, and having him near! What if God should strike him dead! What a relief when he came out again into the fresh air! – though the words of the coveted blessing hardly repaid him for the agony he had passed through. How he must have loathed himself. The sun itself seemed shorn of half its light.

Yet this is the man who became the prince of God. And if he became so, is there not hope for us, who can trace in Jacob many resemblances to ourselves? If the almighty Workman could fashion such clay into so fair a vessel, what may he not do for us?

But remember, God must implant the nature that he educates into Israel the Prince. When we speak of God's education we must be very careful what we mean, and how we express it, lest we should countenance error. Amidst all his sin, there must have been in Jacob a better self, which was capable of receiving the education of God and of being developed into Israel. And it was the possession of this better nature that made Jacob capable of rising to a spiritual level, for which Esau had neither the aptitude nor the taste.

# 4

# The Angel-Ladder

## *Genesis 28*

When Esau found that Jacob had stolen his blessing, he hated him, and vowed to kill him. This was nothing less than might have been expected from his headstrong and impetuous nature. These threats came to Rebekah's ears and filled her with fear, lest she should be deprived of them both in one day – Jacob, the jewel of her eye, by the hand of his brother; and Esau, by being compelled, like a second Cain, to become an outlaw for his brother's murder.

But Rebekah understood Esau's temperament perfectly. If only Jacob absented himself for a short time, all would be forgotten. So Rebekah made up her mind that he should go across the desert to Haran, to abide for a time with her brother Laban. She did not tell her husband all her reasons why Jacob should go to Haran but she adduced very good and obvious ones, in the necessity of preserving from defilement the holy seed, and of procuring for Jacob a suitable wife.

Isaac fell in with the proposal; and 'called Jacob, and blessed him, and charged him, and said unto him, Thou shalt not take a wife of the daughters of Canaan. Arise, go to Padan-aram; and take thee a wife from thence of the daughters of Laban thy mother's brother. And God Almighty bless thee!' And Jacob, not without many a tear, went out from Beersheba, and went toward Haran. And it was on his way that this revelation by means of his dream of the angels and ladder was made to him.

## 1   The circumstances in which this revelation was made to him

Jacob was lonely. He was not what we should call a young man for he reached mature years: but it is almost certain that this was the first time he left the shelter of his home. In the early morning light, as he started forth, there may have been an exhilarating sense of independence, freshness, and novelty; but as night drew its curtains over the world there stole over his mind a sense of loneliness and melancholy. This was God's chosen time, when he drew near to his spirit. And so it has often been with men. Recall, for a moment, your first night away from home – as a schoolboy, or apprentice, or servant, or student, and tell me if that was not a sacred epoch in your history, when God took up the trailing tendrils of your love and twined them around himself, and you realised his presence and clung to him as never before.

Jacob was also in fear. What would hinder Esau, when he heard of his flight, from pursuing him? He was well acquainted with those parts; he was fleet of foot, or might use dogs, so as to track him and run him down. Besides, the country was full of robbers and wild beasts. And it was then that God calmed his fears by showing him that the lone spot was teeming with angel-hosts, willing and eager to encamp about him, with celestial watch and ward. The most lonely spot is as safe for us as the most crowded, since God is there. There comes assurance of one who cannot lie: 'Fear not!' so that we may boldly say, 'The Lord is my helper, and I will not fear what man shall do unto me' (Heb. 13:6).

## 2   The elements of this revelation

The Spirit of God always conveyed his teachings to his servants in language borrowed from their surroundings. Bethel was a bleak moorland that lay in the heart of Palestine. There was nothing remarkable about it. The hillsides and upland slopes were strewn with large sheets of bare rock.

Fleeing northward, the wanderer suddenly found himself overtaken by the swift Eastern night. There was nothing else to do but to lie down on the hard ground, taking the stones as a pillow for his head. Thus he slept, and as he slept he dreamed; and in his dream his mind wove together many of his waking thoughts in fantastic medley. The striking appearance of those huge boulders, the memory that Abraham had built one of his earliest altars there, his last look upward at that wondrous heaven, studded with the brilliant constellations of an Eastern night – all these wove themselves into his dreams. It seemed as if the huge slabs of limestone came near together, and built themselves up into a gigantic staircase, reaching from the spot where he lay to the starry depths above him, and on that staircase angels came and went, peopling by their multitudes that most desolate region, and evidently deeply concerned with the sleeper that lay beneath. Nor was this all; for, from the summit, the voice of God fell like music.

There are here three points of interest:

*a. The ladder.* Jacob may have been oppressed by a sense of his insignificance, and sin, and distance from home. And it was very pleasant to know that there was a link between him and God.

The weakest and most sinful may climb through Jesus from the verge of the pit of hell to the foot of the eternal throne.

Thank God, we are not cut adrift to the mercy of every current; this dark coal ship is moored alongside the bright ship of heavenly grace. Yes, and there is a plank from the one to the other.

*b. The angels.* The angels ascended: there is the ascent of our prayers. The angels descended: there is the descent of God's answers. We are reminded of the afferent and efferent nerves of the body – up which flash the sharp stings of pain from the extremities to the head; and down which come the directions how to act. It would do as well to ponder more frequently the ministering care of the angels. God gives his angels charge concerning us, to keep us in *all* our ways; they bear us up in their hands. They are 'sent forth to minister [to the] heirs of salvation' (Heb. 1:14).

What comfort Jacob must have realised! He found, to his great surprise, that that lone spot was *the gate of heaven,* for it seemed as if the populations of heaven were teeming around him, thronging to and fro. We need never yield to feelings of loneliness again, if we remember that, in our most retired hours, we are living in the very heart of a vast throng of angels; and we should hear their songs, and see their forms, if only our senses were not clogged with sin.

*c. The voice of God.* God answered his thoughts. He felt lonesome, but God said, 'I will be with thee.' He feared Esau; but God said, 'I will keep thee.' He knew not what hardships he might meet with; and God promised to bring him safely back again. Appearances seemed to contradict the divine promise; but God said, 'I will do that which I have spoken to thee of.'

Is it not remarkable that Jacob did not see these glorious realities until he slept? God was as much brooding in the wilderness before he slept as afterward; only he *knew it not.* It was only when he slept that he came to know it.

# 5

# The Noble Resolve

## *Genesis 28*

The revelation of God's love will have five results on the receptive spirit.

### 1   It will make us quick to discover God

Jacob had been inclined to localise God in his father's tents: as many localise him now in chapel, church, or minster; supposing that prayer and worship are more acceptable there than anywhere beside. *Now* he learned that God was equally in every place – on the moorland waste as well as by Isaac's altar, though his eye had been too blind to perceive him. If your spirit is reverent, it will discern God on a moorland waste. If your spirit is thoughtless and careless, it will fail to find him even in the face of Jesus Christ. If only we were full of God, we would find that every spot was sacred, every moment hallowed, every act a sacrament; from every incident we would see a ladder stretching up to heaven; and our happy spirits would be constantly availing themselves of the opportunity to run up the shining way and embrace our dearest Lord.

Up to this moment the Lord has been in many of the moorland wastes of your life; *but you have not known it.* He has been beside you in that lonely chamber of pain; in that irksome situation; on that rugged pathway; but your eyes have been holden. What wonder that your path has been so drear! But if you will only take home to yourself the message of the cross of Jesus, 'God loves me,' then you will never feel lonely or outcast again. You will discover that a desolate moor is one of the mansions of your Father's house. You will be able to commune with him equally on the hillside as amid the congregation. And you will often be compelled to exclaim, as you meet with fresh revelations of himself, in the most unlikely places, '*This* is none other but the house of God; and *this* is the gate of heaven.'

### 2    It will inspire us with Godly fear

'He was afraid, and said, How dreadful is this place!' 'Perfect love casteth out fear' – the fear that has torment; but it begets in us another fear, the fear that reveres God, and shudders to grieve him; and dreads to lose the tiniest chance of doing his holy will. True love is always fearless and fearful. It is fearless with the freedom of undoubting trust; but it is fearful lest it should miss a single grain of tender affection, or should bring a moment's shadow over the face of the beloved.

### 3    It will constrain us to give ourselves to God

The ordinary reading might lead us to suppose that, true to his worst self, Jacob tried to make a bargain with God; and promised to take him as his, on certain conditions. '*If* God will be with me, and keep me in my way, and give me bread to eat and raiment to put on: *then* – '. But a better reading relieves him of this sad imputation; and tones the words down to mean that if the Lord would be his God, then the stone should be God's house. But, however the words may run, this was evidently the moment of his consecration.

### 4   It will prompt us to devote our property to him

'Of all that thou shalt give me, I will surely give the tenth unto thee.' There is no reason to doubt that this became the principle of Jacob's life: and if so, he shames the majority of Christian people – most of whom do not give on principle; and give a very uncertain and meagre percentage of their income. The church would have no lack if every one of its members acted on this principle.

### 5   It will fill us with joy

'Then Jacob lifted up his feet' (29:1, *marg.*). Does that not denote the lighthearted alacrity with which he sped on his way? His feet were winged with joy, and seemed scarcely to tread the earth. And this will be our happy lot, if only we will believe the love that God has for us. 'Our soul shall make her boast in the Lord;
     the humble shall hear thereof, and be glad.'

# 6

# The Education of Home

## *Genesis 29*

Next to the love of God comes the love of man or woman, as a factor in the education of a human spirit. Jacob's encounter with Rachel at the first well he came to, reminds us that though there is nothing more important than the union of heart with heart, there is nothing into which people drift more heedlessly.

### 1   The four conditions of a true home

*a. There must be a supreme affection.*   This was clearly a love-match. 'Jacob loved Rachel' (v.18) is a sufficient explanation. If there is true love, then, though one has been taken from the other by death before they stand together at the marriage altar, yet in the sight of God those two are one forever.

It is needless to show how the necessity of the presence of a supreme love is the ground and justification of monogamy, the union of two. You have no right to marry if this love is absent.

**b.** *Marriage must be 'only in the Lord.'*   Jacob's was so. He might have taken a wife of the daughters of Heth, as Esau did, steeped in the idolatries and impurities that cursed the land. But, guided by his parents' counsels, he crossed the desert to obtain a wife who had been reared in a home in which there still lingered the memory of the worship of the God of Abraham, of Nahor, and of their father Terah (31:53).

**c.** *A true home should be based on the good will of parents and friends.*   There is the halo of a brighter promise encircling the union of two young hearts, when it is ratified amid the congratulations of rejoicing friends. It is wise and right, where practicable, for children to consult, in such matters, those whose love has made them the eager guardians of their opening life; and to do so by courtesy, even when mature years have given them the right to choose and act for themselves. But if parents would have such confidences when their children are old, they must make themselves their confidants while they are young.

## 2   The expulsive power of supreme affection

'Jacob served seven years for Rachel; and they seemed unto him but a few days, for the love he had to her' (v.20). That sentence always charms us for its beauty and its truth. Love has the power of making a rough road easy, and a weary waiting time short. It makes us oblivious to many things, which, for lack of it, would be insupportable.

Do you find it hard to deny yourself, to make the required sacrifices for doing his will, and to confess him? Go to the Holy Spirit, and ask him to shed the love of Christ abroad in your heart, and so teach you to love him who first loved you. Then, as the tides of that love rise within your heart, they will constrain you to live, not for yourself, but for him; then burdens will be light that once crushed; roads will be pleasant that once strained and tired; hours will fly that were once leaden-footed; years will seem as a day. Love's labour is always light.

# 7

# The Mid-Passage of Life

## *Genesis 30*

In our last chapter, we saw how Jacob built for himself a home. But ah – what a home! The presence of the two sisters there was fatal to its peace. They who had been happy enough as sisters before he came, could not now live in such close quarters, as wives of the same husband, without incessant jealousy. Each had her own grievance. Poor Leah knew that Jacob had never loved her, and that she was not the wife of his choice; and though God compensated her by giving her that pride of oriental women, a family of sons, yet even this was a new source of anguish to her; for Rachel envied her. She was frightfully desolate in the home, and the names of her sons are like so many landmarks of her misery. But Rachel must have been equally miserable: true, she had her husband's love, but she could not be sure of keeping it; and she had the mortification of seeing her sister's children growing up as her husband's heirs.

What wonder, then, that the children grew up wild and bad? Reuben, unstable as water, excitable and passionate; Simeon, quiet to obey, but quick to desperate cruelty; and Levi, a willing accomplice in his crime. When children turn out badly, it is often the fault of their home training; and it is more often the result of what they see than of what they are taught. Whatever Jacob may have been – the impressions received in the woman's tents, of high words and evil passion, would be enough to ruin any child.

But it is not so much Jacob's home life, as his business dealings, that we have now to consider.

He served fourteen years, as a dowry for his two wives; and at the time when Rachel gave birth to her firstborn, Joseph, that period had elapsed. As soon as mother and child were able to undertake so long and fatiguing a journey, Jacob declared his intention of returning to Canaan; and this resolve was perhaps precipitated by a message from Rebekah saying that there was now no further reason for his absence.

This proposal alarmed Laban, who had learned to value Jacob's services; and was much too astute to let him go without making an effort to retain so valuable a servant. Jacob at once caught at the opportunity of making an independent provision for his large and increasing family; and the bargin was struck.

Eastern sheep are almost wholly white; the goats black; the multicoloured rare. Jacob proposed, therefore, that all the brown and speckled should be at once removed; and that all of that colour, which the flock produced afterward, should be his wage.

Jacob's double-dealing appeared to be a success. 'The man increased exceedingly; and had much cattle, and maidservants, and menservants, and camels, and asses.' But that which men call success, and which is sometimes a very superficial and temporary thing, proves nothing as to the rightness or wrongness of a life. Many a noble life in the sight of God has been a sad failure when judged by human standards. And many a failure in the judgment of man has been a royal success in the estimation of the angels.

# 8

# The Stirring-up of the Nest

## *Genesis 31*

### 1   The summons to depart

'And the Lord said unto Jacob, Return unto the land of thy

fathers, and to thy kindred; and I will be with thee.' Whether there was voice audible to the outward ear I cannot tell, but there was certainly the uprising of a strong impulse within his heart.

There are many kinds of voices in the world, and none of them is without significance; but the more truly we partake of the nature of 'his own sheep,' the more unerringly will we detect the voice of the Good Shepherd. If you are not quite sure, wait until you are. The only necessity is to be willing to do his will so soon as it is clearly seen. If you are in doubt, wait in faith until every other door is shut, and one path only lies open before you.

God's voice to the heart is generally corroborated by the drift of outward circumstances. 'Jacob beheld the countenance of Laban, and, behold, it was not toward him as before.' For some time their relations had been strained. Ten times in six years Laban had altered the method of computing his wages; and now there were symptoms of open rupture.

It is bitter to behold a change passing over men and women in their behaviour toward us; a change we cannot avert. And yet God is undoubtedly in all this. Take heart; it is only part of the process of making you a prince; in no other way can your mean Jacob-nature be replaced by something better.


## 2   The tenacity of circumstances

When the pilgrim-spirit attempts to obey the voice of God, the house is always filled with neighbours trying to dissuade him from the rash resolve. There was something of this in Jacob's case.

He was evidently afraid that his wives would hinder his return. It would have been natural if they had. Was it likely that they would at once consent to his proposal to tear them from their kindred and land? This fear may have greatly hindered Jacob. He at least thought it necessary to fortify himself with a quiverful of arguments, in order to carry his point. But God had been at work before him; and had prepared their hearts, so that they at once assented to his plan, saying: 'We have no further ties to home; now then, whatsoever God hath said unto thee, do.'

In Laban's endeavours to retain Jacob, we have a vivid picture of the eager energy with which the world would retain us when we are about to turn away from it forever. It pursues us, with all its allies, for seven days and more (v.23). It asks us why we are not content to abide with it (v.27). It professes its willingness to make our religion palatable by mingling with it its own evils (v.27). It appeals to our feelings, and asks us not to be too cruel (v.28). It threatens us (v.29). It mocks us with our sudden compunction, after so many years of contentment with its company (v.30). It reproaches us with our inconsistency in making so much of our God, and yet harbouring some cunning sin. 'Wherefore hast thou stolen my gods?' (v.30). Ah, friends, how sad it is, when we, who profess so much, give occasion to our foes to sneer, because of the secret idols which they know we carry with us! Sometimes it is not we who are to blame, so much as our Rachels – our wives, or children, or friends. But we should never rest until, so far as we know, our camp is clear of the accursed thing.

O that you might break away from that life of worldliness in which you have tarried too long! Make a clean break with it! Call your friends to witness your solemn act; above all, call God to witness your resolve – that never again shall the world, the flesh, or the devil, come over to you, or you pass over to them. This is the true Mizpah of the Lord's watch.

## 3 The divine care

Well might Jacob have thrilled with joy, as he said to his wives, 'The God of my father has been with me.' Blessed is he for whom God fights. He must be more than a conqueror. So Jacob found it; and, at the end of his encounter with Laban, he was able to repeat his assurance that the God of his father had been with him (v.42).

At the head of his flocks and herds, with wives and children and slaves, he struck across the Euphrates and the desert, at the utmost speed possible to his encumbered march; but God's angels accompanied him. He met their radiant hosts afterward (32:1). His flight remained unsuspected for three days; then Laban set off with swift camels in pursuit, and overtook them, while they were still threading their way among the richly wooded and watered hills of Gilead. It was a moment of real danger; and it was then that God interposed. 'God came to Laban the Syrian by night.' That dream laid an irresistible spell on Laban, which prevented him from carrying out his design to do Jacob hurt.

Jacob was an erring and unworthy child; but God did not leave or forsake him. Thus he was able to throw his protection around his erring child; and this was part of the loving discipline that was leading Jacob to a goal of which he never dreamed.

Jacob conceived that he was a model shepherd (v.38), but he little realised how lovingly he was being protected by the shepherd-care of him who keeps Israel, and who neither slumbers nor sleeps. That protection may be ours.

# 9

# The Midnight Wrestle

## Genesis 32

On the morning after his interview with Laban, Jacob broke up his camp on the heights of Gilead, and slowly took his journey southward. He little knew that that day was to be the crisis of his life.

Three events are narrated in this chapter, corresponding to morning, afternoon, and night of that memorable day.

### 1   In the morning

we are told that the angels of God met him. Those words tremble with mystic and indescribable beauty. How did it take place? Did they come in twos or threes? Or, as he turned some corner in the mountain pass, did he see a long procession of bright harnessed angels, marching four abreast, with golden bands girding about them their lustrous robes, while the music of heaven beat time? Would it not remind him of Bethel, that lay across the chasm of twenty-five years? Would it not nerve and prepare him for coming danger?

Doubtless these angel-bands are always passing by us; only our eyes are shut so that we do not see them. But whether we see them or not, we may always depend on their being at hand – especially when some heavy trial is near.

## 2   As the day wore on to afternoon

Jacob's spirit was shaken to the centre by ominous tidings. He had sent messengers to announce to Esau his return, and to ascertain his mind. The messengers now returned in breathless haste to say that Esau was coming to meet him, with four hundred men at his back. Jacob was panic-stricken; and well he might be. His all was at stake – wives and children; herds and cattle; the careful gains of six laborious years. The Mizpah-tower barred the way back; his bridge was, so to speak, burned behind him. Around him were robber tribes, eager to seize on the rich booty if he showed the least sign of vacillation or fear. But to go on seemed to involve a risk of inevitable ruin. There was just one alternative – which most men will only turn to when all other expedients have failed – he could at least pray; and to prayer he betook himself. It may have been a long time since he prayed like this.

There are many healthy symptoms in that prayer. In some respects it may serve as a mould into which our own spirits may pour themselves, when melted in the fiery furnace of sorrow.

He began by quoting God's promise: 'Thou saidst'. Be sure, in prayer, to get your feet well on a promise; it will give you purchase enough to force open the gates of heaven, and to take it by force.

He next went to confession: 'I am not worthy'. There passed before his mind his deceit to his aged father; his behaviour to Esau; his years of trickery to Laban. All the meanness of his heart and life stood revealed, as a landscape is revealed when the midnight sky is riven by the lightning flash. 'I am not worthy'. Great soul-anguish will generally wring some such cry from our startled and stricken hearts.

Then he passed on to plead for deliverance: 'Deliver me, I pray thee, from the hand of my brother, from the hand of Esau.' It was, of course, quite right to pray this, but I cannot feel that it was a wholehearted prayer; for he had hardly finished it when he reverted to the plan on which he had been busy before he turned aside to pray. We are all so apt to pray, and then to try and concoct a plan for our own deliverance. Surely the nobler attitude is, after prayer, to stand still for God to develop his plan, leading us in ways that we had never guessed. The blessed life of our Lord was absolutely planless.

### 3   It was midnight

Jacob had already sent across the Jabbok his property, his children, even his beloved Rachel. 'He caused them to pass over the brook and Jacob was left alone.' There, alone, he considered the past; and anticipated the future; and felt the meanness of the aims for which he had sold his soul. He saw the wretched failure of his life, and so, suddenly, he became aware that a mysterious combatant was at his side, drawing him into a conflict, half literal and half spiritual, which lasted till break of day.

Was this a literal contest? There is no reason to deny it. It would have been as possible for the Son of God to wrestle literally with Jacob, as for him to offer his hands to the touch of Thomas after his resurrection. The physical must have been largely present because, when he resumed his journey, Jacob limped. It was a physical fact, physically commemorated by the Israelites to this day, for they abstain from eating of that part in animals that correspond to the sinew that shrank in Jacob's thigh. Men do not become lame in imaginary conflicts. But, in any case, the outward wrestling was only a poor symbol of the spiritual struggle that convulsed the patriarch's soul.

Remember that the conflict originated not with Jacob, but with the angel: 'There wrestled a man with him.' This passage is often quoted as an instance of Jacob's earnestness in prayer. It is nothing of the sort. It was not that Jacob wished to obtain something from God, but it was that he – the angel Jehovah – had a controversy with this double-dealing and crafty child of his. He was desirous to break up his self-sufficiency forever, and to give scope for the development of the Israel that lay cramped and coffined within.

Has not 'this man' who wrestled with Jacob found you out? Have you not felt a holy discontent with yourself? Have you not felt that certain things, long cherished and loved, should be given up, though it should cost you blood? These convulsive throes, these heaven-born strivings, these mysterious workings – are not of man, or of the will of the flesh, but of God. It is God who works in you, and wrestles with you. Glory be to him for his tender patience, interest, and love!

At first Jacob held his own. 'He saw that he prevailed not against him.' The strength that, years before, had rolled the stone from the well for Rachel's sheep, was still vigorous; and he was in no humour to submit. And thus we do all resist the love of God. Each one of us is dowered with that wonderful power of holding our own against God; and he knows, sorrowfully, that he cannot prevail against us, without taking some severe measures that will give us no alternative but to yield.

Then the angel touched the hollow of his thigh. Whatever it is that enables a soul, whom God designs to bless, to stand out against him, God will touch. And beneath that touch it will shrink and shrivel; and you will limp to the end of life. Remember that the sinew never shrinks except beneath the touch of the Angel-hand – the touch of tender love. This is why your schemes have miscarried; God has touched the sinew of your strength, and it has dried up. Oh, you who are still holding out against him, make haste to yield, lest some worse thing come upon you!

Then Jacob went from resisting to clinging. As the day broke, the Angel wanted to leave; but he could not because Jacob clung to him with a death grip. The request to be let go indicates how tenaciously the limping patriarch clung to him for support. He had abandoned the posture of defence and resistance, and had fastened himself on to the Angel – as a terrified child clasps its arms tightly around its father neck. That is a glad moment in the history of the human spirit, when it throw both arms around the risen Saviour, and hangs on to him and will not let him go. Have you reached the point of self-surrender? If not, ask God to show you what sinew it is that makes you too strong for him to bless you; ask him to touch it so that you will be able to hold out no more. And then you will discover the threefold blessing that is yours.

*a. The changed name.*    In Jacob's time names were given not for euphony, or by caprice, but for character. Now, when Jacob came into the attitude of blessing the Angel immediately said, 'What is thy name?' And he said, 'Jacob. By nature I am a supplanter, a rogue, and a cheat.' Never shrink from declaring your true character: 'My name is Sinner.' 'And he said, thy name shall be no more Jacob, but Israel: a prince with God.' The changed name indicates a changed character. Jacob was clothed with the name and nature of a prince. There is only one way to princeliness – it is the thorn-set path of self-surrender and of faith. Why should you not now yield yourself entirely to God and give him your whole being? It is only a reasonable service.

*b. Power.*    The better rendering of these words would be: 'As a prince hast thou power with God; and with man thou shalt prevail.' We sign for power but we must obtain it from the Creator. The man who would have power with men must first have it with God; and we can get power with God only when our own strength has failed, and we limp. Oh, for the withered sinew of our own strength, that we may lay hold on the strength of God!

*c. The beatific vision.*    'I have seen God face to face.' Our moments of vision come at daybreak, but they are ushered in by the agony of dread, the long midnight vigil, the extreme agony of conflict, the shrinking of the sinew. The price is dear, but the vision is more than worth it all. The sufferings are not worthy to be compared with the glory revealed.

# 10

# Failure

## *Genesis 33–34*

That midnight wrestle made an epoch in Jacob's life. It was the moment in which he stepped up to a new level in his experience – the level of Israel the prince. But let us remember that it is one thing to step up to a level like that; it is quite another to keep it. Some, when they touch a new attainment, keep to it. Some, when they touch a new attainment, keep to it, and are blessed evermore; others, when they have stood there for a moment, recede from it. Jacob, alas! soon stepped down from that glorious level to which the Angel had lifted him.

This descent is indicated by the retention, in the sacred record, of the name Jacob. We should have expected that it would have been replaced by the new title, Israel – as Abram was by Abraham – but it is not so. How could he be called Israel when he had so soon reverted to the life of Jacob; and had gone back to the cringing, crafty, scheming life that he had been leading all too long? The time will come when Israel will become his habitual designation; but not yet – not yet.

We have to consider now the three evidences of failure that are recounted in these chapters.

## 1 The first failure was in his manner of meeting Esau

As the morning broke, 'Jacob lifted up his eyes, and looked; and, behold, Esau came, and with him four hundred men.' Such is life. It is filled with sharply varied experiences.

How often do we find that a great blessing – like that which came to Jacob by the fords of the Jabbok – is sent to prepare us for a great trial. God prevents us, and prepares us, with the blessings of his goodness. Do not be surprised or discouraged if a time of fiery trial should follow a season of unusual blessing; indeed, you may be rather surprised if it does not. But when it comes,be sure to do as Jacob did not do – and draw heavily on all those resources of strength and comfort that have been stored up during the previous days of clear shining and peace.

There are two ways of meeting troubles: the one is the way of the flesh; the other, of the Spirit. The flesh anticipates them with terror; prays in a panic, and then cringes before them – as Jacob, who bowed himself to the ground seven times until he came near his brother. The way of faith is far better. She clings to God; she hears God say, 'I am with thee, and will keep thee'; she believes that he will keep his word; she reviews the past, when the hands of Laban were tied, and argues that God can do as much again.

Some who read this may be dreading a meeting with their Esaus tomorrow; some creditor, some demand for payment, some awkward problem, some difficulty. And you are today worrying, planning, scheming, and contriving, as Jacob did, in arranging his wives and children, and servants, while tomorrow you will go cringing and creeping toward it.

Listen to a more excellent way. Do not lift up your eyes and look for Esaus. Lift them higher – to him from whom our help comes. Then you will be able to meet your troubles with an unperturbed spirit. Those who have seen the face of God need not fear the face of man that will die.

Besides all this, when prayer has preceded trial, the trial turns out to be much less than we anticipated. Jacob dreaded that meeting with Esau, but when Esau came up with him, he ran to meet him, and embraced him, and fell on his neck, and kissed him; and they wept. The heroic Gordon used to say that in his lonely camel rides he often in prayer encountered and disarmed hostile chiefs, before he rode, unaccompanied, into their presence. None can guess, if they have not tried it for themselves, what a solvent prayer is for the difficulties and agonies of life.

It is beautiful to see that, in this, God was better to Jacob than his fears, or his faith. While he was foreboding the worst, his heavenly Friend was preparing deliverance.

## 2 The second failure was in the subterfuge to which Jacob resorted, to free himself from Esau's company

When Esau offered him the protection of his armed men, he was at once in a panic, for he dreaded them even more than the Bedouins of the wilds. He tried to evade the proposal by making many excuses, especially explaining that his flocks and his children could not keep up with their more rapid pace. And finally, still further to reconcile Esau to the separation, he promised to come at last to Seir, where Esau had fixed his abode.

Now I do not believe that Jacob really meant to go to Seir, for as soon as he had seen the rear of Esau's retiring forces, he journeyed in the opposite direction to Succoth. All such subterfuge and lying were utterly unworthy of the man who had seen God's angels face to face.

What wretched failure was here! The bright dawn was all too speedily overcast and if it had not been for the marvellous tenderness of God, there is no telling how much further Jacob would have drifted, or how indefinitely distant the day would have been in which he should be worthy to bear the name of Israel.

## 3 The third failure was in settling at Shechem

God had not said, Go to Shechem; but, 'I am the God of Bethel.'

Bethel, rather than Shechem, was his appointed goal. But we are all too ready to fall short of God's schemes for our elevation and blessedness. So Jacob came to Shalem, a city of Shechem.

But he did worse; he pitched his tent before the city – as Lot did when he pitched his tent before Sodom. What took him there? Whatever may have been his reason, there stands the sad and solemn face that Jacob pitched his tent *before the city.*

Aren't many Christians still doing the same thing today? They live on the edge of the world, just on the border. They are far enough away to justify a religious profession, yet near enough to run into it for sweets. They choose their church, their pastimes, their friendships, on the sole principle of doing as others do; and of forming good alliances for their children. What is all this but pitching the tent toward Shechem?

But Jacob did still worse. Not content with pitching his tent before the city, he bought the parcel of ground 'where he had pitched his tent.' Abraham bought a parcel of ground in which to bury his dead, and this was no declension from the pilgrim spirit – it rather placed it in clearer relief. But Jacob was abandoning the pilgrim spirit and the pilgrim attitude, and was *buying* that which God had promised to *give* to him and to his seed. The true spirit of faith would have waited quietly, until God had made good his repeated promise.

It may be that Jacob sought to conciliate his conscience by building the altar, and dedicating it to the God of Israel. But where the altar and the world are put in rivalry, there is no doubt as to which will win the day: the Shechem gate will appeal too strongly to our natural tendencies, and we will find ourselves and our children drifting into Schechem – while the grass of neglect grows up around the altar, or it becomes broken down and disused.

'And Dinah, the daughter of Leah, which she bare unto Jacob, went out to see the daughters of the land.' It is a startling announcement, but it contains nothing more than might have been expected. Poor girl! Was she lonely, being the only girl? She went along a path that seemed to her girlish fancy ever so much more attractive than the dull routine of home. She took no heed to the warnings that may have been addressed to her. And it all ended – as it has ended in thousands of cases since – in misery, ruin, and unutterable disgrace.

She fascinated the young prince, and fell. It is the old story that is ever new. On the one hand – rank, and wealth, and unbridled appetite; on the other – beauty, weakness, and dallying with temptation. But to whom was her fall due? To Schechem? Yes. To herself? Yes. But also to Jacob. He must forever reproach himself for his daughter's murdered innocence. And all this came because Jacob stepped down from the Israel level back to his old unlovely self.

Let us understand the causes of Jacob's relapse, and see how we may guard against it.

It arises, first, from trusting in the impulse received at a given moment, as though that were sufficient to carry the soul forward through all coming days; and there is therefore a relaxation of watchfulness, and prayer, and Bible study. We are all so apt to substitute an experience for abiding fellowship with the Son of God; to dwell in the past instead of in the living present. This mistake can be obviated only by careful cultivation of the daily, hourly, friendship of the living Saviour. And even this can be attained only by the grace of the Holy Spirit.

Second, it may arise from the energy of the self-life, which the apostle Paul calls *the flesh*. Before regeneration we attempt to justify ourselves; being regenerate, we attempt to sanctify ourselves. There must be more of God in our lives.

Third, these failures arise because we are conscious of the subsidence of the keen emotions that once filled our hearts, and suppose that in losing these we have really lost that spiritual attitude we then assumed. All the deepest experiences in Christian life consist in acts of the will, which may or may not be accompanied by emotion, and which remain when the glow of feeling has passed. God, therefore, withdraws the life of emotion that he may train us to live by faith, and in our wills.

Whatever failure comes may also be associated with our reluctance to confess to others the blessing that has irradicated our inner life. We should not hesitate to tell those with whom we are most intimate what great things the Lord has done for us. To withhold confession is often to staunch the flow of blessing.

If you are conscious of having failed in any of these respects, ask to be forgiven and restored; and trust him, who is the keeper of the faithful soul, trim you as the light of the sacred temple lamps.

# 11

# The School of Sorrow

## *Genesis 35–42*

There was growing on Jacob a realisation that his life was closing; that he must prepare to follow his father into the unseen. His years had been few in comparison with those of his forefathers, and he had the weary sense of failure in that he had 'not attained' (47:9). Such sorrows fell to Jacob's lot: they fall to our lot still; and when they do, let us learn how to receive them.

### 1  Do not judge by appearances

Jacob said, 'All these things are against me.' It was a great mistake. Joseph was alive – the governor of Egypt; sent there to preserve their lives, and to be the stay of his closing years. Simeon was also alive – the blessed link was drawing and compelling his brothers to return into the presence of the strange Egyptian governor. Benjamin would come safely back again. All things, so far from being against him, were working together for good for him. Cultivate the habit of looking at the bright side of things. If there are only a few clouds floating in your sky, do not say that the whole is overcast; and if all the heaven is covered, save one small chink of blue, make much of that; do not exaggerate the darkness.

### 2  Be sure that God has a purpose in all your sorrow

The apparent aimlessness of some kinds of pain is sometimes their sorest ingredient. We can suffer more cheerfully if we can clearly see the end that is being slowly reached. If we cannot, it is hard to lie still and be at rest. But the believer knows that nothing can come to him, save by the permission of God's love. Each calamity has a specific purpose, and the Almighty varies his method of dealing with us: He ever selects the precise trial that will soonest and best accomplish his purposes; and he only continues it long enough to do all that needs to be done. I commend that precious promise to those who think their sorrows past endurance. They will not last forever; they will be suited to our peculiar needs and strength. They will accomplish that on which the great Husbandman has set his heart.

### 3 Remember that nothing can separate you from the love of God

When Jacob reviewed these dark passages of his life from the serene heights of his dying bed, he saw, as he had never seen it before, that God had shepherded him all his life long; and his Angel had redeemed him from all evil (48:15–16). We do not realise this at the time; but there is never an experience in life without the watch of that unsleeping Shepherd-eye, never a peril without the interposition of that untiring Shepherd-hand. Take heart, you who are descending into the dark valley of shadow, the Good Shepherd is going at your side, though you do not see him. His rod and staff will comfort you: yes, his own voice will speak comfortably to you. Fear not!

### 4 Anticipate the 'afterward'

Look not at the things that are seen; but at those that are not seen. Cast into the one scale your sorrows, if you will; but put into the other the glory that will presently be the outcome of the pain. Anticipate the time when every vestige of Jacob shall have been laid aside, and Israel is become the befitting title for your soul. Will that not repay you – because you will have been brought into a oneness with Christ which shall be heaven in miniature?

# 12

# Rest and the Rest-Giver

## *Genesis 49*

There is much of interest in these dying words of Jacob, through which Israel the Prince shines so conspicuously.

It would, for instance, be interesting to mark their accuracy. Reuben, though the firstborn, never excelled; no judge, prophet, or ruler, sprang from his tribe. Simeon was almost absorbed in the nomad tribes of southern Palestine. The cities in which the sons of Levi dwelt were scattered throughout all the tribes. Vestiges of terraced vineyards still attest to how well the hilly province assigned to Judah suited the culture of the vine. Zebulun embosomed the lake of Galilee, and stretched toward the coast of the blue Mediterranean. Esdraelon, the battlefield of Palestine, where Assyria from the North and Egypt from the South often met in deadly feud, lay within the limits of Issachar. Dan was small as an adder but, like it, could inflict dangerous wounds on any invader who had to pass by it toward the heart of the country. Gad, much pressed by border war; Asher, notable for fertility; Naphtali, famous for eloquence; Benjamin, cruel as a wolf. As these justified the prophecy of their dying ancestor, while the mighty tribes of Ephraim and Manasseh sprung from the sons of Joseph, inherited the blessings to the full.

It would be interesting to mark the close connection between the awards and the character of the bearded sons who stood around the withered, propped-up body of that dying man, while his spirit was flaming out in one last splendid outburst of prophetic and princelike glory, too much for the frail tenement to endure. Reuben, for example, had committed a nameless sin years before; he might have hoped that it was all long since forgotten, but no, here it reappears, dragged into inevitable light. That sin deprived him for the primacy – *that one sin.* Was this not arbitrary? Not so, since it was the index of his character, and was the unerring evidence of an unstable nature, for sensuality and instability are one.

But there comes, in these dying words, the announcement of a personality, mysterious, ineffable, sublime, which dwarfs all others, before which that aged spirit bows in worship, illumining the withered face with a light not born of earth. What does he mean by those mystic words, describing the Shiloh, his coming, and the gathering of the peoples to him? There is a power in them that strangely stirs our spirits. We feel instinctively that we are face to face with him before whom angels bow, veiling their faces with their wings. Again the words ring in our hearts: 'The sceptre shall not depart from Judah, nor a lawgiver from between his feet, until Shiloh come; and unto him shall the gathering of the peoples be.'

### 1   Let us try to understand them

The primacy of Israel, forfeited by Reuben, was transferred to Judah. The sceptre, or staff, surely indicates legislative authority; the lawgiver, some kind of legislator, and the drift of meaning in the verse is that Judah should retain the primacy of the tribes; and should not fail to have some kind of government, and some kind of governor, until one came, of whom Jacob spoke as Shiloh.

And who is this Shiloh? The greatest modern Hebrew critics tell us that it is like the German *Frederick* – rich in peace; the restgiver; the man of rest. And of whom can this be true, but of One? The true Shiloh can be none other than the Son of God who, standing among earth's toiling millions, said, 'Come unto me, all ye that labour and are heavy laden, and I will give you rest.'

I have sometimes wondered where Jacob learned this most sweet and true name of our Lord Jesus. Was it flashed into his heart, at that moment, for the first time? It may have been. But there is another supposition, which has often pleased me. You will remember that at Peniel, Jacob asked the mysterious combatant his name. What answer did he receive? The angel simply said: 'Wherefore is it that thou dost ask after my name? And he blessed him there.' I have sometimes thought that, as he blessed him, he whispered in his ear his lovely title, which lingered in the old man's mind as the years went on, and became invested with ever fuller and richer meaning. This is the universal order of Christian living: first the resistance, then the shrunken sinew, then the yielding and clinging, and finally rest.

## 2 Let us note, also, their literal fulfilment

For long centuries, Judah held the proud position assigned by the dying chieftain. The lion of the tribe of Judah brooked no rival. Jerusalem lay in his territory. David sprang from his sons. Throughout the long captivity, princes still claimed and held their right; for we are told that when Cyrus issued the proclamation that gave them liberty, 'there arose up the chief of the fathers of Judah, and numbered unto them Sheshbazzar, the prince of Judah.' It was Judah that returned from the captivity and gave the title *Jew* to every member of the race.

## 3 Let us realise their truth

What a variety of weary eyes will read these words – weary eyes, aching heads, tired bodies, breaking hearts. Would to God that each of these could understand that Jesus Christ, the true Shiloh, is able to give them, now and forevermore, rest! 'Come unto me, *all* ye that are heavy laden, and I will give you *rest*.'

It is a royal word. If this were the only scrap of his words, we would feel him to have been the most royal man that ever trod our world. What certainty is here – no doubt, or question, or fear of failure; no faltering in that clear voice; no hesitancy in that decisive accent. We may trust him brothers and sisters. It will not take him longer to give you rest, than it took him to still the waves: '*immediately* there was a great calm.'

The Shiloh-rest is not for heaven. We need not ask for the wings of a dove to fly away to it. We would not find it hereafter, if we did not first find it here.

The Shiloh-rest is not in circumstances. That thought lies at the root of the teaching of the Epicurean, the Stoic, the worldly philosopher. But circumstances will never bring it, any more than change of posture will bring permanent relief to the pain-racked body.

The Shiloh-rest is not in inaction. In heaven, though they rest, yet they do not rest. They rest in their blessed service. There is the strenuous putting forth of energy, but no strain, no effort, no sense of fatigue. And such is the rest he gives. Does he not speak of a 'burden' and a 'yoke' in the same breath as he speaks of rest?

And it is not hard to get it. See! He gives it; he shows just where to look for and it is easy enough to *find* a thing if we know just where it lies. There seem to me but three conditions to be fulfilled by us.

*a. Surrender all to him.*    As long as you try to wield that sceptre, or permit your will to be the lawgiver of your life, the Shiloh cannot come to you. You must give up your own efforts to save yourself – your own ideas of getting right with God; your own choice; your own way; your own will. You must hand over your sinful spirit to be saved by him; you must surrender the keys of every room in your heart; you must be willing for him to be supreme monarch of every province of your being. So only can you expect rest. And if you cannot bring your nature into this posture, ask him to do it for you.

*b. Trust him, by handing over all to him.*    Hand over to him all your sins and all your sorrows. Do not wait till sins have accumulated into a cloud or a mountain. Do not delay till you are alone. But as swiftly as you are conscious of any burden, pass it on to Jesus; cast all your care on him, for he cares for you. His heart is large enough to hold the troubles of the world. As soon as you give, he takes; and what he takes he also undertakes. This is the blessed rest of faith; the Land of Promise into which our Joshua waits to lead all who trust him.

*c. Take his yoke, and learn of him i.e., do as he did.*    What was his yoke? A yoke means submission. To whom did he submit? To the Father's will. This was the secret of his rest. To live in the will of God – this is rest. Be ever on the outlook for it, and whenever you see it, *take it*. Do not wait for it to be forced on you, as a yoke on a heifer unaccustomed to it, which struggles till a deep wound is cut in its flesh. But *take* the yoke; be meek and lowly; imitate him who said, 'The cup which my Father hath given me, shall I not drink it?' If you say that, you have learned the secret of rest; and Shiloh has already come to you.

# 13

# Home: At Last

## *Genesis 50*

The end has come at last! And we stand with those stalwart men in that hieroglyph-covered chamber, silent with the hush of death, to see the wayworn pilgrim breathe his last. His life has been a stern fight; his pathway not strewn with roses, but set with flints; few and evil the days of the years of his pilgrimage. Compared with the brilliant career of Esau, his life might be almost considered a failure. Better a hundredfold to be Israel the Prince, though an exile; than Esau, the founder of a line of dukes. The name of Israel will be an unfailing inspiration to those who, conscious of untold weakness and unlovableness, shall yet strive to apprehend that for which they were originally apprehended by Christ Jesus.

Before the mind of the dying patriarch three visions seemed to flat in that solemn hour. He was thinking of the City of God, of the gathering of his clan, and of that lone and distant cave in Canaan where his fathers lay, and which he had so often visited.

## 1   The city of God

We are expressly told in the Epistle to the Hebrews that Jacob was one of those 'who died in faith.' He was the heir of promise. The land promised to Abraham and Isaac had not as yet passed into his possession; it was still held by the wandering and settled tribes who had eyed his journeyings with such evident suspicion. All he had was the assured promise that in the coming days it would be his through his seed. He clung tenaciously to the blessed promise, so often reiterated to Abraham, that the land would become his people's, and his assurance that God would keep his word flung a radiance over his dying moments. Oh, glorious faith! What cannot faith do for those whom God has taught to trust!

As it became clear to Jacob that *he* was not to inherit Canaan, he seems to have fixed his mind with increasing eagerness on heaven. He felt that if God had not destined for him an earthly resting place, yet he had prepared for him a city. And it was for that glorius city, the city of the saints, that his pilgrim spirit now yearned. It was his close proximity to it that stirred his aged spirit, and drew it on with breathless eagerness and rapid steps.

The sacred writer employs a beautiful similitude when he says of Jacob and the rest of the patriarchs, that they greeted the promises from afar (Heb. 11:13). So Jacob, as he neared the city of God, so dear to faithful hearts, approved his kinsmanship with the elect spirits of all ages, by reaching forth toward it his aged, trembling hands.

Modern commentators have wrangled fiercely as to how much or how little of the future life was realised by these ancient saints. Into that controversy I have no desire to enter. But Jacob and the men of his type desired 'the better country, that is, a heavenly.' The future was less indistinct to them than we sometimes suppose. They, too, stood on Pisgah-heights and beheld a Land of Promise. On such a Pisgah-height Jacob was standing; and as all earthly objects, even the face of Joseph, grew indistinct to his dimming eyes, those rapturous and celestial scenes grew on his spiritual vision and beckoned to him.

In what relation do you stand to that city of God? Do not imagine that it will gladden your dying gaze, unless it has often been the object of your loving thought in the days of health and vigour. Do you feel the *pull* of that city, as the sailor does of the anchor that keeps him from drifting with the tide? If so, it will gladden your dying moments.

## 2   The gathering of the clan

'I am to be gathered unto my people.' When the dying patriarch spoke this way, he meant something more than that his dust should mingle with all that was mortal of his forefathers. He surely looked upon the city as the gathering-place of his clan, the *rendezvous* of all who were *his* people, because they were the people of God.

What as to the intermediate state? At the best 'we know not what we shall be.' We cannot penetrate the veil that only opens wide enough to admit the entering spirit. It is clear that our spirits will not reach their full consummation and bliss till the morning of the resurrection, when body and spirit will be reunited; but it is equally clear that they will not be unconscious, but will enter into the blessed presence of our Lord.

There is no accent of uncertainty in the New Testament. As soon as the tent is taken down, the mansion is entered (2 Cor. 5:2). Absent from the body, the believer is present with the Lord. Do not puzzle over useless questionings: be content to know that death is not a state, but an act; not a resting place, but a transition to the palace.

What as to the recognition of the departer? It would not have been an object of anticipation to Jacob to be gathered to his people, if he would not know them when he reached their blest society. When the Jew thought of the unseen world, he expected to meet the saints, of whom he had heard from childhood, and especially Abraham. Was not the Jew wiser than most Christians? Has the body powers of recognition, and the spirit none? Can that be a Father's home, where the brothers and sisters do not know each other?

We shall be gathered to our people. Throughout the ages the elect souls of our race have been gathering there. Are they our people? Can we claim kinship with them? There is but one bond, as we are taught in Hebrews 11. Wherever it is found, it designates the owner to be one of those who can claim kinship with the saintly inhabitants of the city of God. The test question of qualification for the franchise of the New Jerusalem is: 'Do you believe in the name of the only-begotten Son of God?'

## 3   The cave of Machpelah

'Bury me with my fathers in the cave that is in the field of Ephron the Hittite.' For seventeen years Jacob had lived in Egypt, surrounded by all the comforts that Joseph's filial love could devise, and his munificence execute. But be must be laid where Abraham and Sarah, Isaac and Rebekah, and the faithful Leah awaited resurrection.

This was something more than the natural sentiment that impels us to request burial in some quiet spot in God's acre, where our family name is inscribed on many of the gravestones around. Jacob felt that Machpelah's cave was the first outpost in the land that was one day to belong to his people; and he wanted, as far as he might, to be there with them, and to share in the land of promise.

The last word was spoken, the last commission given, and he knew the end was come. 'He gathered up his feet into the bed;' i.e., he met death quietly, calmly, manfully. He quietly breathed out his spirit, and was gathered to his people. And at that moment sorrow and sighing, which had been his close companions in life, fled away forever.

How calm and noble that face looked, fixed in the marble of death! The Jacob-look had vanished from it; and it was stamped with the smile with which the royal Israel-spirit had moulded it in its outward passage.

What wonder, then, that Joseph fell on his father's face, and wept on him, and kissed him! He had borne the strain as long as he could; and now nature had to vent herself in manly, filial grief.

The body was carefully embalmed. No time, or pains, or cost, were spared. Egypt herself mourned for him for seventy days. Then one of the most splendid funeral processions that ever gathered to lay saint, or sage, or hero to his rest, carried that precious casket in solemn pomp from Egypt up to Canaan. And the signs of mourning were so great as to impress the inhabitants of the land, the Canaanites.

The stone was rolled away, and Jacob's remains laid on their appointed niche. Many a storm has swept over them – Assyrian, Egyptian, Babylonian, Grecian, Roman, Saracenic, and Mohammedan. But nothing has disturbed their quiet rest; and they hold the land in fee, till God shall fulfil in all its magnificence, the promise that he made and has never recalled – that he would give the land to Jacob's seed for an everlasting inheritance. So rest thee, Israel the Prince!

# JOSEPH

# 1

# Early Days

*Genesis 37*

It is a great mission to rescue truth from neglect; to play the part of Old Mortality, who, chisel in hand, was wont to clear the mould of neglect from the gravestones of the Covenanters, so that the legend might stand out clearly. It is something like this that I attempt for this exquisite story. We think we know it, and yet there may be depths of meaning and beauty which, by their very familiarity, escape us. Let us ponder together the story of Joseph, for in doing so we shall get a foreshadowing of him who was cast into the pit of death, and who now sits at the right hand of Power, a Prince and a Saviour.

### The formative influences of his early life

Seventeen years before our story opens, a child was borne by Rachel, the favourite wife of Jacob. The latter was then living as manager for his uncle Laban, on the ancient pastureland of Charran, situated in the valley of the Euphrates and the Tigris, from which his grandfather Abraham had been called by God. The child received an eager welcome from its parents.

But what a history has passed in that interval! When yet a child he was hastily caught up by his mother and sustained in her arms on the back of a swift camel, urged to its highest speed in the flight across the desert that lay, with only one oasis, between the bank of the Euphrates and the green prairies of Gilead. He could just remember the panic that spread through the camp when tidings came that Esau, the dread uncle, was on his march with four hundred followers. Nor could he ever forget the evening full of preparation, the night of solemn expectancy, and the morning when his father limped into the camp, maimed in body, but with the look of a prince on his face.

More recently still, he could recall the hurried flight from the enraged idolaters of Shechem, and those solemn hours at Bethel where his father had probably showed him the very spot on which the foot of the mystic ladder had rested, and where the whole family formally entered into a new covenant with God. It may be that this was the turning point of his life. Such events make deep impressions on young hearts.

These impressions were soon deepened by three deaths. When the family reached the family settlement, they found the old nurse Deborah dying. She was the last link to those bright days when her young mistress Rebekah came across the desert to be Isaac's bride; and they buried her with many tears under an ancient but splendid oak. And the child could never forget the next event. The long caravan was moving slowly up to the narrow ridge along which lay the ancient village of Bethlehem: suddenly a halt was called, the beloved Rachel could go not another step, and there as the sun was sinking she died. This was the greatest loss he had ever known. A little later the lad stood with his father and brethren before Machpelah's venerable grave, to lay Isaac where Abraham and Sarah and Rebekah awaited him, each on a narrow shelf; and where, after twenty-seven years, he was to place the remains of his father Jacob.

# 2

# The Pit

## *Genesis 37*

To the casual reader the story of Joseph's wrongs and of his rise from the pit to vice-regal power is simply interesting, for its archaic simplicity and the insight into the past that it affords. But to the man on whose heart the cross is carved in loving memory there is a far deeper interest. It is Calvary in miniature. It is the outline sketch of the Artist's finished work. It is a rehearsal of the greatest drama ever enacted among men.

## 1 Joseph's mission

*'Jacob dwelt in the land of his father's sojournings.'* After Jacob had buried his old father he continued to reside in the Vale of Hebron, where Isaac had dwelt for nearly two hundred years, and where Abraham abode before him. This was the headquarters of his vast encampment. But rich as the pastures of Hebron were, they were not sufficient to support the whole of the flocks and herds. The sons were compelled to drive these by slow stages to distant parts of the land. They were even forced, by stern necessity, to brave the anger of the people of Shechem, whom they had grievously wronged, and who had vowed vengeance on them for their foul behaviour.

It was this that gave point to Jacob's question, 'Do not thy brethren feed the flock in Shechem?' He had heard his sons speak of going there in search of pasture; now long weeks had passed since he received tidings of their welfare, and the memory of the past made him anxious about them. And this solicitude became so overpowering that it forced him to do what otherwise would never have entered his thoughts.

He was alone in Hebron with Joseph and Benjamin. They were his darlings; his heart loved them with something of the intense devotion he had felt toward their mother. Joseph was seventeen years old and Benjamin was younger. The old man kept them with him, reluctant to let them from his sight. But the old man yearned with anxious love over his absent sons; and at last, after many battlings and hesitations, he suddenly said to the dearly-loved Joseph, 'Come, and I will send thee unto them . . . go, I pray thee, see whether it be well with thy brethren, and . . . bring me word again.'

On Joseph's part there was not a moment's hesitation. In the flash of a thought he realised the perils of the mission – perils among false brethren, who bitterly hated him. But as soon as he knew his father's will, he said, 'Here am I.' 'So, Jacob sent him . . .

and he came.'

**a.** *Is not all this suggestive of a yet loftier theme?*     Our Lord never wearied of calling himself the Sent of the Father. There is hardly a page in the Gospel of John in which he does not say more than once, 'I came not of myself, but my Father sent me.' Thus it became a constant expression with the New Testament writers, 'God sent forth his Son'; 'The Father sent the Son to be the Saviour of the world.'

**b.** *It must have cost Jacob something to part with the beloved Joseph.*     But who can estimate how much it cost the infinite God to send his only-begotten Son, who had dwelt in his bosom, and who was his Son from everlasting? Let us not think that God is passionless. If his love is like ours (and we know it must be), he must suffer from the same causes that work havoc in our hearts, only he must suffer proportionately to the strength and infinite-ness of his nature. How much, then, must God have loved us, that he should be willing to send his Son! Truly God *so* loved the world! But who shall fathom the depths of that one small word?

**c.** *But our Saviour did not come solely because he was sent.*     He came because he loved his mission. He came to seek and to save those who are lost. If you could have asked him, as you met him traversing those same fields, 'What seekest Thou?' He would have replied in the same words of Joseph, 'I seek my brethren.' Nor was he content with only *seeking* the lost; he went after them *until* he found them. 'Joseph went after his brethren [until] he found them in Dothan.'

## 2  Joseph's reception

'They saw him afar off, even before he came near unto them, [and] they conspired against him to slay him.' He would doubt-less have been ruthlessly slain, and his body flung into some pit away from the haunts of men, if it had not been for the merciful pleadings of Reuben, the eldest brother. 'And it came to pass when Joseph was come unto his brethren, that they stripped Joseph out of his coat, his coat of many colours . . . and they took him, and cast him into a pit.'

The historian does not dwell on the passion of the brothers, or on the anguish of that young heart, which found it so hard to die, so hard to say goodbye to the fair earth, so hard to descend into that dark cistern, whose steep sides forbade the hope that he could ever scramble back into the upper air. But years later they said one to another, 'We are verily guilty concerning our brother, in that we saw the anguish of his soul, when he besought us, and we would not hear.' What a revelation there is in these words! We seem to see Joseph; he struggles to get free; he entreats them with bitter tears to let him go; he implores them for the sake of his old father, and by the tie of brotherhood.

*a. Unforgiven sin is a fearful scourge.* Year passed after year, but the years could not obliterate from the memories of the brothers that look, those cries, that scene in the green glen of Dothan. They tried to lock up the skeleton in their most secret cupboard, but it contrived to come forth to confront them even in their guarded hours. The old father, who mourned for his son as dead, was happier than were they, who knew him to be alive. One crime may thus darken a whole life. God has so made the world that sin is its own Nemesis – sin carries with it the seed of its own punishment. And the men who carry with them the sense of unforgiven sin, will be the first to believe in a vulture forever tearing out the vitals, a worm that never dies, a fire that is never quenched.

*b. But Joseph's grief was a true anticipation of Christ's.* 'He came unto his own, and his own received him not' (John 1:11). They said, 'This is the heir, come let us kill him, and the inheritance shall be ours.' 'They caught him, and cast him out, and slew him.' 'They parted his raiment among them.' They sold him to the Gentiles. They sat down to watch him die. The anguish of Joseph's soul reminds us of the strong cryings and tears wrung from the human nature of Christ by the near approach of his unknown sufferings as the scapegoat of the race. The comparative innocence of Joseph reminds us of the spotlessness of the Lamb who was without blemish, and whose blamelessness was again and again attested to before he died.

*c. Here, however, the parallel ends.* Joseph's sufferings stopped before they reached the point of death; Jesus tasted death. Joseph's sufferings were personal; the sufferings of Jesus were substitutionary and mediatorial: 'He died for us'; 'He gave himself for me.' Joseph's sufferings had no efficacy in atoning for the sin that caused them, but the sufferings of Jesus atone not only for the guilt of his murderers, but for the guilt of all.

# 3

# In the House of Potiphar

## *Genesis 39*

The Midianite merchantmen, into whose hands his brethren sold Joseph, brought him down to Egypt – with its riband of green pasture amid the waste of sand. In some great slave market he was exposed for sale, together with hundreds more, who had been captured by force or stealth from the surrounding countries.

He was bought by Potiphar, 'the captain of the guard', who was, in all likelihood, the chief of the royal bodyguard, in the precincts of the court. The Egyptian monarchs had the absolute power of life and death, and they did not scruple to order the infliction of a variety of summary or sanguinary punishments, the execution of which was entrusted to the military guard.

Potiphar was a member of a proud aristocracy; high in office and in court favour. He would no doubt live in a splendid palace, covered with hieroglyphs and filled with slaves. The young captive must have trembled as he passed up the pillared avenue, through sphinx-guarded gates, into the recesses of that vast Egyptian palace where they spoke a language of which he could not understand a word, and where all was so new and strange. But 'God was with him'; the sense of the presence and guardianship of his father's God pervaded and stilled his soul, and kept him in perfect peace. Who would not rather, after all, choose to be Joseph in Egypt with God, than the brothers with a blood-stained garment in their hands and the sense of guilt on their souls?

Let us consider how Joseph fared in Potiphar's house.

## 1   Joseph's promotion

'The Lord was with Joseph; and he was a prosperous man.' The older versions of the Bible give a curious rendering here: 'The Lord was with Joseph; and he was a lucky fellow.' Everything he handled went well. Success followed him as closely as his shadow, and touched all his plans with her magic wand. Potiphar and his household got to the place where they expected this strange Hebrew captive to untie every knot, disentangle every skein, and bring to successful issues the most intricate arrangements. This arose from two causes.

*a. Though stripped of his coat, he had not been stripped of his character.* He was industrious, prompt, diligent, obedient, reliable. He did his work, not because he was obliged to do it, but because God had called him to do it. He said to himself, as he said in afterlife, 'God did send me before you.' He felt that he was the servant, not so much of Potiphar, as of the God of Abraham and Isaac. There, in the household of Potiphar, he might live a devout and earnest life as truly as when he spent the long, happy days in Jacob's tent; and he did. And it was this that made him so conscientious and careful, qualities that in business must ensure success.

When his fellow-servants were squandering the golden moments, Joseph was filling them with activities. When they worked simply to avoid the frown or the lash, he worked to win the smile of the great Taskmaster, whose eye was ever upon him. They often pointed at him with envy, and perhaps said, 'He is a lucky fellow.' They did not think that his luck was his character; and that his character meant God. There is no such thing as luck, except that luck means character. And if you wish to possess such a character as will ensure your success in this life, there is no true basis for it but Jesus Christ.

*b. The Lord made all that he did to prosper.* 'The Lord blessed the Egyptian's house for Joseph's sake; and the blessing of the Lord was upon all that he had in the house, and in the field.' Such blessing would often be ours if we walked as near to God as Joseph did.

## 2 Joseph's temptation

Years passed on, and Joseph became the steward and bailiff in his master's house. 'He left all that he had in Joseph's hand; and he knew not aught he had, save the bread which he did eat.' And it was just here that Joseph encountered the most terrible temptation of his life.

*a.  There were peculiar elements of trial in Joseph's case.*    The temptation was accompanied by opportunity: 'there was none of the men of the house there within.' It was well timed, and if he had yielded, there was not much fear of detection and punishment; the temptress would never publish her own shame. The temptation was also repeated day by day. How terrible must have been that awful persistency! The temptation that tries to win its way by its very importunity is to be feared most of all.

*b.  Yet Joseph stood firm.*    He reasoned with her. He referred to his master's kindness and trust. He held up the confidence that he dared not betray. He tried to recall her to a sense of what became her as his master's wife. But he did more. He brought the case from the court of reason to that of conscience, and asked in words forever memorable, and which have given the secret of victory to tempted souls in all ages: 'How then can I do this great wickedness, and sin against God!'

If history teaches anything, it teaches that sensual indulgence is the surest way to national ruin. Society in not condemning this sin condemns herself. It is said that the temptations of our great cities are too many and strong for the young to resist. Men sometimes speak as if sin were a necessity. Refuse to entertain such thoughtlessness and dangerous talk. A young man *can* resist; he *can* overcome; he *can* be pure and chaste. We must, however, obey the dictates of Scripture and common sense. Avoid all places, books, and people that minister to evil thoughts. Remember that no temptation can master you unless you admit it *within* your nature; and since you are too weak to keep the door shut against it, look to the mighty Saviour to place himself against it. All hell cannot break the door open which you entrust to the safe keeping of Jesus.

*c.  What a motto this is for us all!*    'How can *I* do this great wickedness?' *I,* for whom Christ died. 'How can I do this great *wickedness?*' Others call it 'sowing wild oats'. I call it SIN. 'How can I do this *great* wickedness?' Many wink at it; to me it is a *great* sin. 'How can I sin *against God?*' It seems only to concern men; but in effect it is a personal sin against the holy God.

**d.  *Joseph did a wise thing when he fled.***    Discretion is often the wisest part of valour. Better lose a coat and many a more valuable possession than lose a good conscience. Do not parley with temptation. Do not stay to look at it. It will master you if you do. 'Escape for thy life; look not behind thee, neither stay in all the plain.'

**e.  *There is no sin in being tempted.***    The sinless one himself was tempted of the devil. The will is the citadel of our manhood; and so long as there is no yielding there, there is none anywhere. I cannot be accused of receiving goods, if I am simply asked to take them in – a request which I indignantly repudiate. The sin comes in when I assent, and acquiesce, and yield.

May we have grace and faith to imitate the example of Joseph, and above all, of our stainless Lord. We may be quite sure that no temptation will be permitted to assail us but such as is common to man, or that we are able to resist. Never forget that we who believe in Jesus are seated with him at the right hand of power; nor that Satan is already, in the purpose of God, a defeated foe beneath our feet. Open your whole being to the subduing grace of the Holy Spirit. And thus we will be more than conquerors through him who loves us.

# 4

# Misunderstood and Imprisoned

*Genesis 39, 40. See also* Psalms 102:17–19

When Potiphar heard the false but plausible statement of his wife, and saw the garment in her hand, which he recognised as Joseph's, his wrath flamed up; he would hear no words of explanation, but thrust Joseph at once into the state prison, of which he had the oversight and charge.

## 1   The severity of his sufferings

It was not a prison like those with which we are familiar – airy, well-lit, and conducted by humane men. To use Joseph's own words, in the Hebrew, it was a miserable 'hole'. 'I have done nothing that they should put me into the "hole".' Two or three little rooms, crowded with prisoners, stifling in air, fetid with ill odours, perhaps half-buried from the blessed sunshine – this was the sort of accommodation in which Joseph spent those two miserable years.

Imagine a large gloomy hall, with no windows, paved with flags black with filth, no light or air, except what may struggle through the narrow grated aperture, by which the friends of the wretched inmates, or some pitying strangers, pass in the food and water which are the sole staff of life. No arrangements of any kind have been made for cleanliness, or for the separation of the prisoners. All day long there is the weary clank of fetters around manacled feet, as the victims slowly drag themselves over the floor, or resolve again and again around the huge stone columns that support the roof, and to which their chains are riveted. In some such sunless 'hole' must Joseph have been confined.

## 2   These sufferings proved to be very beneficial

Taken at the lowest point, *this imprisonment served Joseph's temporal interests.* That prison was the place where state prisoners were bound. There court officials who had fallen under suspicion were sent. Chief butler and chief baker do not seem much to us, but they were titles for very august people. Such men would talk freely with Joseph; and in doing so would give him a great insight into political parties, and a knowledge of men and things generally, which later must have been of great service to him.

But there is more than this. Psalm 105:18, referring to Joseph's imprisonment, has a striking alternative rendering, 'His soul entered into iron.' Put into our language, and it would read, *Iron entered into his soul.* Is there not a truth in this, that sorrow and privation, the yoke borne in youth, are conducive to an iron tenacity and strength of purpose, which are the indispensable foundation and framework of a noble character? Do not flinch from suffering. Bear it silently, patiently, resignedly; and be assured that it is God's way of infusing iron into your spiritual makeup.

As a boy, Joseph's character tended to softness. He was spoiled by his father. He was too proud of his coat. He was given to tell tales. He was too full of his dreams and foreshadowed greatness. None of these were great faults, although he lacked strength, grip, power to rule. But what a difference his imprisonment made in him! From that moment he carried himself with a wisdom, modesty, courage, and manly resolution, that never fail him. He acts as a born ruler of men. He carried an alien country through the stress of a great famine, without a symptom of revolt. He holds his own with the proudest aristocracy of the time. He promotes the most radical changes. He had learned to hold his peace and wait. Surely the iron had entered his soul!

### 3 Joseph's comfort in the midst of these sufferings

*a.* '*He was there in the prison; but the* LORD *was with him.*'
The Lord was with him in the palace of Potiphar; but when Joseph went to prison, the Lord went there too. The only thing that severs us from God is sin: as long as we walk with God, he will walk with us, and if our paths dips down from the sunny upland lawns into the valley with its clinging mists, he will go at our side. The godly man is much more independent of men and things than others. If he is in a palace he is glad, not so much because of its delights as because God is there. And if he is in a prison he can sing and give praises, because God is there and because the God of his love bears him company. To the soul that is absorbed with God, all places and experiences are much the same.

*b. God can also raise up friends for his servants* in most unlikely places, and of most unlikely people. 'The Lord . . . gave him favour in the sight of the keeper of the prison.' He was probably a rough, unkindly man, quite prepared to copy the dislikes of his master, the great Potiphar, and to embitter the daily existence of this Hebrew slave. But there was another Power at work, of which he knew nothing, inclining him toward his ward, and leading him to put him in a position of trust.

*c. Above all, do not avenge yourselves.* When Joseph

recounted his troubles, he did not recriminate harshly on his brethren, or Potiphar, or Potiphar's wife. He simply said: 'I was stolen away out of the land of the Hebrews: and here also have I done nothing that they should put me into the [hole].'

5

# Joseph's First Interview With His Brothers

*Genesis 42*

The fact of Joseph's exaltation from the prison cell in which we left him, to the steps of Pharaoh's throne, are so well known that we need no describe them in detail. The life of Joseph, as the Prime Minister of Egypt, was a very splendid one. Everything that could please the sense or minister to the taste was his. His palaces would consist of numberless rooms opening into spacious courts, where palms, sycamores, and acacia trees grew in rare luxuriance. The furniture would be elegantly carved from various woods, encrusted with ebony and adorned with gilding. Rare perfumes rose from vases of gold and bronze and alabaster; and the foot sank deep in carpets, covering the floors, or trod upon the skins of lions and other ferocious beasts. Troops of slaves and officials ministered to every want. Choirs of musicians filled the air with sweet melody.

Meanwhile, the sons had become middle-aged men, with families of their own. They probably never mentioned that deed of violence to each other. *They did their best to banish the thought from their minds.* Conscious slept. Yet the time had come when God meant to use these men to found a nation. And in order to fit them for their high destiny it was necessary to bring them into a right condition of soul. But it seemed almost impossible to secure repentance in those obtuse and darkened hearts. However, the Eternal brought it about by a number of wonderful providences. This, then, is our theme: God's gracious methods of awakening the consciences of these men from their long and apparently endless sleep.

## 1 The first step toward their conviction was the pressure of want

There was dearth in all lands; and the famine reached even to the land of Canaan. Often before, in the lives of the patriarchs, they had been driven by famine down to Egypt; and Jacob aroused his sons from the hopeless lethargy into which they were sinking by saying, 'Why do ye look one upon another? Behold, I have heard that there is corn in Egypt: get you down and buy for us, from thence; that we may live, and not die. And Joseph's ten brethren went down to buy corn in Egypt.'

*It is so that God deals with us.* He breaks up our nest. He loosens our roots. He sends a mighty famine that cuts away the whole staff of bread. Later those men look back on that time of difficulty as the best thing that could have happened to them: nothing less would have brought them to Joseph. Yes, and the time is coming when you will bless God for your times of sorrow and misfortune. You will say, 'Before I was afflicted I went astray; but now have I kept Thy Word.

## 2 The second step was the rough treatment they received at the hands of Joseph

It would seem that in some of the larger markets he superintended the sale of the corn himself. He may even have gone there on purpose; he may have even cherished, and prayed over, the fancy that his brethren might come themselves. At last the looked-for day arrived. He was standing as usual at his post, surrounded by all the confusion and noise of an Eastern bazaar, when his attention was attracted by those ten men. He looked with a fixed, eager look for a moment, his heart throbbing quickly all the while; and he needed no further assurance: 'he knew them.'

Evidently, however, they did not know him. How should they? He had grown from a lad of seventeen to a man of forty. He was

clothed in pure white linen, with ornaments of gold to indicate his
rank, a garb not altogether unlike that famous coat, which had
wrought such havoc. He was governor of the land, and if they had
thought of Joseph at all when entering that land (and no doubt
they did), they expected to see him in the gang of slaves manacled
at work in the fields, or sweltering in the scorching brickyards,
preparing material for the pyramids. So, in unconscious fulfilment of his own boyish dream, they bowed down themselves
before him with their faces to the earth.

Joseph saw that they failed to recognise him, and partly to
ascertain if his brethren were repentant, partly in order to know
why Benjamin was not with them, he sought to test them. He
spake roughly to them. He accused them of being spies. He
refused to believe their statements, and put them in prison until
they could be verified. He kept Simeon bound.

# 6

# Joseph's Second Interview With His Brothers

## Genesis 43

We will now deal with that moving scene when Joseph caused
everyone to leave him while he cast aside his dignity, stepped
down from his throne, and fell on the necks of his brethren and
wept. We have a lesser task just now, yet full of interest; we have
to consider the successive steps by which that wayward family
was brought into a position in which its members could be forgiven and blessed.

### 1   There was the pressure of poverty and sorrow (43:1)

Jacob would never have turned his thoughts to Egypt if there had been plenty in Canaan. The famine drove the sons of Israel into Egypt to buy corn. And even though poor Simeon was bound in Egypt, the brothers would not have gone a second time if it had not been for the rigour of necessity. At first the aged father strongly opposed the thought of their taking Benjamin, even if they went themselves; and his children lingered.

There is a touching picture given of the conversation between Jacob and his sons, a kind of council of war. Reuben seems already to have lost the priority that his birthright would have secured, and Judah held the place of spokesman and leader among the brethren. He undertook to deal with his father for the rest of his brothers. At the outset, Jacob's request that they should go down to buy food was met with the most distinct refusal, unless Benjamin was permitted to accompany them. And when Jacob complained of their having betrayed the existence of another brother, all of them vindicated their action, and declared that they could not have done otherwise. At last Judah made himself personally responsible for the lad's safety, a pledge which, as we shall see, he nobly redeemed. And so, at last, Jacob yielded, proposing only that they should take a present to mollify the ruler's heart, double money to replace what had been returned in their sacks, and he uttered a fervent prayer to the Almighty on their behalf. Thus God in his mercy closed every other door but the one through which they might find their way to plenty and blessedness. There was no alternative but to go down to Egypt.

*a. So is your life.* You have had all that this world could give. But have you considered your ill-treatment of your great Elder Brother? Have you set your affections on things above? You know you have not. So God has called for a famine on your land. You have lost situation and friends. Your business is broken. Beauty, youth, health – all have vanished. Joseph is gone; Simeon is gone; and Benjamin is on the point of being taken away. Everything has been against you.

*b. It is a severe measure: how will you bear it?* In the first burst of the tempest, you say stubbornly, 'I will not go down; I will not yield; I will stand out to the last.' But, beware! God will have his way at last if not at first. The famine must continue until the wanderer arises to return to the Father, with words of penitent contrition on his lips. Oh that your word might be! – 'Come, and let us return unto the Lord; for he has torn, and he will heal us; he has smitten, and he will bind us up.'

## 2   There was the awakening of conscience

For twenty years conscience had slept. And as long as this was the case there could be no real peace between Joseph and his brothers. *They* could never feel sure that he had forgiven them. *He* would always feel that there was a padlock on the treasure-store of his love. Conscience must awake and slowly tread the aisles of the temple of penitence. This is the clue to the understanding of Joseph's behaviour.

*a. Joseph, to arouse their dormant consciences, repeated as nearly as possible to them their treatment of himself.*     This has already engaged our thought. 'Ye are spies' was the echo of their own rough words to himself. The prison, in which they lay for three days, was the counterpart of the pit in which they placed *him*. Men will best learn what is the true nature of their own iniquities when they experience the treatment they have meted out to others. And Joseph's device was a success. Listen to their moan, 'We are verily guilty concerning our brother.'

*b. Here again is a clue to the mysteries of our own lives.*     God sometimes allows us to be treated as we have treated him, that we may see our offences in true character, and may be obliged to turn to him with words of genuine contrition. Your child has turned to him with words of genuine contrition. Your child has turned out badly. You did everything for him, now he refuses to do what you wish and even taunts you. Do you feel it? Perhaps this will reveal to you what God feels, in that, though he has nourished and brought you up, yet you have rebelled against him. Your neighbour, when in trouble, came to you for help, and promised to repay you with interest. Now he prospers and you ask him to repay you, but he either laughs at you or tells you to wait. Do you feel it? Ah, now you know how God feels, he who helped you in distress, to whom you made many vows, but who reminds you in vain of all the past. That conscience must indeed be deep in sleep that does not awaken at such appeals.

### 3   There was the display of much tender love toward them

As soon as Joseph saw them he invited them to his own table to feast with him. The brothers were brought into his house where every kindness was shown to them. It was as if, instead of being poor shepherds, they were the magnates of the land. Their fears as to the return of the money were allayed by the pious, though misleading, assurance of the steward that if they had discovered it in their sacks it might have been put there by God, because the payment for their corn was in his hands. And when Joseph came they prostrated themselves before him in striking fulfilment of his own boyish dream. He asked them tenderly about the well-being of their father, and there must have been a pathos in his words to Benjamin that would have revealed the whole secret if they had not been so utterly unprepared to find Joseph beneath the strange guise of the great Egyptian governor.

What an inimitable touch that tells us how Joseph's heart welled up into his eyes, so that he needed to hurry in order to conceal the bursting emotions that threatened to overmaster him. 'He sought where to weep; and he entered into his chamber, and wept there. And he washed his face, and went out, and refrained himself, and said, Set on bread.'

The rejected Brother may seem strange and rough. He may cause sorrow. He may bind Simeon before our eyes. But beneath all, he loves us with a love in which is concentrated the love of all parents for their children, and of all friends for their beloved. And that love is constantly devising means of expressing itself. It puts money into our sacks; it invites us to its home and spreads banquets before us. Jesus feels yearnings over us which he restrains, and does not dare to betray until the work of conviction is complete and he can pour the full tides of affection on us, without injury to others or harm to ourselves.

# 7

# Joseph Making Himself Known

## *Genesis 45*

'The cup was found in Benjamin's sack.' What a discovery that was! But how did it get there? The brothers could not tell. They neither could nor would believe that Benjamin had known anything of it. Yet how to explain the mystery was a problem they could not solve. It seemed as if some evil genuis were making them its sport, first in putting the money in their sacks, and then in concealing the cup there.

Each brother must have wished that the cup could have been found in any sack but in Benjamin's. They all remembered their father's unwillingness to let him come. Jacob had seemed to have a premonition of coming disaster. When they first returned from Egypt he said decisively, 'My son shall not go down with you; for his brother is dead, and he is left alone: if mischief befall him by the way in which ye go, then shall ye bring down my grey hairs with sorrow to the grave.' And when the pressure of famine compelled them, the last words of the stricken parent were, 'God Almighty give you mercy before the man, that he may send away your older brother, and Benjamin. If I be bereaved of my children, I am bereaved.' All the time his heart was filled with the presages of coming sorrow; and now those forebodings seemed about to be fulfilled. Oh! how different the road seemed to what it had been a little before! The same sun was shining; the same busy scene surrounded them – but a dark veil was spread over the sky and earth. Let us study the scene that followed.

### 1   Notice their behaviour

*a.* *'They fell before him on the ground.'*   As they did so, they

unconsciously fulfilled his own prediction, uttered when a boy.
How vividly that memorable dream of the harvest field must have
occurred to Joseph's mind! Here were their sheaves making obeisance to his sheaf, standing erect in the midst.

*b. But who was to be their spokesman?* Reuben had always
had something to say in self-justification, and had been so sure
that all would be right that he had pledged the lives of his children
to his father for the safety of Benjamin; but *he* is silent. Simeon
was probably the cruel one, the instigator of the crime against
Joseph; but *he* dares not utter a word. Benjamin, the blameless
one, the prototype of the young man whom Jesus loved, is con-
victed of sin, and has nothing to say. Who then is to speak? There
is only one, Judah, who at the pit's mouth had diverted the
brothers from their first thought of murder. And notice how he
speaks. He throws himself helplessly on Joseph's mercy: 'What
shall we say unto my lord? what shall we speak? or how shall we
clear ourselves?'

*c. We stand on surer ground than ever they did.* They had no
idea of the gentleness of Joseph's heart. They did not understand
why on one occasion he had hastened from their presence; they
could not guess how near the surface lay the fountains of his tears.
They only knew him as rough, and stern, and hard. 'The man,
who is the lord of the land, spake roughly to us.' But we know the
gentleness of the Lord Jesus. We have seen his tears over
Jerusalem; we have listened to his tender invitations to come to
him; we have stood beneath his cross and heard his last prayers
for his murderers, and his words of invitation to the dying thief.
We then need not fear for the issue when we cast ourselves on his
mercy.

*d. In all literature, there is nothing more pathetic than this appeal
of Judah.* The eagerness that made him draw near; the humility
that confessed Joseph's anger might righteously burn, since he
was as Pharaoh; the picture of the elderly man, their father, bereft
of one son, and clinging to this one, the only survivor of his
mother; the recital of the strain that the governor had imposed on
them, by demanding that they should bring their youngest
brother down; the story of their father's dread, only overmas-
tered by the imperious demand of a hunger that brooked no
check; the vivid picture of the father's eagerness again to see the

lad, in whose life his own was bound up; the heartbreaking grief at not seeing him among them; the heroic offer to stay there a slave, as Benjamin's substitute, if only the lad might go home; the preference of a life of slavery rather than to behold the aged man sinking with sorrow into his grave – all this is touched with a master-hand. But if a rough man could plead like this, what must not those pleadings be that Jesus offers before the throne! We have an Advocate in the Court of King's Bench who never lost a case: let us put ourselves into his hands, and trust him when he says, 'I have prayed for you.'

*e. Thus Joseph's object was attained.*   He had wished to restore his brothers to perfect rest and peace, but he knew that this were impossible as long as their sin was unconfessed and unforgiven. But it had now been abundantly confessed. Then, too, he had been anxious to see how they felt toward Benjamin. With this object in view he had given him five times as much as he had given them. Some think that he did this to show his special love. It may have been so, but there probably was something deeper. It was his dream of superiority that aroused their hatred against him: how would they feel toward Benjamin, if he, the younger, were treated better than them all? But notwithstanding the marked favour shown him, they were eager as before for his return with them. Besides, he wanted to see if they could forgive. It was Benjamin who had brought them into all this trouble: had they treated him in the spirit of former days, they would have abandoned him to his fate; but if so, they could not have been forgiven. But so far from showing malice, they tenderly loved and clung to him for the aged father's sake and his own. Evidently then all Joseph's purposes were accomplished; and nothing remained to hinder the great unveiling that was so near.

## 2   Notice the revelation and reconciliation

*a. 'Then Joseph could not refrain himself.'*   When Judah's voice ceased its pathetic pleading, he could restrain himself no more.

*b. And Joseph cried, 'Cause every man to go out from me.'* There was great delicacy here. He did not want to expose his brethren; and yet he wanted to say words that could not be understood by the curious ears of mere courtiers. His brethren, too, must have a chance to be themselves. 'And there stood no man with him, while Joseph made himself known unto his brethren.'

*c. And he wept aloud.* He began to weep so hard that the Egyptians heard the unusual sounds and wondered. Was this joy or grief? I am disposed to think it was neither. It was pent-up emotion. For many days he had been in suspense; so anxious not to lose them, so afraid that they might not stand the test. When from some secret vantage point he had watched them leave the city in the grey light, he may have chided himself for letting them go at all. His mind had been under great pressure; and now that the tension was removed, and there was no further necessity for it, he wept aloud. Ah, sinner, the heart of Christ is on the stretch for you!

*And he said, 'I am Joseph.'* He spoke in deep emotion; yet the words must have fallen on his brothers like a thunderbolt. 'Joseph!' Had they been dealing all the while with their long-lost brother? 'Joseph!' Then they had fallen into a lion's den indeed. 'Joseph!' Could it be? Yes, it must be so; and it would explain many things that had sorely puzzled them. Well might they be troubled and terrified. Astonishment as at one risen from the dead, terror for the consequences, fear lest he would repay them the long-standing debt – all these emotions made them speechless. So he said again, 'I am Joseph, *your brother,* whom ye sold into Egypt'; and he added very lovingly, 'Be not grieved, nor angry with yourselves; for God did send me.' Penitent sinner! in this way your Saviour speaks to you. 'I am Jesus, your Brother, whom you have sold and crucified; yet do not grieve for that. I was delivered by the determinate counsel and foreknowledge of God; though the hands have been none the less wicked by whom I have been crucified and slain. But if you repent, your sins will be blotted out.

*d. 'And Joseph said unto his brethren, Come near to me.'* They had backed farther and farther from him; but now he bids them approach. A moment more saw him and Benjamin locked in each other's arms, their tears freely flowing. And he kissed *all* his *brethren.* Simeon? Yes. Reuben? Yes. Those who had tied his hands and mocked his cries? Yes. He kissed them *all.* And after that they talked with him.

# 8

# Joseph's Father

*Genesis 47:1–11*

We always turn with interest from an illustrious man to ask about his father and his mother. The father of Martin Luther and the mother of the Wesleys hang as familiar portraits in the picture gallery of our fancy. In the story of Joseph we are permitted to glance behind the scenes, and to consider the relations between him and his aged father, Jacob.

### 1   Joseph's undiminished filial love

From the first moment that Joseph saw his brothers in the grain market, it was evident that his love to his father burned with undiminished fervour. Those brethren little guessed how eager he was to learn if his aged father was yet alive, nor what a thrill of comfort shot through his heart when they happened to say, 'Behold, our youngest brother is this day with his father.' Evidently, then, though twenty-five years had passed since he beheld that beloved form, his father was living still.

   And when his brothers came the second time, Judah little realised what a tender chord he struck, and how it vibrated, almost beyond endurance, when he spoke again and again of the father at home, an elderly man, who so tenderly loved the young lad, the only memorial of his mother. He spoke of that father who had been so anxious lest mischief should befall him, and whose grey hairs would go down with sorrow to the grave, unless he came back safe. It was this repeated allusion to his father that wrought on Joseph's felings so greatly as to break him down. 'He could not refrain himself.' And so the very next thing he said, after the astounding announcement, 'I am Joseph,' was, 'Doth my father yet live?' And in the tumultuous words that followed, words throbbing with passion and pathos, sentences about the absent father came rolling out. 'Haste ye, and go up to my father, and say unto him, Thus saith thy son Joseph, God hath made me lord of all Egypt: come down unto me; tarry not . . . And ye shall tell my father of my glory in Egypt, and of all that ye have seen; and ye shall haste, and bring down my father hither.'

The weeks and months that intervened must have been full of feverish anxiety for Joseph; and when at last he heard that his father had reached the frontier of Egypt, in one of the wagons that he had sent to meet him, he 'made ready his chariot, and went up to meet Israel his father.' Oh, that meeting! If the aged man was sitting in some recess of the lumbering wagon, weary with the long journey, how he would revive when they said, 'Joseph is coming'! I think he would surely dismount, and wait, straining his aged eyes at the approaching company, from out the midst of which there came the bejewelled ruler to fall on his neck and weep there a good while. 'Let me die,' said Jacob, as he looked at Joseph from head to foot with glad, proud, satisfied eyes: 'Let me die, since I have seen thy face; because thou art yet alive.'

*Joseph loved his father too well to be ashamed of him.* When Pharaoh heard of the arrival of Joseph's father and brothers, he seemed very pleased, and he directed Joseph to see to their welfare. Then Joseph brought Jacob his father before Pharaoh.

We cannot but admire the noble frankness with which Jacob introduced his father to this great monarch, accustomed to the manners of the foremost court of the world. There was a great social gulf fixed between Egypt and Canaan, the court and the tent, the monarch and the shepherd. And if Joseph had been any less noble or simple than he was, he might have shrunk from bringing the two extremes together. But all these thoughts were forgotten in presence of another: this withered, halting, famine-pursued man was *his father*.

## 2 Pharaoh's question

'How old art thou?' This was Pharaoh's first enquiry, as Jacob entered his presence. It is a question that often rises to our lips, but it is suggested by a very false standard of estimating the length of a man's life. The length of a life is not measured by the number of its days; no, but by the way in which its days have been used.

## 3   Jacob's answer

'And Jacob said unto Pharaoh, The days of the years of my pilgrimage are an hundred and thirty years; few and evil have the days of the years of my life been, and have not attained unto the days of the years of the life of my fathers in the days of their pilgrimage.' Jacob's years had been few in comparison with those of his ancestors. Terah reached the age of 205; Abraham, 175; Isaac, 180. But 'the whole age of Jacob was an hundred forty and seven years.' They had been *evil*. As a young man he was wrenched from his dearest associations of home and friends, and went forth alone to spend the best years of his life as a stranger in a strange land. Arduous and difficult was his service to Laban, consumed in the day by drought, and in the sleepless night vigils by frost. He escaped from Laban with difficulty, and no sooner had he done so than he had to encounter his incensed and impetuous brother. In the agony of that dread crisis he met with the Angel Wrestler, who touched the socket of his hips so that he limped to the end of his life. These calamities had hardly passed when he was involved in extreme danger with the Canaanites of Shechem, and passed through scenes that have blanched his hair, furrowed his cheeks, and scarred his heart. Thus he came to Luz, and Deborah, Rebekah's nurse, died, and was buried beneath an oak, which was thereafter called the Oak of Weeping. 'And they journeyed from Bethel; and there was but a little way to come to Ephrath', and Rachel (his favourite wife) bore a son. It came to pass, as she died, that she called his name 'Ben-oni, the son of my sorrow.' A little further on he came to Mamre, arriving just in time to bear the remains of his own father to the grave. And what sorrows befell him after that, have already touched our hearts, as we have studied the story of his son, Joseph. Reuben involved his name in shameful disgrace. Judah trailed the family honour in the mire of sensual appetite. To all appearance Joseph had been torn to pieces by wild beasts. The dissensions of his sons must have rent his heart. And even after his meeting with his long-lost son he was to linger for seventeen years a pensioner on the bounty of the king of Egypt: far from the glorious heritage that had been promised to his race.

*Such was the exterior of Jacob's life.* You would have called his life a failure. Compare it with the lot of Esau; and what a contrast it presents! Jacob obtained the birthright; but what a life of suffering and disaster was his! Esau lost the birthright; but he had all that heart could wish; wealth, royalty, a line of illustrious sons. The thirty-sixth chapter of Genesis contains a list of the royal dukes of his line. How often must Esau have pitied his brother!

And yet when this same Jacob stands before Pharaoh, the greatest monarch of the world bends eagerly to catch his blessing. 'Jacob blessed Pharaoh'. Jacob in his earlier life was crafty, a mere bargain-maker, a trickster; but all seems to have been eliminated in the fierce crucible of suffering through which he had passed; and he had reached a grandeur or moral greatness that impressed even the haughty Pharaoh. There is a greatness that is wholly independent of those adventitious circumstances that we sometimes associate with it. God himself said, 'Thy name shall be no more called Jacob, but Israel (a prince of God), for as a prince hast thou power with God, and with men'.

Three things made Jacob royal; and will do as much for us.

*a. Prayer.*   On the moorland, strewn with boulders, he saw in his dreams the mighty rocks pile themselves into a heaven-touching ladder. This struck the keynote of his life. Since that day he lived at the foot of the ladder of prayer, up which the angels sped to carry his petitions, and down which they came to bring blessing. Learn to pray without ceasing. It is the secret of greatness. He who is often in the audience chamber of the great King becomes kinglike.

*b. Suffering.*   His nature was marred by selfish, base, and carnal elements. He took unlawful advantage of his famished brother; deceived his aged father; increased his property at the expense of his uncle; worked his ends by mean and crafty means. But sorrow ate away all these things and gave him a new dignity. So does it still work on those who have received the new nature, and who meekly learn the lesson that God's love designs to teach them.

*c. Contact with Christ.*   'There wrestled a man with him until the breaking of the day.' Who was he? Surely none less than the Angel Jehovah, whose face may not be seen, or his name known.

It was the Lord himself, intent on ridding his servant of the evil that had clung so long and so closely to him, sapping his spiritual life. And from that hour Jacob was 'Israel'. Ah, my readers, Jesus, the immortal lover of souls, is wrestling with you, longing to rid you of littleness and selfishness, and to lift you also to a royal life. Yield to him, lest he be compelled to touch the sinew of your strength. If you let him have his way, he will make you truly Princes and Princesses with God; and even those above you in this world's rank will gladly gather around you for the sake of the spiritual blessings you will bestow.

# 9

# Joseph at the Deathbed of Jacob

## *Genesis 47:27–31*

Jacob dwelled in the land of Goshen and there his sons led their flocks over the rich pasture-lands. 'They grew, and multiplied exceedingly.' So seventeen uneventful years went by. And as the elderly man became more and more infirm, his spirit was cheered and sustained by the love of Joseph. Evidently Joseph was the stay of that waning life, and it is not remarkable therefore that the patriarch summoned him not once, or even twice, but three times, to his deathbed. It is on those visits that we dwell now.

## 1   Joseph's first visit

'The time grew nigh that Israel must die.' How inexorable is the 'must' of death! There is no possibility of evading its summons. Jacob exceeded the ordinary span of modern life by many years, and, in spite of much hardship and privation, he had evaded the reach of death; but this could not be forever. The failing powers of his life gave warning that the machinery of nature was on the point of giving way. He must die. Long before our Lord walked this world, men cherished the hope of eternal life.

Daniel teaches in plainest language the truth of a general resurrection to endless life or endless shame. Ecclesiastes closes with an explicit statement of the spirit's return to its giver, and of final judgment. The Book of Job, whatever date may be assigned to it, has been called a hymn of immortality: he knew at least that his 'Redeemer liveth, and that he shall stand at the latter day upon the earth: and though after my skin worms destroy this body, yet in my flesh shall I see God' (Job 19:25–26). In the Book of Psalms we have no uncertain evidence of the tenacity with which pious Jews clung to these hopes. 'Thou wilt not leave my soul in [sheol]; neither wilt thou suffer thine Holy One to see corruption. Thou wilt shew me the path of life' (Ps. 16:10–11). And it is just this faith in and yearning after a life beyond the grave which is the true keynote of the lives of the three great patriarchs who lie together in Machpelah's ancient cave.

Why did they wander to and fro in the land of promise as sojourners in a strange land? Why were they content to have no inheritance – no, not so much as a place to put their feet on? Why did Abraham dwell with Isaac and Jacob in frail, shifting tents, rather than in towns like Sodom and Gomorrah? What did Abraham mean when he said to the sons of Heth, 'I am a stranger and a sojourner with you'? And what was the thought in Jacob's mind when, in the presence of the haughty Pharaoh, he described his life as a 'pilgrimage'? The answer is clearly given in the roll call of God's heroes contained in Hebrews 11: 'They sought a country, a fatherland.' And they were so absorbed with this one thought, that they could not settle to any inheritance in Canaan. Their refusal to have anything more than a grave in the soil of the Promised Land shows how eagerly they looked for the land that was very far off.

At first, no doubt, they thought that Canaan was to be the land of promise. But when they waited for it year after year, and still it was withheld, they looked into the deed of gift again, and instead of a city built by human hands, there arose before them the fair vision of the crystal walls and the pearly gates of the city which hath foundations, whose builder and maker is God.

This belief in the 'city of God', of which later Augustine wrote on the coast of Africa, and which has sustained so many saintly souls, animated their lives, cheered them in death, and cast a bright ray across the gloom of the grave. 'These all died in faith, not having received the promises, but having seen them afar off, and were persuaded of them, and embraced them.' They 'greeted them from afar', as the wanderer greets his longed-for home, when he sees it from afar. With what eagerness, with what earnest yearnings, with what fond anticipation, must these weary wanderers have looked for heaven!

*a. Jacob did not regard the future life as a mere state of existence* stripped of all those associations that make life worth the having. Indeed, in this he seems to have had truer thoughts than many who are found in Christian churches. He said, 'I am to be gathered unto my people.' For him the city to which he went was the gathering-place of his clan, the rendezvous of elect souls, the home of all who were *his* people because they were *God's*.

But it was not simply to express these hopes that the dying patriarch summoned the beloved Joseph to his side. The father wanted to bind the son by a solemn promise not to have him buried in the land of his exile, but to carry him back to that lone cave, which seemed an outpost in the hostile and distant land of Canaan. For seventeen years Jacob had been familiar with Egypt's splendid temples, obelisks, and pyramids; he had been surrounded with all the comforts that Joseph's filial love could devise or his munificence execute. But nothing could make him forget that distant cave that was before Mamre, in the land of Canaan. To him interment in the most magnificent pyramid in Egypt was not for a moment to be compared with burial in that solitary and humble sepulchre, where the mortal remains of Abraham and Sarah, of Isaac and Rebekah, and of the faithful Leah, lay waiting the day or resurrection.

*b. Human nature was not different then from what it is today.* Our truest home is still by the graves of the beloved dead. Many a warrior, dying in some distant land, has asked that his remains might be placed, but in the quiet country graveyard where the moss-covered tombstones repeat in successive generations the family name. It was natural, then, for Jacob to wish to be buried in Machpelah.

*c. But there was something more than natural sentiment.* He was a man of faith. He knew and cherished the ancient promise made by God to his friend, the patriarch Abraham, that Canaan should become the possession of his seed. That promise was the old man's stay. He knew that Canaan and not Egypt was the destined abiding place of his people. They would not always live in Egypt. If then, he was buried in Egypt, he would be left behind, a stranger among strangers. No, this could not be. If they are to leave, he must leave before them. If they are to settle in the land of promise, he will go first as their forerunner. And though he could not share the perils and pains and glories of the Exodus, he would be there to meet them when later descendants would enter on their inheritance.

'Bury me not, I pray thee, in Egypt: but I will lie with my fathers, and thou shalt carry me out of Egypt and bury me in their buryingplace.' What son could resist that appeal? Can any of us resist the last appeals of our beloved? Joseph was too good and tender to hesitate for single moment. 'And he said, I will do as thou hast said.' But the old man was not content with a mere promise. 'And he said, Swear unto me. And he sware unto him. And Israel bowed himself upon the bed's head.' So ended Joseph's first visit to his dying father.

## 2  Joseph's second visit

Tidings came to the Prime Minister of Egypt that his father was sick and wished to see him. And he went to him without delay, taking with him his two sons, Manasseh and Ephraim. When Joseph arrived at his father's dwelling, the aged patriarch seems to have been lying still, with closed eyes, in the extreme of physical exhaustion. He was too weak to notice any of those familiar forms that stood around him. But when one told him and said, 'Behold, thy son Joseph cometh,' the sound of that loved name revived him. He made a great effort, and, propped by pillows, sat up upon the bed.

There was clearly no decay in his power of recollection, as the old man reviewed the past. And as his recollection embraced the past, it was also vividly alive to more recent incidents in the family history. He did not forget that Joseph, who leaned over his dying form, had two sons; and he announced his intention of adopting them as his own. 'Thy two sons . . . which were born unto thee in the land of Egypt before I came unto thee into Egypt, are mine; as

Reuben and Simeon, they shall be mine.' By that act, while Joseph's name was obliterated from the map of Canaan, yet he became possessor of a double portion of his area, because Ephraim and Manasseh would from that day stand there as his representatives.

And when he had said so much, his mind wandered away. He saw again that scene on the hilly road to Bethlehem, just outside the little village, where his onward progress was suddenly halted, and all his camp was hushed into the stillness of a dread suspense, as the life of the beloved Rachel trembled in the balance. He could never forget that moment. His dying eyes could see again the spot where he buried her, 'there in the way of Ephrath.'

When the aged Jacob came back from his reverie, the first sight that arrested him was the presence of the awe-struck boys, who were drinking in every look and word, with fixed and almost breathless heed.

'Who are these?' said Israel.

'They are my sons,' was the proud and immediate reply, 'whom God hath given me in this place.'

And Israel said, 'Bring them, I pray thee, unto me, and I will bless them.'

And so they were brought near, and the aged arms were put feebly round the younger and slender forms. And then again the dying man wandered back to a grief that had left as deep a scar as his sorrow for the beloved Rachel. Then turning to Joseph he reminded him of the long years during which he thought he would never look again on his face. But now God had shown him also his seed.

With prophetic insight he crossed his hands, as the two lads waited before him for his blessing, so that his right found its way to the head of the younger, while his left alighted on that of the elder. By that act he reversed the verdict of their birth, and gave the younger precedence over the elder. It was useless for Joseph to remonstrate, and to urge the claims of his firstborn. Jacob knew quite well what he was doing, and that he was on the line of the divine purpose. 'I know it, my son, I know it; he also shall become a people, and he also shall be great: but truly his younger brother shall be greater than he, and his seed shall become a multitude of nations.'

There was one thing only more to say, before this memorable

interview ended. Years before, Jacob had become embroiled, through the dastardly treachery of his sons, in conflict with the original inhabitants of Canaan, and he had been compelled, in self-defence, to acquire by force a parcel of land, with his sword and with his bow. *This* he gave as an additional portion to his favourite son.

### 3   Joseph's third and last visit

Once more Joseph visited that death chamber. This was the third time and the last. But this time he stood only as one of twelve strong, bearded men, who gathered around the aged form of their father, his face shadowed by death, his spirit aglow with the light of prophecy. How intense the awe with which they heard their names called, one by one, by the old man's trembling voice, now pausing for breath, now speaking with great difficulty! The character of each is criticised with prophetic insight; the salient points of their past history are vividly brought to mind; and some foreshadowing is given them of their future.

This scene is an anticipation of the judgment seat where men shall hear the story of their lives passed under review, and a sentence passed, against which there shall be no appeal.

But the dying patriarch speaks with peculiar sweetness and grace when he comes to touch on the destiny of his favourite son. His words brim with tenderness and move with a stateliness and eloquence which indicate how his heart was stirred to its depths. A few more sentences to Benjamin, and the venerable patriarch drew his feet up into his bed, and quietly breathed his last, and was gathered to his people. But that eager, much-tried spirit passed up into other scenes of more exalted fellowship and ministry, with no pause in his life, for in years to come God attested his continued existence and energy when he called himself 'the God of Jacob', for God is not God of the dead, but of the living. And Joseph fell on his father's face, and wept on him, and pressed his warm lips on the death-cold clay. He commanded the physicians to embalm his body, thus cheating death of its immediate victory.

10

# Joseph's Last Days and Death

## Genesis 50:24–25

'God will surely visit you, and ye shall carry up my bones from hence.' These were the dying words of Joseph. And it is somewhat remarkable that these are the only words in his whole career that are referred to in the subsequent pages of the Scriptures. Of course, I refer to those words in Hebrews 11, where it is said, 'By faith Joseph, when he died, made mention of the [exodus] of the children of Israel; and gave commandment concerning his bones.'

Let us notice:

### 1    The circumstances under which these words were spoken

*a. Joseph was now an old man.*    One hundred and ten years had stolen away his strength, and had left deep marks on his form. It was ninety-three years since he had been lifted from the pit to become a slave. Eighty years had passed since he had first stood before Pharaoh in all the beauty and wisdom of his young manhood. And sixty years had left their papyrus records in the State archives since, with all the pomp and splendour of Egypt's court, he had carried the remains of his old father to Machpelah's ancient cave. He was old when he saw the bright young faces of his great-grandchildren: 'they were brought up upon Joseph's knees.' With long life and many days God had blessed his faithful servant. And now, stopping beneath their weight, he was fast descending to the breakup of natural life.

*b. But the shadows of his own decay were small compared with those that he saw gathering around his beloved people.*    Sixty years before, when Jacob died, all was bright, and he was honoured with a splendid funeral because he had given to the land of Egypt so great a benefactor and saviour in the person of his son. But when Joseph died, all was getting dark, and the shadow of a great eclipse was gathering over the destinies of his people. No notice seems to have been taken in Egypt of his death. No impressive funeral services were voted to him at public expense. No pyramid was placed at the disposal of his sons. And he addresses his brethren gathered about him as being sorely in need of help. They needed an advocate at court, and an assurance of divine visitation.

Three hundred years before, the great founder of the nation had watched all day beside an altar, scaring away the vultures which, attracted by the flesh that lay upon it, hovered around. At length, as the sun went down, the watcher fell asleep – it is hard to watch with God – and in his sleep he dreamed. A dense and awful gloom seemed to enclose him, and to oppress his soul and on it, as upon a curtain, passed successive glimpses of the future of his race – glimpses which a divine voice interpreted to his ear. He saw them exiled to a foreign country, enslaved by the foreigner, and lingering there while three generations of men bloomed as spring flowers, and were cut down before the sharp sickle of death. And as he beheld all the terror of that enslavement, the horror of a great darkness fell on his soul. We know how exactly that horror was justified by the events that were so soon to take place. 'The Egyptians made the children of Israel to serve with rigour: and they made their lives bitter with hard bondage, in mortar, and in brick, and in all manner of service in the field: all their service, wherein they made them serve, was with rigour' (Exod. 1:13–14). The first symptoms of that outburst of popular 'Jew-hate' was already, like stormy birds, settling about the closing hour of the great Eygptian premier.

We cannot tell the precise form of those symptoms. Perhaps he had been banished from the councils of Pharaoh; perhaps he was already pining in neglect; perhaps the murmurs of dislike against his people were already rising; perhaps acts of oppression and cruelty were increasingly rife. In any case, the twilight of the dark night was gathering in; and it was this that made his words more splendid: they shone out as stars of hope.

*c. Moreover, his brethren were around him.*    His forgiveness
and love to them lasted till the testing hour by that great assayer,
Death. Nor did *they* fail. From something narrated in the previous verses of this chapter, it would appear that, for long, his
brethren, judging of him by their own dark and implacable
hearts, could not believe in the sincerity and genuineness of his
forgiveness. They thought that he must be feigning more than he
felt, in order to secure some ulterior object, such as the blessing
and approval of their aged father. And so they feared that, as soon
as Jacob was removed Joseph's just resentment, long concealed
with masterly art, would break forth against them. It seemed
impossible to believe that he felt no grudge, and would take no
action at all with reference to the past; and they said, 'Joseph will
. . . certainly requite us all the evil which we did unto him.' And
Joseph wept when they spoke; wept that they should have so misunderstood him after his repeated assurances; wept to see them
kneeling at his feet for a forgiveness that he had freely given them
years before. 'Fear not,' he said in effect; 'do not kneel there; I am
not God: you thought evil against me; but God meant it for good,
to save many people alive, as it is this day.'

The Lord Jesus, who lights every man coming into the world,
was in Joseph's heart, and his behaviour was a foreshadowing of
incarnate love. Reader! He waits to forgive you in this way.
Though you have maligned, and refused, and crucified him
afresh, and put him to an open shame; yet, for all that, he waits to
forgive you so entirely, that not one of these things shall be ever
mentioned against you again.

*d. Lastly, he was dying.*    He had warded off death from Egypt;
but he could not ward it off from himself. 'I die.' They were
among the last words that he had caught from his father's dying
lips (48:21), and now he appropriates them to himself. Yes, and
in doing so, he touches the zenith of his noble confidence and
hope. O that each of us may go on shining more and more each
day until our last, and that, when heart and flesh are failing most
conspicuously, the life of the spirit may flash out with it most brilliant lights.

It was under all these circumstances that Joseph said, 'God will
surely visit you, and ye shall carry up my bones from hence.'

## 2 Let us investigate the full importance of these words

And we may do so best by comparing them with Jacob's dying wish: 'Bury me with my fathers in the cave that is in . . . the field of Machpelah.' This was most natural: we all love to be buried by the beloved dust of our departed. And Jacob knew that there would be no great difficulty in carrying out his wish. Joseph was then in the height of his power. There was no great faith therefore in asking for that which could so easily be accomplished. But with Joseph it was different. He too wanted to be buried in the land of Canaan; but not at once – not then! There were two things he expected would happen: the one, that the people would go out of Egypt; the other, that they would come into the land of Canaan. He did not know when or how; he was only sure that so it would be: 'surely'.

To Joseph's natural vision these things were most unlikely. When he spoke, Israel was settled in Goshen, and so increasing in numbers and in wealth that any uprooting was becoming daily more unlikely. And as to the oppression that was perhaps beginning to threaten them, what chance would they have of ever being able to escape from the detaining squadrons of Egypt's chivalry, supposing they wished to go? But his anticipation of the future was not founded on human foresight, but on the distinct announcements of the Almighty. He remembered how God had said to Abraham, 'Look from the place where thou art northward, and southward, and eastward, and westward; for all the land which thou seest, to thee will I give it, and to thy seed forever' (Gen. 13:14–15). That promise was repeated to Isaac.

Again that promise was reiterated to Jacob as he lay at the foot of the shining ladder, 'The land whereon thou liest, to thee will I give it, and to thy seed.' These promises had been carefully treasured and handed on. Jacob on his deathbed reassured Joseph that God would certainly bring them to the land of their fathers; and now Joseph reanimated the trembling company that gathered around him with the same hope. Thus he commanded that his bones should be unburied, so that at any moment, however hurried, when the trumpet of exodus sounded, they might be ready to be caught up and borne onward in the glad march for Canaan.

What a lesson must those unburied bones have been to Israel!

When the taskmasters dealt harshly with the people, so that hearts fainted, it must have been sweet to go and look at the mummy case that held those decaying remains, waiting there to be carried forward; and, as they did so, this was doubtless their reflection, 'Evidently then, Joseph believed that we were not to stay here always, but that we should sooner or later leave for Canaan: let us brace ourselves up to bear a little longer, it may only be a very little while!' Yes, and when some were tempted to settle down content with prospering circumstances, it was a check on them to think of those bones, and say, 'Evidently we are not to remain here always: we should do well not to build all our hopes and comfort on the unstable tenure of our sojourn in this place.' And, often, when the Israelites were ready to despair amid the difficulties and weariness of their desert march, those bones borne in their midst told them of the confident hope of Joseph – that God would bring them to the land of rest.

We have no unburied bones to animate our faith, or to revive our drooping zeal; but we have something better – we have an empty grave. It tells us that he is risen. It tells us that not death, but life, is to be the guardian angel of our desert march. It tells us that this world is not our resting place or home; it tells us that resurrection is not possible only, but certain; and that before long we will be where he is. He will go with us along the desert pathway, till we go to be with him.

### 3    Let us realise the spirit that underlay and prompted these words

It was above all a pilgrim spirit. Joseph bore an Egyptian title. He married an Egyptian wife. He shared in Egyptian court life, politics, and trade. But he was as much a pilgrim as was Abraham pitching his tent outside the walls of Hebron, or Isaac in the grassy plains of the south country, or Jacob keeping himself aloof from the families of the land.

We sometimes speak as if the pilgrim spirit would be impossible for us who live in this settled state of civilisation. Our houses are too substantial; our movements too closely tethered to one narrow round. But if that thought should ever cross our hearts again, let us turn to Joseph, and remind ourselves how evidently he was animated by the spirit of those 'who confessed that they were pilgrims and strangers on the earth.' Ah, friends, what are we living for? Are our pursuits bounded by the narrow horizon of earth, and limited to the fleeting moments of time? Are we constantly engaged in lining as warmly as possible the nest in which we hope to spend our old age and die? Are we perpetually seeking to make the best of this world? I fear that these are the real aims of many professing Christians; and, if so, it is simply useless for them to claim kinship with that mighty stream of pilgrims bound to the city that has foundations, their true home and mother city. On the other hand, you may be at the head of a large establishment, engaged in many permanent undertakings, closely attached to the present by imperious duties; and yet, like Joseph, your heart may be detached from things seen and temporal, and engaged, in all its secret longings, to the things unseen and eternal.

*a. The pilgrim spirit will not make us unpractical.* Joseph was the most practical man in his time. Who are likely to be as prompt, as energetic, as thorough, as those who feel that they are working for eternity, and that they are building up day by day a fabric in which they shall live hereafter? Each day is character-building for better or for worse; each deed, well or ill done, is a stone in the edifice; each moment tells on eternity. We will receive a reward according to our deeds.

*b. But the pilgrtim spirit will make us simple.* There are two sorts of simplicity: that of circumstances, and that of heart. Many a person sits down to bread and milk at a wooden table, with a heart as proud as pride can make it; while many others who eat off a golden plate and are as simple as Cincinnatus at his plough. The world cannot understand this. But here in Joseph is an illustration. Ah, my friend, it is not the unjewelled finger, nor the plain attire, nor the unfurnished room, that constitutes a simple unaffected life: but that vision of the spirit, which looks through the unsubstantial wreath-vapours of the morning to the peaks of the everlasting hills beyond and above.

What a contrast there is between the opening and closing words of Genesis! Listen to the closing words, 'A coffin in Egypt.' And is this all? Is all God's work to end in one poor mummy case? Stay. This is only the end of Genesis, the Book of Beginnings. Turn the leaf, and there you will find Exodus, and Joshua, and Kings, and Prophets, and Christ. God is not dependent on any one of us. We do our little work and cease, but God's work goes on. And it is enough for each of us, like Joseph, to have lived a true, pure, strong, and noble life – and to leave him to see after our bodies; our beloved, whom we leave so reluctantly, and our work. Nor will he fail. 'And Moses took the bones of Joseph with him', on the night of the Exodus (Exod. 13:19); 'and they buried the bones of Joseph in Shechem: . . . and it became the inheritance of the children of Joseph' (Josh. 24:32).

# MOSES

# 1

# 'Come to Years'

## *Hebrews 11:24*

It all happened according to the mother's faith. The princess, accompanied by a train of maidens, came to the river bank to bathe. She saw the ark among the flags, and sent her maid to get it. In the midst of the little group the lid was carefully lifted, and their eyes were charmed with the sight of the beautiful face, while their hearts were touched with the whimper of the babe, who missed its mother, and was frightened by its unwonted surroundings and the many unfamiliar faces.

Quickly the woman's heart guessed the secret. The neighbourhood of Hebrew huts, the features and complexion of the babe, the unlikelihood of a mother forgetting her suckling child, the sudden recollection of the stern edict that her father had lately promulgated, all pointed to the inevitable conclusion, 'This is one of the Hebrews' children.' The sudden interposition of Miriam, who had eagerly and breathlessly watched the whole scene, with her naive suggestion of fetching a Hebrew nurse, solved the problem of what should be done with the foundling almost as soon as it could have suggested itself. The child's mother soon stood before the princess, and received the precious burden from her hands; and as she did so, was there not something in her almost convulsive moment that revealed to that quick eye the secret of the little plot? Whether it were so or not, the story does not tell. But with what an ecstasy of joy would that mother pour out her heart when the door was closed on the little group? The child's life was secure beneath the powerful protection of Pharaoh's own daughter, who had said, 'Nurse it for me.' And the wages she had promised would do more than provide for all their need. God had done 'exceedingly abundantly.'

How long the boy stayed in that lowly home we do not know, but it was long enough to know something of the perils and hardships of his people's lot; to learn those sacred traditions of their past, and to receive into his heart the love of the only God, which was to become the absorbing passion and emphasis of his career. Priests, philosophers and scholars might do their best later, but these ideas had been built into the growing structure of his soul, never again to be disintegrated from its fabric. What an encouragement to mothers to make the most of the early years during which children are confided to their charge.

Moses was brought up in the palace, and treated as the grandson of Pharaoh. When old enough he was probably sent to be *educated in the college* which had grown up around the Temple of the Sun, and has been called 'the Oxford of Ancient Egypt.' How wonderfully was God fitting him for the years to come! Stephen says: 'Moses was learned in all the wisdom of the Egyptians' (Acts 7:22). Much of it stood him in good stead when he became the founder of a new state.

But Moses was something more than a royal student: *he was a statesman and a soldier.* Stephen tells us that he was 'mighty in words and deeds': mighty in words – there is the statesman; mighty in deeds – there the soldier. Josephus says that while he was still in his early manhood the Ethiopians invaded Egypt, routed the army sent against them, and threatened Memphis. In the panic the oracles were consulted, and on their recommendation Moses was entrusted with the command of the royal troops. He immediately took the field, surprised and defeated the enemy, captured their principal city, 'the swamp-engirdled city of Meroë,' and returned to Egypt laden with the spoils of victory.

Thus year followed year until he was forty years of age. Already the foremost positions of the state were open to him, and it seemed as if the river of his life would continue in the same bed, undiverted, only waxing ever broader and deeper in its flow.

But beneath all, another thought was always present with him, and gradually dwarfed all others as it grew within his soul. He could not forget that his parents were slaves; that the bondmen who were groaning in the brickfields beneath the lash of the taskmasters were his brethren. He never lost the thought of that God to whom his mother had taught him to pray: and he could not rid himself of the impression that his destiny did not lie amid such surroundings as those, but was in some way to be associated with the fulfilment of that promise that he had heard so often from his mother's lips.

He broke, as gently as he might, the news to his benefactress that he could no longer hold the position to which she had raised him, or be called her son, but must step back to the lowly lot which was his by birth.

### 1   Notice the noble ingredients in this great resolve

**a.** *It was made in the full maturity of his powers.*   With nothing to gain and all to lose, he descended from the steps of the loftiest throne in the world.

**b.** *It was made when the fortunes of the children of Israel were at their lowest ebb.*   They were slaves, were suffering affliction, and were reproached. For a palace there would be a hut; for luxury, hard fare and coarse food; for respect and honour, hatred and contempt; for the treasures of Egypt, poverty and want; for the society of the learned and élite, association with the ignorant and depraved. But with deliberate resolution he bowed his head beneath the yoke even though it was rough and heavy.

**c.** *It was made when the pleasures of sin seemed most fascinating.*   There is nothing gained in saying that there are no pleasures in sin. There are. And Moses was not oblivious to all this; yet, in the heyday of his strength, in the prime of his manhood, in a court where continence and purity must have been unknown, he dared to forgo it all.

**d.** *It was made decisively.*   Many would have tried to retain the proud position and to benefit their enslaved brethren at the same time. But there was no trace of this in the great renunciation that cut Moses off from the least association with the fond and fascinating associations of early life.

### 2   The thought which led to it

'By faith. Moses refused. . . He believed God's promise to Abraham, that after four hundred years of bondage his people would come out; and he knew that that period had nearly expired. He believed that there was a destiny waiting for the chosen people in the long future. He believed that there was a recompense of reward awaiting them beyond the domain and limit of Egypt, more glorious than the dazzling splendour of its highest rewards and honours.

But he did what he did, because he saw by faith what eye had not seen, or ear heard, or the heart conceived; and these things – that wealth and that reward – being so much better than anything Egypt could offer, he cheerfully took the path of affliction, of self-denial and reproach, which led to them.

See, child of God, what is within your reach, if only you will dare to deny yourself and take up your cross! Is the renunciation hard? Do not forget that Christ is suffering with you in it all. He knows every step of the way, because he has so often traversed it in the experience of his own. There is no solace to the agonised soul so sweet as the perpetual mention of his dear name.

And who can estimate the result? The water streams from the smitten rock; and Exodus and the birth of a nation of freemen were the outcome of this great renunciation.

# 2

# Deliverance by Main Force

## *Acts 7:24–25*

There was true heroism in the act, when Moses stepped down from Pharaoh's throne to share the lot of his brethren. At the same time there was a great deal for him to learn. Later he was to be a hand nerved and used and empowered by God himself (Ps. 77:20); but now he was acting in his own self-energy – rash, impetuous, headstrong. Years later he was to be the meekest and least obtrusive of men, conscious to a fault of his own weakness, and at every step looking up for guidance and help; but now he leaned wholly on his own understanding and, without taking counsel of God, thought to secure the emancipation of his people by the assertion of his will, and the putting forth of his might.

But there was the making of a saint in him even though it would take many a long year of lonely waiting and trial before this srong and self-reliant nature could be broken down, shaped into a vessel meet for the Master's use, and prepared for every good work.

## 1 The First Attempt at Deliverance

*a. It sprang largely from human sympathy.* As soon as Moses reached Goshen his first act was to visit his people in the midst of their toils, and to see them work amid conditions of severest hardship. Brick-making in clay pits must always be difficult work, but how much more so when an Egyptian sun shines vertically above you and a taskmaster stands by with his heavy whip to punish the least attempt to rest a moment. As he heard the nation sighing because of its bondage, and groaning under its accumulated sorrows, his soul was filled with tender pity. But it wasn't long before that pity for his people turned to indignation against their oppressors. Before he had gone very far, he came on one of the taskmasters cruelly beating a Hebrew; and as he witnessed the heavy blows falling on the unresisting, quivering body, he could restrain himself no longer, and killed the Egyptian, and buried his body in the nearest sands.

It was a chivalrous act, well meant, and at least significant of the strength of the emotions pent up within him, but the mere impulse of pity would never have been strong enough to bear him through the weary years of the desert march. Beneath the repeated provocations of the people it must have given way. Nothing short of a reception of the divine patience, could suffice for the demands that would be made on him in those coming terrible years.

Is there not a lesson here for many of God's workers? They have not learned to distinguish between passion and principle, between impulse and a settled purpose. If we undertake a definite work because he calls us to it, because it is put before us as a duty for his sake, or because we are channels through which the unebbing torrent of his divine pity is flowing, we have secured a principle of action that will bear us through disappointment, failure, and ingratitude. The way in which men treat us will make no difference to us, because all is done for him.

*b. It was premature.*        God's time for the deliverance of his people was not due for forty years. The iniquity of the Amorites had not reached its full, though it was nearing the brim of the cup (Gen. 15:16). Moses' own education was very incomplete; it would take at least forty years to drain him of his self-will and self-reliance, and make him a vessel meet for the Master's use. The Hebrew people had not as yet come to the pitch of anguish, which is so touchingly referred to, when the death of their principal oppressor seems to have brought matters to a crisis, and they forsook the false gods to which they had given their allegiance in order to return to the God of their fathers (Exod. 2:23).

We all know something of this haste. As Saul, in presence of the Philistine invasion, we suppose that we cannot last for another hour, and we force ourselves to offer the burnt offering. Then we are chagrined to see Samuel's figure slowly pacing up the mountain pass as the fire burns down to its last embers, and to hear from his lips the sentence of deposition for our impatience (1 Sam. 13:12–14).

One blow struck when the time is fulfilled is worth a thousand struck in premature eagerness. It is not for you, O my soul, to know the times and seasons that the Father has put in his own power; wait only on God. Wait at the gates of your Jericho for seven days; do not utter a sound till he says, 'Shout'; but when he gives the signal, with the glad cry of victory you shall pass over the fallen wall into the city.

*c. It was executed in the pride of human strength.*        It was natural that Moses should suppose that he could do something to relieve his people's lot. He would make that nation of oppressors reel before his blows, and of course he would be hailed by his people as their God-sent deliverer.

He was rudely surprised when one day he went out to continue his self-imposed task, and sought to settle a difference between two Hebrews, to find himself repulsed from them by the challenge, 'Who made thee a prince and a judge over us?' He had never expected a rebuff from his own people. Evidently, then, God's time had not arrived; nor could it come until the heat of his spirit had slowly evaporated in the desert air, and he had learned the hardest of all lessons, that 'by strength shall no man prevail.' We must be brought to an end of ourselves before God can begin with us. But when once we have come to that point there is no limit to what may be wrought during a single life by the passage through it of his eternal power and Godhead.

*d. It was too apprehensive of the judgment of other men.*   We are told that he looked this way and that way before he killed the Egyptian; and when he found that his deed of revenge was known, he feared and fled (Exod. 2:12). But suppose that he had felt he had been divinely commissioned to execute judgment on Egypt, would he have cared who was looking, and what was being said? He would have been perfectly indifferent to the praise or blame of men. Whenever men look this way and that to see what other men are doing or saying, you may be quite sure they do not know for certain their Master's plan.

There has been only one perfect Servant of God who has ever trodden our world. He never looked this way or that. He alone could say, 'He that sent me is with me: the Father hath not left me alone; for I do always those things that please him' (John 8:29). Oh, for the single eye, that our whole body also may be full of light!

## 2   The flight to the desert

The news of what Moses had done came to the ears of Pharaoh, and he sought to slay him. But Moses feared, and fled from the face of Pharaoh. Later, under similar circumstances, it is said, 'He forsook Egypt, not fearing the wrath of the king' (Heb. 11:27). And when we ask the reason for his fearlessness, we learn that it was by faith he did so; for 'he endured, as seeing him who is invisible.' But if such were the case later, why was it not so at the time with which we are dealing? Why did he not exercise faith in the invisible God?

Faith is possible only when we are on God's plan, and stand on God's promise. It is useless to pray for increased faith until we have fulfilled the conditions of faith. Faith is as natural to right conditions of soul, as a flower is to a plant. And among those conditions this is the first – find your place in God's plan, and get on to it; and this is the second – feed on God's promises. When each of these is realised, faith comes of itself; and there is absolutely nothing that is impossible.

But Moses was out of touch with God, so he fled, and crossed the desert that lay between him and the eastern frontier. He threaded the mountain passes of the Sinaitic peninsula, through which in later years he was to lead his people; and at last sat down wearily by a well in the land of Midian. There his chivalrous interference was suddenly elicited on behalf of the daughters of the priest of Midian, who seem to have suffered daily from the insolence of shepherds appropriating the water that the shepherd-maidens had drawn for their flocks. That day, however, the shepherds met their match, and were compelled to leave the water troughs to the women, who hurried home, unexpectedly early, to tell of the Egyptian who had delivered them from the hands of the shepherds. It was a good deed that could not pass without repayment in that hospitable land, and it opened the door to the chieftain's tent; ultimately to marriage with one of those same shepherdesses; and finally to the quiet life of a shepherd in the calm open spaces of that wonderful land that, on more than one occasion, has served as a divine school.

# 3

# The Marvellous Conversation

## *Exodus 3:4*

### 1   A memorable day

It began with an ordinary morning. The sun rose as usual in a dull haze over the expanse of sand, or above the gaunt forms of the mountains, seamed and scarred. As the young day opened, the sun began to shine in a cloudless sky, casting long shadows over the plains; and presently, climbing to the zenith, threw a searching, scorching light into every aperture of the landscape beneath. The sheep browsed as usual on the scant herbage, or lay panting beneath the shadow of a great rock. These things were as they had been for forty years, and as they threatened to be, after Moses had sunk into an obscure and forgotten grave. Then, all of a sudden, a common bush began to shine with the emblem of Deity, and from its heart of fire the voice of God broke the silence of the ages in words that fell on the shepherd's ear like a double knock: 'Moses, Moses.'

That voice still speaks to those whose hearts are hushed to hear. Insensibly to ourselves we contract the habit of thinking of God as the God of the dead, who spoke to the fathers in oracle and prophet; whereas the I AM is God of the living – passing through our crowded thoroughfares, brooding over our desert spaces, and seeking hearts that are still enough from their own plannings and activities to listen.

The main point for each of us is to be able to answer his summons with the response, 'Here am I.' If that summons were to come today, too many of us would have to ask for a moment's respite while we went to finish some neglected duty. Oh, for the free, untrammelled, unengaged spirit, to be ready to go at any moment the Lord may appoint.

## 2   A remarkable announcement

Out of the bush came the voice of God, blending past, present, and future, in one marvellous sentence: *the past,* 'I am the God of thy father, the God of Abraham, the God of Isaac, and the God of Jacob'; *the present,* 'I have surely seen the affliction of my people which are in Egypt, and have heard their cry by reason of their taskmasters; for I know their sorrows, and I am come down to deliver them'; *the future,* 'Come now therefore, and I will send thee unto Pharaoh' (Exod. 3:6–10).

## 3   Divine longsuffering under provocation

In the first blush of youthful enthusiasm Moses had been impetuous enough to attempt the emancipation of his people by the blows of his right hand. But now that God proposes to send him to lead an exodus, he starts back in dismay almost petrified at the proposal. Moses, who had run before God in feverish impatience, now lags fainthearted behind him.

*a. At first he expostulated*    'Who am I, that I should go to Pharaoh?' 'And God said, Certainly I will be with thee.' 'I whose glory shines here, who am as unimpaired by the flight of the ages as this fire is by burning; who am independent of sustenance or fuel from man; who made the fathers what they were; whose nature is incapable of change – I will be with you.' What an assurance this was! He seems to say: 'Not an hour without my companionship; not a difficulty without my cooperation; not a Red Sea without my right arm; not a mile of wilderness journeying without the Angel of my Presence.'

*b. In his next excuse*    Moses professed his inability to answer if he were asked the name of God (v.13); and this was met by the proclamation of the spirit-stirring name, Jehovah: 'I AM THAT I AM.' There we have the unity of God to the exclusion of the many gods of Egypt; the unchangeableness of God, who lives in an eternal present; the self-sufficiency of God, who alone in his own equivalent.

The term JEHOVAH was not wholly unknown to Moses, for it entered into his mother's name, Jochebed – *Jehovah my glory;* but now for the first time it was adopted as the unique title by which God was to be known in Israel. It slowly made its way into the faith of the people; and whenever employed, it speaks of the self-existent and redeeming qualities of the nature of God, and is forever enshrined in the precious name of our Saviour, Jesus. The whole subsequent life of Moses and of Israel was inspired by this name.

And for us it is full of meaning. 'This is my name for ever, and this is my memorial unto all generations' (v.15). And as its full meaning opens to our vision, it is as if God put into our hands a blank cheque, leaving us to fill it in as we will. Are we dark? let us add to his I AM the words, *the true Light;* are we hungry? the words, *the Bread of Life;* are we defenceless? the words, *the Good Shepherd;* are we weary? the words, *Shiloh, the Rest-giver.*

*c. Moses' third excuse*    was that the people would not believe him, nor hearken to his voice (Exod. 4:1). But God graciously met this also by showing him miracles that he might perform in Egypt, and that would read deep lessons to himself. 'What is that in thine hand? And he said, A rod.' It was probably only a shepherd's crook. What a history, however, awaited it! It was to be stretched out over the Red Sea, pointing a pathway through its depths, to smite the flinty rock and to win victory over the hosts of Amalek. A rod with God behind it is mightier than the vastest army.

At God's command the rod was cast on the ground, and it became a serpent. The serpent played a very conspicuous part in Egyptian worship, and as it wriggled on the sand and sought to do Moses harm, so that he fled from it, it was an emblem of the might of Egypt before which he had become a fugitive. But when God gave the word, it easily became once more a rod in his hand, as he fearlessly grasped the venomous animal by the tail.

The second sign was even more significant. His hand thrust into his bosom became leprous; and when he did it again it became pure and white. It was as if God met his consciousness of moral pollution and taught him that it could be put away as easily as his flesh was cleansed, through his forgiving grace.

And the third sign, in which it was promised that the water of the Nile should become blood on the dry land, was full of terrible omen to the gods of that mighty country, the people of which depended so entirely on its river, for they worshipped it as a god.

*d.. The last excuse* that Moses alleged was his lack of eloquence. 'O my Lord, I am not eloquent . . . I am slow of speech, and of slow tongue' (v.10). But God was willing to meet this also with his patient grace; and if only Moses had been willing to trust him, it is probable that God would have added the gifts of a persuasive and splendid oratory to the other talents with which Moses was so copiously endowed.

But Moses would not believe it; so at length the Lord ended the conference by saying that he would send Aaron with him, to be his colleague and spokesman. Ah! better a thousand times had it been for him to trust God for speech, than be thus deposed from his premiership! Aaron shaped the golden calf and became a thorn in the side of the saint of God – and probably in the eyes of their contemporaries. Aaron took the greater attention, and had most of the honour and credit of the great deliverance.

## 4  The final assent

It was a very grudging one. We seek every reason for evading the divine will, little realising that he is forcing us out from our quiet homes into a career that includes, among other things, the song of victory on the banks of the Red Sea; the two lonely sojourns for forty days in communication with God; the shining face; the vision of glory; the burial by the hand of Michael; and the supreme honour of standing beside the Lord on the Mount of Transfiguration.

# 4

# The First Four Plagues

## *Exodus 7—8*

### 1   The river of blood

One morning, Pharaoh, accompanied by high officials, court functionaries, and priests, came down either to perform his customary ablutions or to worship. On the river's brink he found Moses waiting for him. There was no hesitation now in the peremptory summons. 'The LORD God of the Hebrews hath sent me unto thee, saying, Let my people go, that they may serve me in the wilderness.' Then follow words which bear out what has been already said of God's purpose in the plagues, 'In this thou shalt know that I am the LORD.'

The summons was met by the curled lip of scorn or imperturbable silence; and as there was no alternative, Aaron smote the water with the rod in the presence of the court. An instantaneous change passed over the appearance and the nature of the water. It became blood. From bank to bank, the tide of crimson gore swept on, hour after hour, day after day, until a week had passed. The fish died and floated on the surface. The air reeked with corruption. And the effects of the visitation extended throughout all the pools, and reservoirs, and cisterns, in places of public resort, as well as in the homes of the people. There was no water in all the land, except the scanty supplies obtained by digging shallow wells, and collecting the brackish surface water.

The magicians in some way counterfeited the marvel; and Pharaoh probably thought that Moses and Aaron were practising some sort of trickery.

## 2 Frogs

It may have been but a few days after the first plague that Moses and Aaron renewed their demand for emancipation,and told the king the penalty of refusal. But there was no response, no proposal, and the inevitable blow fell.

The land suddenly swarmed with frogs. They came up from the river in myriads, till the very ground seemed alive with them, and it was impossible to walk far without crushing scores of them. Frogs in the houses, frogs in the beds, frogs baked with the food in the ovens, frogs in the kneading-troughs worked up with the flour; frogs with their monotonous croak, frogs with their cold, slimy skins, everywhere – from morning to night, from night to morning – frogs. And the aggravation of the plague consisted in the fact of the frog being the emblem of the goddess of fertility, so that it was sacrilege to destroy it.

This plague elicited from Pharaoh the first symptom of surrender. He sent for the brethren and implored their prayers that the scourge might be removed, promising that compliance with his request would secure deliverance: 'I will let the people go.' To make the supremacy and power of God more manifest, Moses bade the monarch fix his own time for the staying of the plague, and then went to cry to the Lord: 'Moses cried unto the LORD . . . and the LORD did according to the word of Moses.'

It is remarkable that though the magicians counterfeited the coming of the frogs, they were evidently unable to remove them; and, indeed, the king does not appear to have appealed to them for help. But what a lesson was taught to Pharaoh – that Jehovah was above all gods, and that he alone could do according to his will!

## 3 Lice

The Egyptians were scrupulously clean in their personal habits, anticipating the habits of our own time. And the priests were specially so. They bathed themselves repeatedly, and constantly shaved their bodies so that no uncleanliness might unfit them for their sacred duties. What horror, then, must have taken hold of them when the very dust of Egypt seemed to breed lice and they found that they were not exempted from the plague, which was as painful as it was abhorrent to their delicate sensibility.

Perhaps there is something more than appears at first sight in the words, 'there was lice in man and *in beast.*' Not only on the bodies of the priests, but on those of the sacred beasts, was there this odious pest. Each revered shrine boasted its sacred bull or goat, whose glossy skin was cleansed with reverent care; and it was an unheard-of calamity that it should become infested with this most disgusting parasite. Thus upon the gods of Egypt did God execute judgment. The magicians themselves seem to have felt that this plague was a symptom of the working of a higher Power than they knew, and even they urged Pharaoh to consider that it was the finger of God.

## 4   The beetle

It is not certain what is meant by the word translated 'flies'. And though it is possible that it is rightly rendered 'flies', it is quite as likely that it stands for a peculiar kind of beetle, which was the emblem of the sun-god. Their most powerful deity seemed now to have turned against them. The beetles covered the grounds, swarmed into the houses, and spoiled the produce of their land.

That it was no mere natural visitation was made clear by a division that was made in this plague between the land of Egypt and that of Goshen, where the Israelites were found. And perhaps this worked on Pharaoh's heart as nothing else had done, for he was prepared to allow the Israelites to sacrifice in the land. It was a concession that Moses could not accept, for the Israelites would be obliged to sacrifice as victims animals that the Egyptians considered sacred, and irritated feeling might provoke some terrible outbreak of violence. Pharaoh yielded to this reason, and promised to let them go if they did not go very far, on the condition that Moses should secure the removal of the plague. 'And the LORD did according to the word of Moses.'

# 5

# The Passage of the Red Sea

*Exodus 14:29–30*

It was not long after the hour of midnight before the entire Israelite host was on the move. From different points the vast host – which, judging from the fact that the number of men amounted to six hundred thousand, and the total could not have been less than two and a half millions – converged toward the central meeting place at Succoth.

Succoth would be about fifteen miles down the road, and there they made their first prolonged halt. They baked unleavened cakes of the dough that they had brought with them; the weary women and children rested in leafy tabernacles hastily improvised from the foliage of that region, so that the whole host, heartened and refreshed, was able to undertake its second stage, which was Etham, on the edge of the wilderness, where the green vegetation of Egypt fades into the wastes of sand. There is one episode that we must not forget to mention, and which shows how largely the whole Exodus was wrought in faith. 'And Moses took the bones of Joseph with him' (13:19). This great ancestor of their race had been dead some four hundred years, but on his deathbed he had made his brethren swear that when God visited them, as he most surely would, and brought them out of Egypt, they should carry his bones with them in their march. In his death, and through that weary waiting time, he had been the prophet of the Exodus; and how often those unburied bones must have been the theme of conversation in Hebrew homes! And now that they were accompanying their march, all the people realised that the anticipations of generations were being fulfilled.

## 1   The guiding pillar

As that Hebrew host broke away from the land of bondage, a majestic cloud gathered in the pure morning atmosphere at the head of the vanguard, never again to desert that pilgrim band until the Jordan was crossed and it had settled down to brood over the house of God. But all through the years, when night fell, it burned with fire at its heart; fire, which was always the symbol and sign of the presence of God.

This served many purposes. It was the guide of their march; it was a shadow from the burning heat of a vertical sun, and at night it provided them with a light as it watched over them like the Eye of God. On one occasion, at least, as we shall see presently, it rendered important service by concealing the movements of Israel, lying between them and the pursuit of their foes.

In the thought of Moses, that cloud by day and night must have been full of reassurance. And it is touching to learn that 'He took it not away,' as if neither sin, nor murmuring, nor disobedience, could ever drive away him who loves us, not because we are good, but to make us so; and who cannot leave or forsake those whom he has taught to lisp, 'Abba, Father.'

## 2   The route

The easiest route to Canaan lay through the Isthmus of Suez and the land of the Philistines. A journey of a little over one hundred miles would have conducted them to their destination. But God did not permit them to go that way, lest the sight of embattled hosts should unnerve them. Years later, when the education and revelations of the desert were finished, they might behold those scenes undismayed. But as yet they must not know war till they had been more deeply taught in the might and care of God. So is our journey ever adapted to our strength. God is always considering what we are able to bear; never leading us into dangers before which heart and flesh would succumb. 'God led them about.'

It must have been a great disappointment when the cloud altered its course and led them due south. On one side of them was Migdol (the modern Muktala) and impassable wastes of sand; on the other was the Red Sea. East of them or, as it might be, in front, was the impassable range of Baal-Zephon.

It was a perfect cul-de-sac. There was no egress from it except the way by which they had entered. Loud and deep must have been the murmurs and protestations of the people. 'Is this the way of Canaan? We know better! How dare you presume to lead us, when your very first tactics prove you to be wholly untrustworthy?'

Such reflections and reproaches are not easy to bear. They can be borne only by a man who has learned utterly to trust his God. They made no impression on Moses. He had learned to obey him implicitly, and to see himself always completely vindicated. Oh, for more of this simple trust in God, which rests so distinctly in his guidance and help!

Often God seems to place his children in positions of profound difficulty – leading them into a wedge from which there is no escape; contriving a situation which no human judgment would have permitted had it been previously consulted. The very cloud leads them. You may be thus involved at this very hour. It does seem perplexing and mysterious to the last degree, but it is perfectly right. The issue will more than justify him who has brought you to this place. You have only to stand still and see his salvation, which is prepared as the morning.


## 3   The pursuit

No sooner had Israel gone than Pharaoh was sorry. The public works stood still for lack of labour. Vast territories were suddenly unoccupied. The labour of this enslaved people was missed on every side, in city and field. There was a sudden loss of revenue and service that he could ill dispense with. And his pride forbade that he should quietly acquiesce in their unhindered Exodus. Besides, in their mad haste to be rid of this people, the Egyptians had loaded them with jewels of silver, and jewels of gold, and raiment; so much so that it is distinctly said, 'they spoiled the Egyptians.' It is clear from the contributions afterward made to the building of the tabernacle, that Israel was carrying off a large amount of treasure and valuables. 'And the heart of Pharaoh and of his servants was turned against the people, and they said, Why have we done this, that we have let Israel go from serving us?' (14:5–6).

At this juncture the king heard of the extraordinary movement southward which seemed to have thrown them again into his power. 'But the Egyptians pursued after them, all the horses and chariots of Pharaoh . . . and overtook them' (14:9).

And so as the afternoon closed in, of perhaps the fifth day of the Exodus, the outposts of the fugitive host beheld the dreaded forms of the Egyptian warriors coming over the ridges of the desert hills; and as the night fell they were aware that the whole Egyptian host was encamped in their vicinity, only waiting for the morning light to swoop down on them, involving them either in a general massacre or, in what was perhaps more dreadful, a return to slavery.

It was an awful plight. Terrible, indeed, was the breaking of that news on those craven hearts. They immediately turned on Moses and spent their fear and anguish on his heart. 'Wherefore hast thou dealt thus with us? Were there no graves in Egypt? Better to have perished there than here! Why did you not leave us alone? Where is your God?' And then that noble spirit rose up in the might of its faith. He was not fearful nor dismayed; he was standing still to see God's salvation. He knew that Jehovah would fight for them, and redeem them, and vindicate his word.

# 6

# The Song of Victory

*Exodus 15:21*

From his chariot-cloud their Almighty looked down on the cowering crowd of fugitives in their great fear as they cried to him.

It would almost seem, from an expression in the Psalms, that the children of Israel yielded to more rebellion at the Red Sea than appears from the narrative of Moses. We are told distinctly that they 'provoked him at the Sea, even at the Red Sea,' because 'they remembered not the multitude of [his] mercies'; so that God saved them in spite of their rebelliousness, for his Name's sake, and 'that he might make his mighty power to be known' (Ps. 106:7–8).

## 1   The song of Moses

'Then sang Moses.' The morning dawn revealed one of the most memorable spectacles of history. A nation of slaves, fleeing from their masters, had suddenly become a nation of freemen, and stood emancipated on the shores of a new continent. The chivalry of Egypt was overwhelmed in the midst of the sea, for there remained not so much as one of them left; and all along the shore lay the bodies of the dead, cast up from the depths of the tide. Here there was given to Israel for all subsequent time an evidence of the trustworthiness of God, which compelled belief, not only in their great Deliverer, but also in his servant Moses.

And from that ransomed host, congregated there in one vast throng, an anthem broke forth. There is no thought of anyone or anything but the Lord throughout the entire piece. It was *he* who had triumphed gloriously, and cast horse and rider into the sea. It was *his* right hand that had dashed in pieces the enemy. It was because *he* blew with *his* wind, that they sank as lead in the mighty waters. It was through the greatness of *his* excellency that they who had risen against him were overthrown.

And the ease of his victory was clearly accentuated. The waters were piled as walls by his breath. He blew with his wind, and a whole army sank as a stone into the depths. He had but to stretch out his right hand, and the sea swallowed the flower of the greatest army of the time.

The women, led by Miriam, replied in a noble refrain, 'Sing ye to the Lord, for he hath triumphed gloriously; the horse and his rider hath he thrown into the sea.' So God turns our anxieties into occasions of singing – weeping endures for a night, but joy comes in the morning.

# 7

# The Gift of Manna

## *Exodus 16:14–16*

### 1   The desert murmurings

It was a great aggravation of the responsibilities that already lay heavily on the heart of Moses, to have to encounter the perpetual murmurings of the people whom he loved so well. It only drove him continually back on his Almighty Friend and Helper. But the repeated outbreak of these murmurings all along the wilderness route only sets in more conspicuous prominence the beauty of his gentle meekness, and the glory of his faith, which probably was the one channel through which the power of God wrought for the salvation and blessing of his people.

**a.** *Murmurers are short of memory.*     It was only one short month since the people had come forth out of Egypt – a month crowded with the wonders which the right hand of the Lord had wrought. The chronicler specially notes that it was the fifteenth day of the second month, and adds, 'The whole congregation of the children of Israel murmured against Moses and Aaron in the wilderness; and the children of Israel said unto them, Would to God we had died by the hand of the LORD in the land of Egypt, when we sat by the fleshpots, and when we did eat bread to the full; for ye have brought us forth into this wilderness to kill this whole assembly with hunger' (vv.2–3). They could well remember the sensual delights of Egypt, but they forgot the lash of the taskmaster and the anguish of heart with which they worked at the kneading of the clay.

Whenever a murmuring fit threatens, let us review the past and recount the Lord's dealing with us in bygone years. Did he deliver in six troubles, and is he likely to forsake us in the seventh? When the psalmist complained, and his spirit was overwhelmed, he tells us that he considered the days of old, the years of ancient times; he remembered the years of the right hand of the Most High.

*b. Murmurers are short of sight.* They fail to see that behind all the appearances of things there lie hid the presence and providence of God. Moses called the attention of the people to this fact, which enhanced so gravely the magnitude of their offence. They thought that they were only venting their frustrations on a man like themselves. Annoyed and apprehensive, it was some relief to expend their spleen on the one man to whom they owed everything. But their faithful leader showed them that their insults were directed not against himself, but against him whose servant he was, and at whose bidding everything was being wrought. 'The LORD heareth your murmurings which ye murmur against him: and what are we? your murmurings are not against us, but against the LORD' (v.8).

## 2 The wilderness food

It is not for us to tell here the whole story of the manna. It is enough to remember:

*a. To look up for our supplies.* 'He gave them bread from heaven to eat.' For the believer there are five sources from which help may come, for in addition to the four quarters of the winds he looks up to the heavens. There came from heaven the sound of the rushing of a mighty wind. Look higher, child of God, to the heart and hand of the Father!

*b. To feed on the heavenly bread daily and early.* 'They gathered it every morning . . . and when the sun waxed hot, it melted.' There is no time like the early morning hour for feeding on the flesh of Christ by communion with him, and pondering his words. How different is that day from all others, the early prime of which is surrendered to fellowship with Christ! Nor is it possible to live today on the gathered spoils of yesterday. Each man needs all that a new day can yield him of God's grace and comfort. It must be daily bread.

*c. To feed on Christ is the only secret of strength and blessedness.* If only believers in Christ would realise and appropriate the lesson so clearly taught in this narrative, as well as in the wonderful discourse our Lord founded upon it (John 6:22–58), they would find themselves the subjects of a marvellous change.

8

# At the Foot of Sinai

*Exodus 19:18*

From Rephidim the children of Israel marched slowly and laboriously through the great thoroughfare of the desert now known as the Wadi-es-Sheykh, the longest, widest, and most continuous of those vast desert valleys. It must have been an astonishing exchange from the flat alluvial land of Egypt, where the only hills were those raised by the hands of man. On either side of the pilgrim host lofty and precipitous mountains reared their inaccessible ramparts of red sandstone and variegated granite, without verdure, or gushing rills, or trace of any living thing. There was nothing to allure them or arrest their steps amid the awful desolation and grandeur of those inaccessible precipices. They would sometimes be almost overwhelmed by the bare sterility of the scene, and by the awful silence that was stirred to resent the intrusion of such a multitude upon its ancient reign. But their course was always onward; and a deepening awe must have grown on their souls.

At last it broke on them. After a march of eighteen miles from the Red Sea, they came out on a perfectly level plain of yellow sand, some two miles long, and half-a-mile wide, nearly flat, and dotted over with tamarisk bushes. The mountains that gather around this plain have for the most part sloping sides, and form a kind of natural amphitheatre; but toward the south there is one pile of jagged cliffs that rise upward in wild precipitousness, while behind lies the granite mass of Gebel Musa, deeply cleft with fissures, and torn, as though it had fought a hard battle with earthquake, storm, and fire. This pile of rocks is called Ras Sufsafeh, and was probably 'the mount that might be touched and burned with fire.' It rises from the plain below as a huge altar, and all that transpired on its summit would have been easily visible to the further limits of the camp of two million souls pitched beneath.

Such was the chosen scene for the giving of the Law. There the hosts of Israel remained stationary for long weeks and there, while clouds veiled the heights, and fire played from peak to peak, God met with his people and gave them his Law, writing his name not on tablets of stone merely, but on the entire course of human history.

## 1 God's object at Sinai

At the time of the Exodus the world was almost wholly given to idolatry. The first objects of idolatrous worship were probably simply the sun and moon and heavenly bodies, or other conspicuous objects of creative wisdom and power. Later, the deity was supposed to reside in men, and even beasts. In dealing with this deluge of idolatry, God acted as he did with the deluge of water that drowned the ancient world. He began with a single family, teaching them the sublime lessons concerning himself. Then when they had understood the lessons, they were to teach others.

Let us notice the successive steps.

*a. First step* God chose from the masses of heathendom one man, 'called him alone', and led him to follow him into a strange land. There, shut away from surrounding peoples, he began to teach him about himself. Jehovah spared no time or pains with the first great Hebrew, so that he, being blessed, might be the means of blessing to the race.

*b. Second step* God welded the Hebrew people together into one that they might be able to receive and retain as a part of their national life those great truths with which they were to be entrusted. This welding was accomplished by the tie of common parentage, of which they were justly proud; by the bond of a common occupation that kept them to themselves as shepherds, apart from the busy traffic of cities and marts of commerce; and last, by

the pressure of a common trial, which together with the marvellous deliverance that was granted them, remained fresh and indel-
ible in all later generations. So perfectly did God do this work,
that while other nations have risen, reigned, and fallen, and their
disintegration has been utter and final, the children of Abraham
endure, like an imperishable rock, undestroyed by the chafe of
waves or the fret of the ages.

c. *Third step*    God revealed his existence. Into the midst of their
bondage tidings came that the God of their fathers was a living
God; that he had met one of their number in the desert and had
called him by name, and had promised to intercede in their behalf.

d. *Fourth step*    God showed by the plagues that he was stronger
than the gods of Egypt. Can you not imagine the children of Israel
saying, 'Our God is great, but perhaps he is not so strong as Isis,
or Osiris, or Serapis, or the sacred bull'? But the wonders that
were wrought on the gods of Egypt settled that question forever.

e. *Fifth step*    God excited their love and gratitude. You can do
anything you like with those you love: but to get, you must give;
to excite love, you must declare it. Hence they were touchingly
reminded of what he had done: 'Ye have seen what I did unto the
Egyptians, and how I bare you on eagles' wings, and brought you
unto myself' (Exod. 19:4).

f. *Sixth step*    God set himself to teach them concerning certain
of those great qualities, the knowledge of which lay at the foundation of all right dealings between the people and himself. And in
order to achieve his purpose, he made use of outward significant
signs.

g. *Seventh step*    God clearly designated Moses to be the organ
and channel of his communications to man. 'Lo, I come unto thee
in a thick cloud, that the people may hear when I speak with thee,
and believe thee for ever' (v.9).

## 2    The lessons of Sinai

a. *The majesty of God*    The natural scenery was sufficiently
majestic; but it became more so as the incidents of the third day
were unfolded. Meanwhile the clouds dropped water, and there
were showers of tropical rain. And it was amid such scenes that

God spoke. Could any combination of natural phenomena have given grander conceptions of the majesty of the divine nature?

*b. The spirituality of God* What was their God like? On that memorable occasion, 'when Moses brought forth the people out of the camp to meet God,' they saw no likeness. He was there, for he spoke. But there was no outward form for the eye to discern. It has not been easy for mankind to learn this lesson so clearly taught on Sinai, that God is a Spirit.

*c. The holiness of God* This primal lesson was also taught in striking fashion by outward signs that impressed the sense. Bounds were erected to keep the beasts from grazing on the thin herbage of the lower slopes: whoever touched the Mount must die, all clothes were to be carefully washed against that third day, absolute purity was to be observed in heart and life, Moses alone was called up to the top of the Mount, and when he had climbed there, he was sent all the way down again for the express purpose of charging the people, and even the priests, not to break through to gaze on the Lord, lest God should break forth on them. All these significant acts converged to give outward and sensible manifestation of the holiness of God.

*d. The royalty of God* The Jewish state was a kingdom, and God was King. And the reality of his government appeared in the way in which Moses himself obeyed his behest. It was a sight never to be forgotten to see how their great leader Moses was absolutely subservient to the command issued from God's pavilion. At the best he was only God's executor, 'the passive instrument of the divine will.' The Decalogue was spoken by God himself 'out of the midst of the fire, of the cloud, and of the thick darkness, with a great voice' (Deut. 5:22). Every ordinance of the Law, every custom and provision for domestic and civil life, every item in the construction of the sanctuary and in the ordering of the priests, was due to the direct will of God, spoken from his mouth. How clear was the testimony to the supremacy of the Most High! Such were some of the lessons taught at Sinai.

The life of fellowship with God cannot be built up in a day. It begins with the habitual reference of all to him, hour by hour, as Moses did in Egypt. But it moves on to more and longer periods of communion. And it finds its consummation and bliss in days and nights of intercession and waiting and holy intercourse. Ah, what patterns are seen on the Mount! Alas for us that we move so far from it! Or at the best are admitted to stand only with the elders,and set paved work of sapphire stone beneath God's feet! Oh, for the closer access, the nearer view, the more intimate face to face intercourse, such as is open still to the friends of God!

# 9

# The Broken Sentence

## Exodus 32:32

This is one of the most pathetic verses of the Bible and bears on its face the evidence of its genuineness. It could not have emanated from the mind or pen of some later scribe, because it is so entirely unexpected, so strange and yet so likely. It is the fragment of a sentence of which we would have given much to hear the conclusion, but who can presume to finish that which in this supreme hour was choked by a paroxysm of grief, a sob of irrepressible emotion?

### 1 The problem with which Moses had to deal

a. *The idolatry of his people*   After the utterance of the ten great words of Sinai, the people, frightened by the thunderings and lightnings, and the voice of the trumpet, and the smoke of the mountain, urged Moses to act as their daysman and mediator. 'They said unto Moses: Speak thou with us, and we will hear; but let not God speak with us, lest we die' (Exod. 20:19). The great lawgiver and leader, acting on their request, thereupon withdrew himself into the divine pavilion, and was absent for about six weeks. After a while, they became uneasy and restless. 'Where is he? He did not take food enough with him to sustain him for so long. Has he met with some mishap on those lonely steeps?' 'As for this Moses, the man that brought us up out of the land of Egypt, we wot not what is become of him' (Exod. 32:1). And then turning to Aaron, the man of words, sure that neither he nor twenty like him could fill the gap which the loss of Moses had caused, they cried, 'Up, make us gods, which shall go before us.'

We may notice in passing the essential nature of idolatry, for in this marvellous chapter we have its entire history. We start from the first cry of the soul, which betrays a yearning for an idol, to the draining of the last bitter dregs with which, when ground to power, the idolater has to drink its very dust. The idolater does not – in the first instance, at least – look on his image as God, but as a representation or manifestation of God. It is an attempt on the part of the human spirit, which shrinks from the effort of communion with the unseen and spiritual, to associate God with what it can own and handle, so as to have a constant and evident token of the presence and favour of God.

This was the case of Israel. It was only three months since they had stood by the Red Sea and seen its waters roll in pride over the hosts of Pharaoh. Every day since then God's love had followed them. And even at the time with which we are dealing the entire summit of the mount was crowned by the pavilion of cloud, which was the emblem of his presence in their midst. But nothwithstanding all, they were carried away before that imperious craving of the human heart, which cries out for a sensible image for its worship.

Their idolatry, then, was a violation, not of the first, but of the second commandment. They did not propose to renounce Jehovah – that was left for the days of Ahab; but they desired to worship Jehovah under the form of a calf, and in distinct violation of the emphatic prohibition which said, 'Thou shalt not make unto thee any graven image, or any likeness of any thing that is in heaven above, or that is in the earth beneath; thou shalt not bow down thyself to them, nor serve them.' This was the sin also of Jeroboam.

*b. Their degradation*    There can be no doubt that the worship of the calf was accompanied by the licentious orgies that were a recognised part of Egyptian idolatry. This is implied in the narrative: 'The people sat down to eat and to drink, and rose up to play.' A striking emendation is given of verse 25: 'Moses saw that the people were broken loose; for Aaron had let them loose for a derision among their enemies.' And from this we may infer that the bonds of continence, that had restrained them since the Exodus, had been suddenly slackened, with the result that they broke from all restraint, and gave themselves up to their unholy riot.

*c. The claims of God*    There was every reason to believe that God would exact the full amount of penalty, not because he was vindictive, but because the maintenance of his authority seemed to demand it. The righteousness of his career, the inviolability of his oath, the authority of the Ten Commandments, so recently given, combined to make it necessary that he should do as he had said.

When Moses reached the camp, he seems to have walked into the astonished throng, broken up their revelry, and overturned their calf, ordering it to be destroyed and the fragments mingled with the water they drank. But as this was not enough to stop the inveterate evil, he was compelled to use more drastic measures, and by the sword of Levi to extinguish it with the lifeblood of three thousand men.

Then when the next day came, when the camp was filled with mourning over those new graves, when the awful reaction had set in on the people and himself, the tide seems to have turned. His indignation was succeeded by bitter sorrow and pity. The pitiable state to which their sin had reduced them aroused his deepest compassion; and he said unto the people, 'Ye have sinned a great sin: and now I will go up unto the LORD; peradventure I shall make an atonement for your sin' (v.30); but he did not tell them the purpose that was in his heart, nor the price he was planning to pay.

## 3   The offer that he made

He returned quietly and thoughtfully to the chamber of God, as the people stood observing. He felt that the sin was very great. He could not see how God could go back from his solemn threatenings. He was convinced that if the merited judgments were averted, it must be in consequence of an atonement. Yet, what atonement could there be? Animals could not avail, though they were offered in slaughter. There was only one thing he could suggest – he could offer himself. This was the secret that he locked in his breast as he climbed the mountain. And it was this that made him say, 'Peradventure'. He could not be sure that the ransom price would be large enough.

Of course, the offer was not accepted. No one can atone for his own sin, much less for the sins of others. Yet the people were spared. The passing by of their transgression was rendered possible by the propitiation that was to be offered in the course of the ages on the cross (Rom. 3:25).

# 10

# Tabernacle Building

*Exodus 25:9,40*

The heart of the Jewish people was the tabernacle, around which their tents circled, and the movements of which determined the journeyings of the host. The tabernacle also taught them some of the deepest thoughts about God, in a kind of picture language.

We must remember that the children of Israel did not possess a language like our own, with many words and a rich vocabulary, capable of expressing all kinds of abstract ideas such as love, wisdom, purity, spirituality, holiness. So before making his revelation God had to provide language for his thoughts. This he did largely in the construction of the tabernacle.

## 1 The conception of the tabernacle

The pattern in the mount! Then clearly there must have been some visible phenomenon, some bright apparition, some glorious picture cast on the clouds or built on the old rocks. There may have been stakes and curtains, cherubs and lamps, gold and silver, altar and candlestick; but they would not bear the touch – they existed as a beautiful dream.

But it is almost inconceivable that God did not at the same time explain to Moses those wonderful conceptions of his own nature, and his relations to men, which were intended to be set forth in this material structure. They were as follows:

*a. God's willingness to share man's life*    If the people had only seen the devouring fire on the top of Sinai, the pavilion of God's presence, they would never have dared to think that there was any community of interest between him and them. To their minds, he would always have seemed distant and unapproachable. So God said, 'Let them make me a sanctuary; that I may dwell among them' (v.8).

Thus it was ordained that this larger tent should be pitched among them, only differing from their own in its proportions and materials; but standing on the same level sand, struck and pitched at the same hour with theirs, and enduring the same vicissitudes of weather and travel. Did this not say, as plainly as words could, that the tabernacle of God was with men, and that he was willing to dwell with them and become their God? Did it not teach that Jehovah had become a pilgrim with the pilgrim host, no longer a God afar off, but a sharer in their national fortunes?

*b. The greatness of God*    To this, too, a visible expression was to be given. The tabernacle must have cost an immense sum for that fugitive nation of slaves. The silver pedestals placed at intervals along the sand to hold the upright boards; the gorgeous tapestry that composed ceiling and walls; the golden furniture, of which the seven-branched candelabra alone weighed one hundredweight of gold; the brass wrought into sixty brazen pillars, with their silver capitals and hooks, from which were suspended curtains so thin that people could see all that was transpiring in the outer court. How costly these were!

On that new year's day, the anniversary of the Exodus (Exod. 40:17), as it stood forth completed in the desert sunshine, it must have furnished new and enlarged conceptions of the divine majesty.

*c. God's unity*    All around them the nations were under the spell of idolatry. But the tabernacle, with all its differing parts, and materials, and accessories, was one. One ark; one incense altar; one altar of burnt offering; one sacred purpose in every order and rite for the putting away of uncleanness. It stood therefore among men as a perpetual protest against idolatry, and as an emphatic witness to the unity of God. 'Hear, O Israel; The Lord our God is one Lord.' Such was the perpetual message that floated on the desert air from that unique structure.

*d. God's spirituality* The concept that God was a Spirit was conveyed to the people in that most striking form.

Enter the holy place; your eye is arrested by the heavy but magnificent curtain, covered with cherubim, that cuts off six feet of the length of the entire structure. Pull that aside, and you pass into a chamber that is a perfect cube, a miniature of the New Jerusalem, whose length, and breadth, and height, are equal. In the Egyptian temple this apartment would contain the crocodile or ibis; but here there was only a box, over which forms of exquisite beauty bent with outspread wings, and between them a light shone that was not borrowed from sun or stars. Could anything more significantly convey the idea that God was a Spirit?

This absence of any visible form in the inner shrine most astonished the rough soldier Pompey, who strode with eager curiosity across the floor, which had never before been pressed by anything but the unsandalled foot of the high priest once a year. He expected to find some visible embodiment of Jehovah, and turned contemptuously away deriding the empty void. But to Moses it must have been an unparalleled conception, overpowering his thoughts.

*e. God's purity* The impression of this was produced by a series of comparisons. First, the tabernacle stood within a courtyard fenced from public approach, the outer part could be trodden only by those men who had passed through certain rites of purification; and as to the inner part, it could be trodden only once a year by the high priest, carefully cleansed by many rites, and clad in garments of special design, while the blood of slain animals, selected out of the herds for their freedom from any blemish or speck, was sprinkled around. All was done to impress upon the people the care with which they should approach God; and in this way impressions of his holiness were wrought into the national mind.

And throughout these arrangements, and notably by these repeated references to the blood of sacrifices that was to be shed and sprinkled, Moses became familiarised with the philosophy of the Atonement.

Such thoughts as these must have penetrated the soul of Moses as he waited before God, oblivious to the flight of time, the waning love and idolatry of his people, or the demands of the body for food. And as we behold the great spectacle of that rapt and spellbound soul, we get some conception of one part at least of the engagements of eternity, and we are stirred to seek after a more intimate knowledge of God.

## 2   The reproduction of the pattern

There is a special interest to us all in this. We are not called to build the Tabernacle again, after that old pattern that has served its purpose and fallen into disuse because it was superseded by the clearer revelations of the Gospel. Yet there is an analogy that is full of instruction and inspiration in the life of every true believer, and deserves our attention for a moment.

As the tabernacle dwelled in the mind of God before it was reproduced on the desert sands, so does the life of each one exist, as a conception of that same infinite intelligence.

When a child is born into the world, there is in the mind of God a perfect picture of what the life may become, an ideal to which it may be conformed. There is a clear anticipation of what it will be, but side by side there is a distinct prevision of what it might be. And if only that pattern could be seen and literally reproduced, if only that life could attain to the divine ideal, there would be no room for regret or disappointment. It would fulfil its complete purpose as a thought of the divine mind, and attain its perfect consummation and bliss. Alas, that with so many of us, as the years have passed, we have wrought our own evil will and followed our own design!

*a. God's pattern was comprehensive*   No tassel, nor socket, nor tiny detail, was left to the fancy or ingenuity of the artificers; all was comprehended in the divine pattern. Of every detail God had a plan, because in each some purpose was hidden and the symmetry of the whole depended on the perfection of each part. So in life God's thought covers all details. Nothing is too trivial to be made a matter of prayer and supplication.

*b. God's plan was unfolded gradually.*   Probably the account of the revelation of the successive parts of the tabernacle is an exact transcript of the method by which the divine sign was unfolded to Moses' thought. Line upon line, precept upon precept – such is ever the divine method.

We will not be able to see far in front, nor the whole completed plan of our life, but as we complete one thing another will be revealed, and then the next and the next. It may be that we will not understand the divine purpose, but at the end of life we will see that it was one complete and exquisite structure, of which no part was wanting.

*c. God's plan was commensurate with the people's resources.*
As the pattern was there on the Mount, there were also the materials for its realisation in the possession of the people below – the gold and silver and precious stones, the blue and purple and scarlet, the fine linen and goats' hair, the rams' skins and badgers' skins, the genius of the artificers, and the willingness of the people.

God never gives a man a pattern without making himself responsible for the provision of all materials needed for its execution. If the materials are not forthcoming, you may seriously question whether you are not working on a plan of your own. God will not provide for a single tassle of your own addition to his scheme.

*d. God's plan must be resolutely obeyed.* Again and again in the last chapter of Exodus we are told that all was done, 'as the Lord commanded Moses.' This was his supreme joy and satisfaction, that he had not added to or diminished from the divine command and so the work was finished.

*e. God's plan is always progressive.* In pursuing the earlier stages of the divine tuition, Moses was especially occupied with elaborating the elementary idea of sacrifice, as in the case of the Paschal Lamb. The next stage was the building of the tabernacle, with which we have now been engaged. But this was not the final form of the divine revelation to which he was called to give visible shape. Years later, when disease was mowing down thousands of victims throughout the camp, as a judgment on the murmurings of the people, their leader was summoned to make a serpent of brass and place it on a pole, that all who looked might live.

In that supreme moment, Moses caught sight of the dying Lord, and discerned not only the fact but also the method of his death.

To no other Old Testament seer, so far as we can learn, was it given to know that Jesus must be lifted up on a cross. But this was permitted to him who had faithfully wrought out the divine plan in its earlier stages; and he too was privileged to set forth, so graphically and simply, the nature of saving faith. 'As Moses lifted up the serpent in the wilderness, so must the Son of man be lifted up; that whosoever believeth in him should not perish, but have everlasting life' (John 3:14–15).

Thus it is always. As we climb the hill, the horizon expands; as we do God's will more thoroughly, we know his doctrine more completely.

# 11

# How He Got Into Trouble

## *Numbers 20:11*

It was but one act, one little act, but it blighted the fair flower of a noble life and shut the one soul whose faith had sustained the responsibilities of the Exodus with unflinching fortitude, from the reward that seemed so nearly within its grasp.

The wanderings of the forty years were almost over. The congregation that had been scattered over the peninsula had converged toward the given meeting place in Kadesh. There the encampment remained for some months, and there Miriam died. She was one of the few with whom that lonely spirit could still converse of that life that lay beyond the desert sands, the valleys of Sinai, and the waters of the Red Sea, in the distant mighty land of the Pharaohs and the Pyramids. Aaron, Caleb, Joshua (and perhaps the Levites), were the only relics and supervisors of that vash triumphant host, whose voices had rung out their challenge on the morning of emancipation.

## 1 How it happened

The demand of the people on the water supply at Kadesh was so great that the streams were drained. Because of this there broke out again that spirit of murmuring and complaint that had cursed the former generation, and was now reproduced in their children. Oblivious to the unwavering care of all the preceding years, the people assembled themselves together against Moses and Aaron, though it was against Moses that they principally directed their reproach.

They professed to wish that they had died in the plague that Aaron's censer had stayed. They accused the brothers of malicious designs to effect the destruction of the whole assembly by thirst. Although the cloud of God brooded overhead and the manna fell day by day, they cursed their abiding place as evil. They taunted Moses with the absence of figs, vines, and pomegranates. They demanded water.

However, he resumed his old position, prostrating himself at the door of the tent of meeting until the growing light that welled forth from the secret place indicated that the divine answer was near. Unlike the injunction on a similar occasion, which now lay back in the haze of years, Moses was urged, though he took the rod, not to use it, but to speak to the rock with a certainty that the accents of his voice, smiting on its flinty face, would have as much effect as the rod had had previously, and would be followed by a rush of crystal water.

Moses might have entered into these thoughts of God in quieter and more tranquil moments, but just now he was irritated, indignant, and hot with disappointment and anger. Therefore, when the assembly was gathered together in their thronging multitudes around him, he accused them of being rebels. He spoke as if the gift of water depended on himself and Aaron. He showed how irked he was at their demand, and then vehemently smote the rock with his rod twice. And as those blows re-echoed through the still air, they shook forever the fabric woven by his dreams and hopes.

What a warning there is here, admonishing us that we sometimes fail in our strongest point, and that a noble career may be blasted by one small but significant and forever lamentable failure! 'The Lord spoke unto Moses and Aaron, Because ye believe me not, to sanctify me in the eyes of the children of Israel, therefore ye shall not bring this congregation into the land which I have given them' (v.12).

The people did not suffer through their leader's sin. The waters gushed from out the rock as plentifully as they would have done if the divine injunctions had been precisely complied with. 'The water came forth abundantly; and the congregation drank, and their beasts also.'

## 2   The principle that underlay the divine decision

*a. There was distinct disobedience.*   There was no doubt as to the divine command; and it had been distinctly disobeyed. Moses was not to strike, but to speak; and he had twice smitten the rock. In this way he had failed to sanctify God in the eyes of the people. He who ought to have set the example of implicit obedience to every jot and tittle, had inserted his own will and way as a substitute for God's. This could not be tolerated in one who was set to lead and teach the people.

It is a solemn question for us all whether we are sufficiently obedient. It is a repeated burden of those sad chapters of Hebrews which tell the story of the wilderness wanderings – the cemetery chapters of the New Testament – that 'they could not enter in because of unbelief.' But throughout the verses the margin suggests the alternative reading of *disobedience*; because disobedience and unbelief are the two sides of the same coin – a coin of the devil's mintage. They who disobey do not believe; and they who do not believe disobey.

*b. There was unbelief.*   It was as if Moses had felt that a word was not enough. He did not realise how small an act on his part was sufficient to open the sluice gates of omnipotence. A touch is enough to set omnipotence in action.

It is wonderful to hear God say to Moses, 'Ye believed me not.' Was this not the man by whose faith the plagues of Egypt had fallen on that unhappy land; and the Red Sea had cleft its waters; and the daily manna had spread the desert floor with food; and the people had marched for thirty-eight years unhurt by hostile arm? What had happened? Had the wanderings impaired that mighty soul, and robbed it of its former strength, and shorn the locks of its might, and left it like any other? Surely, something of this sort must have happened! One act could have wrought such havoc only by being the symptom of unsuspected wrong beneath. Oaks do not fall in a single storm unless they have become rotten at their heart.

Let us watch and pray lest there be in any of us an evil heart of unbelief; lest we depart in our most secret thought from simple faith in the living God; lest beneath a fair exterior we yield our jewel of faith to the solicitation of some unholy passion.

*c. There was the spoiling of the type* 'That Rock was Christ.' It was from his heart, smitten in death on Calvary, that the river of water of life has flowed to make glad the city of God, and to transform deserts into Edens. But death came to him, and can come to him but once. 'Christ was once offered to bear the sins of many' (Heb. 9:28). 'For in that he died, he died unto sin once; but in that he liveth, he liveth unto God' (Rom. 6:10). 'I am he that liveth, and was dead; and, behold, I am alive for evermore' (Rev. 1:18). These texts prove how important it was to keep clear and defined the fact of the death of Christ being a finished act, once for all. It is evident that for the completeness of the likeness between substance and shadow, the rock should have been stricken but once. Instead of that, it was smitten at the beginning and at the close of the desert march. But this was a misrepresentation of an eternal fact, and the perpetrator of the heedless act of iconoclasm had to suffer the extreme penalty, even as Uzzah died for trying to steady the swaying ark.

But there was something even deeper than these things. There was an eternal fitness in the nature of the case in Moses not being permitted to lead the people into the land of rest. Moses represented the Law. It came by him, and he therefore fitly stands before the gaze of the ages as the embodiment of that supreme law, whose eye does not wax dim or its force abate under the wear and tear of time. But the law can never lead us into rest. It can conduct us to the very margin and threshold, but no further. Another must take us in, the true Joshua – Jesus, the Saviour and Lover of people.

## 3 The irrevocableness of the divine decisions

Moses drank deeply of the bitter cup of disappointment. And it seems to have been his constant prayer that God would reverse or mitigate his sentence. 'I pray thee, let me go over, and see the good land that is beyond Jordan, that goodly mountain, and Lebanon' (Deut. 3:25). No patriot ever yearned more to tread the blessed soil of his fatherland as did Moses. With all the earnestness that he had used to plead for the people, he now pleaded for himself. But it was not to be. 'The Lord was wroth . . . and said unto me, Let it suffice thee; speak no more unto me of this matter' (v.26).

At such times our prayer is not literally answered. By the voice of his Spirit, by a spiritual instinct, we become conscious that it is useless to pray further. Though we pray not three times but three hundred times, the thorn is not taken away. But there is a sense in which the prayer is answered. Our suffering is a lesson warning people in years to come. We are permitted from Pisgah's height to scan the fair land we long for, and are then removed to a better land. We have the answer given to us later, as Moses, who had his prayer gloriously fulfilled when he stood with Christ on the Transfiguration Mount.

# 12

# The Death of Moses

## Deuteronomy 34:5–6

The records of Scripture find little room for dying testimonies, words, or experiences; while they abound in stories of the exploits and words of those who have stormed and suffered and wrought in life's arena. This may explain why, contrary to human custom, the death of the great lawgiver is described with such brief simplicity.

But this simplicity is equalled only by the sublimity of the conception. After such a life it was proper that Moses should have a death and burial unparalleled in the story of mankind; and we do not wonder that poet, painter, and preacher have found in that lonely death on Pisgah's summit a theme worthy of their noblest powers.

## 1   Its bearing on sin

We cannot suppose that the sudden outburst of impetuous temper at Meribah – when his spirit was agitated by a fierce whirlwind of wrath, as a storm sweeping down some mountain rent on an inland lake – could remain long unforgiven. As far as the east is from the west, so far had that transgression been removed. But though the remission was complete, yet the result lingered in his life, and shut him out from an experience that should have been the crown of his career.

Nor does sin only entail loss and sorrow on the transgressor; it robs mankind of much of the benefit which otherwise had accrued from his life. If it had not been for his want of faith and his passionate behaviour, Moses would have led his people across the Jordan, and served them for many years.

## 2   Its bearing on death

*a.  Its loneliness*   That majestic spirit had ever lifted itself, like some unscaled peak, amid other men. Into its secrets no foot had intruded, no human eye had peered. But its loneliness was never more apparent than when, unattended even by Joshua, he passed up to die amid the solitudes of Nebo. Alone he trod the craggy steep; alone he gazed up on the fair landscape; alone he lay down to die.

But in that loneliness there is a foreshadowing of the loneliness through which each of us must pass unless caught up to meet the Lord in the air. In that solemn hour human voices will fade away, beloved forms will vanish, familiar scenes will grow dim to the sight. Silent and lonely, the spirit migrates to learn for itself the great secret. Happy the man who, anticipating the moment, can say: 'Alone, yet not alone, my Saviour is with me. He who went this way by himself is now retreading it at my side.'

*b.  Its method*   We die, as Moses did, 'according to the word of the Lord.' Some still substitute 'kiss' for 'word'; so that it seemed as if the Almighty had kissed away the soul of his faithful servant, drawing it back to himself in a long, sweet, tender embrace.

Is not this the manner in which all saints die? Lit in the evening by the rays of a stormy sunset, piercing through the cloud-drift, the tired spirit sinks down, and he bends over it to give it its good-night kiss, as in earliest days the mother had done to the wearied child.

**c.** *Its sepulchre*   We are told that 'the Lord buried him in a valley in the land of Moab', in spite of the opposition of the evil one, who contended with the archangel sent to secure that noble deserted shrine. And so even a band of angels was not permitted to perform the sacred work of interment. We are told that *he* buried him; as if the Almighty would not delegate the sacred office to any inferior hand.

**d.** *Its purpose*   We are told that 'the children of Israel wept for Moses in the plains of Moab thirty days'; and if we connect this statement with the fact of the unknown grave, we will be able to discern the divine purpose in its concealment. Is it not more than likely that, if the Lord had not concealed his grave, the valley of Bethpeor would have become a second Mecca, trodden by the feet of pilgrims from all over the world?

**e.** *Its vision*   From the spot on which he stood, without any extraordinary gift of vision, his eye could range over an almost unequalled panorama. At his feet, the faraway tents of Israel; to the north, the rich pasture-lands of Gilead and Bashan, bounded by the desert haze on the one hand, and on the other by the Jordan valley, from the blue waters of the Lake of Galilee to the dark gorge of the Dead Sea. And beyond the river he could sweep over the fair Land of Promise, from the snow-capped summits of Hermon and Lebanon to the uplands of Ephraim and Manasseh; with the infinite variety of cities perched on their pinnacles of rock, of cornfields and pasture lands, of oil, olives, figs, vines, and pomegranates. Immediately before him, looking west, was Jericho, in its green setting of palm trees, connected by the steep defile with Jerusalem; not far from which Bethlehem, on the ridge of the hills, gleamed as a jewel.

So to dying people still comes the vision of the beautiful land beyond the Jordan. It is not far away – only just across the river. May God grant us the blessedness of dying on the hilltop with that vision in our gaze.

### 3   The bearing on dispensational truth

The Law came by Moses; and Moses stands on the plains of history as the embodiment, as he was also the vehicle, of the moral law.

It was in perfect keeping with this conception that there was no decay in his natural vigour. His eye was as a falcon's, his step limber and elastic, his bearing erect. He did not die of disease, or amid the decreptitude of old age; 'he was not, because God took him'. Time had made him only venerable, but not weak. And thus he represents God's holy law which cannot grow outworn or weak, but always abides in its pristine and perfect strength, though it cannot bring us into God's rest.

This is the beautiful Land of Promise, which can be seen from afar only by those who know nothing except what Moses can teach them; but may be entered by those who follow the ark through the river of death to the self-life, and forward to resurrection ground.

# JOSHUA

# 1

# The Divine Commission

## *Joshua 1:7*

As Joshua stood on the threshold of his great work, he was repeatedly urged to be strong and of a good courage. Some little time before the death of his predecessor, a great convocation of all Israel had been summoned, at which Moses had solemnly transferred his office to his successor, and had given him a charge, saying, 'Be strong and of a good courage; for thou must go with this people unto the land' (Deut. 31:7). And now the voice of God reiterates the charge and repeats the injunction.

At first this startles us. What! must all those whom God uses be strong? Because, if that be so, we who are like Ehud, left-handed; like Gideon, least in our father's house; or like Saul of Tarsus, painfully conscious of weakness, can never get beyond the rank and file in the army of the Lord.

When Moses first received the sentence of death on the other side of Jordan, no one could have been more deeply grieved than his faithful friend and attendant. But the thought of succeeding him never presented itself to his mind.

When therefore the call came to him to assume the office that Moses was vacating, his heart failed him, and he needed every kind of encouragement and stimulus, both from God and man. 'Be strong' means that he felt weak; 'Be of good courage' means that he was frightened; 'Be not thou dismayed' means that he seriously considered whether he would not have to give up the task. He was a worm and no man: how could he deliver Israel?

It is when men are in this condition that God approaches them with the summons to undertake vast and overwhelming responsibilities. Most of us are too strong for him to use; we are too full

189

of our own schemes, and plans, and ways of doing things. He must empty us, and humble us, and then he will raise us up, and make us as the rod of his strength. The world talks of the survival of the fittest. But God gives power to the faint, and increases might to those who have no strength. He perfects his strength in weakness, and uses things that are not, to bring to nothing things that are.

Let us consider the sources of Joshua's strength.

## 1   A faithful past

'After the death of Moses the servant of the Lord . . . the Lord spake unto Joshua the son of Nun, Moses' minister' (Josh. 1:1). In his case, as always, the eternal rule held good, that faithfulness in a few things is the condition of rule over many things; and the loyalty of a servant is the stepping stone to the royalty of the throne.

The previous years of Joshua's past had been full of high and noble endeavour. For forty years, if Josephus is correct in his statement as to his age at the death of Moses, he shared the slavery and sorrows of a captive race. As a descendant of one of the leading families of Ephraim (Num. 13:8, 16), he may have taken some leading part in the marshalling of the Exodus, and there approved himself as worthy of all trust. His conflict with Amalek; his good report of the Land of Promise; his refusal to take any part in the disastrous attack on the Canaanites; his eagerness for the good name and fame of Moses; his patient endurance of the weary years of wandering – all prove that his was no common character. This summons of Joshua to the leader's place in Israel was the reward of more than eighty years of faithful service.

None of us can tell for what God is educating us. We fret and murmur at the daily task of ordinary life, not realising that it is only in this way that we can be prepared for the high and holy office that awaits us. God's will comes to you and me in daily circumstances, in little things equally as in great: dignify the smallest summons by the greatness of your response, so the call will come to you as to Joshua, the son of Nun, Moses' minister.

## 2   A distinct call

'Arise, go over this Jordan, thou, and all this people, unto the land which I do give to them . . . Be strong and of a good courage: for thou shalt cause this people to inherit the land which I sware unto their fathers to give them.' When a man knows that he has been called to do a certain work, he is invincible. He is not unconscious of his own deficiencies, whether they are natural or intellectual. He is not insensible to difficulty; there are none so quick as he to see the great stones, the iron gates, the walled cities, the broad and flowing rivers. He is not invulnerable to the shafts of ridicule and adverse criticism, but for all these he looks steadily to the declared purpose of God and yields himself to be the channel through which it may operate.

Joshua's task was a difficult one. The people of Canaan were well versed in the arts and sciences of the time, acquired from commerce with the Phoenicians on the north and the Egyptians on the south. It seemed preposterous to suppose that a nation of a few years' existence was so soon to dispossess nations that had gained the country by conquest and were prepared to fight for every inch of territory by the most approved methods of warfare. It is clear that the reiterated assurance of God to settle Israel with his help must have been a great source of strength to him.

## 3 The sense of the presence of God

'As I was with Moses, so I will be with thee: I will not fail thee, nor forsake thee.' There was one particular in which Joshua would always come far behind his great predecessor. Both were in necessary and constant communication with God, but Joshua had to seek counsel through the high priest, whereas Moses had enjoyed direct intercourse with God, speaking to him 'face to face, as a man speaketh unto his friend' (Exod. 33:11). Still, Joshua, the son of Nun, was equally sure of the personal companionship of his great ally, though he lacked the direct vision.

All through the arduous campaign that followed, nothing could daunt Joshua's courage while that assurance was ever ringing in his memory: 'I will be with thee.'

## 4 The indwelling of the Word of God

'This book of the law shall not depart out of thy mouth; but thou shalt meditate therein day and night.' We must meditate on the words of God because it is through the Word of God that the Spirit of God comes in fullness to be the mighty occupant of our inner man. This, after all, is the secret of strength – to be possessed of the strong Son of God, strengthened by his indwelling might, and filled by his Spirit.

We can do all things when Christ is in us in unthwarted power. The only limit lies in our faith and capacity or, in other words, in our absolute submission to his indwelling. Our risen Lord is charged with power.

Be strong in your weakness through the strengthening might of Christ. Take weakness, weariness, faintheartedness, and difficulty into his presence; they will melt as frost in the sun. You will make your way prosperous, and have good success; and you will lead a nation to inherit the Land of Promise.

# 2

# Passing the Jordan

## Joshua 3:10

There were several reasons why it was needful for God to drive out the seven nations that dwelled in Canaan. But the chief among them stands that suggested by the memorable interview held between Jehovah and Abraham, the ancestor of the chosen race, four centuries before – the iniquity of the Amorite was now full (Gen. 15:16).

In the first place, the nations of Canaan had given themselves to *the most abominable immorality*. The destruction of the people by the sword of Israel was only the hastening of the natural results of their shameful vice. The reasons that necessitated the deluge of water necessitated this deluge of blood. Plague spot as it was, Canaan would have infected the world had it not been passed through the fire.

In the second place, the Canaanites were *steeped in spiritualism,* and held close communications with the demons of the air, which have always been forbidden to men. When man opens a passage of communication with the fallen spirits around him, he exposes himself to God's direst wrath; and for the sake of the race these black arts must be stopped.

And this last thought gives a new complexion to this conflict. In driving out and destroying these demoralised races, God was in effect waging war with the evil spirits, who from their seat in the heavenlies were ruling the darkness of that land. And thus this old record is invested with a new interest. It is not simply the story of the conquest of Canaan, but it is a fragment from the chronicles of heaven, giving an episode in the eternal conflict between light and darkness, between heaven and hell. What an interesting additional analogy between the Book of Joshua and the Epistle to the Ephesians!

God graciously granted a sign of the ultimate issue of the war, so that through the seven years of coming conflict the people of Israel could be at rest as to the result. 'Hereby ye shall know that the living God is among you, and that he will without fail drive out from before you the Canaanites, and the Hittites, and the Hivites, and the Perizzites, and the Girgashites, and the Amorites, and the Jebusites. Behold, the ark of the covenant of the Lord of all the earth passeth over before you into Jordan.' The passage of the turbulent waters of Jordan was to be the heaven-appointed sign.

## 1   The passage of the Jordan

At the close of the three days of preparation there seems to have been a movement of the camp from Shittim, with its acacia groves, to a spot within a mile of the boisterous rush of the swollen floods. There Israel spent the last memorable night of pilgrimage and wandering. As the dawn broke, the officers again passed through the host, and bade the people watch and follow the movements of the ark. Only a short interval elapsed before the congregation pulled up their slight black tents, packed up their household goods, and adjusted their burdens, and stood in one great host, two and a half million strong, prepared to tread the untried path. The sun was rising behind them, its beams flashing on the Jordan, a mile of water wide, and setting in bold relief the white walls of the houses of Jericho; while all the adjacent hills of Canaan stood around veiled in morning mist, or robed in the exquisite garments of light.

At last the little group emerged from these densely-crowded hosts. It was the chosen band of priests, white-robed, barefooted, who slowly descended the terraced bank of the river, bearing on their shoulders the sacred ark, its golden lid and bending cherubim hidden beneath their covering of blue. How awesome the silence! How fixed the gaze that followed their every step! How hushed the wisecracks and the loud denials of the previous days that protested that the passage was impossible; and that it would be wiser to wait until the mile of water had dwindled to the normal width of thirty yards when the stream was four or six feet deep, and easily fordable!

Nearer the little procession came; but even when it was within a yard of the river brink its approach effected nothing. The waters showed no disposition to flee or fail. But when the feet of the priests touched the tiny wavelets, brown with mud, a marvellous change took place. They began to divide and shrink away. And as the priests pursued them, descending ever further toward the midst of Jordan, they fled before them as if panic-stricken. Nothing could account for so great a wonder except the presence of the God of Jacob, and that the ark of the covenant of the Lord of all the earth was passing through those depths.

Up the river some thirty miles, at Adam, the city that is beside Zaretan, the flow of the river had suddenly stopped, and the waters, unable to hurry forward, gathered into a heap and probably formed a vast lake that spread itself for miles. From that point and downward, the waters, no longer supplied from above, began to fail; they hurried toward the Sea of Death, and were swallowed up in its dark unwholesome depths. 'They were wholly cut off'. As there were none to follow, the river bed for miles was dry; and the people, hurrying down the bank, 'hastened and passed over.' The feet of the priests stood firm until every individual of the redeemed race had crossed the river.

And this was the promised sign, for he who could drive out the waters would drive out their foes. Having done so much, he would perfect that which he had begun.

## 2  The typical significance of this passage

'There shall be a space between you and [the ark]'. Yes, the Lord Jesus preceded his church. He first passed through the grave in resurrection power. 'Every man in his own order: Christ the first fruits, afterward they that are Christ's' (1 Cor. 15:23). In all things, and therefore in this also, he must have the preeminence. 'The priests that bare the ark of the covenant of the LORD stood firm . . . until all the people were passed clean over Jordan.'

The waters of judgment may be accumulating for all who cling to the old Adamstock, but they can never slip from their leash until every trembling laggard soul that will has passed into blessed rest. You may be young, or crippled, or ready to stop, or much afraid, but if you will but cast in your lot with the host of the ransomed, the Priest will lengthen out the dispensation, and hold the waters back for you.

## 3  The bearing of this passage on Christian experience

*a. We have already seen the effect produced on death by the death of the Lord Jesus.*     It is appointed unto man *once* to die. And since we have died in him, we shall find death robbed of its terrors. The darkness of the valley is only that of a shadow, but this is not all. By virtue of our union with him, we have passed through death on to resurrection ground, and have become 'the children of the resurrection'. It is on this fact in our spiritual history that the apostles base many of their most powerful arguments and appeals. 'How shall we that are dead to sin, live any longer therein?' (Rom. 6:2). 'Forasmuch then as Christ hath suffered for us in the flesh, arm yourselves likewise with the same mind: for he that hath suffered in the flesh hath ceased from sin; that he no longer should live the rest of his time in the flesh to the lusts of men, but to the will of God' (1 Peter 4:1-2).

*b. With this truth we can foil the most enticing fascinations of the world.*     We have passed out of it with our dear Lord. We have become citizens of the new Jerusalem, and if we still move amid the world's engagements, it is in the garb of strangers and foreigners – men from the other side of the river who speak the language and wear the attire of the heavenly Canaan – the language, *love*;

the attire, *the white raiment,* pure and clean, washed in the blood of the Lamb.

There is no hope that we shall be able to cope with these things by any might or wisdom of our own. The opposition of that relative; the hatred of that persecutor; the strength of that passion; the tyranny of that habit; the untowardness of our circumstances – these are our Jordan. How easy life would be if only these were other than they are! Give me Canaan without its Jordan! But God permits the Jordans that he may educate our faith. Do not look at the troubled waters rushing past; but at the Priest, who is also the ark of the covenant.

When you come to the dreaded difficulty, you will find that because his feet have been dipped in its brink, it has dwindled in its flow. Its roar is hushed; its waters are shrunken; its violence is gone. The iron gate stands open. The stone is rolled from the sepulchre. The river bed is dry. Jericho is within reach. 'They passed clean over Jordan'.

# 3

# The Stones of Gilgal

## *Joshua 4:5*

On the western side of Jordan, to which the host of Israel had now come, five miles from the river brink, the terraced banks reached their highest point. That was Gilgal. There the first camp was pitched, on the edge of a vast grove of majestic palms, nearly three miles broad and eight miles long, that stretched away to Jericho. In the midst of this forest could have been seen, reaching through its open spaces, fields of ripe corn, 'for it was the time of the barley harvest'; and above the topmost trees you could see the high walls and towers of the city on the farther side, which from that grove derived its proud name, 'Jericho, the City of Palms'.

Gilgal was the base of operations in the war against the people of Canaan. There the camp remained, with the women and children (9:6, 10:6). It ranked with Mizpeh and Bethel among the holy places where Samuel exercised his sacred office (1 Sam. 7:16). It was the rallying point to which the people gathered at solemn times of national crisis (11:14). Saul had reason to remember it; and there Agag was hewed in pieces 'before the LORD'.

Probably to the last of the events and beyond, the twelve stones that had been pitched by Joshua as the last memorial of the passage of the river were visible.

At the time when the book was written, the other heap of stones, laid in the river bed, must have been clearly discernible when the stream, temporarily swollen by the spring floods, had retreated to its normal width (4:9); and there could have been no difficulty in fixing the hill of circumcision where, at the command of God, they had rolled away the reproach of Egypt, and from which the name Gilgal, or Rolling, was derived (5:9).

Gilgal was from the first 'holy ground' (5:15); and as we traverse it again in devout thought, it will also give us themes for deep and holy meditation.

## 1 The stones on the bank

At the divine bidding twelve men, one out of each tribe, went down to the river's bed. From the place where the priests' feet stood firm in Jordan, each man took a stone. For centuries these stones had laid there undisturbed but now, piled together in a heap before the eyes of all men, they were to be a memorial of the passage of Jordan, as the song of Moses was of the passage through the Red Sea.

It is well that forgetful hearts like ours should be stirred up by way of remembrance. We are so apt to grow unmindful of the Rock that begot us, and to forget the God who gave us birth. Therefore it was necessary that these memorial stones be erected beside our Jordans, with their inscription, 'Wherefore remember'.

Consider those twelve stones on the further side of Jordan, and be sure that as they represented the entire people, and commemorated their marvellous transportation from the one side of Jordan to the other, so, in the New Jerusalem, the twelve foundation stones bearing the names of the apostles, and the twelve gates inscribed with the names of the twelve tribes of Israel, are a standing memorial that the church as a whole is on resurrection ground; but her shame and sorrow are that she has not availed herself of her lofty privileges, or descended to earth girded with the power of the risen, living Jesus.

We have crossed the River. Our eternity is begun. In Jesus we are loved and accepted. We are more than conquerors; we occupy a position which, if we would only keep it, is unassailable by our foes. They can prevail only against us when they succeed in attempting us to abandon it. All things are ours in union with our raised and reigning Lord.


## 2   The stones in the bed of the stream

Not content with pitching a pile of stones on the river's bank, Joshua, at God's command, set up twelve stones in the midst of Jordan, in the place where the feet of the priests that carried the ark of the covenant stood. And often, as he came back to Gilgal, he must have gone out by himself to walk and meditate beside the river, turning the outward and the inward gaze to the spot where beneath the flow of the current those stones lay hidden. They were the lasting memorial of the miracle that otherwise might have faded from memory, or seemed incredible. They were aids to faith. Where they lay the people had been, and the feet of the priests had been planted dry. And surely the power that had arrested the Jordan, and brought the people up from its bed, would not fail until it had worked out the whole purpose of God.


## 3   The rite of circumcision

Israel looked for nothing less than to be led from the river brink to the conquest and partition of the land. They suddenly discovered, however, that this was not quite the divine programme for them. But they were required to submit to a painful rite,the seal of the covenant that was made originally to Abraham, and by virtue of which the land had been given to him and to his seed (Gen. 17:8–10).

During the wanderings of the desert – which were due to their unbelief, and practically disinherited them – the observance of this rite had been stopped because the operation of the covenant was for the time in suspense. But now that the new young nation was learning to exercise its faith, the covenant and its seal was again put into operation. 'Their children, whom he raised up in their stead, them Joshua circumcised.'

Even those comparatively unenlightened people must have realised that there was deep spiritual significance in the administration of that rite at that juncture. On more than one occasion they had heard Moses speak of circumcising the heart; and they must have felt that God meant to teach them the vanity of trusting to their numbers, or prowess, or martial array. The land was not to be won by their might, but to be taken from his hand as a gift. Self and the energy of the flesh had to be set aside that the glory of coming victory might be of God, and not of man.

# 4

# Three Successive Days

## *Joshua 5:10–12*

In one of his sonnets, Matthew Arnold tells of an interview he had on a day of fierce August sunshine, in Spitalfields, with a preacher whom he knew, and who looked ill and overworked. In answer to the inquiry as to how he fared. 'Bravely', he said, 'for I of late have been much cheered with thoughts of Christ the *Living Bread.*' He is not the only human soul who, above the ebb and flow of London storm and tumult, has set up a mark of everlasting light to cheer, and to light its course through the night.

In this old record we may discover without effort the Living Bread under three aspects – the Passover; the corn of the land; the manna. Each of these was associated with one of three successive days.

## 1 The Passover

The Passover itself could never be repeated. But the Feast of the Passover, held in commemoration of that event, was destined to perpetual repetition until it gave place to a yet more significant symbol; which, in turn, is to fade into the marriage supper as the love of bethrothal fades into that of marriage.

The Feast of the Passover was held at Sinai, but it was not held again until the forty years had elapsed. In fact, it could not be held while the nation, through unbelief and disobedience, was untrue to the covenant. Had it not been distinctly affirmed, amid other provisions, that no uncircumcised person should eat of it? But as soon as the circumcising of the people was completed there was no longer a barrier; and the Passover was kept between 'the two evenings,' as the sun of the fourteenth day of the month was flinging toward them long shadows from the palm trees and walls of Jericho.

There were two significant parts of the Passover as it was first instituted. First was the sprinkling of blood on the doors without. Second, the family gathered around the roasted lamb, eating it in haste. As years went on and conditions altered, however, blood was no longer sprinkled on the lintel and door posts, but the drinking of wine was substituted for that ancient and significant act. And the family gathered around the table to the sacred feast, not merely with the girded loin and staff in hand as befitted pilgrims, but with the leisured restfulness of home. In point of fact it was a family meal at which the people reviewed the past with thankfulness, and talked together of that mercy that had been so remarkably displayed in their national history. On reaching the Land of Promise, the thoughts of the people were guided back to the great fact of redemption by blood that lay at the basis of their existence.

The other side of the Passover has also a counterpart in our experience. The Israelites feasted, they drank the light Eastern wine, and years later they chanted the Hallel and ate of the flesh of the lamb. The bread was unleavened and the herbs bitter, but joy exceeded sorrow. And this is the type of Christian life.

The Lord's Supper is not simply a memorial of what he did on Calvary, or is doing on the throne; it is a perpetual reminder to the

believing heart of its privilege and duty to eat the flesh and drink
the blood of the Son of Man in a spiritual way. We must eat his
flesh or we will have no life in us. We must drink his blood or we
will not dwell in him, or he in us.

But let us always remember that as no uncircumcised person
was permitted to partake of the Passover, so none who are living
in wilful sin can feed on the flesh and blood that were given for the
life of the world. There must be a Gilgal before there can be a
Passover in the deepest and fullest sense.

## 2   The corn of the land

'And they did eat of the old corn of the land on the morrow after
the passover.' There is no need for the adjective *old*. It would be
sufficient to say that they ate of the corn of the land, though it is
likely that it was the corn of the previous harvest, and not that
which was then ripening throughout the land of Canaan, and
ready for the sickle. The main point is that, with great thankfulness, the Israelites, the majority of whom had never tasted anything but manna, ate of the produce of the Land of Promise.

Is it not significant that on this very day the Lord Jesus arose
from the dead, 'the firstfruits of them that slept'? Surely, then, it is
no straining of the parallel to say that the corn of the Land of
Promise represents him in risen glory. He fell as a seed of corn into
the ground to die, but through death he has acquired the power of
imparting himself to all who believe. He was bruised, as all bread-
corn must be – the wheel of the cart of divine justice ground him
beneath its weight – but he has become thereby as the finest of the
wheat to feed the needs of the world. We must feed on the Paschal
Lamb and learn the full meaning of his cross and passion, his precious death and burial; but we must also feed on the corn of the
heavenly land, and derive life and blessing from his glorious
resurrection and ascension.

The church has in some measure learned to appreciate the
importance of the Incarnation and Crucifixion. But it is comparatively seldom that we hear in treatise or sermon any adequate
treatment of the Ascension from the lowest parts of the earth to
that zenith point of glory from which he fills all things. Oh, to
know what Paul meant by his emphasis when he said, '*yea rather,
that is risen again*'; and to understand his thinking when he said

that though he had known Christ after the flesh, he wished to know him so no more, because he longed to understand the power of his resurrection. The Paschal Lamb is good; but the corn of the land includes the fruits, and honey, and bread-stuffs that grow on the soil of the resurrection life.

The ascension of Christ may be considered in many aspects. The majesty and triumph of the God-man, as he is raised far above all principality and power, whether of angels or of demons, and above every name that is named, whether in this world or that which is to come; the certainty that the same power that raised him from the grave to the right hand of the Father waits to do as much for each of us; the belief that in his ascension he has received gifts for each of us, and the best of all gifts, the fullness of the Spirit, is for us to claim and receive. These are themes that stir our sluggish hearts and make them leap with gladness, which no increase of corn or wine can yield to the men of this world. Happy indeed are they who also in heart and mind ascend, and *with him dwell continually*. To do this is to eat of the corn and fruit of the land.

### 3   The manna

'And the manna ceased on the morrow after they had eaten of the old corn of the land.' There was no break between the two. The corn began before the manna ceased. The one overlapped the other as the thatch of a haystack or the feathers of a bird.

God does not desire that there should be those intervals of apparent desertion and the failure of supplies of which so many complain. It is likely that he may have to withdraw the extraordinary and exceptional, as represented by the manna; but he will wait until we have become accustomed to the ordinary and regular supplies of his grace, as represented by the corn.

We are constantly being forced from the familiar manna that came without anxiety or seeking on our part, to the corn that requires foresight and careful preparation. This is needful because in these we learn invaluable lessons of patience, and self-denial, and co-operation with God. But how we first shrink from the change!

How gracious then is the gentle, thoughtful kindness of God, who lets us see the new before he takes away the old. He allows us to become accustomed to walking before he removes the chair on which we had leaned so long.

This, then, is our main lesson. We must learn to live in such a way as to be nourished with the life of the Son of God. When we eat of Christ, we live by him, as he lived by the Father; and as the Father, dwelling in him, worked through his life, and did his wondrous works, so he, entering into us – the Word by his words – will do through us what had otherwise been impossible.

Do you long for more strength to do or suffer, to witness or turn the foe from the gate? Then feed on Christ, meditating on his word, communing with him, filled by his Spirit, who takes of the things that are his and reveals them to us. 'Blessed are they that hunger and thirst; they shall be filled.' 'He hath filled the hungry with good things.' 'Bread that strengtheneth man's heart.'

# 5

# The Walls of Jericho

## *Joshua 6*

Jericho was filled with faintheartedness. There was no issuing forth of the men of war; no sudden night attack on the brown tents pitched around the central pavilion or tabernacle of God. It was as though some mysterious spell had fallen on king and people, unnerving them, impelling them to stand on the defensive and await the unfolding of events. 'Their heart melted, neither was there spirit in them any more, because of the children of Israel.'

Israel, on the other hand, was probably impatient, eager to be led to the conflict. The men of war, confident in their might, were eager to match themselves against the inhabitants of the land and to wipe out in blood the memory of their fathers' defeat at Hormah. Conscious that the passage of the Jordan had been due to the presence of the priests, it may have been that there was a secret desire in their hearts to show that the time had come for the priests to stand aside, while they approved their prowess and won the land by might.

But they had to learn that the land was a gift, to be received by faith, not won by effort. God required of them only to obey, and wait, and trust, while the divine Captain led his celestial hosts to the assault and achieved the victory. 'And the Lord said unto Joshua, See, I have given into thine hand Jericho, and the king there of, and the mighty men of valour. And ye shall compass the city, all ye men of war, and go round about the city once.'

It certainly was the strangest spectacle ever witnessed by a beleaguered garrison. The besiegers did not make an assault, or rear mounds, or place scaling ladders against the walls. Nor did they afford an opportunity for parley or discussion of terms of capitulation. On each side it seems to have been understood that the war would be to the knife – no quarter asked, no mercy shown. Without delay the host of Israel began encompassing the city.

It was but a little after dawn. The sun had mounted not far above the eastern horizon. Then from out of the camp of Israel a long procession began to unwind itself. First the men of war, marching beneath their tribal banners; then seven priests, white-robed, blowing with seven trumpets of rams' horns; next the ark of God, hidden by its coverings from the gaze of Israelite and Canaanite alike; and last the tribe of Dan, bringing up the rear.

Toward the city this strange procession made its way, preserving an absolute silence, except that the priests went on continually and blew with the trumpets. With that exception no other sound was heard. No challenge! No taunt! No cry as of those who shout for mastery! The entire host wound silently around the city as a serpent, and when the circuit was completed, to the surprise of the Canaanites, who probably expected an immediate assault, it returned quietly to the camp from which it had emerged some hour or two before. And the rest of the day passed without further incident. 'So they did six days.'

On the seventh day, the circuit of the walls was repeated seven times. And at the close of the seventh, Joshua's voice rang out on the still evening air the command, 'Shout, for the LORD hath given you the city.' Then the priests blew a blast on the trumpets; the people shouted with a great shout that reverberated through the hills around, and was perhaps answered by the feebler voices of the women and children from the camp; and the walls of Jericho fell down to the ground, so that the people could go up into the city, 'and they took the city.'

In various directions we may find a counterpart of this remarkable incident.

## 1   In Christian experience

If Egypt represents our conflicts with the world, and Amalek our conflict with the flesh, the seven nations of Canaan represent our conflict with the principalities and powers of wicked spirits who resist our entrance into the heavenlies and dull our practical realisation of what Christ has wrought for us. Entrenched behind the ramparts of some stronghold of difficulty or habit, they defy us and threaten to arrest our progress in the divine life. Who is there among us, or who reads these lines, who does not know, or has not known, of something – a cherished indulgence, a friendship, a pernicious entanglement – reared as an impassable barrier to the enjoyment of those blessed possibilities of Christian experience which are ours in Christ, but which for that reason seem beyond our reach? That thing is a Jericho.

Again, it may be asked, who is there who has not stood, at some period or another, before a Jericho, right in the pass to Canaan? To all such there is comfort in the word spoken by the great Captain to Joshua, standing with bared foot on the holy ground, 'See I have given into thine hand Jericho, and the king thereof, and the mighty men of valour.'

*a.  Be still!*   The hardest of all commandments is this! That our voice should not be heard; that no word should proceed from our mouth; that we should utter our complaints to God alone – all this is foreign to our habits and taste.

It is only the still heart that can reflect the heaven of God's overarching care. Only when we have quieted ourselves as weaned babes can we reach that position in which God can interpose for our help. 'Be still,' says God, 'and know that I am God.' And that soul may well be still and wait, which has learned that the Lord of hosts is beside it, and the God of Jacob its refuge. To that Friend it hastens to pour out its secret agony. In that home it nestles as in the cover of a great rock, sheltered from the blast.

*b. Obey!*    As in this story so in grace, there must be co-opera-tion between God and man. The walls of Jericho could fall down only by the exercise of divine power, but the children of Israel had to encompass them. Only God can give a body as it has pleased him to the seed corn, but man must plough, and sow, and reap, and thresh, and grind. Only God can remove the difficulties that stand in the way of an entirely consecrated and blessed life, but there are commands and duties which we must fulfil.

What are these? In some cases we are withholding obedience that we should give at once. There are things that we ought to do, but which we are not doing. And there is equal danger in doing more than we should – endeavouring to scale walls we are told to encompass; shouting before the word of command has been given; making the circuit of the city more often than the once each day prescribed by the divine ordering.

Whatever then is clearly revealed to us as the will of God, either for us to do or discontinue doing, let us immediately respond, and leave it to him to do all the rest.

*c. Have faith!*    Look from all your preparations, and even from your God-commanded acts to God himself; and as you do so, your difficulties will melt away – that stone will be rolled from the mouth of the sepulchre; that iron gate will open of its own accord; those mighty walls will fall down.

Believe that he is working for you, and all who know you will be compelled to confess that the Lord has done great things for you. He has given you Jericho. Let your heart dwell on that word. Though the walls are yet standing, they are as good as gone; and with their ruins behind you, you can go forward to possess the land.

## 2   In Christian work

The apostle speaks of strongholds that had to be cast down, and of high things that exalted themselves against the knowledge of God. He also asserts that he did not war against such things according to the flesh, and that the weapons of his warfare were not of the flesh, but were mighty before God for the casting down of strongholds, and for the bringing of every high and proud thought into captivity to the obedience of Christ.

What need there is for all Christian workers to ponder these pregnant words! The peril of our time is that we should get away from the simplicity of the early church, which went into the conflict with the mighty superstitions and flagrant sins of its age, with no weapons except those that may be found in symbol in this old-world incident. There were the white robes of priestly purity; the lifting up of the propitiation of Christ; the blowing of the ram's horn; the gospel message proclaimed with no silver cadence, but with rude and startling effect, as a summons to surrender.

With what dismay would the confessors and martyrs, the prophets and apostles of early Christianity view the methods with which we assail the monster forms of vice that confront us!

When confronted with all these things, we are apt to fight the world with weapons borrowed from its arsenals and to adopt methods that savour rather of the flesh than of the spirit. It is a great mistake. Our only hope is to act on strictly spiritual lines. If we can overthrow the dark spirits that abet and maintain, we will see the system that they support crumble as a palace of clouds before the wind.

Let us be pure and holy, giving time to heart searching in the presence of the Captain; let us lift up the sacrifice and work of Jesus; let us blow the gospel trumpet of alarm and summons to surrender; let us be much in silent prayer before God; let us cherish a spirit of unity and love, as the tribes of Israel forgot their differences in one common exedition against their foes; above all, let us believe in the presence and co-operation of God, and we will see the old miracle repeated, and the walls of Jericho fall down.

# 6

# Arrest and Defeat

## Joshua 7:1–2

The conquest of Canaan occupied seven years, and during the whole of that time Israel lost but one battle; indeed, the thirty-six men killed in headlong flight before the men of Ai seem to have been the only loss their hosts sustained. The story of this defeat is told with great detail because it involved lessons of the greatest importance to Israel, and of incalculable value to ourselves.

The experience of defeat is far too common to the majority of Christians. They do not lie on their faces before God, eager to discover the cause of failure, to deal with it, and to advance from the scene of defeat to wider and more permanent success. If we but carefully investigated the causes of our defeats, they would be second only to victories in their blessed results on our characters and lives.

There were three causes for this defeat.

### 1   They were self-confident because Ai was small

Jericho was a heap of smouldering ruins. Man and woman, both young and old, and ox, and sheep, and ass – all had been utterly destroyed with the edge of the sword.

Fearing no attack from the rear, Joshua at once set his face toward the interior of the country, and chose a deep gorge or ravine, which lay a little toward the north, as the route for his army. Eight miles from its opening on the Jordan valley this ravine met another, and near the junction of the two stood the little town of Ai, with a population of twelve thousand persons. The proportion of fighting men has been calculated at about two thousand, but they were strong and commanded the pass, so that Joshua had no alternative but to mete out to Ai the same terrible fate as that with which he had visited Jericho.

Speaking after the manner of men, there was considerable force in the report of the spies sent up the valley to reconnoitre. The place was much smaller than Jericho, and would apparently require much less expenditure of time and strength for its capture. Jericho may have needed the entire host; but for Ai some three thousand men would surely suffice. 'Make not all the people to toil thither; for they [*i.e.*, the men of Ai] are but few.'

But this recommendation went on the supposition that Jericho had been over thrown by the attack of the hosts of Israel; whereas actually they had had singularly little to do with it. They had walked around it and shouted – that was all. It had been taken by their great Captain and Leader, and by him given into their hands. To speak as they did was to ignore the real facts of the case, and to argue as though the victory were due to some inherent qualities in themselves; with the inference that because they had conquered at Jericho they must therefore necessarily conquer at Ai.

There is no experience in the Christian life so full of peril as the hour when we are flushed with recent victory. Counting from our great triumph at Jericho, we despise such a small obstacle as Ai. Surely, we argue, if we have carried the one, we shall easily prevail at the other! And so it frequently happens that a great success in public is followed by a fall in private. We never so need to observe the injunction to 'watch and pray' as when the foe is flying before us.

There is nothing small in Christian life – nothing so small that we can combat it in our own strength. The victories we have won in fellowship with God have imparted no inherent might to us; we are as weak as ever; and as soon as we are brought into collision with the least of our enemies, apart from him, we shall inevitably go down before the shock. The faith, watchfulness, and fellowship with God, which availed before Jericho, can alone serve as the key to Ai.

## 2   They failed to wait on God

An accursed thing in their midst broke the link of fellowship between them and the hosts that served beneath the celestial

Warrior who had appeared to Joshua. There is not the least doubt that if Joshua had been in abiding fellowship with God, the Spirit of God would have indicated the presence of evil in the host, and then Achan and his sin would have been discovered and judged before the march to Ai.

God sees the little tear in the cloth; the spot of decay in the fruit; the ulcer in the flesh, threatening to eat away its vitality. These may not be realised by us, but he knows how inevitably they must lead to defeat. Nor is he slow to warn us of them. Yet of what use is it for him to speak to deaf ears; or to those who are self-confident in their own wisdom; or to those who pride themselves on victories that were wholly his gift?

Where God's children, like Joshua, are oblivious to the warning voices that speak in every fainter tones as they are disregarded, God is compelled to let them take their course until some terrible disaster flings them on their faces to the ground. Ah, if Joshua had only prostrated himself amid the shoutings of victory over Jericho, there would have been no need for him to prostrate himself amid the outcry of a panic-stricken host!

Before we make some new advance, although the point of attack be but an Ai, it is our duty, as it is our best policy, to get back to Gilgal. We ought to seclude ourselves in spiritual converse with our almighty Confederate; asking him to reveal any evil thing that he may see in us, and mustering the tribes of our heart before his scrutiny, that the Achan lurking there may be brought to light before, instead of after, the fight.

## 3   They had committed a trespass 'in the devoted thing'

*a. Joshua was inclined to lay the charge of their failure on God.* But, in point of fact, the blame lay not with God, but wholly with themselves.

There are times in our lives when we are disposed to find fault with God. 'Why have you made me this say? Why was I ever taken out of my quiet home, or country parish, or happy niche of service, to be plunged into this sea of difficulties?' When we are smarting from some defeat, caused by the overpowering might or the clever strategy of the foe, we are prone to blame God. Our Father brings us across the Jordan to give us larger experiences, to open before us vaster possibilities, to give us a better chance of acquiring his unsearchable riches. There is no task without sufficiency of grace.

The defeats we incur in the Land of Promise are not necessary. There is no reason for defeat in the Christian life; always, and everywhere we are meant to be more than conquerors. Child of God, never lay the blame of your failure on God; seek for it within!

*b. Not one of us stands alone; we cannot sin without insensibly affecting the spiritual condition of all our fellowmen.* One Israelite only had trespassed, and yet it is said, '*The children of Israel* committed a trespass in the devoted thing.'

If Israel had but realised how much the safety of the whole depended on the obedience of each, every individual would have watched his brethren, as he watched himself, not for their sakes alone, but for his own; and if the members of Christian communities would understand how vast an influence for good or bad depends on the choice, the decision, the action of any, there would be a fuller and more intelligent obedience to the reiterated injunctions of the New Testament – for the strong to bear the infirmities of the weak; and for all to look not on their own things only, but also on the things of others.

Should these words be read by any person who is conscious of playing an Achan's part, take warning, and while it is called 'today', confess, restore, and repent. Do this not only that you may escape an inevitable judgment, but also that you may not bring disaster and defeat on those with whom you associate, dragging the innocent down into the vortex of a common fate. The hands of Achan were stained with the blood of the thirty-six who perished in the flight to Shebarim.

*c. How careless we are of God's distinct prohibitions!* Nothing could have been more clearly promulgated than the command to leave the spoils of Jericho untouched. The city and its contents were devoted to utter destruction, only a specified number of artices being preserved for tabernacle use. But to Achan, the will of God was overborne by the lust of his eyes and the pride of life. The strong tide of passion swept over the barrier reared by the divine word.

'Israel hath sinned, and they have also transgressed my covenant which I commanded them: for they have even taken of the

accursed thing. . . Therefore . . . they cannot stand . . . before
their enemies . . . neither will I be with you any more, except ye
destroy the accursed from among you.'

# 7

# The Valley of Achor

## Joshua 7

Was it a sudden gust of temptation that swept Achan before it
when, with the rest of the host, he entered Jericho? This, at least,
is clear, that in the late afternoon of the day of Jericho's capture,
he had pilfered one of those robes of exquisite texture for which
the plain of Shinar was famous, together with gold and silver – the
latter coined, the former in a wedge – and had carried them sur-
reptitiously away.

We can imagine him bringing them into his tent. He dug a hole
in the sand and hid the spoil, which by the special order of Joshua
had been devoted to Jehovah.

The whole proceeding had been conducted in such absolute
secrecy, and he was so confident of the collusion of the inmates of
his tent, that amid the general inquiry for the thief he braved
detection and held his peace until the unerring finger of God
pointed him out, as if he said, 'Thou art the man!'

### 1   We should grieve more for sin than for its results

Joshua tore his clothes and fell to the earth on his face before the
ark of the Lord until evening. He was smarting from the disgrace
inflicted on his people, and aghast at the results that would probably ensue as soon as the tidings had been voiced abroad. Judging
simply by human standards, the worst consequences might be
expected when the nations of Canaan suddenly discovered that

the Israelite hosts were not invulnerable. This was Joshua's fear, that the Canaanites and all the inhabitants of the land should hear of it, and encircle them, and cut off their name from the earth.

We dread the consequences of sin, more than the sin itself; what others may say and do, more than the look of pain and sorrow on the face that looks out on us from the encircling throng of glorified spirits.

But it is not so with God. It is our sin that presses him down, as a cart groans beneath its load. Few of us realise what sin is, because we have had no experience of a character without it, either in ourselves or in others.

It is, of course, possible to learn something of the exceeding sinfulness of sin by viewing the agony, heartbreak, and shame, of the dying Lord; by remembering its infinite cost to the love of God. And yet the true way to a proper realisation of sin is to cultivate the friendship of the holy God. The more we know him, the more completely we will enter into his thought about the subtle evil of our heart. We will find sin lurking where we least expected it. We will learn that every look, tone, gesture, word, thought, which is not consistent with perfect love, indicate that the virus of sin has not yet been expelled from our nature; and we will come to mourn not so much for the results of sin, as for the sin itself. This is the godly sorrow that does not need to be repented of.

## 2   We should submit ourselves to the judgment of God

'And the LORD said unto Joshua, Get thee up; wherefore liest thou thus upon thy face?' It was as if he had said, 'You grieve for the effect; grieve rather for the cause.'

Whenever there is perpetual failure in our life, we may be sure that there is some secret evil lurking in heart and life. Somewhere there is a fault in the insulation of the wire through which the currents of divine power and grace come to us; and it is useless to pray that they may be renewed until we have repaired the defect. It is not a question of God's willingness or unwillingness, but of the laws of the spiritual world that make him unable to ally himself with consciously-permitted sin.

*a. In searching out the causes of failure, we must be willing to know the worst.*   As we bare ourselves to the good Physician, let us remember that he desires to indicate the source of our sorrow

only to remove it. 'Be still and know.' The responsibility of showing you your mistake is wholly with him, if you have placed all in
his hands. Leave it there and wait. If he has anything to say, he will
say it clearly, unmistakably, and certainly. If he says nothing, it is
because the set time has not come. But tomorrow in the morning,
it may be, he will speak to you and tell you all. In the meanwhile,
wait and trust.

*b. When God deals with sin he traces back its genealogy.*     To
deal with it thoroughly, we need to go back to its parentage. We
generally deal with the wrong that flames out before the sight of
our fellowmen; we should go behind to the spark as it smoulders
for hours, and to the carelessness that left it there. And by this
insight into small beginnings, our God would forearm us against
great catastrophes.

What we call sin is the outcome of sin permitted, days –
perhaps weeks – before; which, during that time has been gathering strength within the heart. If we would be kept clear from great
transgression, we must see to it that we are cleared from hidden
faults, so subtle and microscopic that they would elude any but a
conscience kept sensitive by the grace of the Holy Spirit.

*c. It is a good thing at times to muster the traits of heart and
life.*     We must make the principal tribes of our being pass before
God – the public and private; our behaviour in the business, the
family, the church – until one of them is taken. Then examine that
department, going through its various aspects and engagements,
analysing it in days or duties; resolving it into its various elements; and scrutinizing each.

This duty of self-examination should be pursued by those who
have least relish for it, as most likely they really need it; while
those who are naturally of an introspective disposition will probably apply themselves to the task without being reminded of the
necessity of so doing, and should guard against its excess and
abuse. Whoever undertakes it should do so in reliance on the
Holy Spirit; and give ten glances to the blessed Lord for everyone
that is taken at the corruptions of the natural heart. It is 'looking
off unto Jesus' which is the real secret of soul-growth.

### 3    We should hold no conference with discovered sin

'And Joshua, and all Israel with him, took Achan the son of

Zerah, and the silver, and the garment, and the wedge of gold, and his sons, and his daughters, and his oxen, and his asses, and his sheep, and his tent, and all that he had: and they brought them unto the valley of Achor. . . And all Israel stoned him with stones, and burned them with fire, after they had stoned them with stones.' Then Jehovah repeated the words that had preceded the capture of Jericho, 'And the LORD said unto Joshua, Fear not! . . . see, I have given into thy hand the king of Ai, and his people, and his city, and his land.'

Then up the long, narrow passage Joshua marched with thirty thousand men – the mighty men of valour. There was a sense in every breast of an integrity that had put away all cause of failure and defeat. The preparations were skilfully made; the appearance of flight on the part of Israel brought the men of Ai to headlong pursuit; and the city was left at the mercy of the ambush, which at the sign of Joshua's uplifted javelin arose, entered the city, and set it on fire. And in that place where Israel had met with so disastrous a defeat, the people took great spoil, especially of cattle, which they drove down in triumph to the camp at Gilgal.

So the Valley of Achor became 'the Door of Hope.' Ah! the metaphor as true as fair! for all our inner life there is no Valley of Achor where the work of execution is faithfully performed, in which there is not a door of hope – entrance into the garden of the Lord; and a song so sweet, so joyous, so triumphant, that it would seem as if the buoyancy of youth were wed with the experience and mellowness of age.

# 8

# Ebal and Gerizim

## Joshua 8:30

This was one of the most impressive scenes that occurred during the occupation of Canaan. Jericho and Ai were heaps of blackened ruins; their kings and people utterly destroyed; their dependent villages mute with terror. And all through the land the rumour ran of the might of Israel's God. The nations of Canaan appear to have been so panic-stricken that they offered no resistance as all Israel went on a pilgrimage of thirty miles to perform a religious duty.

'It shall be', so the word stood, 'on the day when ye shall pass over Jordan unto the land which the LORD thy God giveth thee, that thou shalt set thee up great stones, and plaster them with plaster: and thou shalt write upon them all the words of this law' (Deut. 11:26–32; 27:2). Joshua lost no time in obeying these minute and urgent injunctions; and within two or three days after the fall of Ai – perhaps within three weeks of the passage of the Jordan – the people were assembled in the valley of Shechem, sentinelled on the north by the sterile slopes of Ebal, and on the south by its twin-giant Gerizim.

The valley between these two is one of the most beautiful in Palestine. Jacob's Well lies at its mouth, and all its luxuriant extent is covered with the verdant beauty of gardens, and orchards, and olive groves, rolling in waves of billowy beauty up to the walls of Shechem; while the murmur of brooks flowing in all directions fills the air. There Joshua led the people that, by a solemn act, they might take possession of the land for God.

## 1 The altar on Ebal

Ebal was stern and barren in its aspect. There was a congruity therefore between its appearance and the part it played in the solemn proceedings of the day. For far up its slopes gathered the dense masses of the six tribes who, with thunderous Amens, repeated twelve times, answered the voices of the band of white-robed Levites, as standing with Joshua and the elders and officers and judges in the green valley, they solemnly repeated the curses of the law.

But that was not the first proceeding in the holy ceremonial. Before the people took up their assigned places on the mountain sides, an altar was reared on the lower slopes of Ebal. Special directions as to its construction had been given in Deuteronomy 27. It was to be built of unhewn stones, on which no iron tool had been lifted. This was probably to guard against any attempt to set forth the likeness of God, and to show disapproval of the florid and lascivious ornamentations of which the surrounding heathen were so fond.

There they offered burnt offerings and sacrificed peace offerings. The *burnt offering* was what was known as a sweet savour offering. The entire victim was burned. 'It was an offering made by fire, of a sweet savour unto the LORD' (Lev. 1). In this the Holy Ghost signified our duty to present ourselves without reserve to God.

The *peace offering* also belonged to the sweet savour offerings, but it was not wholly consumed; a part was eaten by the offerers, to testify that in it they had fellowship and communion with God. In the sight of Israel, therefore, Joshua and other chosen representatives partook of portions of the sacrifices, and obeyed the divine injunction, 'Thou shalt eat there, and thou shalt rejoice before the LORD thy God.'

As we pass into the Land of Promise we must see to it that we do not leave behind the devout and loving consideration of that precious blood by which we have been redeemed and which is our life.

Since he died, we need never stand on the mount of cursing. Because he counted not his life dear to himself, those gaunt and forbidding slopes have become the scene of blessed communion with God. We sit and feast with him, and from peak to peak joy chases the terrors of the curse. Because he shed his blood, there will be 'dew, and rain, and fields of offerings', even on Ebal; until its terraced slopes resemble those of the opposite mount of blessing.

## 2   The Law in Canaan

Around the altar strong men reared great stones, and plastered them with a facing of cement, composed of lime or gypsum, on which it was easy to write all the words of the law plainly (Deut. 27:8). In that dry air, where there is no frost to split and disintegrate, such inscriptions would remain for centuries. As time could not have permitted the inscription of the whole law, it is probable that the more salient points were alone committed to the custody of those great stones, to perpetuate to generations following the conditions of the tenure on which Israel held the lease of Palestine.

But when we turn from the literal to the metaphorical, and ask for the underlying typical meaning of this inscription of the law in so prominent a position in the Land of Promise, we are at first startled. What can it mean? Is there a connection after all between law and grace? Are those who sit with Christ in heavenly places still amenable to law – 'under the law', as the apostle puts it?

There is but one answer to all these questions. We are not looking to our obedience to merit the favour of God, or to win any of the blessings of the gospel. But it is also true that faith does not make the law of God of no effect.

When we yield ourselves entirely to the Spirit of life which is in Christ Jesus, and which passes freely through us, as the blood through artery and vein, he makes us very sensitive to the least commandment or desire of him whom he has taught us to love; and so insensibly while we yield ourselves to him, we find ourselves keeping the law after a fashion that was foreign to us when it was a mere outward observance, and we cry with the psalmist, 'O how love I thy law! it is my meditation all the day' (Ps. 119:97).

## 3   The convocation

When these rites were fulfilled, the third and concluding scene of this extraordinary transaction took place. In the centre of the valley the ark rested, with its group of attendant priests and Levites. Nearby were Joshua and the leaders of the tribes, elders, officers, and judges. Then up the slopes of Ebal, finding seats on its terraced sides, were Reuben, Gad and Asher, and Zebulun, Dan, and Naphtali; while up the slopes of Gerizim were the larger and more important tribes of Simeon, and Levi and Judah, and Issachar, and Joseph, and Benjamin. It was as though the voice of blessing had to be louder than that of cursing – a prediction of its final prevalence and triumph.

Then Joshua read aloud 'all the words of the law, the blessings and cursings, according to all that is written in the book of the law'. And as he solemnly read, whether the blessing or the curse, each item was responded to by the Amens that thundered forth from thousands of throats, and rolled in reverberating echoes through the hills. Earth has seldom heard such shouts as those!

It is well worth our while to ponder the list of blessings appended to obedience in that memorable twenty-eighth chapter of Deuteronomy, that we may discover their spiritual counterparts and, having found them, claim them.

Nor can we better close our meditation than by asking that the Holy Spirit may so indwell and guide us that we may choose what he ordains, and not swerve by a hair's breadth to the right or left of the narrow path of obedience; keeping his commandments; obeying his biddings; perfectly conformed to his will. Thus will Ebal cease to frown, and Gerizim rain its blessings on us.

# 9

# A Memorable Day

## Joshua 10:14

'There was no day like that.' It stood alone in the history of the conquest, and of Joshua. Let us notice:

## 1   The confederacy that was gathered against Israel

Israel had previously dealt with separate cities, Jericho and Ai; but now five kings of the Amorites joined together, namely the kings of Jerusalem, Hebron, Jarmuth, Lachish, and Eglon.

The traitor city of Gibeon was the object of the attack of the combined forces. This was due partly because its defection had aroused the fiercest animosity of its former allies, and partly that by its occupation they might be able to interpose one further barrier to the invasion of the Israelites. The royal city of Gibeon lay only six miles to the north of Jerusalem.

Suddenly the men of Gibeon found themselves surrounded by a vast host of infuriated warriors who, not daring to measure themselves against Joshua, were all the more eager to execute their vengeance on those who had dared to make a league with him. Relying on Joshua's fidelity to the covenant so recently formed, a message was sent in breathless haste, summoning him to their help.

## 2   Joshua's heroic faith

There had been great days in his life before but there had never been a day in his life quite like this.

*a. It was a day of vigour.*   As soon as he received the message, he saw the importance of at once vindicating the trust reposed in him. Before the sun went down, orders had passed through the camp that the men of war should be ready for a midnight march; and at dead of night he climbed the pass from Gilgal to Gibeon – fifteen difficult miles – and came on the sleeping host suddenly before they had had time to prepare themselves for fight. Inertness and indolence ill become those who are entrusted with great concerns.

*b. It was a day of fellowship.*   There must have been hard fighting all morning. It was dawn when the battle began, and it would have been toward afternoon when the kings gave the signal for retreat; and the Canaanites, unable longer to sustain the successive onsets of Israel, charging to the battle cry of 'Jehovah, mighty in battle', broke into flight like a flock of panic-stricken sheep. Ten miles they fled, climbing a precipitous ascent to the high ridge of Beth-horon the Upper. From that point the road drops, broken and rugged, seven hundred feet in two miles. The rock is cut into steps. Down this breakneck steep the fugitives fled to reach, if only they might, their fastness and citadels, which lay in the valley below, and longed for night to put a pause on the anguish of the pursuit. It was at this point that the storm, of which we will speak presently, burst on them with irresistible fury, as if the whole artillery of heaven had suddenly opened fire. Over the hills of Gibeon the sun was setting. It needed only an hour or two and its sudden disappearance would bring on the rapid Eastern twilight, while the moon's pale face appearing over the purple waters of the great sea was waiting to lead on the night.

It was under these circumstances that Joshua dared to ask an unprecedented gift of God – that the day might be prolonged.

There are high days in human lives when thought and purpose, which had been quietly gathering strength, suddenly leap from their leash and vent themselves in acts, or words, or prayers. In such hours we realise what Jesus meant when he said, 'Whosoever shall say unto this mountain, be thou removed and be thou cast into the sea; and shall not doubt in his heart, but shall believe that those things which he saith shall come to pass; he shall have whatsoever he saith' (Mark 11:23).

*c. It was a day of triumphant onlook.* Discomfited, weary, vanquished, the kings took shelter in the cave at Makkedah; but Joshua did not stay to send them away; he was too eager to finish what he had begun, and to prevent the Canaanites from reentering their cities. So he took measures to keep them imprisoned in the cave until his return. Presently, flushed with victory, and with (as Josephus tells us) the loss of hardly a single life, he came again. The kings were summoned from their hiding place; and as they crouched abjectly at the feet of their conquerors, Joshua called for all the men of Israel, and said to the chiefs of the men of war, 'Come near, put your feet upon the necks of these kings.'

### 3　The extraordinary interposition of Jehovah

The storm that broke in that late afternoon over the rugged descent to Beth-horon was no common one. Oriental hailstones are of great size: it is said that sometimes lumps of ice, of a pound or more in weight, will fall; and these would naturally kill any on whom they fell. But the remarkable thing in this case was that the storm broke in a moment when its fury could be spent on the Amorites without inflicting injury on Israel. 'It came to pass, as they fled from before Israel, and were in the going down to Beth-horon, that the LORD cast down great stones from heaven upon them unto Azekah, and they died: they were more which died with hailstones than they whom the children of Israel slew with the sword.'

But the stupendous miracle of the day consisted in the arrest of daylight. We place no limit to the divine power. We need not hesitate to accept any well-accredited marvel, but neither should we fail to believe that God could make the clock of the universe stop, if it were necessary that it should do so.

But it is not necessary to believe that he did this. By some process the laws of which are at present unknown to us, but of which we get glimpses, in refraction, in the afterglow of sunset, in the fantastic appearances familiar to travellers in high altitudes and among the loftiest mountains – God was able to prolong the day-light until Israel had finished slaying their foes, so that only a deci-mated remnant entered into the fenced cities. The *how* is not important to our present discussion. It is enough to express our belief in the fact itself. Somehow, the duration of that day's light was lengthened out until the people had avenged themselves of their enemies.

Our present purpose does not require us to follow the steps of the conquerors as they passed from city to city. All were treated with the same unsparing severity. The kings were slain, their bodies gibbeted till the evening; and all the souls smitten, so that none were left remaining, an utter destruction of all and every one by the edge of the sword.

We must remember that the Israelites were the executioners of divine justice, commissioned to give effect to the sentence which the foul impurities of Canaan called for. There is a judgment seat for nations as well as for individuals. And the almighty Judge sees to it that his sentences are carried out.


## 4   The lesson for our own life

There are days so extraordinary for the combination of difficult circumstances, human opposition, and spiritual conflict, that they stand out in unique terror from the rest of our lives. But these days do not come, if we are living in fellowship with God, intent on doing his will, without their coming also his sweet 'Fear them not; for I have delivered them into thine hands!' Our only anxiety should be that nothing divert us from his path, or intercept the communication of his grace. Like a wise commander, we must keep open the passage back to our base of operations, which is God. Careful about that, we need have no anxiety beside.

Moreover, these days may always be full of the realised presence of God. All through the conflict, Joshua's heart was in perpetual fellowship with the mighty Captain of the Lord's host, who rode beside him all the day. So amid all our conflicts, our hearts and minds should there ascend, and there dwell where Christ is seated, drawing from him grace on grace, as we need. Let us put the whole matter into the hands of God, asking him to go before us, to fight for us, to deliver us, as he did for his people on this eventful day. In all such days we may have light that cannot be accounted for on any natural hypothesis. Only let us seek the grace of the Holy Spirit, that we may be kept in such an attitude of soul that we will miss nothing of God's gracious and timely help.

# 10

# A Veteran Comrade

## *Joshua 14*

It was in Gilgal that the apportionment of Canaan took place. There, where the reproach of Egypt had been rolled away, and where the main camp had stood, it was fitting that the rewards of victory should be meted out. It was a great epoch in Israelite story, as the tribes assembled around their veteran leader. Before Joshua and Eleazar stood the urns, the one containing the name of each, and the other the name of some specified portion of that fair land that lay all around.

Judah, first in war and march, was the first to draw near. It was a great people, and was destined yet to play a greater part in the history of Israel and of mankind. But an incident intercepted the casting of the lot that calls for earnest heed; stand still, then, O Christian soul, and see some counterpart of yourself in your best moments, in this demand of the gay headed warrior, this lion's whelp, for that is the underlying thought in the name 'Caleb'. Strong, bold, heroic, there was a great deal of the lion in him beside his name. He had been the young lion of the tribe of Judah some fifty years before, but he was as strong as he stepped out of the ranks of Judah to claim his right as he was when Moses sent him to spy out the land.

### 1    The prime characteristic of Caleb's early life had been his entire devotion to God

Repeatedly we are told both of him and Joshua that they 'wholly followed the LORD'. And there was some trace of this in the words of the old man as he addressed the comrade of many a hard-fought fight, of many a weary march. The rest of the spies had turned aside, dismayed by the spectacle of giants, and walled-up cities, and vast battle array. They had ceased to keep the eye steadfastly fixed on the movements of God's will, and on the might of his hand; and instead of following hard after him, they had yielded to panic and made the hearts of the people melt.

But there had been no panic in the heart of Caleb. He had only been considering that, when God delights in men, he brings them into the land of milk and honey, and makes it theirs by deed of gift.

He followed God completely through the weary years that ensued. Amid the marchings and counter-marchings, the innumerable deaths, the murmurings and rebellions of the people, he retained a steadfast purpose to do only God's will, to please him, to know no other leader, and to heed no other voice. Always strong, and true, and pure, and noble; a man in whose strong nature weaker men could hide.

And two things lit the path of this Greatheart, amid the gloom of the wanderings and the chaos of the conquest. There was first the consciousness that lay on his heart, like sunshine on a summer ocean, that God delighted in him; that the outgoings of God's nature toward him were full of love and joy; and that the peace of God that passes all understanding might be his inalienable possession.

There was next the thought of Hebron. Forty-five years had passed since he had seen the white buildings of that ancient and holy city nestling beneath its terebinths. Hebron, beneath whose oaks Abraham had pitched his tent; Hebron, whose soil had been trodden by the feet of the incarnate God, as with two angel attendants, he visited the tent of Abraham; Hebron, where Sarah and Abraham, Isaac and Rebekah, Jacob and Leah, lay buried; each in a little niche, holding the land in trust, as the graves of the dead always hold the land for the living, until the promise of God was realised, and the seed of Abraham could return to claim its heritage.

God had read his secret, and had arranged that what his heart loved best his hand should take, and hold, and keep. Often, as he lay down to sleep beside the campfire, his last thought would be of Hebron; and amid the noontide haze, when the mirage gleamed on the horizon, it would sometimes seem to him as if the green hills of Hebron were calling to him across the waste.

We have trace of the attitude of Caleb's heart through those long years in the words he spoke at this memorable juncture, when he said: 'Behold, the Lord hath kept me alive, *as he said. . .* Now therefore give me this mountain, *whereof the LORD spake* in that day . . . as the LORD said.' The promise of God was his stay and comfort and exceeding great reward. He had to wait for its fulfilment, and it seemed long; as waiting times always do, especially when man waits for God. But God was working for him while he was waiting.

## 2 Such devotion as Caleb's has marvellous results

*a. It is the soil from which such a faith springs as can claim the realisation of promise.* 'Now therefore give me this mountain, whereof the LORD spake in that day.' No common faith was needed to make so large a claim. Think of the Anakim that held it in their giant hands! But faith triumphed; and if the words, 'It may be', come into his speech, words with a falter in them, the tremor, as it were, of fear, we must understand that they did not spring from any doubt of God; but of that mistrust of self which is a trait in all moral greatness. There is waiting for you an inheritance – some promised Hebron, some blessed gift of God's infinite love in Christ. It is for you to say, with the faith of a Caleb, 'Give me this mountain'.

**b.** *It leads to fellowship.*    Hebron stands for friendship, fellowship, love. The old word means that, and perhaps that is why Caleb was so eager to strike out the recent giant's name of Kirjath-arba, and to bring back the word that Abraham had often had on his lips. It spoke to him of that communion with his unseen Friend whom he had enjoyed through the wanderings and vicissitudes of his long life, and which was not to end now; because in the seclusion of his estate, beneath the shadow of his own vine and fig tree, he would speak with him as a man with his friend.

Those who follow God know him. He turns and sees them following, and hears their inquiry to know his secret place, and bids them 'Come and see'.

**c.** *It leads to strength.*    'Lo', said Caleb, 'I am this day fourscore and five years old. As yet I am as strong this day as I was in the day that Moses sent me: as my strength was then, even so is my strength now, for war, both to go out, and to come in.' Consecration is the source of undecaying strength. The soul must learn to take the power that God gives to the faint, and to receive the strength he increases to such as have no might.

But this strength is accessible only through obedience. God cannot and will not bestow it except where there is a thoughtful and deliberate purpose to do his will, to follow his path, and to execute his work.

**d.** *It gives victory.*    Of all the Israelites who received their inheritance in the Land of promise, Caleb appears to have been the only one who succeeded in perfectly expelling the native occupants of the country. The Israelites generally seem to have made poor headway against their strong and mighty foes, with their chariots of iron and fenced walls. Repeatedly we encounter the sorrowful affirmation, *they were not able to drive them out.* But Caleb was a notable exception. The man who wholly followed the Lord was alone wholly victorious.

How precious and searching is the conclusion! Our failures in expelling the giants of the heart, in dealing with inbred corruption and the assaults of Satan, are almost entirely due to some failure in consecration. But when, so far as we know, we are entirely yielded to God, then no sin can stand before us, because nothing can stand before him.

*e. It enables us to give blessings to others.* Twice we are told how Achsah got off her donkey to ask a blessing from her father's hands. 'Give me also springs of water. And he gave her the upper springs, and the nether springs.'

Follow the Lord fully: so will you dwell in the land; so will you be able to obtain promises, not for yourself only, but also for others. The Othniels and Achsahs of your home circle will gather around you to ask a blessing, and you will have power to open springs of spiritual blessing in the heights of the heavenly places, and in the depths of daily practical ministry, in the valley of human life.

# 11

# The Conclusion of the Task

## Joshua 18

The two great tribes were thus at last settled – Judah, as Dean Stanley suggests, like a lion to guard the south, and couch in the fastness of Zion; while Ephraim, like the more peaceful but not less powerful bullock, was to rove the rich vales of central Palestine, and defend the frontier of the north. And Joshua was able to turn his attention to the several items that claim a passing notice.

## 1  Joshua erected the tabernacle in Shiloh

During the march through the wilderness, when the camp was pitched, the tabernacle occupied the centre of the camp. Around it were grouped the tents of the priests and Levites, while the tribes occupied specified places, three to each quarter of the compass. An attentive comparison of those positions with the territories allocated to them in the Land of Promise will reveal a striking similarity. It was as though the encampment were, in its main features, repeated in their final settlement in the land. And to complete the parallel, the tabernacle was now removed from Gilgal and pitched in Shiloh, which lay as nearly as possible at the heart of Canaan.

Here, then, in the centre of the land, embosomed in the keeping of the strongest tribes, on the east side of the highway that led from Bethel to Shechem, was the chosen spot where the tabernacle of God was among men; and he dwelled with them.

## 2   Joshua rebuked the inertness of the people

And Joshua said to the children of Israel, 'How long are ye slack to go in to possess the land, which the LORD God of your fathers hath given you?' (18:3). At that point the twenty-one commissioners arose to walk through the land and surveyed it. They embodied the results in a book, in which the land was described by cities in seven portions. This they brought to Joshua. It may be that the account of what they had seen was the means under God of arousing the people from the apathy into which they had sunk.

There is the portion of Benjamin, the beloved of the Lord, a place of safety with him, covered all the day long, and borne between his shoulders – the place where Eastern mothers cradle their babes, giving them warmth and easy carriage. There is the portion of Zebulun, to whose shores the illimitable ocean washes the treasures of the deep; in whose heart Gennesaret lies, with its fragrant memories of God manifest in the flesh. There is the portion if Issachar, which derived treasures from the sands, emblems of the precious stones, the pearls and crystals of spiritual character. There is the portion of Asher, the oil of whose wine-presses bespeaks the unction of the Holy Ghost; the strength of whose shoes speaks of that invincible might that treads down serpent and scorpion. There is the portion of Naphtali, satisfied with favour, and full of the blessing of the Lord; owning rich forests, the circle of Galilee, and the garden of Palestine. Each of these is significant of spiritual endowment, which we ought to arise to possess.

Too long have we been slack to go in to possess that fullness of the Holy Spirit that might be in us as a living spring, making us perfectly satisfied; like the fountain in the courtyard of a beleaguered castle that enables the garrison to defy the siege. There is a knowledge of Jesus, a participation in his victory, a realisation of blessedness, which are as much beyond the ordinary experience of Christians as Canaan was better than the wilderness. But how sad, that of all this we know so little.

How much we miss! The nomad life could not afford those seven tribes so much lasting enjoyment as their own freehold in Canaan. But the comparison is utterly inadequate to portray the loss to which we subject ourselves in refusing to appropriate and enjoy the blessedness that is laid up for us in Jesus. Let us come to our Joshua at Shiloh, and ask him to lead us into each of these.

### 3   Joshua received his own inheritance

'[The children of Israel] gave him the city which he asked, even Timnath-serah in mouth Ephraim' (19:50). In the following book it is spoken of as Timnath-heres (Judges 2:9). It was 'the portion of the sun'.

The old veteran had deserved well of his people, and must have been glad to retire to his estate on which the remaining twenty years of his life were spent. And the greatness of his influence may be inferred by considering the evils that overwhelmed Israel when he was taken. His very presence among the people was a restraint. What a significant testimony to his consistency and steadfastness is furnished by the record, 'The people served the Lord all the days of Joshua.'

### 4   Joshua also made provision for the manslayer

Six cities were apportioned, three on each side of the Jordan, easily accessible. There the manslayer, who had killed any person unwittingly and unawares, might flee from the pursuit of the next of kin. Once within the city walls, all breathless with his flight, the manslayer waited at the entering of the gate of the city, until he had stated his case to the elders, who had the right of admitting him provisionally into the city. On the appearance of the avenger of blood, the cause seems to have been finally adjudicated; and if it were clearly shown that there was no animosity in the blow that caused death, the manslayer was permitted to remain there, until the death of the high priest then in office.

Take heart, O Christian soul! you have done many evil things in your ignorance or thoughtlessness. Get thee to the City of Refuge; you will not only be safe, but shall enjoy your inheritance also, for the High Priest has died, and in his death has put away your sin for ever; there is therefore now no condemnation for you, because you are in him.

The Jews killed the Prince of Life, but they did it in ignorance (Acts 3:17–18). Therefore they have lost their heritage; but they exist still as prisoners of hope, finding refuge among the cities of the priests, until such time as the Lord Jesus will inaugurate that new and glorious reign in which he will take to himself the kingdom. Then Israel will return, each to his own house, and to the city he fled from.

### 5   Joshua appointed cities for the Levites

There was an ancient curse hanging over the lots of Simeon and Levi. Brethren by birth, they had been joint perpetrators in a dark crime that had given Jacob, their father, a bad name among the inhabitants of the land, among the Canaanites and Perizzites. The dying patriarch could not forget that deed of treacherous cruelty, and as it rose before his eyes he said:

> Weapons of violence are their swords,
> Cursed be their anger, for it was fierce;
> And their wrath, for it was cruel;
> I will divide them in Jacob,
> And scatter them in Israel.

But this curse was not fulfilled in each case in the same way. With Simeon, it ran its course. Settled at the south of Canaan, between Judah and Philistia, this tribe became more and more nomadic, and finally faded out of corporate existence. In the case of Levi, it was transformed into blessing. At Sinai, when Moses called on all who were loyal to Jehovah to gather in the gate of the camp, the Levites, to a man, answered his appeal. Phinehas, also, who took such decisive action in the matter of Baalpeor, was a Levite. Therefore Jehovah entered into a covenant of life and peace with them, took them as a subsitute for the firstborn sons of Israel, and pledged himself to be their inheritance (Num. 18:20; Josh. 13:33).

At the divine command, forty-eight cities were given to the Levites, with one thousand cubits of pasture land measured outward from the city walls. There they dwelled when not required for temple service, or when they were incapacitated by age from attending to their sacred office.

As Jacob predicted, they were scattered; but the effect was salutary. They permeated the whole land with the hallowing influence of Shiloh. Moreover, the teaching of the law was a special prerogative of the Levites, who appear to have travelled through their apportioned districts.

So the work was finished. 'There failed not aught of any good thing which the LORD had spoken unto the house of Israel; all came to pass' (Josh. 21:43–45).

# 12

# Evensong

## *Joshua 24*

The veteran leader, who was soldier, judge, statesman, and prophet combined, desired to see his people face to face. His meeting with their representatives was therefore followed, almost immediately, by a gathering of all the tribes of Israel to Shechem. It was here they had stood together years before in solemn convocation, while from the heights of Ebal and Gerizim had rolled the Amens of the people in answer to the blessing and the curse.

The stones on which the law had been written were still clearly in evidence, and the whole scene must have come back vividly to the memory of the majority of those assembled. But from that moment the valley would be associated especially with this touching farewell scene in which Joshua uttered his last exhortations and appeals.

## 1   Joshua's narrative

He told again the wonderful story of Israel's past; beginning where God began, with their father in their native land beyond the Euphrates, in the dim dawn of history.

Isaac, Jacob, Esau – names that made the deepest chords vibrate in his hearers' hearts – were successively recalled in the deep hush that had fallen on the vast assembly. Then the speaker reached more familiar ground, as he recalled names and events that had played a part in his own wonderful career – the mission of the two brothers; the plagues of Egypt; the cry and deliverance of the Red Sea; the wilderness; Balak, son of Zippor, and Balaam, son of Beor; the passage of the Jordan; the fall of Jericho; the overthrow of the seven nations of Canaan; the possession of their land.

But throughout the story, the entire stress is laid on the grace of God. *I* too; *I* gave; *I* sent; *I* brought; *I* destroyed; *I* gave; *I* delivered. Not a mention is made of Israel's mighty men. All is attributed to the ultimate source of nature, history, and grace – the supreme will of God.

There is nothing more beneficial than to stand on the height of the years in life's golden evening, and review the way by which our God has led us. The faraway home, where faces glimmer out in the daybreak of life's morning, on which we shall not look again until the veil of eternity rends; the hard bondage of early life; the many difficult situations and deliverances; the guiding cloud of the pilgrimage; the daily provision for incessant needs; the human love; the goodness and mercy that have followed all our days. Ah me! what a romance lies behind the meanest life, of sin and forgiveness, of provocation and pity, of grace and gift! Not one of us that will not hold his own history to be the most wonderful of all, when we exchange experiences in that land that we will not get by our own sword or bow, dwelling in mansions we did not build, eating of vineyards and oliveyards we did not plant.

## 2  Joshua's appeal

It would appear that the people largely maintained the worship of
household gods, like those Rachel stole from Laban. This practice
was probably perpetuated by stealth. But the germs of evil were
only awaiting favourable conditions to manifest themselves, and
Joshua had every reason to dread the further development of the
insidious taint. Therefore, with marked emphasis, Joshua
appealed to the people to put away the gods which Terah and
others of their ancestors had served beyond the river, and those
which they had vainly invoked in the slave huts of Egypt. He did
this first at the close of his address (v. 14), and again just before
the memorable interview closed (v. 23).

## 3  The people's first reply

They professed that they had no desire to forsake Jehovah and
serve other gods. They freely acknowledged that they owed everything to him from the Exodus to the possession of Canaan. They
also expressed their determination to serve the Lord.

## 4  Joshua's answer

Whether they uttered all these vows in thunderous unison, or by
the mouth of chosen representatives, or whether the historian
gathered the consensus of their feeling as it passed from lip to lip,
we cannot tell. But surely Joshua detected some traces of insincer-
ity in their voice. Perhaps he felt the unreality of their professions
because they gave no sign of abandoning their strange gods. Had
he hoped for a repetition of the scene that had taken place on that
spot so many years before when, at the challenge of Jacob, his
household gave to him all the strange gods that were in their
hands, and the rings that were in their ears, and Jacob hid them
beneath the oak that was by Shechem?

But there was no such response. The people contented themselves with their affirmations, but made no sacrifices. There was
no holocaust, and Joshua was deeply conscious of the unreality of
profession that went no deeper than words. This, he said in effect,
is no way to serve the Lord. He is a holy God; he is a jealous God.

He will search out these secret sins of yours; he will not be content with the service of the lip; he will not pass over transgression and sin.

## 5   The people's second reply

They were full of self-confidence, and vowed, come what might, that they would serve the Lord. Standing there with Joshua they forgot the many failures of the past, mocked at his fears, derided his suggestions of possible declension, and cried, 'Nay; but we will serve the LORD.'

What a commentary on those proud words is given by the Book of Judges! Serve the Lord! The first sentence that follows the record of Joshua's death in that book tells us that 'the children of Israel did evil in the sight of the LORD, and served Baalim: And they forsook the LORD the God of their fathers' (Judg. 2:11–12). And this record recurs with melancholy monotony on nearly every page.

In point of fact, resolution, however good and however strongly expressed, is not sufficient to carry us forward into a life of obedience. Our moral nature has become so weakened by repeated failure that it is not able to resist the appeals of sense. To will is present with us, but how to perform that which is good we don't have. No one can look thoughtfully into the workings of his own nature without realizing the terrible paralysis that has befallen it. Consecration is possible only when it is conceived, prosecuted, and consummated in power not our own, and in the energy of the Holy Spirit.

## 6   Joshua's second answer

'Ye are witnesses,' he said, 'against yourselves, that ye have chosen you the LORD, to serve him.' In other words, he appealed to them on the ground of their own declarations, and sought to bind them to the vows they had made. Did he not intend to prove them deeper, to make them realize the solemnity of the occasion, to compel them to face the greatness of the responsibility they had assumed?

## 7 The people's third reply

'We are witnesses,' they cried; as years later the people met Pilate's repeated challenge by the imprecation on themselves of the blood of Jesus. Alas, for their self-confident boast, for their headstrong pride of purpose! O my soul, be warned, that when you are challenged as to your resolves, make your boast in God. Only by your God can you leap over a wall, or run through a multitude. Ask the Holy Spirit to bind you by cords to the altar of self-surrender by the blood-red cord of Calvary; by the silver cord of hope in the Second Advent; by the golden cord of daily fellowship.

## 8 Joshua's response

Further words were fruitless, and so he set up a memorial of the pledges by which the people had bouind themselves. He wrote their words in the book of the law of God; and he took a great stone, and set it up there under the slab. 'Behold,' he said, 'this stone shall be a witness unto us; for it hath heard all the words of the LORD which he spake unto us: it shall be therefore a witness unto you, lest ye deny your God.' Then he dismissed the people so they could return to their homes.

There is comfort suggested to us by contrast with this solemn scene. Even in the Land of Promise, the people introduced the old Sinaitic spirit of duty and obedience as the condition of their tenure. They had said at Sinai, 'All that the LORD says, we will do.' And they said it again in Canaan.

Joshua did not give the people rest. Had he done so, David would not have spoken of another day. Canaan was only the *type* of the Sabbath-keeping of the people of God, but he did not exhaust it. At the best it was only a material and unsatisfying type. It afforded rest from the fatigues of the march, but not rest to the infinite capacities of the soul. The produce of cornfields, and vineyards, and oliveyards, could not appease the appetite for the infinite that must have made itself felt even in the heart of Israel, as the nation settled in its God-given land. Therefore, as the Holy Spirit tells us, there remained over and above a rest that is open by faith to the people of God of every age.

It is only when we apprehend the provisions of the New Covenant, which does mention man, but is full of the *I wills* of God, that we come into the true blessedness of rest and peace. When you confess yourself powerless to maintain the attitude of consecration, and are content to work out in the strength of his Spirit, you will experience the fullness of that rest that is deep as God's, like the azure sky that slumbers behind the bars of gold, which encase the glory of sunset.

His task ended, Joshua retired to his inheritance, but the influence of his character and life was felt as long as he lived, and afterwards. At last he died, one hundred and ten years old, and they buried him. He richly merited all the honour he received. He had none of the gifts of Moses. He may be compared to the man of two talents, while his great master was dowered with five. But he was strong and wise and true to the great trust committed to his care by the people and by God; and amid the stars that shine in the firmament of heaven, not the least bright or clear is the lustre of Joshua, the son of Nun, the antetype of the risen and ascended Saviour.

# SAMUEL

# 1

# An Age of Transition

## *1 Samuel 16:1*

The story of Samuel is a divine interlude between the days of the Judges and those of David the king.

Up to now the high priesthood had been the supreme authority recognized in the Hebrew commonwealth. To Moses, its founder, there could be of course no successor; but Aaron was the first of an unbroken line of priests. No other office stood for the whole of Israel. The Mosaic era, however, was not destined to culminate in the rule of the priest who had seldom combined the sacerdotal functions with the special qualifications that constitute a great leader and ruler. The priest was to make way for the king.

A suggestion that a fresh development of the Hebrew polity was near occurs in the closing verses of the Book of Ruth, with which this book is connected by the conjunction *now*. The genealogy, which is the evident climax of that sweet pastoral story, has no connection with Aaron or his line. It expressly deals with the tribe of Judah, of which nothing was spoken concerning the priesthood. Evidently the divine purpose was moving forward – but where? From the vantage point of accomplished fact, we can see that it was slowly moving toward the establishment of the kingdom under David; and veiled from all eyes there was the yet profounder movement toward the revelation of 'that Proper Man,' in whose nature, fitly known as Wonderful, the priestly, the prophetic, and the royal, blend in perfect symmetry and beauty.

## 1 The urgent need for a strong man

Every age takes up the cry, 'Give us men'; but if ever a strong man

239

was needed, it was in the days of which the Book of Judges affords some startling glimpses.

Canaan had been conquered, but the ancient inhabitants were far from being subdued. In the South, the Philistines held their five cities. The mountain fortress, which was later known as Mount Zion, garrisoned by Jebusites, was proudly defiant up to the days of David. Nearly all the seacoast, and all the strongholds in the rich plain of Esdraelon, were in the hands of the Canaanites. The little kingdom of Gezer remained independent until it was conquered by the king of Egypt, and given as a dowry to Solomon's queen. On the northern frontier were the remains of those mighty nations that Joshua had overthrown in the great battle of the Waters of Merom, but which probably only gave a nominal allegiance to the Israelite suzerainty. Had it not been for the presence of these warlike tribes, we would never have heard of Gideon, of Barak, or Jephthah, of Samson, or of David.

In Israel, their incessant exposure to attack was aggravated by the absence of a strong central government. The priesthood had evidently fallen into the hands of weaklings from the days of Phinehas. Of this there is striking confirmation in the fact that Eli sprang, not from the house of Eleazar, the eldest son of Aaron, in which the succession ought to have been continued, but from the family of the younger son, Ithamar. There is a strong probability that the representatives of the elder branch had proved themselves so unable to cope with the disorders of the time that they had been set aside in favour of any one who showed he was equipped enough to take the field and marshal the forces of Israel. Perhaps Eli, in his young life, had done some stirring deed of prowess that raised him to the supreme position his fellow-countrymen could give; though, when we are introduced to him, he is pitiful in his senile decrepitude and weakness (1 Chron. 6:4–15; 24:4). From time to time prophets had been raised up as a temporary expedient. 'He gave them judges until Samuel the prophet.' The reign of a judge was, however, a very transient gleam of light in that dark and stormy age.

Thus the nation was in danger of desolation by internal anarchy and external attack. With no principle of cohesion, no rallying point, no acknowledged leader, what was there to resist the pressure of the Canaanites from within its borders, and of the hostile nations from without? 'In those days there was no king in

Israel, but every man did that which was right in his own eyes'; 'The children of Israel did evil in the sight of the Lord'; 'The children of Israel cried unto the Lord.' These three sentences, repeated frequently and emphatically, are the keynotes of the whole book. The religious ties, also, were very weak. We find, for instance, the name of Baal, a Phoenician deity, occurring three times in the names of members of the family of Saul (1 Chron. 8:30, 33, 34). The stories of Micah, of Ruth, and of the extermination of the Danites, supply graphic pictures of the disunion, independence, and wildness of the time; of wild license, and of exposure to attack.

It was necessary, therefore, to introduce a new order of things. The task demanded a preeminently strong man; and the person was superbly supplied, as we shall see, in the prophet Samuel, who conducted his people from one age to another without a revolution, and almost without the excitement that naturally accompanies so great a change.

## 2 How the need was met

God's greatest gifts to man come through travail. Before Samuel could be given to his people, Hannah had to be a woman of a sorrowful spirit.

Some few miles to the north of Jerusalem, on the confines of the territories of Ephraim and Benjamin, was situated the town of Ramathaim-Zophim. It was also known as Ramah, and has passed into New Testament history as Arimathea, the town from which came Joseph who begged of Pilate the body of the Lord. Ramathaim means the two Ramahs, as there were probably an upper and a lower city, to which reference is made in a later story (1 Sam. 9:13). Zophim recalls the name of an ancestor of Elkanah, named Zuph, who appears to have been a man of considerable importance (1 Chron. 6:35; 1 Sam. 9:5). In this mountain city a child was to be born who was to give the city interest and importance, not only during his lifetime, when it became the focus of the national life, but for centuries of years.

Toward the close of Samson's career in southern Judah, a family resided at Ramah consisting of Elkanah, a Levite, and his two wives, Hannah (Grace) and Peninnah (Pearl or Margaret). He had formerly lived in Ephraim, and was therefore considered to belong to that tribe (Josh. 21:20). That he had two wives was not a violation of the Levitical law, which did not forbid polygamy, but carefully regulated the marriage law.

It is supposed that Elkanah brought a second wife into his home because of Hannah's childlessness; but, whatever had been the cause, the step had been filled with misery. The house at Ramah was filled with bickering and strife, which was augmented as Peninnah had child after child, while Hannah was still childless. Apart from all else, her desolate condition was an almost intolerable affliction (Gen. 30:1); but that it should be made the subject of biting sarcasm and bitter taunts was the occasion of the most poignant grief. Her soul was pierced as by the sword of the Lord, and drew near to the grave; then it was that the hunger of her soul could not be appeased even by the consciousness of Elkanah's fond affection (1 Sam. 1:5, 8; 2:5–8). But out of his soul-travail the joy of her life and the saviour of her country were to be born.

# 2

# A Woman's Anguish of Heart

## 1 Samuel 1:15

We may infer that Hannah's barrenness, and the provocation of her rival, were not the only reasons for Hannah's sorrow. As her noble song proves, she was saturated with the most splendid traditions and hopes of her people; her soul was thrilling with the conceptions that inspired the songs of Moses. Stricken with an agony of grief for the anarchy and confusion around her, she longed to enshrine her noblest self in a son, who should resuscitate the ebbing prosperity of the nation, and set it on a solid foundation. What if she were to be deprived of his presence and support from his earliest years, would she not be compensated a thousand times if only the Lord would accept him as his own, and use him to be the channel through which his redemptive plans might be achieved? Levites ordinarily were consecrated to the Lord's service between the ages of thirty and fifty, but her son, if only she might have one, would be given to the Lord all the days of his life, and no razor would ever touch his flowing locks.

On one occasion, while the feast was proceeding at Shiloh, it seemed as though Hannah could restrain herself no longer, and after her people had eaten and drunk – she fasting, except from tears – she rose up and returned to the outer court of the tabernacle. Most of its ancient glory had departed. 'And she was in bitterness of soul, and prayed unto the LORD, and wept sore.' Others went with burnt offerings, but she with the broken heart, which God will not despise.

We are told that 'she prayed', and it becomes us to study her prayer and its result.

## 1   It was heart prayer

It is the custom of Orientals to pray audibly, but as she stood beside Eli's seat (v. 26) she spoke in her heart; her lips moved but her voice was not heard. This indicates that she had made many advances in the divine life, and had come to know the secret of heart fellowship with God.

## 2   It was based on a new name for God

She appealed to the Lord under a new title, 'LORD of hosts'. She asked him to look down from the myriads of holy spirits who circled his throne, to her dire affliction and anguish. She vowed in words that Elkanah by his silence of consent afterward ratified (Num. 30:6–15), that she did not want this inestimable boon for herself merely, but for the glory of God; and that her son should be a Nazarite from his birth, abstaining from intoxicating drink, his locks unshorn, his body undefiled by contact with the dead.

## 3   It was definite prayer

'Give unto thine handmaid a manchild.' 'For this child I prayed.' So many of our prayers miscarry because they have no special goal. Experienced saints who are versed in the art of intercessory prayer tell us of the marvellous results that have accrued when they have set themselves to pray definitely for the salvation of individuals, or for some good and perfect gift on their behalf.

### 4   It was prayer without reserve

'I have poured out my soul before the LORD.' Ah, how good it would be if we could more often follow Hannah's example. When the heart is breaking, when its frail machinery seems unable to sustain the weight of its anxiety, when its cords are strained to the point of snapping, then, as you remember these things, pour out your soul in you (Ps. 42:4).

### 5   It was persevering prayer

'It came to pass, as she *continued* praying before the LORD.' Not that either she or we can claim to be heard for our much speaking, but when the Lord lays some burden on us we cannot do other than wait before him.

### 6   It was prayer that received its coveted request

Eli was seated in his place at the entrance to the sanctuary, and he noticed Hannah. At first his attention was probably arrested by the signs of her excessive sorrow, and he expected that she would pour out her prayers in an audible voice, as so many other burdened souls would do. But since her lips moved, while her voice was not heard, the high priest thought she was drunk, and rather rudely and coarsely broke in on her with the rebuke, 'How long wilt thou be drunken? put away thy wine from thee.' Eli judged after the sight of his eyes, and clearly the mind of God had not been revealed to him. He had degenerated into the mere official, from whom the divine purposes were concealed.

  Hannah answered the unjust reproach with great meekness. 'No,' she said, 'it is not as you think. I have drunk neither wine nor strong drink, but have poured out my spirit to the LORD.' She realized, even before Eli replied, that the merciful Burden bearer had heard and answered her prayer. She had entered into the spirit of the prayer, which not only asks, but takes. She anticipated those wonderful words which, more than any others, disclose the secret of prevailing supplication, 'What things soever ye desire when ye pray, believe that ye receive them, and ye shall have them (Mark 11:24). She knew that she had prevailed, and the peace of God, which passes all understanding, filled and kept her mind and heart. And she said, 'Let thine handmaid find grace in thy sight. So the woman went her way, and did eat, and her countenance was no more sad.'

The next day was fixed for their return home. But what a changed woman she was! How differently she had borne herself in that last brief visit to the holy shrine! And with what a glad face she entered the home that had been associated with such sorrow. Peninnah must have wondered what had happened to make so great a change; but Elkanah was the confidant of her secret, and his faith was made stronger by her unquestioning trust (v. 23).

## 7 The workings of sorrow

In this prayer we can trace the harvest sown in years of suffering. Sorrow gives an indefinable beauty to the soul. It may be that the long sharp pain, which has been your lot for these many years, the heart hunger, the disappointed hopes, the silent waiting, the holding your peace, even from good, have been necessary to teach you how to pray, to lead you into the secret of a childlike faith, and to fit you to be the parent of some priceless gift to the world.

It fell to Hannah according to her faith. 'The LORD remembered her, and . . . when the time was come about . . . that she bare a son, and she called his name Samuel, saying, Because I have asked him of the LORD.'

The good Elkanah had a new joy in his heart as he went up to offer to the Lord his yearly sacrifice; but Hannah stayed at Ramah until the child was weaned, which would probably be on his completion of his third year, when Levite children were permitted to be enrolled and to enter the house of the Lord (2 Chron. 31:16).

At last the time arrived when the child should be openly presented to the Lord. The parents set out on their solemn journey with their child. The mother's heart was now as full of praise as it had formerly been of sorrow. She had learned that there was no Rock like her God. Her song, on which the mother of our Lord modelled the Magnificat, is the outburst of a soul whose cup was overflowing with the loving kindness of the Lord.

Presently the memorable journey from Ramah was finished. The sanctuary was again in sight, where she had suffered so poignantly and prayed so fervently. How it all rushed to her memory! 'I am the woman that stood by thee here,' she said to Eli; 'For this child I prayed; and the LORD hath given me my petition.'

Take heart, man or woman of a sorrowful spirit! Only suffer according to the will of God, and for no wrong of sinful cause! Suffer for his church, for a lost world, for dying men! Travail in birth for souls! And if you do abide your Lord's time, he will bring you again to tread in garments of joy, where you have stood in the drapery of woe. They who go forth and weep, bearing precious seed, shall doubtless come again with rejoicing, bringing their sheaves with them.

# 3

# The Vision of God

## *1 Samuel 3*

It is touching to notice the various references to the child Samuel as they recur during the progress of the narrative, especially those in which an evident contrast is intended between his gentle innocence and the wild license of Eli's sons – it is like a peal of sweet bells ringing amid the crash of a storm.

Hannah said, '. . . I will bring him, *that he may appear before the LORD, and there abide for ever.*' 'And she . . . brought him unto the house of the LORD in Shiloh; *and the child weas young.*' 'As long as he liveth he is lent to the LORD. *And he worshipped the LORD there.*' 'And *the child ministered unto the LORD before Eli.*' 'Now the sons of Eli were sons of Belial; they knew not the LORD: *But Samuel ministered before the LORD, being a child.*' 'Now Eli was very old, and he heard all that his sons did unto all Israel. . .

*And the child Samuel grew on, and was in favour with the* LORD,
*and also with men.' 'And Samuel grew, and the* LORD *was with
him, and did let none of his words fall to the ground.'*

His life seems to have been one unbroken record of blameless
purity, integrity, and righteousness. One purpose ran through all
his years, threading them together in an unbroken series. There
were no gaps nor breaks; no lapses into sensuality or selfishness;
no lawless deeds in that wild, lawless age. Toward the end of his
long life he was able to appeal to the verdict of the people in
memorable words, which attested his consciousness of unsullied
moral virtue.

Samuel was not a prophet in the sense of foretelling the long
future, but it was by his saintliness, the moral grandeur of his
character, that he arrested the ruin of his people.

The noblest gift that any of us can make to our country or age
is an undefiled character and a stainless life.

## 1   The transition of a young soul

For Samuel, however, a great change was necessary and imminent. Up to this moment he had lived largely in the energy and
power of his mother's intense, religious life. His faith had to rest,
not on the assertions of another person's testimony, but on the
fact that for himself he had seen and tasted, and handled the
Word of Life. It is a great hour in the history of the soul when the
traditional, which has become a habit from long use, is suddenly
exchanged for the open vision of God; when we say with Job, 'I
have heard of thee by the hearing of the ear; but now mine eye
seeth thee' (Job 42:5).

Will you believe then that God may be coming near you, and is
about to reveal himself to you in the Lord Jesus, as not to the
world? He is about to transform your life and lift it to a new level.

## 2   The vision of the young eyes

*a.* When God came near his young servant, it seemed as though
*he placed his seal on his faithfulness.*   Up to now only small services had been required of him. It was right that he who had
shown himself faithful in little should have a larger and wider
area of responsibility assigned to him.

*b. The vision*  came as night was beginning to yield to dawn; but the lamp had not yet gone out 'in the temple of the LORD, where the ark of God was.' Three times the boy was startled from his innocent slumbers. He heard his name called and, sure that Eli needed him, three times sped across the intervening space to report. Once, and again, and yet again, he ran to Eli, and said, 'Here am I, for thou calledst me.'

*c. Eli was very wise in his treatment of the young boy.*  He might have posed as the sole trustee of the divine secrets, might have stood on the dignity and pride of office. But he took the boy's hand in his and led him into the divine presence. The aged man said sweetly, 'Go, lie down: and it shall be, if he call thee, that thou shalt say, Speak, LORD, for thy servant heareth.'

*d. The message entrusted to the boy was a terrible one.*  We cannot but wonder if Samuel was afraid to show Eli the vision. With *a beautiful modesty and reticence* he set about the duties of the day, and opened, as usual, the doors of the house of the Lord. It was not for him to blurt out the full thunder that had burst on him. This was another beautiful trait in the boy's character. But he had misread Eli's character; he did not realize that men like him will resign themselves without a word of defence, determined to know the worst, and when they know it, meekly answer, 'It is the LORD; let him do what seemeth him good.'

# 4

# Misfortune on Misfortune

## *1 Samuel 4—6*

The scanty records of these chapters (4:1–7:7) bridge a considerable tract of scripture; covering, perhaps, forty years. It was an age of disunion and anarchy. After the deaths of Joshua, Caleb, and of all that generation, 'there arose another generation after them, which knew not the LORD, nor yet the works which he had done for Israel' . . . (Judg. 2:10). There was no man, and no tribe, able to unite the people under one leadership, or recall them to the worship of the one Jehovah. The heart of the national life beat feebly and, in the expressive phrase that so completely represents the age of the judges, 'Every man did that which was right in his own eyes.'

The only common tie was afforded by the tabernacle, the ark, and the high priesthood; but even the influence of these had become greatly reduced. 'The children of Israel forsook the LORD . . . and followed other gods, of the gods of the people that were round about them, and bowed themselves unto them.'

There was therefore nothing to hinder the steady encroachments of the neighbouring nations. Now it was the children of Ammon on the east, then the Amalekites and Midianites from the desert, and again the Philistines on the southwest, that broke in on the Land of Promise. From time to time judges were raised up, but their authority was only temporary and limited.

Our story is especially connected with the southern and middle districts of Canaan which, notwithstanding Samson's heroic exploits – for he was contemporary with Samuel's early years – lay under the tyrannous yoke of the Philistines, who seem about this time to have been largely reinforced from the original seat of their empire in the neighbouring island of Crete, and to have made the position of the Hebrews almost intolerable.

## 1   An ill-fated attempt

'Now Israel went out against the Philistines to battle, and pitched beside Eben-ezer, and the Philistines pitched in Aphek.' From these words we infer that the war was begun by Israel because the yoke of Philistia was too galling to be endured; but it is almost certain that from the first it was an ill-starred and badly-managed campaign.

Distinct directions were issued by Moses as to the way in which a campaign should be begun and conducted (Deut. 20), but none of them seems to have been put in force on this occasion. No priest was called in to ask counsel of God; not even Samuel. It was the sudden flaming out of a spirit of hatred and revenge from a race of slaves, who were stung to the depths by the taunts, the insults, and the whips of their masters.

The Israelitish hosts, hastily summoned and insufficiently armed, suffered a heavy defeat. Four thousand men lay dead on the battlefield, and a spirit of intimidation and dismay spread though the entire host. Such will always be the result when God's people leave him out of their plans.

## 2   The ark, but not God, to the rescue

On the evening of that disastrous day the elders of Israel held a council of war (v. 3). It was evident that their defeat had to be attributed to some failure in their relations with the Lord. They said, 'Wherefore hath *the* LORD smitten us to-day before the Philistines?' They were conscious that they had left him out of their plans, and suddenly thought of an idea by which they might almost compel him to take sides with him against their foes. 'Let us fetch the ark of the covenant of the LORD out of Shiloh unto us, that when it cometh among us, it may save us out of the hand of our enemies.'

They remembered the wonderful scenes in which that ark had played a part: Its going forth had always meant the scattering and flight of Jehovah's foes. Surely it would do the same again. They did not realize that God's very present help depended not on the presence of a material symbol, but on moral and spiritual conditions, which they should have set themselves to understand and fulfil.

The arrival of the ark, in due course, borne by the Levites, and accompanied by the sons of Eli as its custodians, was received with the exultant shouts of the entire host. Eli had evidently been unwilling to allow it to leave the sacred enclosure – 'his heart trembled for the ark of God' – but he had yielded too often and too long to be able to sustain a successful protest; and probably no one else had any misgivings, for 'when the ark of the covenant of the LORD came into the camp, all Israel shouted with a great shout, so that the earth rang again.'

As soon as the Philistines were acquainted with the cause of this exuberant outburst, they were correspondingly depressed, for they too identified the presence of the God of Israel with the advent of the ark. It had always been associated in their minds with the hand of 'these mighty gods . . . that smote the Egyptians.' 'Woe unto us!' they cried, 'for there hath not been such a thing heretofore. Woe unto us! who shall deliver us?'

The Philistines seem to have stirred themselves to deeds of desperate valor. They advanced to the conflict with the words of their leaders ringing in their ears. 'Be strong, and quit yourselves like men, O ye Philistines, that ye be not servants unto the Hebrews, as they have been to you! quit yourselves like men, and fight' (see 1 Cor. 16:13).

The issue of that terrible day was extremely disastrous. 'Israel was smitten, and they fled every man into his tent: and there was a very great slaughter; for there fell of Israel thirty thousand footmen.' Around the ark the ground must have been heaped with corpses, as the Hebrews fought desperately in the defence of the symbol of their faith; but in vain, for the ark of God was taken, and the two sons of Eli were slain. Samuel had foretold it, and so it happened.

That afternoon a Benjamite, with his clothes rent and dust on his head, bore the tidings to the hamlets and villages that lay along the open road to Shiloh; and a wail arose that grew in volume as he sped onwards until it reached its climax in the city of the high priest. 'When the man came into the city, and told it, all the city cried out.' On the still evening air arose a piercing outburst of lamentation, for what was there to hinder the immediate march of the victorious army on the city, deprived in one day of its warriors, and apparently of its God!

The old man, Eli, blind and anxious, had caused himself to be seated on his throne, facing the main thoroughfare. When the noise of the tumult arose, he anxiously enquired of the attendant priests and Levites and, perhaps, of Samuel, waiting as usual to respond to his last appeal for help, 'What meaneth the noise of this tumult?' At the same moment the messenger appears to have burst into the presence of the little group, telling Eli who he was. In answer to the eager enquiry of the high priest, 'How went the matter, my son?' without warning or preface, and with no care to soften the harsh words, he blurted out, with an ever-rising climax of dread awfulness: 'Israel is fled before the Philistines, and there hath been also a great slaughter among the people, and thy two sons also . . . are dead, and the ark of God is taken.'

The old man received the tidings in silence. The three first shots hit him severely, but not mortally; but 'when he made mention of the ark of God, he fell from off the seat backward by the side of the gate, and his neck brake, and he died.' With her last gasp the wife of Phinehas gathered up the horror of the situation in the single word that she uttered as the name of her child, prematurely born – Ichabod. It was sad indeed that she was a widow; sad that her father-in-law had died at the moment when he was needed so sorely; but sad most of all that the ark was taken, for with it the glory had departed. She was a true soul and was worthy to be classed with Hannah in her loyal devotion to the name and house of God!

But worse troubles befell them. In frantic haste the Israelites bore away the remnants of the sacred tent and its furniture, and concealed them. In subsequent years they were at Nob (1 Sam. 21:1). The removal of these precious relics was hardly completed before the Philistine invasion burst on the deserted city as an overflowing flood.

## 3   The awful name of God

This part of the history more closely concerns the growing understanding of the surrounding nations as to the true nature of the God of Israel.

There was no other way in which the Spirit of God could inform the people of Philistia as to his holiness and power, than that which he adopted in this event. They bore the ark from the battlefield to the temple of Dagon in exuberant triumph. They would not have been impressed by the message of a prophet; but they could not resist the conclusions forced on them when, on two following mornings, they found his image prostrate before the emblem of Jehovah, and on the second occasion the head and arms were severed from the body so that the only part that was left intact was the fish's tail with which the figure ended. A terrible plague of 'tumours' broke out on each successive city to which the ark was removed, and a visitation of destructive vermin on the country districts where it may have been deposited.

We must not suppose, of course, that God had no love toward these untutored souls, but there was not other way of convincing them of his real nature and prerogatives. The prostrated form of Dagon, the painful disease by which they were smitten, and the devastation of their crops, caused them to cry to heaven (v. 12), as though they realized that they were being dealt with by a greater than Dagon.

If the Philistines could have understood Epistles like those of John, they would without doubt have been written and communicated to them by some man of God; but since they could not understand such means of instruction, they were reached by the overthrow and shattering of their idol, the plagues that accompanied the progress of the ark, and the direction taken by the cows which, while crying for their little ones, bore their sacred burden along the straight road that led them from their home toward Beth-shemesh.

Similarly, the inhabitants of that frontier town had to learn by a stern lesson that God was a holy God, and that he could not permit them to manifest a wanton curiosity and irreverence in handling the sacred emblem of his presence. To pry into the ark as they did, was forbidden to the priests, and even the high priest himself; how much more to them? The swift retribution that followed on this act of irreverence extorted the reverent acknowledgment of the awesome holiness of God, as the men of Beth-shemesh said, 'Who is able to stand before this holy Lord God?' When, on the other hand, the ark had been reverently borne to Kirjath-jearim, and had been carefully entrusted to the custody of Abinadab and his son Eleazar, the blessing that befell his house was an indication of the tender love and pity of the divine nature, who is willing to dwell with those who are of a humble and lowly heart, and who tremble at his word.

# 5

# The Victory of Faith

## *1 Samuel 7:1–14*

After twenty years of quiet and unobtrusive toil, Samuel led his people to desire both to feel and manifest the old unity, and there was a distinct yearning after Jehovah. The sacred writer tells us that all the house of Israel 'was drawn together' after Jehovah (v. 2, *marg.*). In being drawn to God they were drawn toward each other, as the spokes of a wheel centre in the hub.

In verses 3 and 4 we probably have the substance of innumerable exhortations that Samuel delivered to all the house of Israel. From end to end he traversed the country, urging the people to return to Jehovah, to put away the false gods and Ashtaroth. On every hand idols were cast from their pedestals, and the vicious orgies were brought to an end in the groves and valleys.

## 1   The convocation at Mizpeh

The movement at last demanded a public demonstration, and Samuel summoned all Israel to Mizpeh.

The day was devoted to fasting, as the law required on the great Day of Atonement. The people confessed their sins, afflicted their souls, and humbled themselves before Jehovah. In addition, a somewhat novel rite was introduced. Water was brought from a neighbouring well and solemnly poured out before the Lord, as afterward at the Feast of Tabernacles.

The pouring of water may have implied that they poured forth from their full hearts floods of penitence and tears; that they desired by the heaviness of their grief to wash their land free from the accumulated evil of the past years; or that the people realized their utter helplessness, so that they were as water spilled on the ground, which could not be gathered up. But whatever it may have signified, it must have been a very striking spectacle. It was a worthy act for his manhood's prime, and we are not surprised to learn that, as by a sudden outburst of acclamation, he was appointed judge (v. 6).

Oh, who will induce the professing church of God to put away the evil things by which her testimony is now impaired! What would not be the blessed result if the children of God would come to another Mizpeh and confess, as Israel did, 'We have sinned against the LORD'!

## 2   The victory of faith

The tidings of this great convocation reached the Philistines, who looked on it as an unmistakable sign of the returning spirit of national life, and 'the lords of the Philistines went up against Israel' (v. 7). From every part the contingents of a great army were assembled, and there was every reason to fear that the terrible experiences of Aphek would be renewed. A panic of fear spread through the multitudes of Israel. There appeared but one hope: God had to arise to his people's help, or they would be trampled beneath the heel of the conqueror. 'Cease not to cry unto the LORD our God for us,' the people said to Samuel, 'that he will save us out of the hand of the Philistines.'

The power of Samuel's prayers was already known throughout the land, like those of John Knox in the days of Queen Mary. The people had come to believe in them; they felt them to be the palladium of their liberties. If only Samuel would pray, they might count on deliverance. They knew that he had prayed; they now begged that he not cease.

But Samuel did more than pray. He took a sucking lamb, and offered it as a whole burnt offering to the Lord, symbolizing thus the desire of Israel to be wholly yielded to the divine will. There must be consecration before there can be faith and deliverance. It is not enough simply to put away sin; we must also give ourselves absolutely and entirely to God. Failure in the walk always denotes failure in the heart-life. If you are perpetually overcome by the Philistines, be sure that there is a flaw in your inner consecration.

While the smoke of this offering was rising in the calm air, and the eyes of tens of thousands were fixed on the figure of Samuel, and while his piercing cries for divine help were rising to heaven, the Philistines drew near to battle against Israel. But suddenly the voice of God answered the voice of the prophet. 'The LORD thundered with a great thunder [Hebrew, *the voice of God*] on that day upon the Philistines, and discomfited them.' The sky was suddenly black with tempest, peal after peal rolled through the mountains. Then at a signal from Samuel, the men of Israel flung themselves on the flying foe. Josephus tells of another circumstance that added to the horrors of that irresistible onslaught. 'God destroyed their ranks with an earthquake; the ground trembled under their feet, so that there was no place whereon to stand in safety. They either fell helpless to the earth, or into some of the chasms that opened beneath them.'

The pursuit only stopped when the Philistines came beneath the shadow of their own fortress of Bethcar, the Well of the Vineyards, as it is now called.

This is the great message of the whole story for us. If only the church of God would put away the evils that grieve his Holy Spirit; if only we would ourselves come out and be separate, the Spirit would interpose for us too. The Lord would deliver us, fighting on our behalf against our foes, so that we would be more than conquerors through him who loves us.

# 6

# The Stone of Help

## *1 Samuel 7:12*

'Then Samuel took a stone, and set it between Mizpeh and Shen, and called it Eben-ezer [the stone of help], saying, Hitherto hath the LORD helped us.' This was the same spot on which Israel had suffered the great defeat that led to the capture of the ark (4:1). How wonderful this was, that the story of the victory should be told on the plain that had been the scene of defeat!

From that moment Samuel's supremacy in the country was established. During his judgeship the Philistines did not return within the border of Israel. The alienated cities that the Philistines had taken from Israel were restored to Israel, from Ekron even to Gath. The Amorites, who had taken part with the Canaanites, found it to their advantage to side with Samuel and abstain from hostilities (v. 14).

It's amazing what prayer can do. It not only can open and close heaven, but will give the soul that prays an undisputed supremacy over his times, so that people will acknowledge that the saviour of the city is not so much the politician, the man of intellect, or the man of affairs, but he who has learned how to walk with God.

At the foot of this stone let us linger for a little, to learn one or two more lessons, for stones have ears and voices. Joshua said that the stone he reared, at the end of his life's work, had *heard;* and our Lord said that the stones around him might be expected to cry *out* (Josh. 24:27; Luke 19:40).

## 1  Its site

It stood on ground that had witnessed a terrible defeat and disaster. We are told, in the fourth chapter, that the great battle of Aphek was fought on this spot. 'Israel went out against the Philistines to battle, and pitched beside Eben-ezer, and the Philistines pitched in Aphek.' 'Now the Philistines took the ark of God, and they brought it from Eben-ezer unto Ashdod' (4:1; 5:1).

Many who gathered around Samuel, when he raised and named this stone, must have been present twenty years before on that fatal field, the Flodden of Israel's glory. Here the fight had been fiercest, the slain thickest; in the distance the fight had raged around the ark of God as it was taken and retaken, and taken again. At this point, desperate deeds of valor had been done to turn back Israel from a shameful fight, but in vain. There Hophni fell, and Phinehas.

Notwithstanding all this, and though the spot was associated with the memories of disgrace and shame, yet there the stone was erected that spoke so eloquently of divine help.

What living encouragement there is in this for us! We too may be travelling at this very hour battlefields that have been sadly marked by defeat. Again and again we have met the foes of our peace in mortal conflict, only to be repulsed. We have been overthrown by our adversary, and overpowered, in spite of all our efforts, by our besetting sin. Be of good cheer! The stone of Ebenezer will be raised on the very field of the fatal battle of Aphek.

## 2  Its retrospect

What a story this stone had to tell, if all were unfolded, of the wonderful dealings of God with his people. It looked back on the twenty years of patient work by which the prophet Samuel had been leading the people homeward to the God of their fathers.

It looked back on many a scene of iconoclasm as, from Dan to Beersheba, there had been a general putting away of the Baalim and Ashtaroth, the cutting down of groves and overthrow of altars. It looked back on that memorable convocation of all Israel at Mizpeh, when water was poured out before the Lord in confession of sin and humble penitence.

It looked back especially to the offering of the burnt offering, which declared Israel's resolve to be from that point on wholly devoted to God and to Samuel's piercing cry of intercession. Above all, it looked back on that memorable moment when, as the Philistines drew near to battle against Israel, 'the LORD thundered with a great thunder upon the Philistines, and discomfited them, and they were smitten down before Israel.'

Has anything like this taken place in your life? On your answer much will depend. If since your last failure and defeat there have been no acts of the soul, like those that took place at Mizpeh, there is no probability of there being any break in the long monotony of your reverses, unless there is the pouring out of your heart before God, the putting away of idols, and the resolve to follow him fully.

I must bear witness to the incessant failure of my life, as long as I cherished things in my heart that were alien to God's holy will. Rules for holy living, solemn and heart-stirring conventions, helpful books and addresses, produced but small result. There was temporary amendment, but little else. But when the scene at Mizpeh had been reflected in the inner mirror of the soul, then victory took place on the very spot marked by defeat. I would like to have you ponder this. You will never raise your stone of Ebenezer until you have stood on the watchtower of Mizpeh and put away all known sin, all complicity with what is grievous in the eyes of Christ. Then only will his keeping power avail.

You say that you cannot. Ah, that is the point where the Great Physician is willing to interpose for your rescue and deliverance! What you cannot do for yourself, he will do. The only question is, *Are you willing?* or, Are you willing to be made willing? Then tell him that you cannot be as you would, or that you will not be as you should, and pray him to undertake your difficult and almost desperate case. Do not doubt the result.

### 3   Its inscription

'Hitherto hath the LORD helped us.' Surely if the stone had a retrospect, as we have seen, it had also a prospect. It looked forward as well as backward. It seemed to say, As God has helped, so he will continue to help.

As we go through life let us be careful to erect our Ebenezer stones, so that when new responsibilities begin to crowd on us, or fresh and unforeseen difficulties threaten, we may be emboldened to sing with Newton:

> His love in time past forbids me to think
> He'll leave me at last in trouble to sink;
> Each sweet Eben-ezer I have in review
> Confirms his good pleasure to help me quite through.

All through life, if you will only trust God, you will have occasions to raise these stones of help. The last stone that we shall erect will be on the edge of the river. As we turn our back forever on the land of our pilgrimage, and enter on the work and worship of eternity, we will set up a great stone to the glory of our God, saying once more, with a deep sigh of perfected satisfaction, 'Hitherto hath the LORD helped.'

# 7

# A Great Disappointment

## *1 Samuel 7—8*

The supreme test of character is disappointment and apparent failure. We are now to see how Samuel carried himself in the face of a great disappointment. This at least may be said of him, as of old it was said of Job, that he still held fast his integrity.

## 1 How the disappointment came about

During the years that followed the glorious victory of Aphek,

Samuel set himself to build up in the hearts of his fellow-countrymen something of that profound belief in the reign of the divine King, which we know as the Theocracy, and which was so dear to all devout Hebrews.

His headquarters and home were at Ramah, the scene of the years of his happy childhood. From there he went on itinerating journeys. Who was he but the messenger and minister of the Lord of Hosts? With all the force of his character and eloquence of his speech he insisted that the people were the subjects of Jehovah, owing allegiance to him alone, and receiving from him direction in times of perplexity, and deliverance in days of battle. They needed no king – Jehovah was King; no officials, but those who uttered his messages; no code of laws, but those that emanated from him. It was a beautiful and inspiring concept.

*a.  The same object was in his mind as he instituted the schools of the prophets.*    To Samuel's wise interpretation of his times we must attribute the institution of these seats of learning. The priesthood had forfeited its right to stand between Jehovah and his people. It was clear that some other religious body must be called into existence. The times demanded an order of men who would be trained in the law of God, who would be fitted to interpret the holy oracles to the people, and from the midst of whom men would arise from time to time to proclaim on the housetops what God had whispered to their ears in secret. We find these schools flourishing in the days of Elijah and Elisha – some apparently on the same sites where they had been instituted by Samuel (10:3–5; 19:23–24; 2 Kings 2).

*b.  But the failure to realize his high purpose seems to have happened because of the failure of his sons.*    As Samuel became old, he was less able to administer justice; the burden of administering the government became too heavy for him, and he appointed his sons to assist him. The experiment proved however to be a disastrous failure. They 'walked not in his ways, but turned aside after lucre, and took bribes, and perverted judgment.'

This precipitated the catastrophe; and 'all the elders of Israel' came to Samuel at Ramah. 'Behold, thou art old, and thy sons walk not in thy ways; now make us a king to judge us like all the nations.'

Looked at from the human standpoint, there was much to

warrant the request. The Philistines were pushing their outposts into the heart of the country (13:3, 5); Nahash the Ammonite was a dangerous neighbour on the Eastern frontier (11:1); there was fear that disintegration might again separate the people on Samuel's death. But, on the other hand, the request shattered the prophet's hopes.

## 2   How Samuel bore his disappointment

'The thing displeased Samuel, when they said, Give us a king to judge us.' It was not so much that they had rejected him, but that they had rejected God – that he would not be King over them. They had failed to grasp the right concept and had fallen to the level of the nations around them.

Under these bitter circumstances, he made for the one harbour of refuge: 'Samuel prayed unto the LORD.'

Then the Lord answered his servant. He always does, and will, answer. 'Be careful for nothing; but in every thing by prayer and supplication with thanksgiving let your requests be made known unto God. And the peace of God, which passeth all understanding, shall guard your hearts and your minds through Christ Jesus' (Phil. 4:6).

## 3   The divine answer and encouragement

When Samuel cried to the Lord about his deep trouble, in the divine answer it was made clear that the cherished ideal of a lifetime would have to be abandoned. The distinct impression was made on the prophet's mind that he had to renounce his high purpose, and step down to become subordinate to a king. 'Now therefore' said his almighty Friend and Confidant, 'hearken unto their voice.'

At the same time his sorrow was greatly mitigated because he discovered that God was his Fellow-Sufferer, and that the sorrow of the divine heart was infinitely greater than his own. 'They have not rejected thee, *but they have rejected me* (v. 7). It is a great honour when a person is summoned to enter into fellowship with God in the awful pain and grief that we bring on his tender and Holy Spirit.

*The suffering of God.* Surely no one will count the phrase

extravagant that attributes suffering to God, on account of his rejection by human hearts, and who refuse his reign and belittle the Spirit of his grace. Christ taught us that God was not impassive; but that he yearned, sorrowed, loved, as human fathers do, only with heights and depths of intensity that are indeed divine.

The prophet says that God was pressed beneath the sin and rebellion of men, as the groaning cart is pressed beneath its load.


### 4    Samuel's noble behaviour toward the people

demands our attention. The request of the people for a king was, no doubt, in part based on Deuteronomy 17:14, which seemed to anticipate just such a crisis as had now arisen. But the present request had been sprung on Samuel prematurely. Instead of seeking to understand the mind of God, the people had made up their own mind; instead of consulting the aged prophet, they dictated the policy on which they had set their hearts.

Under these circumstances, and with the express direction of God, Samuel protested solemnly to the deputation of elders, and through them to the people, showing the manner of the king that would reign. It was impossible that a king demanded in such a spirit as characterized the people could be a man after God's own heart. They wanted one who, in his stature and bearing, in his martial prowess and deeds, would be worthy to compare with neighbouring monarchs. This was much more to them than character, obedience to God, or loyalty to the Mosaic code. And as they desired, to it was done to them. Ah! how often it happens that God gives us according to our request, but sends leanness into our souls (Ps. 106:15).

*Dangers that Samuel foresaw*    All the Oriental extravagance and prodigality of human life, which were the familiar accompaniment of royalty in neighbouring countries, were destined to reappear in the court of the kings of Israel. They would enforce the service of the young men to make their weapons, fight their battles, and minister to their royal state. They would exact unremunerated labour in the tillage of their lands. From the daughters and wives of the people they would demand confectionaries and bakemeats, and other elaborate luxuries for the royal appetite. Vineyards and oliveyards, farms and lands, would be confiscated at their desire. A system of heavy taxation would be imposed on the produce of the land, and on the flocks and herds that covered the pasture lands; while the people would have to stand still and see their hard-earned money squandered on the pleasures and self-indulgence of the palace. A brief experience of this kind would lead to a universal outcry, as the nation awoke to its grievous mistake; but the step so rashly taken would be found to be irreparable.

Samuel's protest and remonstrance were, however, alike in vain. 'The people refused to hearken unto the voice of Samuel; and they said, Nay; but we will have a king over us.' They trusted in man, and in the arm of flesh; their heart departed from the Lord; and in the sequel they were destined to see their king slain, their land overrun, and the national fortunes reduced as low as possible.

When Samuel saw that the people had made up their mind, he dismissed the assembly and took it upon himself to do the best he could for them. He set himself to build up an entirely new organisation. In doing this he had to sacrifice his previous convictions, and do violence to his better judgment; but when once he realised that there was no alternative, he became the most devoted and efficient organizer of the new age.

# 8

# The Voice of Circumstances

## *1 Samuel 9–10*

It was the spring of the day. The dawn was breaking in the Eastern sky, when three men descended the steep ascent on which Ramah stood, and emerged from the city gate (19:11–12, 14, 26). The group was a remarkable one, comprising the aged seer; 'a young man, and a goodly,' who was the king elect, though he did not realise it; and a herdsman, Doeg, so tradition states, who later achieved an unhappy notoriety, but was at that time simply a servant in attendance on his master's son. 'As they were going down at the end of the city, Samuel said to Saul, Bid thy servant pass on before us, but stand thou still a while, that I may shew thee the word of God.'

## 1   The circumstances that led up to this incident

*a. The asses of Kish, Saul's father, were lost.*   'And Kish said to Saul, his son, Take now one of the servants with thee, and arise, go seek the asses.'

But when they left home they little realized how far their search would lead them. 'And he passed through mount Ephraim, and passed through the land of Shalisha, but they found them not: then they passed through the land of Shalim, and there they were not: and he passed through the land of the Benjamites, but they found them not.' Three days were consumed in this fruitless search, in stopping every traveller, asking many questions, scrutinizing every trail – but all to no avail.

*b. By God's providence, which some call chance, the seekers found themselves in the land of Joseph,*   and there the thought of his father's possible anxiety arrested the steps of the young farmer, and he said, 'Come, and let us return, lest my father leave caring for the asses, and take thought for us.' This remark indicated a good and commendable trait in Saul's character. On the whole, a man who cares for the feelings of those nearest to him is likeliest to be a good ruler of men.

*c.* Having arranged for the offering of the piece of silver that was discovered in the bottom of the servant's pocket, as their gift to the seer, *the two men made for the gate of the little city*, 'which was set on a hill,' its white houses glistening in the intense sunshine. The young women of whom they made inquiries, the fact that Samuel was in the city and on his way to a feast in the high place, the encounter with Samuel himself in the main street, and news that the asses were found – were like so many signposts that pointed them by the way they should go, until they came to the place that awaited them, the seat and portion prepared by the instruction of the prophet.

Can we say anything that is too trivial to be a part of God's divine plan? Let it never be forgotten that straying asses, an unexpected encounter in the street, the presence of a coin in the pocket, or its absence, are all part of a divine plan, and it only awaits the quick eye, the ready ear, and the obedient heart, to detect the things that God has prepared for those that love him.

## 2  The incident of Saul's first anointing

Saul slept at Samuel's house that night, and on the housetop. The prophet had prepared his couch there with a special purpose, which burned like a clear flame in his heart; for when the house was quiet, he went upstairs to the young man, who was pondering the strange events of the day, and 'communed with Saul upon the top of the house.'

With careful skill Samuel awoke the sleeping soul of the young son of the soil, who probably had lived in a narrow, circumscribed area, and who was interested in flocks and herds, in vines and crops, in the talk of the countryside, but with few thoughts of the national welfare.

He was awakened by Samuel before the breath that announced the dawn had stirred the leaves of the sleeping woods. 'Samuel called Saul to the top of the house, saying, Up, that I may send thee away.' Then as they reached the edge of the city the servant was sent on, and as the two stood together, Samuel took from out of his breast the vial of oil, and poured it upon the strong young head bent beneath his touch. 'Is it not because the LORD hath anointed thee to be captain over his inheritance?' he said.

It was a great hour in Saul's life. No wonder that 'when he had turned his back to go from Samuel,' it was with '*another heart*.' In a sense, though not the deepest, old things had passed away, and everything had become new.

# 9

# Forsaken? Never!

## *1 Samuel 12:22*

While the entire land was ringing with the news of Saul's exploit in the deliverance of Jabesh-gilead, it appeared to Samuel to be an auspicious moment for confirming the kingdom in his hand; and therefore he summoned a great convocation of the nation at Gilgal.

On that spot Israel had encamped for the first night after crossing the Jordan, and the twelve great stones commemorating that event were still visible. There the act of circumcision had been performed, cleansing the people of the neglect of the wilderness; and there too the first Passover in the Land of Promise had been celebrated. Amid these great memorials and memories of the past the people gathered from far and near to crown Saul king. He had been designated at Mizpeh; he was to be crowned at Gilgal. It was the inauguration of his reign, its ratification and confirmation by the entire people. After this great ceremony, Saul and his people rejoiced together with peace offerings and thank offerings before God; and this was the moment that Samuel chose to lay down his office as judge – the last of the judges, and the first of the prophets.

## 1  Samuel's resignation

Standing bare-headed before the vast audience of the men of Israel, and pointing to his white locks, Samuel said, 'I am old and grey headed ... and I have walked before you from my childhood unto this day.' He was anxious to obtain from the people a vindication of the blamelessness of his career. He therefore protested:

'I have not defrauded you, nor oppressed you. Whose ox have I taken? Whose ass? Can any man confront me with having taken from his hand even a sandal, as a bribe, that I should turn away my eyes from his misdoing?' And all the people, with one unanimous consent, cried: 'Thou hast not defrauded us, nor oppressed us, neither hast thou taken aught of any man's hand.'

But the old man was not content; he wanted to bind the people by a solemn oath, as in the very sight of God and the king; and therefore he said, lifting his hand to heaven, 'I call God to witness against you this day, and his anointed king, that what you have said is true.' And again, from the lips of all the people, with one unanimous shout, there came the response, 'He is witness.' The old man was comforted and added, 'Yes, God is witness: the very God who brought our people out of Egypt, and appointed Moses and Aaron.'

## 2    He designated his people's sin

It was a great opportunity to show them where they had done wrong; and a man whose own hands are clean is permitted to be the sincere critic of others' misdoing. In several particulars he pleaded with that dense mass of people, and dared to hold up the crimes of his nation, that they might see them as they were.

First, he showed them the difference between their former and their latter method of procedure. He carried their thoughts back to Egypt and, in effect, said: When your fathers were in bondage to the Egyptians, and under the oppression of Pharaoh, you cried to Jehovah, and in gracious answer he raised up deliverance. And when in the days of the Judges you were oppressed first by Sisera, then by the Philistines, and then by the people of Moab, you cried to God for deliverance, and it came; but now, when the threatened invasion of Nahash, the king of the Ammonites, is filling the horizon with thunderclouds, instead of holding a great convocation for prayer, you insist on my appointing a king. Why have you deteriorated? Why was prayer your natural resort three hundred years ago, and now it is neglected? Is it not because you are prayerless that you have drifted from your ancient moorings? In this is a great sin.

Second, in his dealing with the people, he put a new reading on past history. On their side, they pointed out the successive catastrophes that had befallen their country. Samuel, of course, admitted the successive afflictions that had befallen his people, but he made it clear that it was not the presence or absence of a monarchy, but the want of singleness of purpose, and devotion to Jehovah, that had been the cause and root of all their troubles.

Third, he indicated to the people that God had never failed to send them a man when a man was wanted. 'See how perpetually in the dark hour, in answer to prayer, God has sent you the man who was needed. Could you not have trusted him; and instead of being so urgent for a king, have waited for him to do for you as he has done in the past?'

Last, he said: 'My countrymen, you have greatly deteriorated; you have failed your faith; you have demanded a visible king, but have forgotten the invisible Lord. You have taken shelter under the idea of a new royalty, whereas God was your King, your true Head, the Leader and Patron of the nation. You should have rested only on him.'

It was brave thing, a noble thing, a right thing, for Samuel to show to his people how they had drifted from the old true standing ground of faith into practical atheism and unbelief.

### 3   Samuel's assurance

Having handed over his office to Saul, who from then on was to be the shepherd and leader of the chosen people, and having dealt with their failure and deterioration, he went on to say with inimitable sweetness, 'The LORD will not forsake his people for his great name's sake.' Oh, take these words to heart, and let them sink, like a refrain of music, into your soul.

The old prophet went on to say: 'It hath pleased the LORD to make you his people.' God hides his reasons. He loves because he will. This assurance applies to men.

# 10

# Not Ceasing in Prayer

*1 Samuel 12:16–25*

In all Samuel's career there is nothing finer than the closing scene of his public action as the judge and leader of the Hebrew nation. Naturally he found it difficult to step down from his premiership, and inaugurate a régime with which he had no sympathy, since it seemed to be a setting aside of Israel's greatest glory in having God for King. But he suppressed his strong personal feelings, and did his best to start the nation on the new path it had chosen, selecting a king with the utmost care, bridging over the gulf between the old order and the new.

We cannot turn from the record of the great convocation, assembled before the Lord at Gilgal to ratify Saul's election, without noticing the repeated allusions to Samuel's power in prayer. His whole career seems to have been bathed in the spirit of supplication.

As a boy, with hands meekly clasped, as Sir Joshua Reynolds has depicted him, he asked God to speak, while his ear was quick and attentive to catch his lowest whispers. In the Psalms he is mentioned as chief among those who call on God's name, and as having been answered (99:6). Jeremiah alludes to the wonderful power he exercised in intercessory prayer when he pleaded for his people (15:1). All Israel knew the long, piercing cry of the prophet of the Lord. In their perils his intercession had been their deliverance, and in their battles his prayers had secured them victory (1 Sam. 7:8; 8:6). There was 'an open road' between God and him, so that thoughts of God's thinking were able to come into his heart; and he reflected them back again with intense and burning desire.

### 1   Samuel's prayer for thunder and rain

The heart of man cries out for divine authentication. If our nature realized its divine ideal, it would discern God in the ordinary and common incidents of providence. But the eyes of the soul are blinded, and men do not see the traces of the divine footprints across the world day by day.

In default of the faculty of detecting God's presence in the noiseless and ordinary providence of life, man asks for some startling phenomena to prove that God is speaking. Samuel knew this, and he perhaps longed for some divine corroboration of his words. He had surrendered his prerogatives, and introduced his successor; had confronted his people with their sins, and announced the heavy penalties that must follow on disobedience; now he desired that they should hear another voice, affirming his words, and pressing them home on conscience and on heart.

He concluded his address and appeal with the announcement, 'Now therefore stand and see this great thing, which the LORD will do before your eyes. Is it not wheat harvest today? I will call unto the LORD, and he shall send thunder and rain; that ye may perceive and see that your wickedness is great, which ye have done in the sight of the LORD, in asking you a king.'

During the wheat harvest, lasting from the middle of May to the middle of June, rain is almost unknown in Palestine, and the occurrence of a thunderstorm, coming as it did at *the call* of the aged prophet, was too startlingly unusual to be viewed as other than the divine authentication of his claims.

We cannot be too thankful for the witness of the Holy Spirit, whose voice is to the faithful servant of God all, and more, than the thunder was to Samuel. It was this that armed the primitve saints with irresistible power.

May I ask if my fellow servants realize this – that the Holy Spirit is in the church today, that he is prepared to bear his witness to every true word that is spoken in the name of Jesus, and that he will convict of sin, righteousness, and judgment; so that the faith of our hearers should not stand in the wisdom of man, but in the power of God.

This is often the fatal lack of our preaching. We speak earnestly and faithfully, but we do not sufficiently look for nor rely on the divine co-witness; we do not understand the communion and fellowship of the Comforter; and our hearers do not hear his voice thrilling their souls, as thunder in the natural world, with the conviction that the things that we speak are the truths of God. Only let the passionate longing of our heart be, 'Father, glorify thy name,' and voices will come as from heaven, saying, 'I have both glorified it, and will glorify it again.' While some that stand by may say that 'it thundered,' others will say, 'an angel spake' (John 12:28–29).

## 2   Samuel's unceasing intercessions

Terrified by the loud thunder peals and the torrents of rain, the people were eager to secure Samuel's intercession on their behalf. 'Pray for thy servants unto the LORD *thy* God,' they said, 'that we die not'; and the emphasis they laid on the word *thy* seemed to indicate that they felt no longer worthy of their ancient prerogative as the chosen people. Touched with their appeal, and confident that Jehovah only desired to corroborate his word, the aged seer calmed their fears, urged them never to turn aside to vain idols, which could neither profit nor deliver, assured them that the Lord would not forsake them, and ended with the striking words: '*Moreover as for me, God forbid that I should sin against the LORD in ceasing to pray for you.*'

*a.  Samuel realized that prayer was action in the spiritual plane.*
He could no longer exert his energies for his people, as he had done. The limitations imposed by his advancing years, and by the substitution of the kingdom for his judgeship, made it impossible that he should make his yearly rounds as before; but he was able to translate all that energy into another method of helpfulness. The prayers of God's saints were equivalent, from then on, to battalions of soldiers.

*b.  Samuel viewed prayer as a divine instinct.*   For him to thwart the promptings toward prayer that arose within his soul would be nothing short of sin. 'God forbid,' he said, 'that I should sin against [him] in ceasing to pray.'

Let us recognize that, logic or no logic, men pray, and they want to pray. The instinct to do so seems to be part of ourselves. To thwart this instinct is to do violence to our noblest nature, to grieve the Holy Spirit of God, and to sin against the divine order. Prayer is the response of the soul to God, the return tide from us to him, the sending back in vapour what we receive in showers of heavenly rain.

c. *Samuel viewed prayer as a trusteeship.*    He could no longer act as judge, but he felt that the interests of the nation had been entrusted to his hands for the highest ends, and it would be treachery to fail in conserving and extending them, at least by his intercessions. The failure of Saul to realize his ideal only elicited the more strenuous appeals to God to save both king and people, and the victory we must record in our next chapter must have been due to his eager urgings.

# 11

# The Cause of Saul's Downfall

## 1 Samuel 13:13–14

This chapter is the story of a great tragedy, since it contains the history of the incident that revealed Saul's unfitness to be the founder of a line of kings.

Let us gather around this story, not only because it has so much to do with the history of God's people, but because it is full of instruction for ourselves. Turning from Saul to David, Samuel said, 'The LORD hath sought him a man after his own heart.' It is therefore clear that in some way Saul had ceased to be 'a man after God's own heart,' and it becomes us to carefully inquire the reason so we may avoid the rocks on which this good ship split and foundered.

You will notice that the chapter that tells the history of this tragedy also contains the story of the unutterable distress to which the chosen people had been reduced by another invasion of the Philistines. We are told, for instance, in verse 6, that the people of Israel were in a difficult situation, that they were distressed, that they hid themselves in caves and thickets, in rocks and in pits. Indeed, some of them even crossed the Jordan, and forsook their people in the hour of their extremity; while those who were yet associated with Saul and Jonathan, as the nucleus of the royal army, followed him trembling (v. 7). A spirit of fearfulness had settled down on the entire people; the old national spirit had decayed; it seemed as though they could never again be induced to stand against the Philistines, any more than a flock of sheep against a pack of wolves.

A further proof of the hapless misery of the people is adduced in verse 19: there was no smith to be found throughout the entire land of Israel, and the Hebrews had to take their implements of agriculture down to the blacksmiths of the Philistines so that they might be sharpened for their use. Never in the history of the chosen people were there more dire calamity, more absolute hopelessness and despair, than reigned around Saul and throughout the entire country at this hour.

At this juncture Saul seems to have withdrawn his troops, such as they were, from Michmash, and to have taken up his position on the ancient site of Gilgal, where the act of circumcision was performed after Israel had crossed the Jordan under Joshua. There on the level land, and therefore exposed to the assault of the Philistine hosts at any moment, Saul seems to have pitched his camps; while his heroic son, Jonathan, kept up a post of observation in the vicinity of the Philistine hosts.

While Saul with his soldiers remained at Gilgal, every day marked the reduction of his host. This man and that stole away, either across the Jordan as a refugee, or to hide in some hole and corner of the hills.

It may be asked why, at such a time, Saul did not make one desperate effort against the Philistines. Why did he wait there day after day, while his army evaporated before his eyes? Ah! thereby hangs a story – to understand it we must turn back a page or two in the inspired record. In 10:8, in that early morning interview when Samuel designated Saul for the crown, he told him that the crisis of his life would overtake him at Gilgal – a prophecy the fulfilment of which had now arrived. 'Thou shalt go down before me to Gilgal; and, behold, I will come down unto thee, to offer burnt offerings, and to sacrifice sacrifices of peace offerings: seven days shalt thou tarry, till I come to thee, and shew thee what thou shalt do.'

## 1   Saul's mistake

This command, uttered three years before to Saul, as he stood on the threshold of his vast opportunities, involved two things, and each of them constituted a supreme test.

First, whether or not he was prepared to act. Not as absolute monarch determining his own policy, but as God's servant, receiving the marching orders of his life through the prophet's lips; not acting as an autocrat, but as one to whom there had been a delegation of divine authority.

Second, whether he could control his impetuous nature, put the curb on his impulse, and hold himself well in hand.

It was this embargo that Samuel had laid on him that made him wait day after day. Can you imagine how his chosen advisers and warriors would come to him and urge him to do something? But he waited day after day. 'He tarried seven days, according to the set time that Samuel had appointed: but Samuel came not to Gilgal; and the people were scattered from him.' Then it would seem that shortly after the expiration of the allotted time he could wait no more. He thought that Samuel must have forgotten the appointment, or had been intercepted in making his way from Ramah through the Philistine lines. He had waited until within half an hour (because to offer a burnt offering and a peace offering could not take much longer), and then spoiled the whole by his inability to delay further; and he said to the priest, who still lingered by the ancient site where God had been worshipped and the tabernacle posted, 'Bring hither a burnt offering to me, and peace offerings.' 'And it came to pass, that as soon as he had made an end of offering the burnt offering, behold, Samuel came.'

The person who is after God's heart is the person who will obey God to the letter, who will wait for God to the last moment, who will stand still, until God sets him free.

We become so weary of waiting, and it seems as though God is so slow. God's mighty processes sweep around so wide an orbit. One day is as a thousand years, but his coming is as the morning, as the spring, as the millennium. 'His going forth is prepared as the morning; and he shall come unto us as the rain, as the latter and former rain unto the earth' (Hos. 6:3).

## 2   Saul's insincere plea

Notice Saul's explanation to Samuel. He said: 'Therefore said I,
The Philistines will come down now upon me to Gilgal, and I have
not made supplication unto the LORD: I forced myself therefore,
and offered a burnt offering.' That surely was insincere. He laid
the blame on circumstances; he as much as said: 'The circumstances of my lot forced my hand; I did not want to do it; I was
most reluctant, but I could not help myself; the Philistines were
coming.'

O soul of man, you are greater than circumstances, greater than
things, greater than the mob of evil counsellors. You are meant to
be God's crowned and enthroned king; rouse yourself, lest it
should be said of you also that your kingdom will not continue.

## 3   Mark the alternative to this

In answer to all this Samuel, speaking in the name of God, said: 'I
have chosen a man after my own heart, who will perform all my
will.' In Jesse's home the lad was being prepared who could
believe, and who would not hurry.

Wait for the Lord. Let your heart stop its feverish beating, and
your pulse register no more its tumultuous waves of emotion! To
act now would only disappoint the highest hopes, mar the divine
purposes, and set stones rolling that will never be stopped. Wait
for God; stand still, and see his salvation. His servant is coming
up the pass; his steps may not be quite so speedy as we would have
them, but he will arrive to the moment – not a moment too soon,
but not a moment too late. Oh, wait, my soul, wait on God; for he
cannot be behind, as he will not be before, the allotted and
appointed moment.

# 12

# 'Two Putting Ten Thousand to Flight'

## *1 Samuel 14*

Just two young men, with the glow of patriotism in their hearts, and trust in God as their guiding star – imagine what they can do!

Jonathan was a true knight of God, who anticipated some of the noblest traits of Christian chivalry. We may almost say of him that he was the Hebrew Bayard, a soldier without fear and without reproach. He lived pure, spoke true, righted wrong, was faithful to the high claims of human love, and followed the Christ, though as yet he did not know him. His character serves as a bright background on which that of his father is but a sorry contrast.

From the Jordan bank, a noble valley, twelve miles in length, leads up into the hill country of central Palestine. Two miles from the head of this narrow passage, and about eight miles due north of Jerusalem, the cliffs on either side become very precipitous, and approach each other almost to touching.

The ridge on the north was called Bozez, or 'shining,' because it reflects all day the full light of the Eastern sun; while that on the south, a few yards away, was known as Seneh, 'the acacia,' being constantly in the shade. Michmash crowned the former, and there the Philistines were encamped; while the little village of Geba lay above the latter, and there Saul had moved his army, such as it was, withdrawing from the plains of the Jordan to watch the movements of the hostile force.

How long the armies watched each other we have no means of knowing, nor can we guess what the result might have been had it not been for the heroic episode we are to recount.

## 1    Jonathan entered into the divine purpose

Jonathan chafed at the inaction and the disgrace that the entire situation caused his countrymen. He was animated also by a profound faith in God, and was prompted by the divine Spirit to an act that issued in a glorious victory and deliverance.

Saul, on the other hand, had no perception of these things. Discouraged by what met his eye and ear from morning to night, he had no power to arouse himself to lay hold on the divine promise of deliverance. The sentence of deposition, which Samuel had pronounced, seemed to shut him up to despair. Happy are they who, like Jonathan, raise themselves above the depression of the moment and ally their weakness with the march of God, as he is always going forth to establish righteousness and judgment in the earth, which has been redeemed by precious blood.

## 2    He yielded himself as an instrument to God

God is always on the outlook for believing souls who will receive his power and grace on the one hand, and transmit them on the other. Happy are they who are not insensible to the divine impulse, nor disobedient to the heavenly vision.

Jonathan was one of those blessed souls who are as sensitive to God as the retina of the eye to light, or the healthy muscle to the nerve; and 'it came to pass upon a day, that Jonathan said unto the young man that bare his armour, Come, and let us go over to the Philistines' garrison, that is on the other side.' In all probability the two slipped away silently in the grey dawn while their comrades were still wrapped in slumber. The imitation of a divine purpose thrilled the ardent spirit of the young prince, of which he gave some clue in the words, 'It may be that the LORD will work for us: for there is no restraint to the LORD to save by many or by few.'

Notice where Jonathan laid the emphasis. He had the smallest possible faith in himself, and the greatest faith in God. All that he aspired to was to be the humble vehicle through which the delivering grace of God might work. This is what God wants – not our strength, but our weakness, which in absolute despair turns to him; not our armies, but two or three elect souls who expect great things and dare them.

Saul, the chosen king, had no such vision and no such faith. He was not sensitive to the divine voice speaking in his soul, but had to depend on the interposition of the priest (vv. 19, 36); he spoke and acted as though the victory depended wholly on the efforts that he and his men might put forth; and in forbidding the use of such simple refreshment as the wild honey of the woods might yield, he forfeited the full results of God's interposition. Throughout the whole day, and especially in this senseless command, which was meant to save time, but really hindered the full result, Saul showed himself oblivious of the one thought that animated the heart of his noble son – that God was working through human instruments to inflict his own judgment on the invading hosts.


### 3    Jonathan trusted in God and God did not fail him

As they ascended the steep cliff, the young men agreed on the sign that should indicate that they were indeed in the line of the divine will, and that God would not fail them. This was graciously granted in the mocking voices of the advanced outposts, which ridiculed the idea that the Hebrews were to be feared (v. 11), even though they would succeed in scaling the crags. 'Behold,' they said, 'the Hebrews come forth out of the holes where they had hid themselves. And the men of the garrison answered Jonathan and his armour-bearer, and said, Come up to us, and we will show you a thing [or we should like to make your acquaintance].'

This was the heaven-given sign, and conveyed the assurance that the Lord had already delivered them into the hand of Israel (v. 10).

The soul that counts on God cannot be ashamed. When the two young Benjamites reached the top they used their slings with such precision that twenty men fell dead to the ground. Because of this, a heaven-sent panic spread from them to the main army behind them, and to the bands of spoilers returning from their night raids. The Philistines could not know that the two who faced them were absolutely alone. It seemed as though they were precursors of a host of resolute and desperate men, and suddenly, in panic, each man suspected his neighbour of being in league against him; 'every man's sword was against his fellow, and there was a very great discomfiture.' Meanwhile, the Hebrews who had been allied to the Philistines, or silently acquiescent in their rule, even they also turned against them; and all who had hid themselves in the hill country of Ephraim, when they heard that the Philistines fled, ran after them and met them in battle.

From his outlook at Gibeah, Saul beheld the wild confusion, and how the multitude swayed to and fro, and melted away. Without delay he hurled himself with his soldiers on the fleeing foe, who fled in order to gain the Philistine frontier by the valley of Aijalon. Every town through which the fugitives passed joined the pursuit, so that the fleeing host was greatly reduced, and thousands of warriors dyed the highways of the land, which they had so grievously oppressed, with their hearts' blood. Thus did God deliver his people in answer to Jonathan's faith.

The unwise prohibition of the king against food had a terrible sequel; first, in the exhaustion of the troops, and, second, in the famished eating of the spoils of the day, without the proper separation of the blood. Still worse, when the day closed in, and Saul asked counsel of God, the divine Oracle was silent. Some sin had silenced it, and the monarch realized that some sin was crying for discovery and expiation. He did not look for that sin in his own heart, where he would have assuredly found it, but in the people who stood around him. Finally he and Jonathan stood before the people as the objects of his divine displeasure, and Saul was prepared even to sacrifice his own son in his moody wrath.

But the people saved him. They cried indignantly, 'Shall Jonathan die, who hath wrought this great salvation in Israel? God forbid: as the LORD liveth, there shall not one hair of his head fall to the ground; for he hath wrought with God this day.' Saul had not only missed the greatest opportunity of his life, but he was already wrapping himself in the unbelief, the jealousy, and the moroseness of temper in which his sun was to be enshrouded while it was yet day.

# 13

# A Remarkable Dialogue

## *1 Samuel 15:12–35*

An intimation of Saul's lapsed obedience was made in the secret ear of Samuel in the dead of night, when God came near him and said, 'It repenteth me that I have set up Saul to be king: for he is turned back from following me, and hath not performed my commandments.'

The faithful soul of Samuel was deeply moved. We are told he was '*angry* – a righteous indignation that one who had been appointed with such solemn sanctions, and had started out so well to achieve glorious deliverances for his people, had so seriously missed his mark. 'He cried unto the LORD all night.'

Samuel travelled some fifteen miles to find Saul, following him from Carmel where, as we have seen, Saul set up a monument, to Gilgal, the site of the ancient shrine where, as one of the versions informs us, the king was engaged in offering sacrifices to Jehovah; and there this most remarkable dialogue took place.

**Saul**   It was begun by the king who, seeing the prophet coming toward him, went out to meet him with an unctuous phrase on his lips, 'Blessed be thou of the LORD'; and, with great complacency in his demeanour, added, 'I have performed the commandment of the LORD.' Whether Saul was blinded and did not really know how far he had deteriorated, or whether he desired to gloss over his failure, and to appear as a truly obedient son so as to deceive the prophet, we cannot tell; but that 'Blessed be thou of the LORD' from *his* lips, and at *such* a moment, has an ugly sound.

**Samuel**   At that moment the sheep began to bleat and the oxen to low. A breath of wind, carrying with it the unmistakable indication of the near presence of a great multitude of flocks and

herds, was wafted to the prophet's ear. It is an unfortunate
occurrence when, just as a man is becoming loud in his protestations of goodness, some such untoward incident suddenly takes
place, so that the lowing of the oxen and the bleating of the sheep
belie his words. With sad irony the prophet said, 'What meaneth
then this bleating of the sheep in mine ears, and the lowing of the
oxen which I hear?'

**Saul** The king excused himself by laying emphasis on the word
*they* – 'They have brought them from the Amalekites: for *the
people* spared the best of the sheep and of the oxen, to sacrifice
unto the LORD thy God'. Notice the subtle effort to conciliate the
prophet by the emphasis laid upon the word *thy* – 'thy God; and
the rest we have utterly destroyed.' It was unroyal and contemp-
tible to lay the blame on the people, and it was an excuse that
could not be allowed.

**Samuel** The royal backslider would probably have gone on
speaking, but Samuel interrupted him, saying, 'Stay, and I will tell
thee what the LORD hath said to me this night.' Then the faithful old
prophet went back to the past. He reminded Saul how insignificant
his origin had been, and how he had shrunk from undertaking the
great responsibility of the station to which God had summoned
him. He reminded him how he had been raised up to the throne,
and how the almighty King of Israel had delegated to him his
authority, requiring that he should act as his designated viceregent.
He reminded him also that a distinct charge had been given him,
and that the responsibility of determining his line of action had
been transferred from himself, as the agent, to the divine Being,
who had issued his mandate of destruction. In spite of all, Saul had
allowed his greed to hurry him into an act of disobedience.

**Saul** The king reiterated his poor excuse: 'Yea, I have obeyed the
voice of the LORD, and have gone the way which the LORD sent me,
and have brought Agag the king of Amalek, and have utterly
destroyed the Amalekites. But *the people* took of the spoil, sheep
and oxen, the chief of the [devoted things] . . . to sacrifice unto the
LORD thy God in Gilgal.' It was as though he had said, 'You have
judged me wrongfully. If you would wait for a little while, you
would see the result of my act of apparent disobedience.' He may
even have persuaded himself into thinking that he meant to sacrifice these spoils now that he had reached Gilgal; or he might have
mentally resolved there and then to sacrifice them, and so relieve

himself of the complicated position into he found himself drifting.

**Samuel**  In answer to this last remark, God's messenger uttered one of the greatest sentences in the earlier books of the Bible, a sentence that is the seed germ of much to the same purpose in the prophets: 'Hath the Lord as great delight in burnt offerings and sacrifices, as in obeying the voice of the Lord? Behold, to obey is better than sacrifice, and to hearken than the fat of rams.'

Then, tearing the veil aside, Samuel showed the enormity of the sin that had been committed by saying: 'Rebellion is as the sin of witchcraft, and stubbornness is as iniquity and idolatry.' These sins were universally reprobated and held up to the contempt of good men; but in God's sight there was nothing to choose between them and the sin of which the king had been guilty. Then, facing the monarch, and looking at him with his searching eyes, the prophet, in the majesty of his authority as God's representative, pronounced the final sentence of deposition, saying, 'Because thou hast rejected the word of the Lord, he hath also rejected thee from being king.'

**Saul**  In a moment the king realized the brink of the precipice on which he stood; and with the cry not of a penitent, but of a fugitive from justice he cringed before Samuel, saying, 'I have sinned: for I have transgressed the commandment of the Lord, and thy words: because I feared the people, and obeyed their voice. Now therefore, I pray thee, pardon my sin, and turn again with me, that I may worship the Lord.'

There is a great difference in the accent with which men utter those words, 'I have sinned.' The prodigal said them with a faltering voice – not because he feared the consequences of his sin, but because he saw its heinousness in the expression of his father's face, and the tears that stood in the beloved eyes. Saul, however, feared the consequences rather than the sin; and that he might avert the sentence he said, as though Samuel had the power of the keys to open and unloose, to pardon or to refuse forgiveness, 'pardon my sin.'

**Samuel**  The prophet saw through the subterfuge. He knew that Saul's penitence was not genuine, but that the king was deceiving him with his words, and he turned about to go away. Then Saul, in the extremity of his anguish, in fear that in losing him he might lose at once his best friend and the respect of the nation, seems to have sprung forward and seized the skirt of Samuel's cloak, and as he did so with a strong masterful grasp, as if to restrain and draw back to himself the retreating figure of the prophet, it tore. When Samuel felt and heard the tear, he said: 'The LORD hath rent the kingdom of Israel from thee this day, and hath given it to a neighbour of thine, that is better than thou.' And he told Saul to remember that the 'Strength of Israel will not lie nor repent' for his sentence is irrevocable. The word had gone out of his lips and could not be called back. There was no opportunity of changing his mind, though Saul would seek it bitterly with tears.

**Saul** Again the king repeated the sentence, 'I have sinned'; but his real meaning was disclosed in the following words: 'Yet honour me now, I pray thee, before the elders of my people, and before Israel, and turn again with me, that I may worship the LORD thy God.' His inner thought was still to stand well with the people, and he was prepared to make any confession of wrongdoing as a price of Samuel's apparent friendship.

Finally Samuel stayed with him, so the elders would not become disenchanted with their king, and that the people generally might have no idea of the deposition of Saul, lest the kingdom itself totter to its fall before his successor was prepared to take his place. The two knelt side by side before God; but what a contrast! *Here* was darkest night; *there* was the brightness of the day. *Here* was the rejected; *there* the chosen faithful servant.

At last the aged man summoned Agag, the king of the Amalekites, to his presence, and Agag came to him 'cheerfully,' hoping without doubt that he would be spared; and saying, as he advanced, 'Surely the bitterness of death is passed – there is no reason for me to fear it.' Then Samuel, strengthened with some paroxysm of righteous indignation, seized a sword that lay within his reach, and cut Agag in pieces before the Lord – a sign of the holy zeal that will give no indulgence to the flesh; and we are reminded of the words of the apostle, 'Make not provision for the flesh, to fulfil the lusts thereof' (Rom. 13:14). To Amalek we must give no indulgence.

May God help us to read deeply into this tragic story. Whenever God our Father puts a supreme test into our lives, let us at any cost obey him. Let us walk circumspectly and wisely, redeeming each opportunity, that God may make the most possible of us and that, above all, we may not become castaways.

# 14

# 'Sin Bringing Forth Death'

## *1 Samuel 18:12*

Never has there been a truer illustration of the words in which the apostle James (Jas. 1:15) describes the genealogy of sin and her fateful family than that furnished by the life history of Saul. No sooner are we told that he had begun to yield to the spirit of evil, than the historian hastens to tell us of the successive steps by which its early suggestions grew into a headlong passion, sending the monarch to one breach after another of the divine law.

It happened this way. About this time, while Saul was smarting under Samuel's sentence of deposition, David for the first time crossed his path. Two accounts are given of the introduction of the young shepherd to the God-forsaken and moody monarch, but they are not mutually inconsistent. The one tells of his entering the royal palace as a minstrel; the other of his prowess in war, which rendered his presence an indispensable asset to the court.

The attacks of Saul's depression and despondency become more frequent and severe; and at last it was suggested by his servants – tradition says, by Doeg the Edomite – that the effect of music should be tried on the poor diseased brain.

The king instantly fell in with the suggestion, and presently David's name was mentioned. The young shepherd was possessed of the qualities that were most captivating for the king. He was a skilful musician. He had already come to be known as a man of valor in the border skirmishes that he engaged in with robbers for the integrity of his father's flock. He was skilful in judgment, and eloquent in speech. Manly beauty characterized his countenance and bearing. It seems as though what happens in measure to all God's servants had happened to David – the unction and abiding of the Holy Spirit had brought out into fair and living prominence his natural traits.

The description of David given to him greatly pleased the king, who was always on the outlook for promising youths; and he sent a summons to Jesse to send him his son David, who was with the sheep. Such a summons could not be disregarded, and making up a present of the produce of his farm, the aged father sent his Benjamin to begin to tread the difficult and intricate paths of royal favour. 'And David came to Saul, and stood before him: and he loved him greatly.' And whenever Saul was overtaken by one of his fits of melancholy, David, then probably about eighteen years of age, played the harp for Saul, so that he was refreshed, and the evil spirit left him.

It is probable that the spell of music with which David sought to relieve the king's dark moods was greatly successful. Saul's fits of insanity became less and less frequent; the need for David's attendance at court was greatly relaxed; and the king may almost have ceased to think of him, amid the many suitors for his royal favour.

How long a period elapsed in this way we cannot tell, but another series of events brought Saul and David into closer and more tragic contact. The Philistines had never forgiven the Hebrews for having discarded the yoke, which for so long they had meekly borne; and at last, after a series of forays and raids on the southern borders of Canaan, the tide of invasion could no longer be restrained. It rolled across the frontiers, and poured through the valleys, until the Philistine hosts were gathered together in the valley of the Terebinth, which belonged to Judah, and pitched their camp at Ephes-dammin, 'the Boundary of Blood,' so called, probably from the dark and bloody encounters that had taken place there. The valley, or wadi, is broad and open, and about three miles long. It is divided in the centre by a remarkable ravine, or trench, formed by a mountain torrent, which is full of foaming water in the winter, though dry in summer. It was the presence of this gorge or channel, some twenty feet wide, with steep vertical sides, and with a depth of ten or twelve feet, that prolonged the issue for so long, so that the two hosts lay watching each other for forty days, neither of them daring to face the hazard involved in crossing the valley and its ravine, in the face of the other.

The full story of the combat with Goliath belongs to the life of

David; we touch on it here only as it concerns the ill-fated and hapless Saul.

When the gigantic Philistine champion strode forth, and even dared to come near the lines of the Hebrew troops, and when he boldly challenged the armies of Israel to produce a man worthy to take up the gage of battle, Saul was as dismayed and panic-stricken as any of his soldiers. It is said that he was 'greatly afraid' (17:11). Though he was God's chosen king, and in his earlier life he had stood in the might of a simple faith, his disobedience had severed the source of his power, and he had become as weak as any other person. All that Saul could do, in the face of the brag-gart blasphemy of Goliath, was to hold out the most lavish prom-ises of what he would do for the hero who would take up the chal-lenge, and make the proud Gittite bite the dust.

When David finally was brought into his presence, avowing his determination to go alone to fight the Philistine, Saul sought to dissuade him. 'Thou art not able to go against this Philistine to fight with him.' The point of David's narrative of his successful conflicts with the lion and bear was entirely lost on him. Saul looked on them as the result of superior agility and sinewy strength; he did not fathom David's meaning as he spoke of the great deliverance that Jehovah had given him (17:37). Already the young psalmist was saying to himself:

> The LORD is my light and my salvation,
> Whom shall I fear?
> The LORD is the strength of my life,
> Of whom shall I be afraid?

On the ground of expediency, after his return to Gibeah, Saul set David over the men of war. The harp was exchanged, for the most part, for the sword; and as he went forth on his expeditions against the hereditary foes of Israel, he became more and more necessary to the stability of the throne, as he became increasingly the darling of the nation. 'Whithersoever Saul sent him, he behaved himself wisely.' Out of this popularity originated the great sin of Saul's life.

On one occasion, as Saul and David were returning from some final and decisive victory over the Philistines (v. 6), the people crowded to meet them and the troops; and the women, dressed in gay attire, danced around, singing to the music of their tambourines and three-stringed instruments. As they performed the usual sacred dance they sang responsively, 'answering one another,' an ode of victory, of which this was the refrain:

> Saul hath slain his thousands,
> And David his ten thousands.

The king was instantly smitten with the dart of jealousy. His soul was set on fire with the thought that it was probably that David was the neighbour of whom Samuel had spoken as being the divinely designated successor to the kingdom, which was even now passing from his hand. 'And Saul was very wroth, and the saying displeased him; and he said . . . What can he have more but the kingdom?'

'And Saul eyed David from that day forward.' All the love and admiration he had entertained toward him turned to gall and bitterness. His old malady, which had been charmed away from him, came back with stronger force than before; and on the day after the incident, brooding over his fancied wrongs, it seemed as though his entire nature were suddenly thrown open to an evil spirit. Raving in a mad fit of frenzy, he caught up the spear that stood beside him as the emblem of his royal state, and hurled it at David who was sitting before him, endeavouring to charm away his malady. Not once, but twice, the murderous weapon quivered through the air; but David 'avoided out of his presence twice,' no doubt imputing the attempt on his life to the king's illness, and having no idea of the jealousy that was burning in his soul like fire.

# 15

# The Sin of Jealousy

## 1 Samuel 18

Among the most terrible of human sins is jealousy – and of all the delineations of it none is more absolutely true to life colouring than this portrait of the first king of Israel.

### 1   Jealousy opens the door to the devil

In Saul's case the interval was the briefest possible. On the next day, after the song of the women, which first aroused in his heart the feeling of jealousy toward David, we learn that 'an evil spirit' came with force on the ill-fated monarch.

This evil spirit is said to have been 'from God' – a phrase that can only be interpreted on the hypothesis that God permitted it to come, and that this was an obvious result of his sinful life.

### 2   Jealousy defeats its own good

With almost a single bound, David had leaped into the throne of universal homage and affection. 'All Israel and Judah loved David' (v. 16). Not only they, but the court was enamoured of him. He was set over the men of war, and his promotion was good not only 'in the sight of all the people,' but also 'in the sight of Saul's servants'; while Jonathan loved him with a love passing the love of women; and Michal, Saul's daughter, was attracted to him. There must have been something of a spell in the influence of that pure bright soul over all who came into contact with it.

Besides this, the Lord was evidently with him. Note how constantly the sacred chronicle touches that note: 'Saul was afraid of

David, because the LORD was with him' (v. 12); 'David behaved himself wisely in all his ways; and the LORD was with him' (v. 14); 'And Saul saw and knew that the LORD was with David' (v. 28). Moreover, he behaved himself wisely, or prospered (v. 5); 'wisely in all his ways' (v. 14); 'very wisely,' so much so that Saul stood in awe of him (v. 15); 'more wisely than all the servants of Saul, so that his name was much set by' (v. 30).

Under these circumstances, how judicious it would have been for Saul to bind the son of Jesse to himself! Admitting frankly that he was his designated successor, and that he was enjoying the special favour of Jehovah, the king might have used David for the rehabilitation of his waning fortunes. It was evidently impossible to reverse the divine choice, but he might have postponed the infliction of the inevitable sentence. Nothing could have been easier, nothing more politic. But instead of this, Saul allowed his mad passion to smoulder and sometimes burst into a flame, until it broke out in irresistible fury, and consumed the house of his life.

### 3    Jealousy is very inventive of methods of executing its purpose

Trace this in the history before us. First Saul, under the excuse of his sickness, attempts to take David's life with his own hand. He knew that the murderous deed would be charged to the deranged condition of his mind, and therefore, with impunity, twice threw the javelin at the minstrel who sought to charm away his illness.

Then he sought to throw him into positions of extreme peril, by inciting him to valiant deeds on the field of battle, and in border warfare. For a bribe he promised him his elder daughter, Merab, and to this was added the appeal of religion, and no motive could be more potent with this devout and chivalrous soul. 'And Saul said to David, Behold my elder daughter Merab; her will I give thee to wife: only be thou valiant for me, and fight the LORD's battles.' Then, with unsparing hand, the sacred writer draws aside the veil, and recites to us the secret thoughts that were passing in that dark and evil-haunted nature – 'For Saul said, Let not mine hand be upon him, but let the hand of the Philistines be upon him.'

The stratagem had failed, but it seemed too insidious, and too likely to realize the royal purpose, to be abandoned without being put to one further proof; and Michal, Saul's younger daughter, who really loved David, at this time at least, was made the prize to allure the young unsuspecting warrior to fresh encounters with the Philistines. To his servants, Saul must have seemed to be sincerely attached to David, and to desire, with genuine earnestness, to enrol him in his family. He was playing clearly a game of unusual adroitness. On the one hand, his servants really believed that the king delighted in David, and wanted the alliance; on the other, 'Saul thought to make David fall by the hand of the Philistines.'

It was only after the plot had failed, and it seemed as though, through the providence of God, David was possessed of a charmed life, that Saul spoke to Jonathan his son, and to all his servants, that they should slay David; again he hurled his javelin at him with such force that it stuck, quivering in the palace wall. He later pursued him, first to his own home, and finally to Samuel's home in Naioth (see chap. 19).

### 4   Jealousy of the innocent is unable to avail against God

It was remarkably so with David. Saul was set on alluring him to his ruin. Through God's interposition, however, each murderous intent was foiled, and became the cause of the still greater popularity to his rival. If he is set over the men of war, he prospers wherever he is sent; if he is separated from the immediate proximity of the king, and permitted to go in and out before the people, the whole nation loves him (18:13, 15). If he is sent to fight the Philistines, he slays not one hundred but two, so that his name is 'much set by' (v. 30). If Saul urges Jonathan to slay him, he drives his own son into a closer friendship, and forces him to plead the cause of the twin soul with which his own was knit. Everything that is meant for ill turns out for good.

# 16

# A Great Sunset

## *1 Samuel 25:1*

Samuel finally came to his end, as far as this world at least was concerned; and was borne to his grave, as a shock of corn fully ripe. Though he had spent the last years in retirement, partly because of his great age, and partly because of the breach between the king and himself, he had never lost the love and respect of his people. So when the tidings sped through the country that he had fallen into that blessed sleep that God gives to his beloved, the event was felt to be a national calamity, so that from Dan in the far north to Beersheba on the southern frontier, 'all the Israelites were gathered together, and lamented him, and buried him.'

The impression made on his contemporaries lingered, as an afterglow, long after his death. Again and again he is referred to in the sacred record.

First Chronicles 9:22 suggests that he laid the foundations of that elaborate organization of Levites for the service of the sanctuary that was perfected by David and Solomon.

First Chronicles 26:27–28 asserts that he began to accumulate the treasures by which the house of the Lord was ultmately erected in the reign of David's mighty son.

Second Chronicles 35:18 contains a passing reference to some memorable Passover Feast, which he instituted.

Psalm 99:6, and Jeremiah 15:1, commemorate the fragrance of his perpetual intercessions.

Acts 3:24 and 13:20 indicate what a conspicuous landmark was furnished by his life and work in the history of his people.

Hebrews 11:32–33 places him in the long gallery of time. 'The time would fail me to tell . . . of Samuel . . . who through faith . . . wrought great righteousness . . .'

## 1   The blessedness of his life

Though Samuel's career was an arduous one, it must have been filled with the elements of true blessedness.

*a. He was pre-eminently a man of prayer.*    This was his perpetual resort; he never ceased to pray. Many a sleepless night he spent in tears and prayers for the king whom he had set up, and into whose hands he had committed the national interests as a precious charge.

All books, says an eloquent writer, are dry and tame compared to the great unwritten book prayed in the closet. The prayers of exiles! The prayers of martyrs! The prayers of missionaries! The prayers of the Waldenses! The prayers of the Covenanters! The sighs, the groans, the inarticulate cries of suffering men, whom tyrants have buried alive in dungeons, whom the world may forget, but God never! Can any epic equal those unwritten words which pour into the ear of God out of the heart's fullness? But these prayers have been deeds. In the words of James 5:16, they have availed much in their working. An energy passes from the holy soul, striving mightily in prayer, which becomes a working force in the universe, an indestructible unit of power, not apart from God, but in union with his own mighty energies.

Let us pray more, especially as life advances. 'More things are wrought by prayer than this world dreams of.'

*b. Samuel was also characterized by great singleness of purpose.*    He could court without flinching the most searching scrutiny (1 Sam. 12:3). His had been a career of stainless and irreproachable honour. The interests of his people had been his all-absorbing concern. The troubles that had befallen his land had only led him nearer God, and bound him more tightly to his fellow countrymen; but when he discovered that they desired him to give up his position, it required all the gifts of God's grace, and all the qualities of a naturally noble nature, to sustain the shock with equanimity. But he set himself to secure the best successor the age could afford, and humbly stepped down from the supreme place of power.

Oh, to be so absorbed in a consuming passion for the glory of God in the salvation of others, that we may be oblivious of ourselves, willing to take second place.

c. *Samuel was also careful to construct.* When the whole land
was disorganized, he began to lay the foundations of a new State.
The time and care he expended on the schools of the prophets, his
administration of justice in his itineraries, his appeals to the
people in their convocations, formed a great policy that resulted
in a consolidated and united people.

As first of the prophets, as the connecting link between the first
days of the settlement in Palestine and the splendour of Solomon's
reign, by his unblemished character, by his sympathy and
strength, by his evident fellowship with the God if Israel from his
boyish days to his old age, Samuel won from his people the most
profound veneration; and it is not to be wondered at that one of
them – who owed everything to him, though he was unable to
appreciate the majesty of his personality – in the supreme hour of
his desperate need, when all beside had deserted him, turned for
help to the great prophet, though he had been withdrawn for a
considerable time from earthly scenes, and cried, 'Bring me up
Samuel.'

## 2 His blessed death

Death is not a state, but a step; not a chamber, but a passage; not
an abiding place, but a bridge over a gulf. We should speak of the
departed as those who, for a moment, passed through the shadow
of the tunnel, but are now living in the intensity of a vivid existence on the other side. 'God is not the God of the dead, but of the
living, for all live unto him.' None are dead, in the sense of
remaining in a condition of *deadness*. Those whom we call *dead*
are those who died, and passed through death into the other life.

Remember how the apostle Peter describes death. Speaking of
his death, he uses the very word that had been employed in the
conversation on the Mount of Transfiguration, when Moses and
Elijah spoke with the Master of the decease he was to experience
at Jerusalem. 'After my decease' (Luke 9:31; 2 Peter 1:15). The
Greek word is *exodos*. There is only one other place in which that
word occurs in the whole New Testament, when reference is
made to the going out of the people from Egypt (Heb. 11:22).

Death, under this conception, is a going out, not a coming in.
It begins. If it ends, it ends the life of slavery and pain, and opens

the way into a world where the development of the soul will be unrestrained. The Lord justly claims the title, 'the resurrection and the life.' He has abolished death, and brought life and immortality to light through his gospel. We are not now left to the dim light of a surmise, of supposition, or of hesitating guesswork. We *know* that there is a life beyond death, because men saw him after he was risen.

Yes, he lives; and because he lives we shall live also. He has gone to prepare mansions for us in the Father's house. In that world we will see his face; and, in company with kindred spirits, we will do his commandments. Even now I suppose Moses and Aaron are among his priests, and Samuel among those who call on his name, 'in the solemn troops, and sweet societies' of eternity.

# 17

# An Epilogue

### *2 Samuel 1:19–27*

'The Song of the Bow,' for that is the title of the touchingly beautiful elegy with which David's poet mourned over the tragedy of Gilboa, is very pathetic and inspiring. It seemed as though the singer had forgotten the rough experiences that had fallen to his lot through the jealous mania of the king; and, passing over recent years, he was a minstrel-shepherd once more, celebrating the glory and powers of his King.

> *Thy glory, O Israel, is slain upon thy high places!*
> *How are the mighty fallen!*
> *Saul and Jonathan were lovely and pleasant in their lives,*
> *And in their death they were not divided.*

It makes us think of the love of God to hear David sing like that. It reminds us that God has said, 'Their sins and iniquities will I remember no more.' Here at least, long before the Christian era, was a love that bore all things, believed all things, hoped all things, endured all things, and never failed; which thought only of what had been noble and beautiful in them, and refused to consider anything that had been base and unworthy. This is the way that we also would think of Saul, the first king of Israel.

It is a very solemn thought! No career could begin with fairer, brighter prospects than Saul had, and none could close in a more absolute midnight of despair; and yet such a fate may befall us, unless we watch, and pray, and walk humbly with our God.

The reign of Saul would be almost too bitter to contemplate, unless under its rough covering we could detect the formation of the luscious fruit of David's kingdom, destined to sow eternal seed over the world. Similarly, we might despair of the condition to which the 'trinity of evil' has reduced our world if we did not know that in the days of these kings the God of heaven will set up a kingdom that will never be destroyed, nor will the sovereignty of it be left to another people; but it will break in pieces and consume all these kingdoms, and it will stand forever (see Dan. 2:44).

'Samuel the prophet' thus practically bridges the gulf between Samson the judge and David the king; and there is deep significance in the fact that his name is identified with the two books of Scripture that describe this great transitional period, every event of which was affected by his influence.

# DAVID

# 1

# Taken From the Sheep-cotes

## *1 Samuel 16:1*

The story of David opens with a dramatic contrast between the
fresh hope of his young life and the rejection of the self-willed
king Saul, whose course was rapidly descending toward the fatal
field of Gilboa.

Few have had a fairer chance than Saul. Choice in gifts, handsome in appearance, favoured by nature and opportunity, he
might have made one of the greatest names in history. His first
exploit, the relief of Jabesh-gilead, justified the wildest anticipations of his friends. But the fair dawn was soon overcast.

The final announcement of his deposition was made at Gilgal.
Saul, it is said, rejected the word of the Lord; and the Lord
rejected him from being king.

From Gilgal Saul went up to his house at Gibeah, in the heights
of Benjamin: while Samuel went to Ramah, a little to the south –
his house was there; there he had judged Israel for twenty years.

In the selection of every man for high office in the service of
God and man, there are two sides – the divine and the human. We
must consider, therefore: (1) The Root of David in God; (2) The
Stem of Jesse – that is, the local circumstances that might account
for what the boy was; and (3) The White Bud of a Noble Life.

## 1  The root of David

Once in the prophecy of Isaiah, and twice in the Book of Revelation, our Lord is called the 'Root of David.' 'The Lion of the Tribe
of Juda, the Root of David, hath prevailed to open the book, and
to loose the seven seals thereof' (Rev. 5:5).

The idea suggested is of an old root, hidden deep in the earth, which sends up its green scions and sturdy stems. David's character may be considered as an emanation from the life of the Son of God before he took on himself the nature of man, and an anticipation of what he was to be and do in the fullness of time. Jesus was the Son of David, yet in another sense he was his progenitor. Thus we return to the ancient puzzle, that Jesus of Nazareth is at once David's Lord and Son (Mark 12:35–37).

There are four great words about the choice of David, the last of which strikes deeply into the heart of that great mystery.

*a.* *'The LORD hath sought him a man'* (1 Sam. 13:14).    No one can know the day or hour when God will pass by, seeking for chosen vessels and goodly pearls. Let us be always on the alert, with our lamps burning and our nets mended and cleansed.

*b.* *'I have found David my servant'* (Ps. 89:20).    There is ecstasy in the voice, like the thrice-repeated 'found' of Luke 15. David was found long before Samuel sent for him. What was the moment of that blessed discovery? Was there not some secret glad response to the Master's call, like that which the disciples gave, when Jesus found them at their nets, and said, 'Follow me'?

*c.* *He chose David to be his servant* (Ps. 78:70).    The people chose Saul; but God chose David. This made him strong. The thought that he was divinely commissioned was his standby (2 Sam. 7:21). We are immovable when we touch the bedrock of God's choice, and hear him say, 'He is a chosen vessel unto me, to bear my name' (Acts 9:15).

*d.* *The LORD has appointed him to be Prince* (1 Sam. 13:14). Appointments are not due solely to human patronage, nor won by human industry; they are of God. Fit yourself for God's service; be faithful. He will presently appoint you; promotion comes neither from the east nor the west, but from above.

*e.* *'I have provided me a king'* (1 Sam. 16:1).    That answers everything. The divine provision meets every need, silences every anxiety. God has provided against all contingencies, and has his prepared and appointed instrument. As yet the shaft is hidden in his quiver, in the shadow of his hand; but at the precise moment it is needed the most and can be most effective, it will be produced and launched on the air.

## 2  The stem of Jesse

We turn for a moment to consider the formative influences of David's young life. The family dwelled on the ancestral property to which Boaz, that mighty man of wealth, had brought the Rose of Moab. His wealth may have been somewhat decayed through the exactions of the Philistine garrison, which seems to have been posted in the little town.

David says nothing of his father, but twice speaks of his mother as 'the handmaid of the LORD'. From her he derived his poetic gift, his sensitive nature, his deeply religious character. To the father he was the lad who kept the sheep, whom it was not worth while to summon to the religious feast; to his mother he was David the beloved. He honoured both of his parents with dutiful care; and when it seemed possible that they might suffer serious hurt, amid the pelting storm of Saul's persecution, he moved them to the safe-keeping of the king of Moab, the land of his ancestress.

Young David may have owed something to the schools of the prophets, established by Samuel's wise prescience to maintain the knowledge of the law in Israel. They appear to have been richly endued with the gracious power of the Holy Ghost.

But nature was his nurse, his companion, his teacher. Bethlehem is situated six miles south of Jerusalem, by the main road leading to Hebron. Its site is two thousand feet above the level of the Mediterranean, on the northeast slope of the long grey ridge, with a deep valley on either side; these unite at some little distance to the east, and run down toward the Dead Sea. On the gentle slopes of the hills the fig, olive, and vine grow luxuriantly; and in the valleys are the rich cornfields, where Ruth once gleaned, and which gave the place its name, the House of Bread. The moorlands around Bethlehem, forming the greater part of the Judaean plateau, do not however present features of soft beauty; but are wild, gaunt, strong – character-breeding.

Such were the schools and schoolmasters of his youth. But pre-eminently his spirit lay open to the Spirit of God, which brooded over his young life, teaching, quickening, and ennobling him, opening to him the books of nature and revelation, and pervading his heart with such ingenuous trust as the dumb animals of his charge had in him.

# 2

# 'From That Day Forward'

## *1 Samuel 16:13*

Few have had so varied a career as he: shepherd and monarch; poet and soldier; champion of his people, and outlaw in the caves of Judaea; beloved of Jonathan, and persecuted by Saul; vanquishing the Philistines one day, and accompanying them into battle the next. But in all he seemed possessed of a special power with God and man. The secret still eludes us, until we read the momentous words that sum up the result of a memorable day in the obscure years of opening youth. 'The Spirit of the LORD came mightily upon David from that day forward.'

## 1   It began like any ordinary day

No angel-trumpet heralded it; no faces looked out of heaven; with the first glimmer of light the boy was on his way to lead his flock to pasture lands heavy with dew. As the morning hours sped onward, many duties would engross his watchful soul.

A breathless messenger suddenly broke on this pastoral scene, with the tidings of Samuel's arrival at the little town, and that the prophet had refused to eat of the hastily-prepared banquet until the young shepherd had joined the invited guests. How the young eyes must have flashed with pleasure! Never before had he been wanted and sent for in this way. It was a genuine pleasure to feel that the family circle in great Samuel's eyes was not complete until he had come. He therefore left his sheep with the messenger, and started at full speed for home.

## 2   It was the consummation of previous training

We must not suppose that now, for the first time, the Spirit of God worked in David's heart, and that he had probably never experienced, before the day of which we treat, that special unction of the Holy One symbolized in the anointing oil. This blessed anointing for service cannot be ours before we have experienced a previous gracious work on the heart. And it was because all these had been wrought in David by the previous work of the Holy Spirit, that he was prepared for this special unction. It may be, reader, that in the obscurity of your life you are being prepared for a similar experience.

## 3   It was ministered through Samuel

The old prophet had conferred many benefits on his native land, but none could compare in importance with his eager care for its youth. The creation of the schools of the prophets was due to him.

Driving a heifer before him, he entered the one long street of Bethlehem, and summoned the elders to a feast, so as not to arouse the suspicions of the jealous, moody king, who would have tried to take his life if he had suspected the real object of his visit.

When David reached the village, a strange scene met his eye. There he saw his father Jesse, and his seven brothers, who were probably waiting for him in the ancestral home, preparatory to their all going together to the public banquet to which the leading men of the village had been invited. No sooner had he entered, flushed with exertion, health glowing on his face, genius flashing from his eye, royalty in his mien, than the Lord said to Samuel, 'Arise, anoint him: for this is he!' Then Samuel took the horn of oil he had brought with him from Nob, and poured its contents on the head of the astonished lad.

It is likely that the bystanders did not realize the significance of that act; but David probably understood. Josephus indeed tells us that the prophet whispered in his ear the meaning of the sacred symbol. Did the aged lips approach the young head, and as the trembling hand pushed back the clustering locks, did they whisper in the young man's ear the thrilling words, 'Thou shalt be king'? From that memorable day David returned to his sheep; and as the months went by slowly, he sometimes must have wondered when the hour of achievement would arrive. When would he have an opportunity to display and use his new-found force? He had to learn that we are sometimes strengthened with all might to patience and long-suffering as the prelude to heroic deeds; we have to wrestle with the lion and the bear on the hills of Bethlehem, that we may be prepared to meet Goliath in the valley of Elah.

### 4   It was a day of rejection

Seven of Jesse's sons were passed over. Seven is the perfect number: the seven sons of Jesse stand for the perfection of the flesh. This has to be cut down to the ground, lest it should glory in God's presence. The lesson is hard to learn, but its acquisition is imperative.

# 3

# Summoned to the Palace

## 1 Samuel 16:18–19

After his anointing, David returned to his sheep. When Saul, advised by his courtiers, sent for him years later to charm away his melancholy, this was the specific indication he gave to Jesse, his father, 'Send me David thy son, which is with the sheep.' It says much for the simplicity and innocence of the boy's character that he should have returned to the fold, to lead and guard his helpless charge, faithfully fulfilling the routine of daily duty, and waiting for God to do what Samuel had spoken to him of.

A contemporary hand has given a brief picture of his character as it presented itself at this period to casual observers. One of Saul's young men said, 'Behold, I have seen a son of Jesse the

Bethlehemite, that is cunning in playing, and a mighty valiant man, and a man of war, and prudent in matters, and a comely person, and the LORD is with him.'

## 1   The minstrel

He had the poetic temperament, sensitive to nature, and he had the power of translating his impressions into speech and song. Thus we admire his marvelous power in depicting the sacred hush of dawn, where there is neither speech nor language, just before the sun leaps up as a bridegroom to run his race, and the solemn pomp of night, where worlds beyond worlds open to the wondering gaze. And to these we might add the marvellous description of the thunderstorms that broke over Palestine, rolling peal after peal, from the great waters of the Mediterranean, over the cedars of Lebanon to the far-distant wilderness of Kadesh, until the sevenfold thunders are followed by torrents of rain, and these by the clear shining in which Jehovah blesses his people with peace (Pss. 23, 19, 8, 29).

The Psalm began with David. The psalms that he composed in those early days were destined to be sung throughout the world, working on men effects like those worked on the king, of whom it is said that when David took the harp and played with his hand, Saul was refreshed.

## 2   The young warrior

There was abundant opportunity for the education of his prowess. The Philistines' frontier was not far away from his native town. Many skirmishes the men of Bethlehem had with the border warriors, who would sweep down on the produce of their vineyards and cornfields when the harvest was ripe. In these David acquired the character of being a man of valour and a mighty man of war.

But he would have been the last to attribute his exploits to his sinewy strength. By faith he had learned to avail himself of the might of God. Was he not his servant, designated for a great mission, summoned to wage uncompromising war with the uncircumcised?

*For by Thee have I run through a troop;*
*And by my God have I leaped over a wall. . .*
*It is God that girdeth me with strength. . .*
*He maketh my feet like hinds' feet. . .*
*He teacheth my hands to war. . .*
*Thou hast subdued under me those that rose up against me.*

Psalm 18

### 3   Prudent in speech

The discernment of David will appear as our story proceeds. He was as prudent to advise and scheme as he was swift to execute. Whatever emergency threatened, he seemed to know just how to meet it. And this was no doubt due to the fact that his spirit rested in God. The sad mistakes he made may be traced to his yielding to the sway of impulse and passion, to his forgetfulness of his habit of drawing near to God and inquiring of him before taking any important step.

When men live like that, they cannot fail to be prudent in speech, discerning in counsel.

### 4   The charm of his presence

He was David the beloved. Wherever he moved, he cast the spell of his personal magnetism. So he passed through life, swaying the sceptre of irresistible potency over men and women. Beloved of God and man, with a heart timid to the touch of love, the soil of his soul was capable of bearing crops to enrich the world; but it was also capable of the sharpest suffering possible to man.

### 5   God was with him

He thought of God as his Rock, Redeemer, Shepherd, and Host in the house of life, his Comforter in every darksome glen. In weariness he found green pastures; in thirst, still waters; in perplexity, righteous guidance; in danger, sure defence – in what the Lord was to his soul. God's Word, though he knew but a part of it, was perfect, right and pure. He set the Lord always before him; because he was at his right hand, he could not be moved; and therefore his heart was glad.

# 4

# The Faith of God's Elect

## *1 Samuel 17*

Having recovered from the chastisement inflicted on them by Saul and Jonathan at Michmash, the Philistines had marched up the valley of Elah, encamping on its western slope. Saul pitched his camp on the other side of the valley. Three figures stand out sharply defined on that memorable day.

### 1 The Philistine champion

Goliath was tall – nine feet six inches in height; he was heavily armed. His armour became a spoil for Israel; it was eagerly examined and minutely described. They even weighed it and found it to weigh five thousand shekels of brass, equivalent to two hundred pounds. He was protected by an immense shield, carried by another in front of him so as to leave his arms and hands free. He wielded a ponderous spear, while sword and javelin were carried at his side. He was quite a braggard, for he talked of the banquet he proposed to give to the fowls and beasts, and defied the armies of the living God.

### 2 Saul

There was not among the children of Israel a better person than he; from his shoulders and upward he was taller than any of the people. He had also a good suit of armour, a helmet of brass, and a coat of mail; but he dared not adventure in conflict with what he considered were utterly overwhelming odds. He intimidated David with his materialism and unbelief: 'Thou art not able to go against this Philistine to fight with him: for thou art but a youth, and he a man of war from his youth.'

## 3  David

He was only a boy, ruddy and handsome. He carried no sword in his hand; he carried a staff, probably his shepherd's crook; he wore no armour, no weapon except a sling in his hand and five smooth stones that he had chosen out of the torrent bed and put in his shepherd's bag. But he was in possession of a mystic spiritual power; the living God was a reality to him. He had no doubt that the Lord would vindicate his glorious name, and deliver into his hands this uncircumcised Philistine.

Let us study the origin and temper of this heroic faith.

*a. It had been born in secret, and nursed in solitude.*    God was as real to him as Jesse, or his brothers, or Saul, or Goliath. His soul had so rooted itself in this conception of God's presence, that he took it with him, undisturbed by the shouts of the soldiers as they went forth to the battle, and the searching questions addressed to him by Saul.

This is the unfailing secret. Thus alone can the sense of God's presence become the fixed possession of the soul, enabling it to say repeatedly with the psalmist, 'Thou art near, O God.'

*b. It had been exercised in lonely conflict.*    With a beautiful modesty David probably would have kept to himself the story of the lion and the bear, unless it had been extracted from him by a desire to magnify Jehovah. Possibly there had been many conflicts of a similar kind, so that his faith had become strengthened by use, as the sinews of his wiry young body by exertion.

*c. It stood the test of daily life.*    There are some who appear to think that the loftiest attainments of the spiritual life are incompatible with the grind of daily toil and the friction of the home. It was not so with David. When Jesse, eager to know how it fared with his three elder sons, who had followed Saul to the battle, asked David to take them rations, and to take a present to the captain of their division, there was an immediate and ready acquiescence in his father's proposal; 'he rose up early in the morning . . . and took, and went, as Jesse had commanded him.' And before he left his flock he was careful to entrust it with a keeper. We must always be careful that we do not neglect one duty for another; if we are summoned to the camp, we must first see to the care of the flock. He who is faithful in the greater must first have been faithful in the least.

**d.** *It bore meekly misconstruction and rebuke.*　Reaching the camp, he found the troops forming in battle array, and ran to the front. He had already found his brothers and greeted them, when he was arrested by the braggart voice of Goliath from across the valley and saw, to his chagrin, the men of Israel turn to flee, stricken with panic. When he expressed surprise, he learned from bystanders that even Saul shared in the general panic, and had issued rewards for a champion. So he passed from one group of soldiers to another, questioning, gathering further confirmation of his first impressions, and evincing everywhere the open-eyed wonder of his soul that 'any man's heart should fail because of him.'

Eliab had no patience with the words and bearing of his young brother. How dare he suggest that the behaviour of the men of Israel was unworthy of them and their religion! What did he mean by inquiring so minutely after the particulars of the royal reward? Was he thinking of winning it? It was absurd to talk like that! 'Why art thou come down? With whom,' he said, with a sneer, 'hast thou left those few sheep in the wilderness?' Ah, what venom lay in those few words! David, however, ruled his spirit, and answered softly. 'Surely,' he said, 'my father's wish to learn of your welfare was cause enough to bring me here.' It was at this point that the victory over Goliath was really won. To have lost his temper in this unprovoked assault would have broken the alliance of his soul with God, and drawn a veil over the sense of his presence. But to meet evil with good, and maintain an unbroken composure, only cemented his alliance with the Lamb of God.

**e.** *It withstood the reasoning of the flesh.*　Saul was eager for David to adopt his armour, though he dared not put it on himself. He was taken up with the boy's ingenuous earnestness, but advised him to adopt the means. 'By all means trust God, and go; but be wise. We ought to adopt ordinary precautions.'

But an unseen hand withdrew David from the meshes of temptation. He had already yielded so far to Saul's advice as to have put on his armour and girded on the sword. Then he turned to

Saul and said, 'I cannot go with these'; and took them off. It was not now Saul's armour *and* the Lord, but the Lord alone; and he was able, without hesitation, to accost the giant with the words, 'The LORD saveth not with sword and spear.' Now let Goliath do his worst; he will know that there is a God in Israel.


# 5

# 'In the Name of the Lord of Hosts'

## *1 Samuel 17:45*


While the two armies, on either side of the ravine, waited expectantly, every eye was suddenly attracted by the slight young figure which, staff in hand, emerged from the ranks of Israel, and descended the slope. For a little while David was hid from view, as he bent intent on the pebbles that lined the bottom, of which five smooth stones were presently selected and placed in his shepherd's bag. Then, to the amazement of the Philistines, and especially of their huge champion, he sprang up on the opposite bank, and rapidly moved toward him.

Goliath cursed David as he did so, and threatened him that his blood would colour the mountain grass, while his unburied body would be a feast to the wild things of the earth and air. 'Then said David to the Philistine, Thou comest to me with a sword, and with a spear, and with a shield: but I come to thee in the name of the LORD of hosts, the God of the armies of Israel whom thou hast defied.'


### 1   The talisman of victory

'The name of the LORD of hosts.' Throughout the Scriptures, a name is not simply, as with us, a label; it is a revelation of character. Thus the name of God, as used so frequently by the heroes and saints of sacred history, stands for those divine attributes and qualities that combine to make him what he is. The special quality that David had extracted from the bundle of qualities represented by the divine name of God is indicated in the words, *the Lord of hosts.*

To come in the name of the Lord of hosts implied his own identification by faith with all that was comprehended in this sacred name. A person in a foreign country speaks in a very different tone as an ordinary traveller, or if he acts as representative and ambassador of his country. In the former case he speaks in his own name, and receives what respect and obedience it can obtain; in the latter he is conscious of being identified with all that is associated with the name of his country. For a man to speak in the name of England means that England speaks through his lips; that the might of England is ready to enforce his demands; and that every sort of power that England wields is pledged to avenge any affront or indignity to which he may be exposed.

There is much for us to learn concerning this close identification with God before we will be able to say with David, 'I come to thee in the name of the LORD of hosts.' It would be well worthwhile to become so absolutely identified with God that his name might be our strong tower, our refuge, our battlecry, our secret of victory.

## 2   The conditions on which we are warranted in using the name

*a. When we are pure in our motives*   There was no doubt as to the motive that prompted David to this conflict. It is true that he had spoken to the men of Israel, saying. 'What shall be done to the man that killeth the Philistine?' but no one supposed that he acted as he did because of the royal reward. His one ambition was to take away the reproach from Israel, and to let all the earth know that there was a God in Israel.

We must be wary here. It is so easy to confuse issues that are as wide apart as the poles, and to suppose that we are contending for the glory of God, when we are really combating for our church, our cause, our prejudices or opinions.

To fall into this sin, though unconsciously, is to forfeit the right to use his sacred name. How constantly we need to expose our hearts to the inspiration of the Holy Spirit, that he may wholly cleanse them, and fill them with an all-consuming devotion to the glory of God.

**b.** *When we are willing to allow God to occupy his right place.*
David said repeatedly that the whole matter was God's. And David's attitude has been that of every man who has done great things on behalf of righteousness. We must recognize Jesus Christ as the essential warrior, worker, organizer, and administrator of his church through the Holy Spirit. Whatever is rightly done, he must do. We are not called to work for him, but to let him work through us. His skill must direct us; his might empower us; his uplifted hands bring us victory.

**c.** *When we take no counsel with the flesh*     It must have been a hard thing for a young man to disagree with Saul, especially when the king was so solicitous for his welfare. It was well for him, indeed, that David withstood the siren song, and remained unaffected by the blandishments of royal favour. To have yielded to Saul would have put him beyond the circle of the divine environment.

### 3   The bearing of those who use the name

**a.** *They are willing to stand alone.*     The young man asked no comradeship in the fight. He was perfectly prepared to bear the whole brunt of the fray without sympathy or succour; so sure was he that the Lord of hosts was with him, and that the God of Jacob was his refuge.

**b.** *They are deliberate.*     David was free from the nervous trepidation that so often unfits us to play our part in some great scene. Calmly and quietly he went down the slope and selected the pebbles that best suited his purpose. In this quietness and confidence he found his strength. He did not flee because the Lord went before him, and the Holy One of Israel was his protection.

**c.** *They are fearless.*     When the moment came for the conflict, David did not hesitate, but ran toward the Philistine army to meet their champion. There was no fear of the result in that young heart; no tremor in the voice that answered the rough taunt; no falter in the arm that wielded the sling; no lack of precision in the aim that drove the stone to the one part of the Philistine's body that was unprotected and vulnerable.

*d. They are more than conquerors.* The stone sank into the giant's forehead; in another moment he fell stunned to the earth. There was no time to lose; before Goliath could recover himself, or his startled comrades overcome their stupefied amazement, his head had been separated from his body by one thrust of his own sword. And when the Philistines saw that their champion was dead, they fled. The spoils of victory lay with the victor. David took the head of the Philistine as a trophy, and put his armour in his tent.

Let us live alone with God. The weakest man who knows God is strong to do exploits. This is the victory that overcomes the world, the flesh, and the devil – even our faith.

# 6

# Jonathan

## *1 Samuel 18:1*

In heaven's vault there are what are known as binary stars, each probably a sun, but blending their rays so that they reach the watcher's eye as one clear beam of light. So do twin souls find the centre of their orbit in each other, and there is nothing in the annals of human affection nobler than the bond of such a love between two pure, high-minded and noble men. Nowhere is it more fragrant than on the pages that contain the memorials of the love of Jonathan and David.

David was in all probability profoundly influenced by the character of Jonathan, who must have been considerably older. It seems to have been love at first sight. 'When [David] had made an end of speaking unto Saul, the soul of Jonathan was knit with the soul of David, and Jonathan loved him as his own soul.' That night a royal messenger may have summoned David to Jonathan's pavilion, on entering which he was amazed to be greeted with the warm embrace of a brotherly affection, which was never to wane. The young soldier must have shrunk back as unworthy; he must have ruefully looked down at his poor apparel as unbefitting a royal alliance. But all such considerations were swept away before the impetuous rush of Jonathan's affection, as he stripped himself of robe and apparel, of sword and bow and girdle, and gave them all to David. 'Then Jonathan and David made a covenant, because he loved him as his own soul.'

## 1   Consider the qualities of this friend

whom Jehovah chose for the moulding of the character of his beloved.

*a. He was every inch a man.*     The prime condition of two men walking together is that they should agree. And the bond of a common manliness knit these twin souls from the first. Jonathan was every inch a man; as dexterous with the bow as his friend with his sling. He was able to flash with indignation, strong to bear without quailing the brunt of his father's wrath, fearless to espouse the cause of his friends at whatever cost. He was also capable of inspiring a single armour-bearer with his own ardent spirit of attacking an army, of turning the tide of invasion, and of securing the admiration and affection of the entire people who, standing between him and his father, refused to let him die.

*b. He was very sensitive and tender.*     It is the fashion in some quarters to emphasise the qualities supposed to be especially characteristic of men – those of strength, courage, endurance – to the undervaluing of the more tender graces often associated with women. But in every true man there must be a touch of woman, as there was in the ideal Man, the Lord Jesus. In him there is neither male nor female, because there is the symmetrical blending of both: and in us, too, there should be strength and sweetness, courage and sympathy.

*c. Jonathan had a marvellous power of affection.*     He loved David as himself; he was prepared to surrender without a pang his succession to his father's throne, if only he might be next to his friend. We judge a man by his friends and the admiration he excites in them. Any man whom David loved must have been possessed of many of those traits so conspicuous in David himself.

*d. He was distinctly religious.*     When first introduced to us he is accompanied by his armour-bearer. He climbs single-handed to attack the Philistine garrison strongly entrenched behind rocky crags, he speaks as one familiar with the ways of God, to whom there is no restraint 'to save by many or by few'; and when the appointed sign is given, it is accepted as a sign of the victory that the Lord is about to give (1 Sam. 14).

When the two friends are about to be torn from each other, with little hope of renewing their blessed intercourse, Jonathan finds solace in the fact of the divine appointment, and the Lord being between them. Between them, not in the sense of division, but of connection; as the ocean unites us with distant lands. However far we are parted from those we love, we are intimately near in God.

And when, in the last interview the friends ever had, they met by some secret arrangement in a wood, 'Jonathan came to David there, and strengthened his hand in God.' All that those words imply it is not easy to write: our hearts interpret the words, and imagine the stream of holy encouragement that poured from that noble spirit into the heart of his friend.

## 2  Consider the conflict of Jonathan's life.

He was devoted to his father. He was always found associated with that strange dark character.

When his father first ascended the throne of Israel, the Lord was with him, and Jonathan knew it (1 Sam. 20:13). It must have been a delight to him to feel that the claims of the father were identical with the claims of God, and the heart of the young man must have leaped up in a blended loyalty to both. But the fair prospect was soon overcast. The Lord departed from Saul, and his power to hold the kingdom immediately waned. The Philistines invaded his land, his weapons of defence failed him, his people followed trembling, and Samuel told him that his kingdom could not continue. Then followed that dark day when Saul intruded on the priestly office in offering sacrifice. The ominous sentence was spoken, 'The LORD hath sought him a man after his own heart, and the LORD hath commanded him to be captain over his people.'

From that moment Saul's course was always downward; but Jonathan clung to him as if he hoped that by his own allegiance to

God he might reverse the effects of his father's failure, and still hold the kingdom for their race.

At first this was not so difficult. There was no one to divide his heart with his father. But when he woke up to find how truly he loved David, a new difficulty entered his life. Not outwardly, because though Saul eyed David with jealousy, there was no open rupture. David went in and out of the palace, was in a position of trust, and was constantly at hand for the intercourse for which each yearned. But when the flames of hostility, long smouldering in Saul's heart, broke forth, the true anguish of his life began. On the one hand, his duty as son and subject held him to his father, though he knew his father was doomed, and that union with him meant disaster to himself; on the other hand, all his heart cried out for David.

His love for David made him eager to promote reconciliation between his father and his friend. It was only when repeated failure had proved the fruitlessness of his dream that he abandoned it; and then the thought must have suggested itself to him: Why not join your fortunes with his whom God has chosen? The new fair kingdom of the future is growing up around him – identify yourself with it, though it be against your father.

The temptation was pleasing and masterful, but it fell blunt and ineffectual at his feet. In some supreme moment he turned his back on the appeal of his heart and elected to stand beside his father. From that choice he never flinched. When David departed where he would, Jonathan went back to the city. His father might sneer at his league with the son of Jesse, but he held his peace; and when finally Saul started for his last battle with the Philistines, Jonathan fought beside him, though he knew David was somehow involved in alliance with them.

Jonathan died as a hero; not only because of his prowess in battle with his country's foes, but also because of his victory over the strangest passion of the human heart, the love of a strong man, in which were blended the strands of a common religion, a common enthusiasm for all that was good and right.

# 7

# Songs Born of Sorrow

## *1 Samuel 23*

It is remarkable how many of David's psalms date from those dark and sad days when he was hunted as a partridge on the mountains. His path may be tracked through the Psalter, as well as in the sacred narratives of his wanderings. Keilah, Ziph, Maon, Engedi, yielded themes for strains that will live forever. We will now trace the parallel lines of David's history and song.

### 1   A cluster of Psalms

*a. Keilah*   While hiding in the forest of Hareth, tidings came to David of a foray of the Philistines on one of the hapless border towns. 'Behold, the Philistines fight against Keilah, and they rob the threshingfloors.' The year's harvest was at that time spread out for threshing; it was an opportune moment therefore for the plunderer. The labours of the year were being carried off, and the cattle 'lifted by Israel's bitter and relentless foe.' David arose and went down from the hill country of Judah into the plains, met the marauders on their return journey, heavily laden with booty and impeded with cattle. He slaughtered many of them and brought back all the spoil to the rejoicing townsfolk who, in return for his services, gladly lodged and entertained him and his men.

It must have been very welcome to the weary little band. To again be in a town that had 'gates and bars' was a welcome exchange to life in the dens and caves of the earth. And this gleam of comfort probably elicited from the minstrel-chieftain Psalm 31, 'Blessed be the LORD: for he hath shewed me his marvellous kindness in a strong city.'

*b. Ziph*     His stay in Keilah was brought to a close by the tidings, given perhaps by Jonathan, that Saul was preparing an
expedition to take him. These tidings were confirmed through the
ephod, by which David appealed to the God of Israel; and other
information was communicated that the cowardly and ungrateful
townspeople, when forced to choose between the king and himself, did not hesitate to save themselves by surrendering their deliverer. Then David and his men, in number about six hundred,
arose and departed out of Keilah, and went wherever they could
go. They perhaps broke up into small parties, while the leader,
with the more intrepid and devoted of his followers, made his way
to the neighbourhood of Ziph, about three miles south of Hebron.

This was about the lowest ebb in David's life. The king was
searching for him every day with a malice that made it evident
that he had come out to seek his life. In addition to this relentless
hate, there was the meditated treachery of the Ziphites, who
sought to obtain favour with the king by betraying David's hiding
place. Tidings of their intended treachery came to David and he
moved further south to the wilderness of Maon, where a conical
hill gives an extended view of the surrounding country. But the
men of Ziph conducted the king to the spot with such deadly
accuracy, that before David and his band could escape, the little
beleaguered group found the hill on which they gathered surrounded by the royal troops, and their escape rendered impossible. It was fortunate for them that at this juncture a breathless
messenger burst in on Saul with the words, 'Haste thee, and
come; for the Philistines have invaded the land.'

Then David drew a long sigh of relief, and sang Psalm 54: 'Save
me, O God, by thy name, and judge me by thy strength.'

*c. Engedi*     From Maon, when the heat of the pursuit was over,
David moved his quarters eastward to the strongholds of the wild
goat on the shores of the Dead Sea. It is said that grey weather-
beaten stones mark the site of an ancient city, and traces of palms
have been discovered encrusted in the limestone. This was
David's next resort – Engedi, the haunt of the wild goat. Here,
again the psalmist sets his experiences to music in two priceless
songs. Psalm 57, 'Be merciful to me, O God, for my soul trusteth
in thee'; and Psalm 142, 'I cried unto the LORD with my voice;

with my voice unto the LORD, did make my supplication.'

Wilderness experiences also gave rise to other psalms, all of them marked by a recurrence of the same metaphors borrowed from the wilderness and rocky scenery; of the same protestations of innocence; of the same appeals for the overshadowing wing of the most high; of the same delicately-worded references to Saul. Among these are Psalms 11, 13, 17, 22, 25, 64.

## 2   Some characteristics of these Psalms

We cannot deal with these psalms in detail, but one or two features arrest the most superficial glance.

**a.** *There is a conscious rectitude.*    His conscience was void of offence toward God and man. If challenged as to his absolute sinlessness, he would have acknowledged that he was constantly in need of the propitiating sacrifices that would plead for him with God. But, in respect to Saul, or to any treachery against him or his house, he protested his absolute innocence, and turned confidently to God with clean hands and a pure heart, as one who had not lifted up his soul unto vanity, or sworn deceitfully (Ps. 7:3–5; 24).

**b.** *There is great evidence of suffering.*    Of all sources of pain, there is none so hard to bear as the malice of our fellows. This is what David suffered from most of all: that though he was absolutely innocent, though he was willing to give himself to prayer and ministry on their behalf, yet his slanderers pursued him with unrelenting malice – 'Their teeth are spears and arrows, and their tongue a sharp sword' (Ps. 57:4).

**c.** *But his appeal was to God.*

> *Save me, O God, by thy name,*
> *And judge me by thy might!* (Ps. 54:1)

> *Behold, God is mine helper.* (Ps. 54:4)

> *I will cry unto God most high;*
> *Unto God that performeth all things for me.*
> *He shall send from heaven, and save me. . .*
> *God shall send forth his mercy and truth.* (Ps. 57:3)

*Refuge failed me; no man cared for my soul.*
*I cried unto thee, O L*ORD.
*I said, 'Thou art my refuge.'* (Ps. 142:4–5)

What depths of pathos lie in these stanzas of petition! He commits himself to him who judges righteously. If any should read these lines who are unjustly maligned and persecuted, let them rest in the Lord and wait patiently for him. Some little time may elapse before the hour of deliverance may strike, but soon God will arise and lift the poor out of the dust, 'to make them sit with princes and inherit the throne of glory.'

# 8

# The Mercy of God That Led to Repentance

## *1 Samuel 29–30*

Throughout David's season of declension and relapse, the loving mercy of God hovered tenderly over his life. This is illustrated by the present period of David's history. There was a special focusing of divine gentleness and goodness to withdraw him from his purpose, to keep back his soul from the pit. We now trace the successive stages in this loving process of divine restoration.

### 1    In inclining strong and noble men to identify themselves with David's cause

'Now these are they,' says the chronicler, 'that came to David to Ziklag, while he yet kept himself close because of Saul the son of Kish: and they were among the mighty men, helpers of the war' (1 Chron. 12:1). And he proceeds to enumerate them. Some came from Saul's own tribe, experienced marksmen, who could use with equal dexterity the right hand and the left in slinging stones and handling the bow and arrow. Some came from the eastern bank of the Jordan, swimming it at the flood, mighty men of calor, men trained for war. Some came from Benjamin and Judah, assuring David that there was no ground for his suspicions of their loyalty.

Evidently the spirit of discontent was abroad in the land. The people, weary of Saul's oppression and misgovernment, were beginning to realize that the true hope of Israel lay in the son of Jesse. Thus from day to day 'there came to David to help him, until it was a great host, like the host of God' (1 Chron. 12:22).

## 2 In extricating his servant from the false position into which he had drifted

The Philistines suddenly resolved on a forward policy. They were aware of the disintegration that was slowly dividing Saul's kingdom; and had noticed with secret satisfaction the growing numbers of mighty men who were leaving it to seek identification with David, and therefore, presumably, with themselves. Not content with the border hostilities that had engaged them so long, they resolved to strike a blow in the very heart of the land, the fertile plain of Esdraelon, destined to be one of the greatest battlefields of the world. It became drenched with the blood of great leaders such as Sisera, Saul, and Joash, and of vast hosts such as Philistine and Hebrew, Egyptian and Assyrian, Roman and Maccabean, Saracen and Anglo-Saxon. 'The Philistines gathered together all their armies to Aphek; and the Israelites pitched by a fountain which is in Jezreel.'

When this campaign was being meditated, the guileless king assured David that he would accompany him. This was perhaps said as a mark of special confidence. He had seen no fault in his *protégé* from the first hour of his coming into his court; he had no hesitation, therefore, in summoning him to march beside him, and even to be captain of his bodyguard. 'Therefore will I make thee keeper of mine head for ever.' It was a relief to the gentle nature of the king to turn from his imperious lords to this generous, open-hearted soul, and entrust himself to his strong care.

However, it was a very critical juncture for David. He had no alternative but to follow his lord into the battle, but it must have been with a sinking heart. It looked as though he would be forced to fight Saul, from whom for so many years he had fled; and Jonathan, his beloved friend; and the chosen people, over whom he hoped one day to rule. He could not but reply evasively, and with forced composure and gaiety: 'Thou shalt know what thy servant can do'; but every mile of those fifty or sixty that had to be traversed must have been trodden with sad face and troubled heart. There was no hope for him in man. It may be that his heart already was turning in eager prayer to God, asking him to extricate him from the net that his sins had woven for his feet.

If by your mistakes and sins you have reduced yourself to a false position like this, do not despair; hope still in God. Confess and put away your sin, and humble yourself before him, and he will arise to deliver you.

An unexpected door of hope was suddenly opened in this valley of Achor. When Achish reviewed his troops in Aphek, David and his men passed on in the rear with the king. This aroused the jealousy and suspicion of the imperious Philistine princes, and they came to Achish with fierce words and threats. 'What do these Hebrews here? Make this fellow return, that he may go again to his place which thou hast appointed him, and let him not go down with us to battle.' In vain Achish pleaded on behalf of his favourite; the Philistines would have none of it. They pointed out how virulent a foe he had been, and how tempting the opportunity for him to purchase reconciliation with Saul by turning traitor in the fight. In the end, therefore, the king had to yield. It cost him much to inform David of the inevitable decision to which he was driven; but he little realized with what a burst of relief his announcement was received. It was with unfeigned satisfaction that he received the stringent command to depart from the camp with the morning light.

### 3  By the divine dealings with him in respect to the burning of Ziklag

It was by God's great mercy that the Philistine lords were so set against the continuance of David in their camp. They thought that they were executing a piece of ordinary policy, dictated by prudence and foresight; little realizing that they were the shears by which God was cutting the meshes of David's net. Their protest was lodged at exactly the right moment; had it been post-poned but for a few hours, David would have been involved in the battle, or have not been back in time to overtake the Amalekites, redhanded in the sack of Ziklag.

As David was leaving the battlefield, a number of the men of Manasseh, who appear to have deserted to Achish, were assigned to him by the Philistines, lest they also should turn traitors on the field. Thus he left the camp with a greatly increased following. Here, too, was a proof of God's tender thoughtfulness, because at no time of David's life was he in greater need of reinforcements than now.

Contrary to custom, David had left no men to defend Ziklag during his absence. It is difficult to understand the laxity of his arrangements for its safeguard in those wild and perilous times; but apparently not a single soldier was left to protect the women and children. Yet it turned out well, for when a band of Amale-kites fell suddenly on the little town, there was none to irritate them by offering resistance.

In the first outburst of grief and horror, nothing but the gra-cious interposition of God could have saved David's life. On reaching the spot they considered home, after three days' exhausting march, the soldiers found it a heap of smouldering ruins; and instead of the welcome of wives and children, silence and desolation reigned supreme. Those who sometime earlier had cried, 'Peace, peace to thee, thou son of Jesse, thy God helpeth thee,' now spoke of stoning him. The loyalty and devotion that he had never failed to receive from his followers were suddenly changed to vinegar and gall.

*But this was the moment of his return to God.* In that dread hour, with the charred embers smoking at his feet, with the cold hand of anxiety for the fate of his wives feeling at his heart, he suddenly sprang back into his old resting place in the bosom of God.

From this moment David is himself again, his old strong, glad, noble self. For the first time, after months of disuse, he asks Abiathar to bring him the ephod, and he inquires of the Lord. With marvellous vigour he arises to pursue the marauding troop, and he overtakes it, leading them to the work of rescue and ven-geance with such irresistible impetuosity that not a man of them escaped, except four hundred young men who rode on camels and fled. And when the greed of his followers proposed to withhold the rich plunder from those whose fear had caused them to stay back by the brook Besor, he dared to stand alone against all of them, and insisted that it should not be so, but that he who went down to the battle, and he who stayed back with the supplies should share alike. Thus he who had power with God had power also with man.

And when, shortly after, the breathless messenger burst into his presence with the tidings of Gilboa's fatal rout, though it meant the fulfilment of long-delayed hopes, he was able to bear himself humbly and with unaffected sorrow, to express his lament in the most exquisite funeral ode in existence, and to award the Amalekite his deserts.

He was sweet as well as strong, courteous as well as brave. For when he returned to Ziklag, his first act was to send of the spoil taken from the Amalekites to the elders of all the towns on the southern frontier where he and his men were accustomed to staying, acknowledging his indebtedness to them, and so far as possible repaying it.

Thus the sunshine of God's favour rested afresh on his soul. God had brought him up from the horrible pit and the miry clay; had set his feet on a rock, and established his going; and had put a new song of praise in his mouth. Let all backsliders give heed and take comfort.

# 9

# Thrice Crowned

## 2 Samuel 1—4

Two whole days had passed since that triumphant march back from the slaughter of Amalek to the charred and blackened ruins of Ziklag. What should he do next? Should he begin to build again the ruined city? Or was there something else in the divine programme of his life?

On the third day a young man rushed breathless into the camp, his clothes torn and earth on his head. He headed straight for David, and fell to the ground at his feet. In a moment more his tidings were told, each word stabbing David to the quick. Israel had fled before their enemy; large numbers had fallen on the battlefield; Saul and Jonathan were dead also. That moment David knew the expectations of years were on the point of being realized; but he had no thought for himself or for the marvellous change in his fortunes. His generous soul, oblivious to itself, poured out a flood of the noblest tears man ever shed, for Saul and for Jonathan his son, and for the people of the Lord, because they had fallen by the sword.

## 1 David's treatment of Saul's memory

There could be no doubt that Saul was dead. His crown and the bracelet worn on his arm were already in David's possession. The Amalekite had made it appear that the king's life had been taken, at his own request, by himself. 'He said to me,' so the man's tale ran, 'Stand, I pray thee, upon me, and slay me: for anguish is come upon me, because my life is yet whole in me. So I stood upon him, and slew him,' because I was sure that he could not live after that he was fallen.' David seems to have been as one stunned until evening, and then he aroused himself to show respect to Saul's memory.

*a. He gave little attention to the Amalekite.* The bearer of the sad news had been held under arrest, because he admitted he had slain the Lord's anointed; and as the evening fell the wretched man was again brought into the chieftain's presence. David asked, an expression of horror in his tone, 'How wast thou not afraid to stretch forth thine hand to destroy the LORD's anointed?' Then calling one of the young men, he told him to slay the Amalekite.

*b. He next poured out his grief in the Song of the Bow.* This has passed into the literature of the world as an unrivalled model of a funeral dirge. The Dead March in *Saul* is a familiar strain in every national mourning.

The psalmist bursts into pathetic reminiscences of the ancient friendship that had bound him to the departed. He forgets all he had suffered at the hands of Saul; he thinks only of the ideal of his early manhood. His chivalrous love refuses to consider anything but what had been brave and fair and noble in his king. 'Lovely and pleasant,' such is the epitaph he inscribes on the memorial stone.

But for Jonathan there must be a special stanza. Might had also been given to him. Had he not, singlehanded, attacked an army, and brought about a great deliverance? But with all his strength, he had been gentle. A brother-soul; every memory of whom was very pleasant. A knightly nature; dreaded by foe, dearly loved by friend; terrible as a whirlwind in battle, but capable of exerting a woman's love, and more.

> *Thy love to me was wonderful,*
> *Passing the love of women.*

*c. Moreover, he sent a message of thanks and congratulation to the men of Jabesh-gilead.* The indignity with which the Philistines had treated the royal bodies had been amply expiated by the devotion of the men of Jabesh-gilead. They had not forgotten that Saul's first act as king had been to deliver them from a horrible fate. They had organized an expedition that had taken the bodies of Saul and his three sons from the walls of Bethshan, to which, after being beheaded, they were affixed; they had carried them through the night to their own city, where they had burned them to save them from further dishonour – the ashes being reverently buried under the tamarisk tree in Gilead.

As soon as David heard of this act, he sent messengers to the men of Jabesh-gilead, thanking them for their chivalrous devotion to the memory of the fallen king, and promising to reward the kindness as one done to the enitre nation, and to himself.

## 2  David's attitude with respect to the kingdom

There is something very beautiful in his movements at this juncture, evidencing how completely his soul had come back to its trust in God.

This was the more remarkable when so many reasons might

have been given for immediate action. The kingdom was overrun by Philistines; indeed it is probably that for the next five years there was no settled government among the northern tribes. It must have been difficult for David's patriot heart to restrain itself from gathering the scattered forces of Israel and flinging himself on the foe. He knew, too, that he was God's designated king, and it would have been only natural for him to step up to the empty throne, assuming the sceptre as his right. Possibly none would have disputed a vigorous decisive policy of this sort. Abner might have been outmanoeuvred, and have shrunk from setting up Ishbosheth at Nahaniam. So mere human judgment might have reasoned. But David was better advised. He inquired of the Lord, Shall I go up into any of the cities of Judah? And when the divine oracle directed him to proceed to Hebron, he does not appear to have gone there in any sense as king or leader, but settled quietly with his followers among the towns and villages in its vicinity, waiting until the men of Judah came, and claimed him king. Then for a second time he was anointed.

## 3  The characteristics of David's reign in Hebron

For seven years and six months David was king in Hebron over the house of Judah. He was in the prime of life, thirty years of age, and seems to have given himself to the full enjoyment of the quiet sanctities of home. Sandwiched between two references to the long war that lasted between his house and that of Saul is the record of his wives and the names of his children (3:2–5).

Throughout those years he preserved that same spirit of waiting expectancy that was the habit and temper of his soul, and which was so rarely broken in on. He sat on the throne of Judah, in the city of Hebron – which means *fellowship* – waiting until God had smoothed the pathway to the supreme dignity he had promised. The only exception to this policy was his request that Michal should be returned to him; it would perhaps have been wiser for them both if she had been left to the husband who seemed really to love her. But David may have felt it right to insist on his legal status as the son-in-law of the late king, and as identified by marriage with the royal house.

The overtures for the transference of the kingdom of Israel were finally made by Abner himself, in entire independence of

David; it was he who had communications with the elders of Israel, and spoke in the ears of Benjamin, and went finally to speak in the ears of David in Hebron all that seemed good to Israel and to the whole house of Benjamin.

Throughout these transactions David quietly receives what is offered; and only asserts himself with intensity and passion on two occasions, when it was necessary to clear himself of complicity in dastardly crimes, and to show his abhorrence of those who had perpetrated them.

It was a noble spectacle when the king followed the bier of Abner, and wept at his grave. He forgot that this man had been his persistent foe, and remembered him only as a prince and a great man. Then followed the dastardly assassination of the puppet king, Ishbosheth. His had been a feeble reign throughout. Located at Mahanaim, on the eastern side of Jordan, he had never exercised more than a nominal sovereignty. All his power was due to Abner, and when he was taken away the entire house of cards crumbled to pieces, and the hapless monarch fell under the daggers of traitors. David solemnly swore that he would require at their hands the blood of the murdered man.

Then came all the tribes of Israel to that 'long stone town on the western slope of the bare terraced hill,' and offered him the crown of the entire kingdom. They remembered his kinship with them as their bone and flesh; they recalled his former services when, even in Saul's days, he led out and brought in their armies. Then David made a covenant with them, and became their constitutional king and was solemnly anointed, for the third time; king over the entire people.

It is to this period that we must attribute Psalm 18, which undoubtedly touches the highwater mark of thankfulness and adoration. Every precious name for God is laid under contribution; the figure of his coming to rescue his servant in a thunderstorm is unparalleled in sublimity, but there is throughout an appreciation of the tenderness and love of God's dealing with his children.

> Thou hast given me the shield of thy salvation;
> Thy right hand hath holden me up,
> And thy gentleness hath made me great. (Ps. 18:35)

# 10

# The Sin of His Life

## *2 Samuel 11—19*

The chronicler omits all reference to this terrible blot on David's life. The older record sets down each item without extenuation or excuse. The gain for all penitents would so much outweigh the loss to the credit of the man after God's own heart.

### 1 The circumstances that led to David's sin

The warm poetic temperament of the king especially exposed him to a temptation of this sort; but the self-restrained habit of his life would have prevailed, had there not been some failure to trim the lamp.

For seventeen years he had enjoyed an unbroken spell of prosperity; in every war his was successful, and on every great occasion he increased the adulation of his subjects. But such prosperity is always filled with peril.

In direct violation of the law of Moses, he took more concubines and wives; fostering in him a habit of sensual indulgence, which predisposed him to the evil invitation of that evening hour.

He had also yielded to a fit of sluggishness, unlike the martial spirit of the Lion of Judah; he allowed Joab and his brave soldiers to do the fighting around the walls of Rabbah, while he waited at Jerusalem.

One sultry afternoon the king had risen from his afternoon siesta, and was lounging on his palace roof. In that hour of enervated ease, to adopt Nathan's phrase, a traveller came to him, an evil thought. To satisfy this hunger he entered into the home of a poor man and took his one ewe lamb, although his own folds were filled with flocks. We will not extenuate his sin by dwelling on Bathsheba's willing complicity, or on her strict ceremonial purification; it is enough to say she despised her marriage vows to her absent husband. The Scripture record lays the burden of the sin on the king alone, before whose absolute power Bathsheba may have felt herself obliged to yield.

One brief spell of passionate indulgence, and then! – his character blasted irretrievably; his peace vanished; the foundations of his kingdom imperilled; the Lord displeased; and great occasion given to his enemies to blaspheme! Moments of leisure are more to be dreaded than those of strenuous toil.

A message came one day to David from his companion in sin that the results could not be hidden. It made his blood run with hot fever. The law of Moses punished adultery with the death of each of the guilty pair. Instant steps must be taken to veil the sin! Uriah the Hittite must come home! He came, but his coming did not help the matter. He refused to go to his home, though on the first night the king sent him there a meal of meat straight from his table, and on the second made him drunk. The chivalrous soul of the soldier shrank even from sleeping with his wife while the great war was still in process.

There was no alternative but that he should die; for dead men tell no tales. If a child was to be born, Uriah's lips, at least, should not be able to disown it. He bore to Joab, all unwitting, the letter that was his own death warrant. Joab must have laughed to himself when he got it. Uriah was set in the forefront of the hottest battle and left to die; the significant item of his death being inserted in the bulletin sent to the king from the camp. It was supposed by David that only he and Joab knew of this thing; Bathsheba probably did not guess the costly method by which her character was being protected. She lamented for her dead husband, as was customary of a Hebrew matron, congratulating herself meanwhile on the fortunate coincidence; and within seven days was taken into David's house. What a relief! The child would be born under cover of lawful wedlock! There was one fatal flaw, however, in the whole arrangement: 'The thing that David had done displeased the LORD.' David and the world were to hear more of it. But oh, the bitter sorrow that he should have fallen in this way! The psalmist, the king, the man, the lover of God, all trampled in the mire by one dark, wild, passionate outburst. My God, grant that I may wear the white flower of a blameless life to the end!

## 2 Delayed repentance

The better the man, the dearer the price he pays for a short season of sinful pleasure. For twelve whole months the royal sinner wrapped his sin in his bosom, closed his lips, and refused to confess. But in Psalm 32 he tells us how he felt. His bones wasted away through groaning all day long. Day and night God's hand lay heavily on him.

Nathan's appearance on the scene must have been a positive relief. The prophet, by right of old acquaintance, sought a private audience. He told what seemed to be a real and pathetic story of high-handed wrong; and David's anger was greatly worked up against the man who had perpetrated it. The spirit that always characterizes the sullen, uneasy conscience, flamed out in his sentence. The Levitical law in such a case only demanded fourfold restoration (Exod. 22:1). The king pronounced sentence of death. Then, as a flash of lightning on a dark night suddenly reveals to the traveller the precipice over which he is about to step, the brief, awful, stunning sentence, 'Thou art the man!' revealed David to himself and brought him to his knees. Nathan reminded him of the unstinted goodness of God. 'Thou hast despised his word; thou hast slain Uriah; thou hast taken his wife. The child shall die; thy wives shall be treated as thou hast dealt with his; out of thine own house evil shall rise against thee.' 'I have sinned against the LORD,' was David's only answer.

When Nathan had gone, David beat out that brief confession into Psalm 51, that all the world might use it. But long before his pathetic prayer was uttered, as soon as he acknowledged his sin, without the interposition of a moment's interval between his confession and the assurance, Nathan had said, 'The LORD also hath put away thy sin.'

Penitent soul! Dare to believe in the instantaneous forgiveness of sins. You have only to utter the confession, to find it interrupted with the outbreak of the Father's love. As soon as the words of penitence leave your lips, they are met by the hurrying assurances of a love which, while it hates sin, has never ceased to yearn over the prodigal.

# 11

# Sunset and Evening Star

## *1 Chronicles 20—29*

A period of ten years of comparative rest was granted David, between the final quelling of the revolts of Absalom and Sheba and his death. The recorded incidents of those years are few. It is probable that David walked softly and humbly with God, concentrating his attention of the erection of the temple. If he might not build it himself, he would strive with all his might to help him who would.


### 1   Its site

This was indicated in the following manner. David conceived the plan of numbering Israel and Judah. The chronicler says that Satan moved him to it, while the older record attributes the suggestion to the anger of the Lord. The sin of numbering the people probably lay in its motive. David was animated by a spirit of pride and prestige.

In spite of the remonstrances of Joab and others, the king persisted; and the officers went throughout the land, numbering the people. Excluding the tribes of Levi and Benjamin, and the city of Jerusalem, the fighting men of Israel numbered about a million, and those of Judah five hundred thousand.

When the enumeration was nearly complete, and the officers had reached Jerusalem, David's heart struck him, and he said to the Lord: 'I have sinned greatly in that I have done.' A night of anguish could not, however, wipe out the wrong and folly of nine months. David might be forgiven, but he had to submit to one of three modes of chastisement. It was wise on his part to choose to fall into the hands of God; but the plague that devastated his people with unparalleled severity hurt him deeply.

Sweeping through the country, it came at last to the holy city, and it seemed as if the angel of the Lord were hovering over it, sword in hand, to begin his terrible commission. Then it was that David cried to the Lord, pleading that his judgments might be stopped: 'Better let they sword be plunged into my heart, than that one more of my people should perish. I have done perversely; but these sheep, what have they done?' And the angel of the Lord stayed by the threshingfloor of Araunha, or Ornan, a Jebusite, who is thought by some to have been the deposed king of the old Jebusite city. There on Mount Moriah, where centuries before the angel had stopped the uplifted knife of Abraham, God said: 'It is enough; stay thine hand.' That spot became the site of the temple. At the direction of the prophet Gad, David purchased the threshingfloor, the threshing instruments, and the oxen that trod out the grain. He insisted on paying the full price that he might not give God that which cost him nothing; and from that day forward Mount Moriah became the centre of national worship, the site of successive temples, and the scene of the manifestation of the Son of Man.

## 2   Its builder

The last year of David's life, and the fortieth of his reign, was embittered by a final revolt of the discordant elements that had so often given him trouble. Joab at last turned traitor to his old master; and Abiathar, instigated probably by jealousy of Zadok, joined him in embracing the cause of Adonijah, the eldest surviving son.

When the account of the revolt was brought to David, it stirred the old lion heart, and though he had reached the extreme point of physical exhaustion, he aroused himself with a flash of his former energy to take measures for the execution of the divine will communicated to him years before. Not many hours passed before tidings broke in on Adonijah's feast at Enrogel, that Solomon had been anointed king in Gihon, by the hand of Zadok the priest and Nathan the prophet, and that he had ridden through the city on the royal mule, escorted by Benaiah and his men-at-arms. Within an hour all of Adonijah's supporters had melted away, and he was clinging, as a fugitive, to the horns of the altar.

It was probably about this time that David gave Solomon the charge to build the house for God. He enumerated the treasures he had accumulated, and the preparatory works that had been set on foot. It is almost impossible for us to realize the immense weight of precious metal, the unlimited provision of brass, iron, and timber, or the armies of workmen. The surrounding countries had been drained of their wealth and stores to make that house magnificent.

At the close of this solemn charge, he added instructions to direct Solomon in his behaviour toward Joab and Shimei. These charges have the appearance of vindictiveness, but we must give the dying monarch credit for being animated with a single purpose for the peace of his realm. Had vengeance been in his heart, he might have taken it then.

### 3   Its pattern

The Jewish polity required that the king should not only be anointed by the priest but also recognized by the entire people. It was therefore necessary that David's choice should be ratified in a popular assembly, which gathered at the royal command (1 Chron. 28:1). For the last time monarch and people stood together before God. Again he recited the circumstances of his choice, of his desire to build the temple, and the substitution of Solomon for himself. Then turning to the young man that stood beside him, he urged him to be strong and carry out the divine purpose.

Next followed the gift of the pattern of the house that had been communicated to David by the Spirit of God, and an inventory of the treasures from which each article was to be constructed. To David's imagination the splendid temple stood before him complete in every part. The contribution from his private fortune had been most generous, and with this as his plea he turned to the vast concourse, asking princes and people to fill their hands with gifts. The response was beautiful. It is probable that never before or since has such a contribution been made at one time for religious purposes; but, better than all, the gifts were made willingly and gladly.

With a full heart David blessed the Lord before the congregation. His lips were touched with the old fire. Standing on the threshold of the other world, his days seemed as a shadow in which there was no abiding; and then the king and father pleaded for Solomon that he might keep the divine statutes and build the house. Last, he turned to the people, and urged them to join in ascriptions of praise, and there was such a shout of jubilation, of blessing and praise, that the sky rang again; while a great religious festival crowned the proceedings.

It was a worthy conclusion to a great life! How much longer David lived we cannot tell. One record says simply that 'David slept with his fathers, and was buried in the city of David'; another, that 'he died in a good old age, full of days, riches, and honour.'

# ELIJAH

# 1

# The Source of Elijah's Strength

## *1 Kings 17*

This chapter begins with the conjunction 'And': it is therefore an addition to what has gone before, and it is *God*'s addition. When we have read to the end of the previous chapter, we might suppose that was that, and that the worship of Jehovah would never again acquire its lost prestige and power. And, no doubt, the principal actors in the story thought so too. Ahab thought so; Jezebel thought so; the false prophets thought so; the scattered remnant of hidden disciples thought so.

But they had made an omission in their calculations – they had left out Jehovah himself. When men have done their worst, and finished, it is time for God to begin. And when God begins, he is likely, with one blow, to reverse all that has been done without him.

Things were dark enough. After the death of Solomon, his kingdom split into two parts – the southern under Rehoboam his son; the northern under Jeroboam. Jeroboam was desperately eager to keep his hold on his people, but he feared he would lose it if they continued to go, two or three times a year, to the annual feasts at Jerusalem. He resolved therefore, to set up the worship of Jehovah in his own territories. So he erected two temples, one at Dan, in the extreme north, the other at Bethel, in the extreme south. And in each of these he placed a golden calf, that the God of Israel might be worshipped 'under the form of a calf that eateth hay'. This sin broke the second commandment, which forbade the children of Israel making any graven image; or bowing down before the likeness of anything in heaven above, or in the earth beneath. Jeroboam's wickedness was never forgotten in Holy

Scripture. Like a funeral knell, the words ring out again and again: 'Jeroboam, the son of Nebat, who made Israel to sin.'

After many revolutions, and much bloodshed, the kingdom passed into the hands of a military adventurer, Omri. The son of this man was Ahab, of whom it is said, 'he did more to provoke the LORD God of Israel to anger than all the kings of Israel that were before him'. This came to pass because he was a weak man, the tool of a crafty, unscrupulous, and cruel woman.

When the young and beautiful Jezebel left Tyre to become the consort of the newly-crowned king of Israel, it was no doubt regarded as a splendid match. Tyre at that time sat as queen on the seas, in the zenith of her glory: her colonies dotted the shores of the Mediterranean as far as Spain; her ships whitened every sea with their sails; her daughter, Carthage, nursed the lion-cub Hannibal, and was strong enough to make Rome tremble. But, like many a splendid match, it was filled with misery and disaster.

As she left her palace home, Jezebel would be vehemently urged by the priests – beneath whose influence she had been trained – to do her utmost to introduce into Israel the rites of her hereditary religion. Nor was she slow to obey. First, she seems to have erected a temple to Astarte in the neighbourhood of Jezreel, and to have supported its four hundred and fifty priests from the revenues of her private purse. Then Ahab and she built a temple for Baal in Samaria, the capital of the kingdom, large enough to contain immense crowds of worshippers (2 Kings 10:21). Shrines and temples then began to rise in all parts of the land in honour of these false deities, while the altars of Jehovah, like that at Carmel, were ruthlessly broken down. The land swarmed with the priests of Baal and of the groves. The schools of the prophets were shut up; grass grew in their courts. The prophets themselves were hunted down and slain by the sword. 'They wandered about in sheepskins and goatskins, being destitute, afflicted, tormented' (Heb. 11:37); so much so, that the pious Obadiah had great difficulty in saving a few of them, by hiding them in the limestone caves of Carmel, and feeding them at the risk of his own life. But God is never at a loss. The land may be overrun with sin; the lamps of witness may seem all but extinguished; but he will be preparing a weak man in some obscure highland village; and in the moment of greatest need will send him forth as his all-sufficient answer to the worst plottings of his foes. So it has been; and so it shall continue to be.

## 1   Elijah was of the inhabitants of Gilead

Gilead lay east of the Jordan; it was wild and rugged. The inhabitants partook of the character of their country – wild, lawless, and unkempt. They dwelt in rude stone villages, and subsisted by keeping flocks of sheep.

Elijah's childhood was like the other young men of his time. In his early years he probably did the work of a shepherd on those wild hills. As he grew to manhood, his erect figure, his shaggy locks, his cloak of camel's hair, his muscular, sinewy strength – which could outstrip the fiery horses of the royal chariot, and endure excessive physical fatigue – distinguished him from the dwellers in lowland valleys.

As he grew in years, he became characterised by an intense religious earnestness. He was 'very jealous for the LORD God of hosts'. As messenger after messenger told how Jezebel had thrown down God's altars, and slain his prophets, and replaced them by impious rites of her Tyrian deities, his indignation burst all bounds; he was 'very jealous for the LORD God of hosts.'

But what could he do – a wild, untutored child of the desert? There was only one thing he could do – the resource of all much-tried souls – he could pray; and he did: 'he prayed earnestly' (James 5:17). And in his prayer he seems to have been led back to a denunciation made, years before, by Moses to the people, that if they turned aside and served other gods and worshipped them, the Lord's wrath would be sent against them; and he would shut up the heaven so that there should be no rain (Deut. 11:7). And so he set himself up to pray that the terrible threat might be literally fulfilled. 'He prayed earnestly that it might not rain' (James 5:17).

And as Elijah prayed, the conviction entered his mind that it should be even as he prayed; and that he should go to acquaint Ahab with the fact. Whatever might be the hazard to himself, both king and people must be made to connect their calamities with the reason for them. That the drought was due to his prayer is also to be inferred from the words with which Elijah announced the fact to the king: 'There shall not be dew nor rain these years, *but according to my word*'.

This interview needed no ordinary moral strength. What chance was there of his escaping with his life? Yet he went and came back unhurt, in the panoply of a might that seemed invulnerable.

What was the secret of that strength? If it can be shown that it was due to something inherent in Elijah, and peculiar to him, then we may as well turn away from the inaccessible heights that mock us. But if it can be shown, as I think it can, that this splendid life was lived, not by its inherent qualities, but by sources of strength that are within the reach of the humblest child of God who reads these lines, then every line of it is an inspiration.

Elijah's strength did not lie in himself or his surroundings. He was of humble extraction. When, through failure of faith, he was cut off from the source of his strength, he showed more cowardice than most men would have done; he lay down on the desert sands and asked to die.

## 2    Elijah gives us three indications of the source of his strength

'As the LORD God of Israel liveth.' To everyone else Jehovah might seem dead; but to him, he was the one supreme reality of life. And if we would be strong, we too must be able to say: 'I know that my Redeemer liveth.' The person who has heard Jesus say, 'I am he that liveth,' will also hear him say, 'Fear not! be strong, yea, be strong.'

'Before whom I stand.' Elijah was standing in the presence of Ahab, but he was conscious of the presence of a greater than any earthly monarch, the presence of Jehovah. Gabriel himself could not employ a loftier designation (Luke 1:19). Let us cultivate this habitual recognition of the presence of God, for it will lift us above all other fear. Besides this, a conviction had been impressed on his mind that he was chosen by God as his servant and messenger, and in this capacity he stood before him.

The word 'Elijah' may be rendered – Jehovah is my God; but there is another possible translation – Jehovah is my strength. This gives the key to his life. What a revelation is given us in this name! Oh, that it were true of each of us. Yet, why should it not be? Let us from this day forth cease from our own strength which, at best, is weakness; and let us appropriate God's by daily, hourly faith.

# 2

# Beside the Drying Brook

## *1 Kings 17*

We are studying the life of a man of like passions with ourselves
– weak where we are weak, failing where we would fail; but who
stood singlehanded against his people, stemmed the tide of
idolatry and sin, and turned a nation back to God. And he did it
by the use of resources that are within reach of us all. This is the
fascination of the story.

Faith made him all he became, and faith will do as much for us
if only we can exercise it as he did. Oh, for Elijah's receptiveness,
that we might be as full of divine power as he was, and as able
therefore to do exploits for God and truth!

But, before this can happen, we must pass through the same
education as he. We must go to Cherith and Zarephath before we
can stand on Carmel.

Notice, then, the successive steps in God's education of his servants.

## 1 God's servants must learn to take one step at a time

This is an elementary lesson, but it is hard to learn. No doubt
Elijah found it so. Before he left Tishbe for Samaria, to deliver the
message that burdened his soul, he would naturally inquire what
he should do after he had delivered it. How would he be received?
What would be the outcome? If he had asked those questions of
God, and waited for a reply before he left his highland home, he
would never have gone at all. Our Father shows us only one step
at a time – and that, the next; and he bids us take it in faith.

But as soon as God's servant took the step to which he was led, and delivered the message, then 'the word of the Lord came unto him, saying, Get thee hence . . . and hide thyself by the brook Cherith.' And it was only when the brook had dried up that the word of the Lord came to him saying, 'Arise, get thee to Zarephath.'

I like that phrase, 'the word of the LORD came unto him.' He did not need to go to search for it; it *came* to him. And so it will come to you. It will find you out, and tell you what you are to do.

It may be that for long you have had on your mind some strong impression of duty; but you have held back, because you could not see what the next step would be. Hesitate no longer! Step out on what seems to be the impalpable mist: you will find a slab of concrete beneath your feet, and every time you put your foot forward you will find that God has prepared a stepping stone, and the next, and the next; each as you come to it. God does not give all the directions at once, lest we should get confused; he tells us just as much as we can remember and do. Then we must look to him for more; and so we learn the sublime habits of obedience and trust.

## 2   God's servants must be taught the value of the hidden life

'Get thee hence, and turn thee eastward, and hide thyself by the brook Cherith.' The man who is to take a high place before his fellowmen must first take a low place before God. And there is no better way of bringing a man down than by dropping him suddenly out of an area in which he was beginning to think himself essential, teaching him that he is not at all necessary to God's plan, and compelling him to consider in the sequestered vale of some Cherith how mixed are his motives, and how insignificant his strength.

Every saintly soul that would wield great power with people must win it in some hidden Cherith. We cannot give out unless we have previously taken in. Our Lord found his Cherith at Nazareth and in the wilderness of Judaea, amid the olives of Bethany and the solitudes of Gadara. Not one of us can dispense with a Cherith where we may taste the sweets and imbibe the power of a life hidden with Christ, and in Christ by the power of the Holy Ghost.

### 3 God's servants must learn to trust him absolutely

We give at first a timid obedience to a command that seems to involve many impossibilities; but when we find that God is even better than his word, our faith grows exceedingly, and we advance to further feats of faith and service. At last nothing is impossible. This is the key to Elijah's experience.

How strange to be sent to a brook, which would of course be as subject to the drought as any other! How contrary to nature to suppose that ravens, which feed on carrion, would find such food as man could eat; or, having found it, would bring it regularly morning and evening! How unlikely, too, that he could remain hidden from the search of the bloodhounds of Jezebel anywhere within the limits of Israel! But God's command was clear and unmistakable. It left Elijah no alternative but to obey.

There is strong emphasis on the word *there*. 'I have commanded the ravens to feed thee *there*.' Elijah might have preferred many hiding places to Cherith, but that was the only place to which the ravens would bring his supplies; and, as long as he was there, God was pledged to provide for him. Our supreme thought should be: 'Am I where God wants me to be?' If so, God will work a direct miracle rather than allow us to perish for lack. God sends no soldier to war on his own strength.

We will not stay to argue the probability of this story being true. The presence of the supernatural presents no difficulties to those who can say 'Our Father', and who believe in the resurrection of our Lord Jesus. But if corroboration were needed, it could be multiplied many times from the experience of living people who have had their needs supplied in ways as marvellous as the coming of the ravens to the lonely prophet. God has infinite resource; and if you are doing his work, where he would have you, he will supply your need, though the heavens fall. Only trust him!

### 4 God's servants are often called to sit by drying brooks

'It came to pass after a while, that the brook dried up.' What did Elijah think? Did he think that God had forgotten him? Did he begin to make plans for himself? We will hope that he waited quietly for God. Many of us have had to sit by drying brooks;

perhaps some are sitting by them now – the drying brook of popularity, ebbing away as it did from John the Baptist. The drying
brook of health, sinking under a creeping paralysis, or a slow
decline. The drying brook of money, slowly dwindling before the
demands of sickness, bad debts, or other people's extravagance.
The drying brook of friendship, which for long has been
diminishing, and threatens soon to cease. Ah, it is hard to sit
beside a drying brook – much harder than to face the prophets of
Baal on Carmel.

Why does God let them dry? He wants to teach us not to trust in
his gifts but in himself. Let us learn these lessons, and turn from
our failing Cheriths to our unfailing Saviour. All sufficiency
resides in him.

# 3

# The Test of the Home Life

## *1 Kings 17*

### 1    Elijah teaches us contentment

The fare in the widow's home was frugal enough, and there was
only just enough for their daily needs. Human nature, which was
as strong in the prophet as in the rest of us, would have preferred to
be able to count sacks of meal and barrels of oil. But this is usually
not God's way; nor is it the healthiest discipline for our better life.

God's rule is – day by day. The manna fell on the desert sands
day by day. Our bread is promised to us for the day. And they
who live like this are constantly reminded of their blessed dependence on their Father's love.

If God were to give us the choice between seeing our provision
and keeping it ourselves, or not seeing it and leaving him to deal it
out, day by day, most of us would be almost sure to choose the
former alternative. But we would be far wiser to say, 'I am content

to trust you, Father. You keep the stores under your own hand; they will give me less anxiety; they will not lead me into temptation; they will not expose me to jealousy of others more favoured than myself.'

And those who live this way are not worse off than others. No, in the truest sense they are better off. Better off, because the responsibility of maintaining them rests wholly on God; and they are delivered from the fret of anxiety, the strain of daily care, and the temptations that make it almost impossible for a rich man to enter the kingdom of God. The main thing is to understand the precious promise, 'Seek ye first the kingdom of God and his righteousness, and all these things shall be added unto you'. Then let us go on doing our duty, filling our time, working out the plan of our life. Our Father has ample resources: His are the cattle on a thousand hills; and his the waving cornfields, and the myriad fish of the ocean depths. He has prepared a supply for our need, and he will deliver it in time, if only we will trust him.

If these words are read by those who are dependent on daily supplies – with little hope of ever owning more than the daily handful of meal, and the little oil at the bottom of the cruse – let them be comforted by the example of Elijah. The bottom of the barrel may have been scraped today, but on going to it tomorrow there will be just enough for tomorrow's needs. The last drop of oil may have been drained today, but there will be more tomorrow, and enough. Anxiety will not do you good; but the prayer of faith will. 'Your Father knoweth what things ye have need of'.

## 2   Elijah also teaches us gentleness under provocation

We do not know how long the mother watched over her dying child, but she spoke unadvisedly and cruelly to the man who had brought deliverance to her home: 'Art thou come unto me to call my sin to remembrance, and to slay my son?'

A remark so uncalled-for and unjust might well have stung the prophet to the quick, or prompted a bitter reply. And it would have doubtless done so had his goodness been anything less than inspired by the Holy Spirit. But without further remark Elijah simply said, 'Give me thy son'.

If the Holy Spirit is really filling the heart, a marvellous change will come over the rudest, the least refined, the most selfish person. There will be a gentleness in speech, in the very tones of the voice; a tender thoughtfulness in the smallest actions; a peace passing understanding on the face; and these will be the evident seal of the Holy Ghost. Are they evident in you?

> Gentle Spirit, dwell with me,
> I myself would gentle be;
> And with words that help and heal,
> Would Thy life in mine reveal.

### 3    Elijah teaches also the power of a holy life

Somewhere in the background of this woman's life there was a dark deed that dwarfed all other memories of wrongdoing, and stood out before her mind as her sin – 'my sin' (1 Kings 17:18). What it was we do not know; it may have been connected with the birth of that son. It had probably been committed long years before, and had filled her with agony of mind, but in later years the sharp sense of remorse had become dulled; sometimes she even lost all recollection of her sin for weeks and months together.

It is remarkable how different the mental stimulus is that is required by different casts of mind, to awaken dormant memories. In the case of the woman of Zarephath it was Elijah's holy life, combined with her own terrible sorrow. Beneath the spell of these two voices her memory gave up its dead, and her conscience was quickened into vigorous life. 'Art thou come unto me to call my sin to remembrance?'

### 4    Elijah teaches, lastly, the secret of giving life

It is a characteristic of those who are filled with the Holy Spirit that they carry with them everywhere the spirit of life, even resurrection life. Thus was it with the prophet. But mark the conditions under which alone we will be able to fulfil this glorious function.

*a. Lonely wrestlings*    'He took him out of her bosom, and carried him up into a loft, where he abode, and laid him upon his own bed. And he cried unto the LORD.' We are not specific enough in prayer, and we do not spend enough time dwelling with holy fervour on each beloved name. What wonder that we achieve so little!

*b. Humility*    'He stretched himself upon the child.' How

wonderful that so great a man should spend so much time and thought on that slender frame, and be content to bring himself into direct contact with that which might be thought to defile! We must seek the conversion of children, winning them before Satan or the world get them. But, to do so, we must stoop to them; becoming as little children to win little children for Jesus.

*c. Perseverance* 'He stretched himself ... three times, and cried unto the LORD.' He was not soon daunted. It is in this way that God tests the genuineness of our desire. These deferred answers led us to lengths of holy boldness and persistence of which we should not otherwise have dreamed, but from which we shall never go back.

And his supplications met with the favour of God. 'The LORD heard the voice of Elijah; and the soul of the child came into him again, and he revived.' And as the prophet presented him to the grateful and rejoicing mother, he must have been beyond all things gratified with her simple testimony to the reality and power of the life that the Holy Spirit had established in him: 'Now by this I know that thou art a man of God, and that the word of the LORD in thy mouth is truth.'

# 4

# The Conflict on the Heights of Carmel

## *1 Kings 18*

It is early morning on Mount Carmel. From all sides the crowds are making their way toward this spot which, from the earliest times, has been associated with worship. No work is being done anywhere; every thought of young and old is concentrated on that mighty convocation to which Ahab has summoned them. See how the many thousands of Israel are slowly gathering and taking up every vantage spot from which a view can be had of the proceedings.

The people are nearly gathered, and there is the regular tread of marshalled men; four hundred prophets of Baal, conspicuous with the sun symbols flashing on their brows; but the prophets of Astarte are absent: the queen, at whose table they ate, has over-ruled the summons of the king. And now, through the crowd, the litter of the king, borne by stalwart carriers, threads its way, sur-rounded by the great officers of state.

We fix our thought on that one man, of sinewy build and flow-ing hair who, with flashing eye and compressed lip, awaits the quiet hush that will presently fall on that mighty concourse. One man against a nation! See, with what spiteful glances his every movement is watched by the priests.

The king alternates between fear and hate; but he restrains himself because he feels that somehow the coming of the rain depends on this one man. And if there are sympathisers in the crowd they are hushed and still. Even Obadiah discreetly keeps out of the way. But do not fear for Elijah! He is only a man of like passions with ourselves, but he is full of faith and spiritual power; he can avail himself of the very resources of Deity, as a slender rod may draw lightning from the cloud. This very day, by faith – not by any inherent power, but by faith – you will see him subdue a kingdom; nothing shall be impossible to him. He spoke seven times during the course of that memorable day, and his words are the true index of what was passing in his heart.

## 1    Elijah remonstrated

'Elijah came unto all the people, and said, How long halt ye between two opinions! If the LORD be God, follow him; but if Baal, then follow him.'

At present their position was illogical and absurd. Their course was like the limp of a man whose legs are uneven; or like the device of a servant employed to serve two masters – doing his best for both, and failing to please either. His sincere and simple soul had no patience with such glaring folly. The time had come for the nation to be stopped in its attempt to combine the worship of Jehovah and of Baal; and to be compelled to choose between the two issues that presented themselves.

The people seemed to have been stunned and ashamed that such alternatives should be presented to their choice, for they 'answered him not a word'.

## 2   Elijah threw out a challenge

'The God that answereth by fire, let him be God.' It was a fair proposal, because Baal was the lord of the sun and the god of those productive natural forces of which heat is the element and sign. The priests of Baal could not therefore refuse.

And every Israelite could recall on many occasions in the glorious past when Jehovah had answered by fire. It was the emblem of Jehovah, and the sign of his acceptance of his people's service.

When Elijah therefore proposed that each side should offer a bullock, and await an answer by fire, he secured the immediate agreement of the people. 'All the people answered and said, It is well spoken.'

The proposal was made in the perfect assurance that God would not fail him. God will never fail the man who trusts him completely. Be sure that you are in God's plan; then forward in God's name! – the very elements will obey you and fire will leap from heaven at your command.

## 3   Elijah dealt out withering sarcasm

The false priests were unable to insert the secret spark of fire among the wood that lay on their altar. They were compelled therefore to rely on a direct appeal to their patron deity. And this they did with might and strength. Round and round the altar they went in the mystic choric dance, breaking their rank sometimes by an excited leap up and down at the altar; and all the while repeating the monotonous chant, 'Baal, hear us! Hear us, Baal!' But there was no voice, nor any that answered.

Three hours passed in this way. Their Sun-god deity slowly drove his golden car up the steep of heaven, and ascended his throne in the zenith. It was surely the time of his greatest power, and he must help them then, if ever. But all he did was to bronze to a deeper tinge the eager, upturned faces of his priests.

Elijah could hardly conceal his delight in their defeat. He knew it would be so. He could afford to mock them by suggesting a cause of the indifference of their god: 'Cry aloud: for he is a god; either he is talking, or he is pursuing, or he is in a journey, or peradventure he sleepeth, and must be awaked.'

'And they cried aloud, and cut themselves after their manner with knives and lancets, till the blood gushed out upon them.' Surely their sincere efforts were enough to touch the compassion of any deity, however hard to move! And, since the heavens still continued silent, did it not prove to the people that their religion was a delusion and a sham?

Thus three more hours passed by until the hour had come when, in the temple of Jerusalem, the priests of God were accustomed to offer the evening lamb. But 'there was neither voice, nor any answer, nor any that regarded.' The altar stood cold and smokeless, the bullock unconsumed.

## 4   Elijah issued an invitation

His time had come at last; and his first act was to invite the people nearer. He wanted the answer of fire to be beyond dispute; he therefore invited the close scrutiny of the people as he raised up the broken altar of the Lord. As he sought, with reverent care, those scattered stones, and built them together so that the twelve stood as one – meet symbol of the unity of the ideal Israel in the sight of God – the sharp glances of the people, in his close proximity, could see that there was no inserted torch or secret spark.

## 5   Elijah gave a command

His faith was exuberant. He was so sure of God that he dared to heap difficulties in his way, knowing that there is no real difficulty for infinite power. The more unlikely the answer was, the more glory there would be to God. Oh, matchless faith! which can laugh at impossibilities and can even heap them one upon another, to have the pleasure of seeing God vanquish them.

The altar was raised; the wood laid in order; the bullock cut in pieces: but to prevent any possibility of fraud and to make the coming miracle still more wonderful, Elijah said, 'Fill four barrels with water, and pour it on the burnt sacrifice, and on the wood'. This they did three times, until the wood was drenched and the water filled the trench, making it impossible for a spark to travel across.

How sad that few of us have faith like this! We are not so sure of God that we dare to pile difficulties in his way. Yet what this man had, we too may have, by prayer and fasting.

## 6 Elijah offered a prayer

Such a prayer! It was quiet and assured, confident of an answer. Its chief burden was that God would vindicate himself that day in showing himself to be God indeed, and in turning the people's heart back to himself.

Is it not wonderful that 'the fire of the Lord fell, and consumed the burnt sacrifice, and the wood, and the stones, and the dust, and licked up the water that was in the trench'? It could not have been otherwise! And let us not think that this is an old story, never to be repeated. Our God is a consuming fire; and when once the unity of his people is recognised and his presence is sought, he will descend, overcoming all obstacles.

## 7 Elijah issued an order for execution

The order went forth from those stern lips: 'Take the prophets of Baal; let not one of them escape.' The people were in the mood to obey. Only a moment before they had rent the air with the shout, 'The LORD, he is the God, the LORD, he is the God!' They saw how hideously they had been deceived. And now they closed around the cowed and vanquished priests, who saw that resistance was in vain, and that their hour had come.

'Elijah brought them down to the brook Kishon, and slew them there.' One after another they fell beneath his sword while the king stood by, a helpless spectator of their doom, and Baal did nothing to save them.

And when the last was dead, the prophet knew that rain was not far off. He could almost hear the footfall of the clouds hurrying up toward the land. He knew what we all need to know, that God himself can only bless the land or heart that no longer shelters within its borders rivals to himself. May God impart to us Elijah's faith, that we also may be strong and do great things!

# 5

# Rain at last!

## *1 Kings 18*

We can in a very inadequate degree realise the horrors of an Eastern drought. The anguish of the land was directly attributable to the apostasy of its people. The iniquities of Israel had separated from them their God, and Elijah knew this right well. This prompted him to act the part of executioner to the priests of Baal, who had been the ringleaders in the national revolt from God, but whose bodies now lay in ghastly death on the banks of the Kishon, or were being carried out to sea.

Ahab must have stood by Elijah in the Kishon gorge and been an unwilling spectator of that fearful deed of vengeance, not daring to resist the outburst of popular indignation or to attempt to shield the men whom he had himself encouraged and introduced. When the last priest had died, Elijah turned to the king and said, 'Get thee up, eat and drink; for there is a sound of abundance of rain.' It was as if he said, 'Get up to where your tents are pitched on the broad upland sweep; the feast is spread in your gilded pavilion; feast on its dainties; but be quick! for now that the land is rid of these traitor priests and God is once more enthroned in his rightful place, the showers of rain cannot be delayed any longer. Be quick! or the rain may interrupt your feast.'

What a contrast between these two men! 'Ahab went up to eat and to drink. And Elijah went up to the top of Carmel; and he cast himself down upon the earth, and put his face between his knees.' It is no more than we might have expected of the king. When his people were suffering the extremities of drought, he cared only to find grass enough to save his horses; and now, though his faithful priests had died by hundreds, he thought only of the banquet that awaited him in his pavilion. I think I can see Ahab and Elijah ascending those heights together: no sympathy, no common joy; the king turns off to his tents while the servant of God climbs steadily up to the highest part of the mountain, and finds an oratory at the base of a yet higher promontory.

Such contrasts still show themselves. The children of this world will spend their days in feasting and their nights in revelry, though a world is rushing to ruin. Woe to the land when such men rule! May our beloved country be preserved from having such leaders as these! And may our youth be found, not garlanded and scented for the Ahab feasts, but with Elijah on the bleak mountains, where there may be no fancy feasts but where the air is fresh, and life is free, and the spirit is braced to noble deeds.

## 1 There are certain characteristics in Elijah's prayer that we must notice as we pass, because they should form part of all true prayer

*a. It was based on the promise of God*   When Elijah was summoned from Zarephath to resume his public work, his marching orders were capped by the specific promise of rain: 'Go, shew thyself unto Ahab; and I will send rain upon the earth.' God's promises are given, not to restrain, but to incite to prayer. They are the mould into which we may pour our fervid spirits without fear. Though the Bible is crowded with golden promises from cover to cover, yet they will be inoperative until we turn them into prayer.

When we are asked therefore *why* men should pray, and *how* prayer avails, we should answer no more than this: 'Prayer is the instinct of the religious life; it is one of the first principles of the spiritual world'. It is clearly taught in the Word of God to be accepted by the Almighty. It has been practiced by the noblest and saintliest of men, who have testified to its certain efficacy. We are content therefore to pray, though we are as ignorant of the philosophy of the *modus operandi* of prayer as we are of any natural law.

When your child was a toddling, lisping babe, it asked many things wholly incompatible with your nature and its own welfare; but as the years passed, increasing experience has moulded its requests into shapes suggested by yourself. So, as we know more of God through his promises, we are led to set our hearts on things that lie on his open palm waiting to be taken by the hand of an appropriating faith. This is why all prayer, like Elijah's, should be based on promise.

*b. It was definite.*　　This is where so many prayers fail. We do not pray with any expectation of attaining definite and practical results. Let us correct this. Let us keep a list of petitions that we will plead before God. Let us direct our prayer, as David did (Ps.5:3), and look up for the answer; and we will find ourselves obtaining new and unwonted blessings. Be definite!

*c. It was earnest.*　　'Elijah prayed earnestly.' The prayers of Scripture all glow with the white heat of intensity. Prayer is not answered unless it is accompanied with such earnestness as will prove that the blessing sought is really needed.

Such earnestness is, of course, to be dreaded when we seek some lower benefit for ourselves. But when, like Elijah, we seek the fulfilment of the divine promise – not for ourselves, but for the glory of God – then it is impossible to be too much in earnest, or too full of the energy of prayer.

*d. Elijah's prayer was humble.*　　'He cast himself down upon the earth, and put his face between his knees'. It is not always so – that the men who stand straightest in the presence of sin bow lowest in the presence of God? True, you are a child; but you are also a subject. True, you are redeemed man; but you cannot forget your original name, *sinner.* True, you may come with boldness; but remember the majesty, might, and power of God, and take your shoes from off your feet. Our only plea with God is the merit and blood of our great High Priest. It becomes us to be humble.

*e. It was full of expectant faith.*　　It beat strongly in Elijah's heart. He knew that God would keep his word, and so he sent the lad – possibly the widow's son – up to the highest point of Carmel, and urged him to look toward the sea, because he was sure that before long his prayer would be answered, and God's promise would be kept. We have often prayed, and failed to look out for the blessings we have sought.

There is a faith that God cannot refuse, a faith to which all things are possible. It laughs at impossibility, and can move mountains and plant them in the sea. May such faith be ours!

Such faith was Elijah's.

*f. It was very persevering.*　　He said to his servant, 'Go up now, look toward the sea.' And he went up, and looked, and said, 'There is nothing.' How often have we sent the lad of eager desire to scan the horizon! And how often has he returned with the answer, *There is nothing!* And because there is nothing when we have just begun to pray, we stop praying. We leave the mountain brow. We do not know that God's answer is even then on the way.

Not so with Elijah. 'And he said, Go again seven times.' He came back the first time, saying, 'There is nothing – no sign of rain, no cloud in the clear sky': and Elijah said, 'Go again'. And that was repeated seven times. It was no small test of the prophet's endurance, but with the ordeal there came sufficient grace so that he was able to bear it.

Our Father frequently grants our prayer and labels the answer for us, but keeps it back that we may be led on to a point of intensity. He from which we shall never recede. Then when we have outdone ourselves, he lovingly turns to us, and says, 'Great is thy faith: be it unto thee even as thou wilt!' (Matt. 15:28).

*g. And the prayer was abundantly answered.*　　For weeks and months before, the sun had been gathering up from lake and river, from sea and ocean, the drops of mist, and now the gale was bearing them rapidly toward the thirsty land of Israel. 'Before they call, I will answer; and while they are yet speaking, I will hear' (Isa. 65:24). The answer to your prayers may be nearer than you think. On the wings of every moment it is hastening toward you. God will answer you, and soon!

Soon the boy, from his tower of observation, beheld on the horizon a tiny cloud, no bigger than a man's hand, moving quickly across the sky. No more was needed to convince an Oriental that rain was near. It was, and is, the certain precursor of a sudden hurricane of wind and rain. The boy was sent with an urgent message to Ahab, to come down from Carmel to his chariot in the plain beneath, lest Kishon, swollen by the rains, should stop him on his way home. The boy barely had time to reach the royal pavilion before the heavens were black with clouds and wind, and there was a great rain.

The monarch started amid the pelting storm, but faster than his swift horses were the feet of the prophet, energised by the hand of

God. He snatched up his streaming mantle and twisted it around his loins; and amid the fury of the elements, with which the night closed in, he outran the chariot, and ran like a common courier before it to the entrance of Jezreel, some eighteen miles away.

Thus by his faith and prayer this one man brought back the rain to Israel. Why should we not learn and practise his secret? Then we too might bring from heaven spiritual blessings that would make the parched places of the church and the world rejoice and blossom as the rose.

# 6

# How the Mighty Fell!

## *1 Kings 19*

Amid the drenching storm with which the memorable day of the convocation closed in, the king and the prophet reached Jezreel. They were probably the first to bring tidings of what had occurred. Elijah went to some humble lodging for shelter and food; while Ahab retired to the palace where Jezebel awaited him. All day long the queen had been wondering how matters were going on Mount Carmel. She cherished the feverish hope that her priests had won the day, and when she saw the rain clouds steal over the sky she attributed the welcome change to some great interposition of Baal, in answer to their pleadings. We can imagine some scene such as this taking place between the royal pair when they met.

'How have things gone today? No doubt, well; the rain has anticipated your favourable reply.'

'I have nothing to tell you that will give you pleasure.'

'Why?'

'The worst has happened.'

'What do you mean? Where are my priests?'

'You will never see them again. They are all dead; by this time their bodies are floating out to sea.'

'Who has dared to do this thing? Did they not defend themselves? Did you not raise your hand? How did they die?'

'And Ahab told Jezebel all that Elijah had done, and withal how he had slain all the prophets with the sword.'

Jezebel's indignation knew no bounds. Ahab was sensual and materialistic; if only he had enough to eat and drink, and the horses and mules were cared for, he was content. In his judgment there was not much to choose between God and Baal. Not so Jezebel. She was as resolute as he was indifferent. Crafty, unscrupulous, and intriguing, she moulded Ahab to her mind.

To Jezebel the crisis was a grave one. Policy as well as indignation prompted her to act at once. If this national reformation were permitted to spread, it would sweep away before it all that she had been labouring at for years. She must strike, and strike at once; so that very night, amid the violence of the storm, she sent a messenger to Elijah, saying 'So let the gods do to me, and more also, if I make not thy life as the life of one of them by tomorrow about this time.' That message betrays the woman. She did not dare kill him, though he was easily within her power; so she contented herself with threats. Her mind was set on driving him from the country, so that she might be left free to repair the havoc he had caused. And, sad to say, in this she was only too successful.

Elijah's presence had never been so necessary as now. The work of destruction had begun, and the people were in a mood to carry it through to the bitter end. The tide had turned, and was setting toward God; and Elijah was needed to complete the work of reformation by a work of construction. From what we have seen of him, we should have expected that he would receive the message with unruffled composure; but, 'he arose, and went for his life.'

Accompanied by his servant, and under cover of night, he hurried through the driving storm, across the hills of Samaria; nor did he slacken his speed until he had reached Beersheba. He was safe there; but even there he could not stay, so he plunged into that wild desert waste that stretches southward to Sinai.

Through the weary hours he plodded on beneath the burning sun, his feet blistered by the scorching sands; no ravens, no Cherith, no Zarephath were there. At last the fatigue and anguish overpowered even his sinewy strength, and he cast himself beneath the slight shadow of a small shrub of juniper, and asked to die. 'It is enough: now, O LORD, take away my life; for I am not better than my fathers.'

What might have been! If only Elijah had held his ground he might have saved his country; and there would have been no necessity for the captivity and dispersion of his people. The seven thousand secret disciples would have dared to come forth from their hiding places, and show themselves; and would have constituted a nucleus of loyal hearts, by whom Baal had been replaced by Jehovah; his own character would have escaped a stain that still remains.

The Bible saints often fail just where we would have expected them to stand. Abraham was the father of those who believe, but his faith failed him when he went down to Egypt and lied to Pharaoh about his wife. Moses was the meekest of men, but he missed Canaan because he spoke unadvisedly with his lips. So Elijah shows himself to be indeed 'a man of like passions with ourselves.'

What proof there is here of the veracity of the Bible! Had it been merely a human composition, its authors would have shrunk from delineating the failure of one of its chief heroes. Is there not even a gleam of comfort to be had out of the woeful spectacle of Elijah's fall? If it had not been for this, we would always have thought of him as being too far removed from us to be in any sense a model. But now as we see him stretched under the shade of the juniper tree asking for death, we feel that he was what he was, only by the grace of God, received through faith. And by a similar faith we may appropriate a similar grace to ennoble our unimposing lives.

### Several causes account for this terrible failure

*1. His physical strength and nervous energy were completely overtaxed.*    Consider the tremendous strain he had undergone since leaving the shelter of the quiet home at Zarephath. The long excitement of the convocation, the slaughter of the priests, the intensity of his prayer, the eighteen miles swift run in front of Ahab's chariot, followed by the rapid flight that had hardly been relaxed for a single moment until he had cast himself upon the desert sand – all had resulted in sheer exhaustion. He was suffering deeply from reaction.

*2. He was deeply sensitive to his lonely position.* 'I only, am left.' Some men are born to loneliness. It is the penalty of true greatness. At such a time the human spirit is apt to falter unless it is sustained by a heroic purpose, and by an unfaltering faith. You remind me that Elijah might have had the company of the young boy. But remember that there is company which is not companionship. We need something more than human beings; we need human hearts, and sympathy, and love.

*3. He looked away from God to circumstances.* Up to that moment Elijah had been animated by a great faith, because he had never lost sight of God. 'He endured, as seeing him who is invisible' (Heb. 11:27). Faith always thrives when God occupies the whole field of vision. But when Jezebel's threats reached him, we are told most significantly, '*when he saw that,* he arose, and went for his life.' While Elijah set the Lord always before his face, he did not fear, though a host was camped against him. But when he looked at his peril, he thought more of his life than of God's cause. '*When he saw that,* he arose, and went for his life.'

Let us refuse to look at circumstances even though they roll before us as a Red Sea and howl around us like a storm. Circumstances, natural impossibilities, difficulties, are nothing in the estimation of the soul that is occupied with God.

It is a great mistake to dictate to God. Elijah did not know what he said when he told God that he had had enough of life, and asked to die. If God would have taken him at his word, he would have died under a cloud; he would never have heard the still small voice; for he would never have founded the schools of the prophets, or commissioned Elisha for his work; he would never have swept up to heaven in a fiery chariot.

What a mercy it is that God does not answer all our prayers! How gracious he is in reading their inner meaning and answering them! This, as we shall see, is what he did for his tired and complaining servant.

How many have uttered those words, 'It is enough!' The Christian worker, whose efforts seem in vain: 'It is enough. Let me come home. The burden is more than I can bear. The lessons are tiresome. School life is tedious; holidays will be so welcome. I cannot see that anything will be gained by longer delay. It is enough!'

Little do we know how much we would miss if God were to do as we request. To die now would be to forgo immeasurable blessings that await us within forty days' journey from this; and to die like a dog, instead of sweeping, honoured and beloved, through the open gates of heaven. It is better to leave it all in the wise and tender thought of God, and we will yet live to thank him that he refused to gratify our wish when, in a moment of despondency, we cast ourselves on the ground and said, 'Let us die, It is enough!'

7

# The 'Still, Small Voice'

## *1 Kings 19*

Refreshed by sleep and food, Elijah resumed his journey across the desert to Horeb. Perhaps no spot on earth is more associated with the manifested presence of God than that sacred mount. There the bush burned with fire; there the law was given; there Moses spent forty days and nights alone with God. It was a natural instinct that led the prophet there, and all the world could not have furnished a more appropriate school.

Forty times the prophet saw the sun rise and set over the desert waste. Thus, at last, the prophet came to Horeb, the mount of God. We have to consider how God dealt with his dispirited and truant child.

### 1   God spoke to him

In some dark cave, among those jagged precipices, Elijah lodged; and as he waited in lonely reflection, the fire burned in his soul. But he didn't have to wait long. 'Behold, the word of the Lord came to him.'

That word had often come to him before. It had come to him at Tishbe. It had come to him in Samaria, after he had given his first message to Ahab. It had come to him when Cherith was dry. It had come to summon him from the solitudes of Zarephath to the stir of active life. And now it found him out, and came to him again. There is no spot on earth so lonely, no cave so deep and dark, that the word of the Lord cannot discover us and come to us.

But though God had often spoken to him before, he had never spoken in quite the same tone – 'What doest thou here, Elijah?' The accent was stern and reproachful.

If the prophet had answered that searching question of God with shame and sorrow; if he had confessed that he had failed, and asked for forgiveness; if he had cast himself on the pity and tenderness of his almighty Friend – there is not the least doubt that he would have been forgiven and restored. But instead of this, he evaded the divine question. He did not try to explain how he came there, or what he was doing. He chose rather to dwell on his own loyalty for the cause of God; and to bring it out into striking relief by contrasting it with the sinful backslidings of his people. 'I have been very jealous for the Lord God of hosts: for the children of Israel have forsaken thy covenant; thrown down thine altars, and slain thy prophets with the sword; and I, even I only, am left; and they seek my life, to take it away.'

There was no doubt truth in what he said. He was full of zeal and holy devotion to the cause of God. He had often mourned over the national degeneracy. He keenly felt his own isolation and loneliness. But these were not the reasons why at that moment he was hiding in the cave; nor were they the real answer to that searching question, 'What doest thou here, Elijah?'

How often that question still put! When a person endowed with great faculties digs a hole in the earth, and buries the God-entrusted talent, and then stands idle all day, again the question must be asked, 'What doest thou here?'

Life is the time for doing. There is plenty to do. Evil to put down; good to build up; doubters to be directed; prodigals to be won back; sinners to be sought. 'What doest thou here?' Up, Christians, leave your caves, and do! Do not do in order to be saved, but being saved, *do!*

## 2   God taught him by a beautiful natural parable

He was commanded to stand at the entrance to the cave. Presently there was the sound of the rushing of a mighty wind; and in another moment a violent tornado swept past. Nothing could withstand its fury. It tore the mountains, and broke in pieces the rocks before the Lord; the valleys were littered with splintered fragments; *but the Lord was not in the wind.* And when the wind had died away, there was an earthquake. The mountain swayed to and fro, yawning and cracking; the ground heaved as if an almighty hand were passing beneath it; *but the Lord was not in the earthquake.* And when the earthquake was over, there was a fire. The heavens were one blaze of light, each pinnacle and peak glowed in the kindling flame; the valley beneath looked like a huge smelting furnace, *but the Lord was not in the fire.*

How strange! Surely these were the appropriate natural symbols of the divine presence. But listen! a still small whisper is in the air – very still, and very small; it touched the listening heart of the prophet. It seemed to be the tender cadence of the love and pity of God that had come in search of him. Its music drew him from the cave, into the innermost recesses of which he had been driven by the terrible convulsions of nature. 'And it was so, when Elijah heard it that he wrapped his face in his mantle, and went out, and stood in the entering in of the cave.'

What was the meaning of all this? It is not difficult to understand. Elijah was most eager that his people should be restored to their allegiance to God; and he may have spoken often this way with himself: 'Those idols will never be swept from our land unless God sends a movement swift and irresistible as the *wind,* which hurries the clouds before it. The land can never be awakened except by a moral *earthquake.* There must be a baptism of *fire.*' And when he stood on Carmel, and beheld the panic among the priests and the eagerness among the people, he thought that the time – the set time – had come. But all that had died away. That was not God's chosen way of saving Israel.

But in this natural parable God seemed to say: 'My child, you have been looking for me to answer your prayers with striking signs and wonders; and because these have not been given in a marked and permanent form, you have thought me heedless and inactive. But I am not always to be found in these great visible movements; I love to work gently, softly, and unperceived; I have been working so; I am working so still; and there are in Israel, as the results of my quiet gentle ministry, "seven thousand, all the knees that have not bowed to Baal, and every mouth that has not kissed him".' Yes, and was not the gentle ministry of Elisha, succeeding the stormy career of his predecessor, like the still small voice after the wind, the earthquake, and the fire? And is it not probable that more real good was effected by his unobtrusive life and miracles than was ever wrought by the splendid deeds of Elijah?

We often fall into similar mistakes. When we wish to promote a revival, we think we need large crowds, much evident impression, powerful preachers; influences comparable to the wind, the earthquake, and the fire. But surely Nature herself rebukes us. Who hears the roll of the planets? Who can detect the falling of the dew? Whose eye has ever been injured by the breaking of the wavelets of daylight on the shores of our planet? 'There is no speech, nor language; their voice is not heard.' At this moment the mightiest forces are in operation around us, but there is nothing to betray their presence. And thus it was with the ministry of the Lord Jesus. He did not strive, nor cry, nor lift up, nor cause his voice to be heard in the streets. He comes down as showers on the mown grass. His Spirit descends as the dove, whose wings make no tremor in the still air. Let us take heart! God may not be working as we expect; but he is working. If not in the wind, then in the breeze. If not in the earthquake, then in the heartbreak. If not in the fire, then in the still, small voice. If not in crowds, then in lonely hearts; in silent tears; in the broken sobs of penitents; and in multitudes who, like the seven thousand of Israel, are unknown as disciples.

But Elijah refused to be comforted. It seemed as if he could not shake off the mood in which he was ensnared. And so when God asked him the second time: 'What doest thou here, Elijah?' he answered in the same words with which he had tried to justify himself before. 'And he said, I have been very jealous . . .'

It is pleasant to think of those seven thousand disciples, known only to God. We are sometimes sad as we compare the scanty number of professing Christians with the masses of ungodly. But we may take heart: there are still other Christians. That harsh-seeming governor is a Joseph in disguise. That wealthy owner of the garden in Arimathea is a lowly follower of Jesus. That member of the Sanhedrin is a disciple; but secretly, for fear of the Jews. But if you are one of that number, I urge you, do not remain so: it robs the cause of God of your help and influence; it is an act of treachery to Christ himself. Beware lest, if you are ashamed of him, the time may come when he will be ashamed of you.

It is quite true that confession means martyrdom in one form or another; and sometimes our heart and flesh shrink back as we contemplate the possible results of refusing the act of obeisance to Baal. But at such times, let us encourage ourselves by anticipating the august moment when the dear Master will speak our names before assembled worlds, and own us as his. And let us also ask him in us and through us to speak out and witness a good confession.

# 8

# Naboth's Vineyard

## *1 Kings 21*

In a room of the palace, Ahab, king of Israel, lies upon his couch, his face toward the wall, refusing to eat. What has taken place? Has disaster befallen the royal arms? Is his royal consort dead? No; the soldiers are still flushed with their recent victories over Syria. The worship of Baal has quite recovered the terrible disaster of Carmel; Jezebel – resolute, crafty, cruel, and beautiful – is now standing by his side, anxiously seeking the cause of this sadness.

The story is soon told. Jezreel was the Windsor of Israel; and there stood the favourite residence of the royal house. On a certain occasion, while Ahab was engaged there, his eye lighted on a neighbouring vineyard, belonging to Naboth the Jezreelite; which promised to be so valuable an addition to his property that he resolved to procure it at all cost. He therefore sent for Naboth and offered either a better vineyard in exchange or the worth of it in money. To his suprise and indignation, Naboth refused both.

And Naboth said to Ahab, 'The LORD forbid it to me, that I should give the inheritance of my fathers unto thee.'

At first sight this refusal seems churlish and uncourteous. But by the law of Moses, Canaan was considered as being, in a peculiar sense, God's land. The Israelites were his tenants; and one of the conditions of their tenure was that they should not alienate that which fell to their lot, except in cases of extreme necessity; and then only until the year of Jubilee. Naboth anticipated that if it once passed out of his hands, his patrimony would become merged in the royal possession, never to be released. Taking his stand then on religious grounds, he might well say: 'The Lord forbids me to do it.' His refusal was in part, therefore, a religious act.

But there was, without doubt, something more. In his mention of 'the inheritance of his fathers,' we have the suggestion of another, and most natural reason, for his reluctance; his fathers had for generations sat beneath those vines and trees; there he had spent the sunny years of childhood. He felt that all the juice ever pressed from all the vineyards of the neighbourhood would never compensate him for the heartache from those clustered memories.

Naboth's refusal made Ahab leap into his chariot and drive back to Samaria; and turn his face to the wall in a sulk, 'heavy and displeased.' At the close of the previous chapter (1 Kings 20:43) we learned that he was displeased with God; now he is agitated by the same strong passions toward man. In a few more days the horrid deed of murder was perpetrated; which at one stroke removed Naboth, his sons, and his heirs, and left the unclaimed property to fall naturally into the royal hands. There are many lessons here that would claim our notice if we were dealing with the whole story, but we must pass them by, to centre our attention exclusively on the part played by Elijah amid these terrible translations.

## 1   He was called back to service

How many years had elapsed since the word of the Lord had last come to Elijah, we do not know. Perhaps five or six. All this while he must have waited wistfully for the well-known accents of that voice, longing to hear it once again. And as the weary days, passing slowly by, prolonged his deferred hope into deep and yet deeper regret, he must have been driven to continued soul-questionings and searchings of heart; to bitter repentance for the past, and to renewed consecration for whatever service might be imposed on him.

It may be that these words will be read by some, once prominent in Christian service, who have lately been cast aside. The Great Master has a perfect right to do as he will with his own, and takes up one and lays down another; but we should inquire whether the reason may not lie within our own hearts in some inconsistency or sin that needs confession and forgiveness at the hands of our faithful and merciful High Priest, before ever again the *word* of our Lord can come to us.

It is also possible that we are left unused for our own deeper teaching in the ways of God. Hours, and even years, of silence are full of golden opportunities for the servants of God. In such cases, our conscience does not condemn us or accost us with any sufficient reason arising from ourselves. Our simple duty then is to keep clean, and filled, and ready; standing on the shelf, meet for the Master's use; sure that we serve if we only stand and wait; and knowing that he will accept, and reward, the willingness for the deed.

## 2   Elijah was not disobedient

Once before, when his presence was urgently required, he had arisen to flee for his life. But there was no vacillation, no cowardice now. He arose and went down to the vineyard of Naboth, and entered it to find the royal criminal. It was nothing to him that there rode behind Ahab's chariot two ruthless captains, Jehu and Bidkar (2 Kings 9:25). He did not for a moment consider that the woman who had threatened his life before might now take it, maddened as she was with her recent spilling of human blood. Who does not rejoice that Elijah had such an opportunity of wiping out the dark stain of disgrace. His time of waiting had not been lost on him!

## 3   He was acting as an incarnate conscience

Naboth was out of the way; and Ahab may have comforted himself, as weak people do still, with the idea that he was not his murderer. How could he be? He had been perfectly quiet. He had simply put his face to the wall and done nothing. He did remember that Jezebel had asked him for his royal seal, to give validity to some letters that she had written in his name, but then how was he to know what she had written? Of course if she had given instruction for Naboth's death it was a great pity, but it could not now be helped; and he might as well take possession of the inheritance! With such excuses he succeeded in stilling the fragment of conscience that alone survived in his heart. And it was then that he was startled by a voice he had not heard for years, saying, 'Thus saith the Lord. Hast thou killed, and also taken possession?' 'Hast thou killed?' The prophet, guided by the Spirit of God, put the burden on the right shoulders.

If an employer, by paying an inadequate and unjust wage, tempts his employees to supplement their scanty pittance by dishonest methods, he is held responsible, in the sight of heaven, for the evil he might have prevented if he had not been wilfully and criminally indifferent.

Acts of high-handed sin often seem at first to prosper. Naboth meekly dies; the earth sucks in his blood; the vineyard passes into the oppressor's hands; but there is One who sees and will most certainly avenge the cause of his servants. 'Surely I have seen yesterday the blood of Naboth, and the blood of his sons, saith the LORD; and I will requite thee in this plat' (2 Kings 9:26). That vengeance may tarry, for the mills of God grind slowly; but it will come as certainly as God is God. And in the meanwhile in Naboth's vineyard stands Elijah the prophet. This lesson is enforced again and again by our great dramatist, who teaches men who will not read their Bibles that sin does not pay in the end; that however successful if may seem at first, in the end it has to reckon with an Elijah as conscience and with God as an avenger – and he never misses his mark.

## 4   He was hated for the truth's sake

'And Ahab said to Elijah, Hast thou found me, O mine enemy?' Though the king did not know it, Elijah was his best friend; Jezebel his direst foe. But sin distorts everything.

When Christian friends remonstrate with evildoers, and rebuke their sins, and warn them of their doom, they are hated and denounced as enemies. The Bible is detested, because it so clearly exposes sin and its consequences. It cannot be otherwise.

Let us not be surprised if we are hated. Let us even be thankful when men detest us – not for ourselves, but for the truths we speak. Let us 'rejoice, and be exceeding glad.' When bad men think thus of us, it is an indication that our influence is opposite their lives.

### 5　He was a true prophet

Each of the woes that Elijah foretold came true. Ahab postponed their fulfilment, by a partial repentance, for some three years; but at the end of that time he went back to his evil ways, and every item was literally fulfilled. He was wounded by a 'chance' arrow at Ramoth-gilead, 'and the blood ran out of the wound into the midst of the chariot'; and as they washed his chariot in the fountain of Samaria, the dogs licked his blood. Twenty years later there was nothing of Jezebel left for burial; only her skull, and feet, and palms escaped the voracious dogs as she lay exposed on that very spot. The corpse of Joram, their son, was cast forth unburied on the same plot, at the command of Jehu, who never forgot those memorable words. God is true, not only to his promises, but also to his threats.

Every word spoken by Elijah was literally fulfilled. The passing years amply vindicated him. And as we close this tragic episode in his career, we rejoice to learn that he was stamped again with the divine imprimatur of trustworthiness and truth.

# 9

# The Translation

## *2 Kings 2*

We now turn to one of the most sublime scenes of Old Testament story. We would have been glad to learn the most minute particulars concerning it, but the historian contents himself with the simplest statements. Just one or two broad, strong outlines, and all is told that we may know. The veil of distance, or the elevation of the hills, was enough to hide the receding figures of the prophets from the eager gaze of the group that watched them from the neighbourhood of Jericho. And the dazzling glory of the celestial cortege made the only spectator unable to scrutinise it too narrowly. What wonder, then, if the narrative is given in three brief sentences! 'They still went on, and talked, that, behold, there appeared a chariot of fire, and horses of fire, and parted them both asunder; and Elijah went up by a whirlwind into heaven.'

The two friends halted for a moment before the broad waters of the Jordan, which threatened to bar their onward steps; and Elijah took off his well-worn mantle, and wrapped it together and struck the waters, and they parted here and there, leaving a clear passage through which they went.

## 1 The fitness of this translation

*a. There was fitness in the place.*    Not Esdraelon, not Sinai, not the schools of Gilgal, Bethel, or Jericho; but amid the scenery familiar to his early life; in view of localities forever associated with the most memorable events of his nation's history; surrounded by the lonely grandeur of some rocky gorge – *there God chose to send his chariot to bring Elijah home.*

*b. There was fitness in the method.*    He had himself been as the whirlwind that sweeps all before it in its impetuous course, leaving devastation and ruin in its track. It was fitting that a whirlwind-man should sweep to heaven in the very element of his life. Nothing could be more appropriate than that the stormy energy of his career should be set forth in the rush of the whirlwind, and the intensity of his spirit by the fire that flashed in the harnessed seraphim. What a contrast to the gentle upward motion of the ascending Saviour!

*c. There was fitness in the exclamation*    with which Elisha bade him farewell. He cried, 'My father, my father! the chariot of Israel, and the horsemen thereof!' That man, whom he had come to love as a father, had indeed been as an armed chariot of defence to Israel. Alas, that such men are rare! But in our time we have known them, and when they have been suddenly swept from our side we have felt as if the church had been deprived of one main source of security and help.

## 2   The reasons for this translation

*a. One of the chief reasons was, no doubt, as a witness to his times.*   The men of his day had little thought of the hereafter. At the very best the Jews had but vague notions of the other life. But here a convincing evidence was given that there was a spiritual world into which the righteous entered; and that, when the body sank in death, the spirit did not share its fate, but entered into a state of being in which its noblest instincts found their befitting environment and home – fire to fire; spirit to spirit; the man of God to God.

A similar testimony was given to the men of his time by the rapture of Enoch before the Flood, and by the ascension of our Lord from the brow of Olivet. Where did these three wondrous journeys ends, unless there was a destination that was their befitting terminus and goal? And as the tidings spread, thrilling all listeners with mysterious awe, would there not break on them the conviction that they likewise would have to take that wondrous journey into the unseen, soaring beyond all worlds, or sinking into the bottomless pit?

*b. Another reason was evidently the desire on the part of God to give a striking sanction to his servant's words.*   How easy it was for the men of that time to evade the force of Elijah's ministry by asserting that he was an enthusiast, an alarmist, a firebrand! And if he had passed away in decrepit old age, they would have been still further encouraged in their impious conjecturings. But the mouths of blasphemers and gainsayers were stopped when God put such a conspicuous seal on his servant's ministry. The translation was to the life work of Elijah what the resurrection was to that of Jesus – it was God's undeniable testimony to the world.

## 3   The lessons of this translation for ourselves

*a. Let us take care not to dictate to God.*   This was the man who lay down on the ground and asked to die. How good it was of God to refuse him the answer he craved! Was it not better to pass away, missed and beloved, in the chariot his Father had sent for him?

This is no doubt one reason why our prayers go unanswered. We do not know what we ask. When next your request is denied, reflect that it may be because God is preparing something for you as much better than your request as the translation of Elijah was better than his petition for himself.

*b. Let us learn what death is.* It is a translation: we pass through a doorway; we cross a bridge of smiles; we flash from the dark into the light. There is no interval of unconsciousness, no parenthesis of suspended animation. 'Absent from the body,' we are instantly 'present with the Lord.' As by the single act of birth we entered into this lower life, so by the single act – which men call death, but which angels call birth (for Christ is the firstborn from among the dead) – we pass into the real life. The fact that Elijah appeared on the Mount of Transfiguration in holy communion with Moses and with Christ proves that the blessed dead are really the living ones, and they entered that life in a single moment the moment of death.

Was it not some reference to this august event that was in the mind of the great Welsh preacher Christmas Evans who, when dying, majestically waved his hand to the bystanders, and looked upward with a smle, and uttered these last words, *'Drive on!'* 'The chariots of God are twenty thousand.'

# JEREMIAH

# 1

# 'The Word of the Lord Came Unto Me'

## *Jeremiah 1:4, 12–13*

If the days of David and Solomon may be compared to spring and summer in the history of the kingdom of Israel, it was late autumn when the events in Jeremiah's life open. The influence of the spiritual revival under Hezekiah and Isaiah, which had for a brief interval arrested the process of decline, had spent itself; and not even the reforms of the good king Josiah, which affected rather the surface than the heart of the people, would avail to avert inevitable judgment. King and court, princes and people, prophets and priests, were infected with abominable vices.

Every high hill had its thick grove of green trees, within whose shadow the idolatrous rites and abominable license of nature worship were freely practised. The face of the country was thickly covered with temples erected for the worship of Baal and Astarte and all the host of heaven, and with lewd idols. In the cities, the black-robed chemarim, the priests of these unhallowed practices, flitted to and fro in strange contrast to the white-stoled priests of Jehovah.

But it was in Jerusalem that these evils came to a head. In the streets of the holy city, the children were taught to gather wood, while the fathers kindled the fire and the women kneaded dough to make cakes for Astarte, 'the queen of heaven', and to pour out drink offerings to other gods.

In such a Sodom God's voice must be heard. Yet if God speaks, it must be through the yielded lips of you and me. He seeks such today. We are still the vehicles of his communications to others.

In the call of Jeremiah we may discover the sort of person whom God chooses as the medium for his speech. It is not to be expected that a superficial gaze will comprehend the special qualifications that attracted the divine choice to Jeremiah. There are several reasons why Jeremiah might have been passed over.

## 1   He was young

How young we do not know, but young enough for him to hold back at the divine proposal with the cry, 'Ah, Lord God! behold I cannot speak: for I am a child.'

God has often selected the young for posts of eminent service: Samuel and Timothy; Joseph and David; Daniel and John the Baptist; Calvin, who wrote his *Institutes* before he was twenty-four; and Wesley, who was only twenty-five when he inaugurated the great system of Methodism.

## 2   He was naturally timid and sensitive

By nature he seemed cast in too delicate a mould to be able to combat the dangers and difficulties of his time. The bitter complaint of his later years was that his mother had brought him into a world of strife and contention. And it was in allusion to the natural shrinking of his disposition that Jehovah promised to make him a 'defenced city, and an iron pillar, and a brasen wall against the whole land.'

Many are moulded on this type. Yet such, like Jeremiah, may play a heroic part on the world's stage, if only they will let God lay down the iron of his might along the lines of their natural weakness. Happy is the soul who can look up from its utter helplessness, and say with Jeremiah, 'O LORD, my strength . . . in the day of affliction.'

## 3   He especially shrank from the burden he was summoned to bear

His chosen theme would have been God's mercy – the boundlessness of his compassion, the tenderness of his pity. In the earlier chapters, when he pleads with the people to return to God, there is a tenderness in his voice, and pathos in his speech, which proves how thoroughly his heart was in this part of his work.

But to be charged with a message of judgment; to announce the woeful day; to oppose every suggestion of heroic resistance; to bring charges on the prophetic and the priestly orders, to each of which he belonged, and the anger of each of which he incurred, the crimes of which they were disgraced – this was the commission that was furthest from his choice.

### 4   He was conscious of his deficiency in speech

Like Moses, he could say, 'O Lord, I am not eloquent, neither heretofore, nor since thou hast spoken unto thy servant: but I am slow of speech, and of a slow tongue.'

Do not then despair because of apparent disqualifications. Notwithstanding all, the Word of the Lord shall come to you. The one thing that God demands of you is absolute consecration to his purpose, and willingness to go on any errand on which he may send you. If these are yours, all else will be given you. He will assure you of his presence – 'I am with thee, to deliver thee.' He will equip you – 'Then the Lord put forth his hand, and touched my mouth. And the Lord said unto me, Behold I have put my words in thy mouth.' Oh, for the circumcised ear, and the loyal, obedient heart!

# 2

# 'I Formed Thee'

## *Jeremiah 1:5*

God has a plan for each of his children. The path has ben prepared, it is for us to walk in it. There is no emergency in the path for which there has not been provision made in our nature; and there is no faculty stored in our nature which, sooner or later, will not have its proper exercise and use. From the earliest inception of being, God had a plan for Jeremiah's career, for which he prepared him. Before the dawn of consciousness, in the very origin of his nature, the hands of the great Master Workman reached down out of heaven to shape the plastic clay for the high purpose he had in view.

## 1    The divine purpose

'I knew thee ... I sanctified thee ... I have appointed thee a prophet'. In that degenerate age the great Lover of souls needed a spokesman; and the divine decree determined the conditions of Jeremiah's birth, and character, and life.

It is wise to discover, if possible, while life is yet young, the direction of the divine purpose. There are four considerations that will help us. First, the indication of our natural aptitudes, for these, when touched by the divine Spirit, become talents or gifts. Second, the inward impulse or energy of the divine Spirit, working in us both to will and to do his good pleasure. Third, the teaching of the Word of God. Fourth, the evidence of the circumstances and demands of life. When these concur and focus in one point, there need be no doubt as to the divine purpose and plan. It was thus that God disclosed to Samuel, and Jeremiah, and Saul of Tarsus, the future for which they were destined. Perhaps the noblest aim for any of us is to realise that word which was addressed by God to Jeremiah, when he as much as said to him, 'On whatsoever errand I shall send thee, thou shalt go; and whatsoever I shall command thee, thou shalt speak.'

## 2    Formative influences

It is interesting to study the formative influences that were brought to bear on the character of Jeremiah. There were the character and disposition of his mother, and the priestly office of his father. There was the near proximity of the holy city, making it possible for the boy to be present at all the holy festivals, and to receive such instruction as the best seminaries could provide. There was the companionship and association of godly families. His uncle, Shallum, was the husband of the illustrious and devoted prophetess, Huldah; and their son Hanameel shared with Baruch, the grandson of Maaseiah, the close friendship of the prophet, probably from the days they were boys together. There were also the prophets Nahum and Zephaniah, who were burning as bright constellations in that dark sky, to be soon joined by Jeremiah himself.

His mind was evidently very sensitive to all the influences of his early life. His speech is saturated with references to natural emblems and national customs, to the life of men, and the older literature of the Bible. Many chords made up the music of his speech.

It is thus that God is ever at work, forming and moulding us. The plan of God threads the maze of life. The purpose of God gives meaning to many of its strange experiences. Be brave, strong, and trustful!

### 3  There was also a special preparation and assurance for his life's work

'The LORD put forth his hand, and touched my mouth. And the LORD said unto me, Behold, I have put my words in thy mouth.' In a similar manner the seraph had touched the lips of Isaiah years before. Words are the special gift of God. They were the endowment of the church at Pentecost. And it is always an evidence of a Spirit-filled man when he begins to speak as the Spirit gives him utterance.

God never asks us to go on his errands (1:7) without telling us what to say. If we are living in fellowship with him, he will impress his messages on our minds, and enrich our life with the appropriate utterances by which those messages will be conveyed to others. If only God's glory is our object, his hand will touch our mouth, and he will leave his words there.

Two other assurances were also given. First, 'Thou shalt go to all that I shall send thee.' This gave a definiteness and directness to the prophet's speech. Second, 'Be not afraid of their faces: for I am with thee to deliver thee, saith the LORD.' An assurance that was remarkably fulfilled, as we shall see, in the unfolding of this narrative.

As long as we are on the prepared path, performing the appointed mission, he is with us. We may defy death. We bear a charmed life. Men may fight against us, but they cannot prevail; for the Lord of Hosts is with us, the God of Jacob is our refuge (1:19).

**4   Last, God promised a twofold vision to his child.**

On the one hand, the swift-blossoming almond tree assured him that God would watch over him, and see to the swift performance of his predictions; on the other, the seething cauldron, turned toward the north, indicated the breaking out of evil. So the pendulum of life swings to and fro; now to light and then to darkness. But happy is the man whose heart is fixed, trusting in the Lord. Men may fight against him, but they will not prevail; he is encircled in the environing care of Jehovah. As God spoke to Jeremiah, so he addresses us: 'They shall fight against thee; but they shall not prevail against thee; for I am with thee, saith the LORD, to deliver thee' (1:19).

There was a period in Jeremiah's life when he seems to have swerved from the path of complete obedience (15:19), and to have turned from following the God-given plan. But as he returned again to his allegiance, these precious promises were renewed, and again sounded in his ears.

It may be that you have stepped back before some fearful storm of opposition, as a fireman before the belching flames. Thus Cranmer signed his recantation. Yet return again to your post; the old blessing will flood your soul; God will bring you again that you may stand before him, and you shall be as his mouth. Thus it was with Peter on the day of Pentecost.


# 3

# Cistern making

## Jeremiah 2:13


There was probably little interval between Jeremiah's call and his entrance on his sacred work. We are told that to this young ardent soul 'the word of the Lord came' (2:1). Coming, it thrilled him.

He dwelt lightly on the ominous mention of the inevitable conflict which the divine voice predicted. He did not stay to gauge the full pressure of opposition indicated in the celestial storm signal. He had been told that the kings and princes, priests and people, would fight against him; but in the first blush of his young faith he thought more of the presence of Jehovah, who had promised to make him 'a defenced city, and an iron pillar, and brasen walls against the whole land.'

## 1 The prophet's twofold burden

When Jeremiah began his ministry, going from Anathoth to Jerusalem for that purpose (2:2), Josiah, though only twenty-one years of age, had been on the throne for thirteen years. He was beginning those measures of reform that were used to postpone, though not to avert, the doom of city and nation. 'They brake down the altars of Baalim in his presence; and the images, that were on high above them, he cut down; and the groves and the carved images, and the molten images, he brake in pieces, and made dust of them, and strowed it upon the grave of them that had sacrificed unto them. And he burnt the bones of the priests upon their altars, and cleansed Judah and Jerusalem' (2 Chron. 34:4–5).

For seventy years the grossest forms of idolatry had held almost undisputed sway. The impious orgies and degrading rites, which licensed vice as a part of religion, were in harmony with the depraved tastes of the people.

The result was first, that the work of reform was largely superficial; it did not strike beneath the surface nor change the trend of national choice. And second, this policy compacted together a strong political party, determined to promote a closer alliance with Egypt, which had just asserted her independence against the king of Assyria. In these two directions the young prophet was called to make his influence felt.

*a. He protested against the prevalent sin around him.* The one thought of the people was to preserve the outward acknowledgment of Jehovah by the maintenance of the temple services and rites. If these were rigorously observed, they figured that there was no sufficient cause of charging them with the sin of apostasy.

They insisted that they were not polluted (2:23); and reiterated with wearisome monotony, 'The temple of the LORD, The temple of the LORD, The temple of the LORD, are these' (7:4). This accounts for the plain denunciations of sin that came burning from the lips of the young prophet. He included the priests and expounders of the law, pastors and prophets, in his scathing words (2:8). Every metaphor is adopted that human art can suggest to bring home to the people their infidelity to their great Lover and Redeemer, God (3:20).

*b. He also protested against the proposal to form an Egyptian alliance.*     The little land of Canaan lay between the vast rival empires founded on the Nile and the Euphrates. It was therefore constantly exposed to the transit of immense armies, like locusts, destroying everything, or to the hostile incursions of one or other of its belligerent neighbours. It had always been the policy of a considerable party at the court of Jerusalem to cultivate alliance with Egypt or Assyria. In Hezekiah's and Manasseh's time the tendency had been toward Assyria; now it was toward Egypt, which had in a remarkable way thrown off the yoke that the great King Esarhaddon in three terrible campaigns had sought to rivet on its neck. The prophet strenuously opposed these overtures. Why should his people bind themselves to the fortunes of any heathen nation whatsoever? Was not God their King? Surely their true policy was to stand alone, untrammelled by foreign alliances, resting only on the mighty power of Jehovah.

This, then, was Jeremiah's mission – to stand almost alone; to protest against the sins of the people, which were covered by their boasted reverence to Jehovah; and to oppose the policy of the court, which sought to cultivate friendly relations with the one power that seemed able to give aid to his fatherland in the awful struggle with the northern kingdom that he saw to be imminent (1:15). And this ministry was carried out in the teeth of the most virulent opposition. Here was a priest denouncing the practices of priests, a prophet the lies of prophets. Small wonder therefore that the most powerful parties in the state conspired against him.

## 2   The imagery he employed

It is a scene among the mountains. In that green glade a fountain rises icy cold from the depths, and pours its silver stream downward through the valley. It is flowing in abundance, but its banks are unvisited, neither cup nor bucket descends into its crystal depths; for all practical purposes it might as well cease to flow.

Far away from that verdant valley you hear the clink of the chisel, and presently discover people of every age and rank engaged in making cisterns to supply their homes. Each man has his own scheme, his own design. After years of work he may achieve his purpose, and wait expectantly for the shower. It soon descends, and he is filled with pride and pleasure to think of the store of water that he has been able to secure. But lo! it does not stay. He finds that with the utmost care the cisterns made in the quarry can hold no water.

What an infinite mistake to miss the fountain freely flowing to quench the thirst, and cut out the broken cistern in which is disappointment and despair! Yet this, said the prophet, was the precise position of Israel. In resorting to false religions and heathen alliances, they were cutting out for themselves broken cisterns that would fail them in their hour of need.

## 3   Its application to ourselves

Many cistern makers may read these words – each with soul-thirst craving satisfaction; each within easy reach of God, but all attempting the impossible task of satisfying the thirst for the infinite and divine, with men and things.

There is the cistern of *pleasure,* the cistern of *wealth,* the cistern of *fame,* and the cistern of *human love,* which, however beautiful as a revelation of the divine love, can never satisfy the soul that rests in it alone – all these, made at infinite cost of time and pain, deceive and disappoint. They are 'broken cisterns that can hold no water.' And in the time of trouble they will not be able to save those who have constructed and trusted them.

At your feet, O weary cistern-cutter, the fountain of God's love is flowing through the channel of the divine Man! Stoop to drink it. 'The Spirit and the bride say, Come. And him that heareth say, Come! And let him that is athirst come: And whosoever will, let him take the water of life freely' (Rev. 22:17).

# 4

# On the Potter's Wheel

## *Jeremiah 18:4*

One day, beneath the impulse of the divine Spirit, Jeremiah went beyond the city precincts to the Valley of Hinnom, on the outskirts of Jerusalem, where he found a potter, busily engaged at his handicraft.

As the prophet stood quietly beside the potter, he saw him take a piece of clay from the mass that lay beside his hand, and having kneaded it to rid it of the bubbles, place it on the wheel, rapidly revolving at the motion of his foot driving the treadle. From that moment his hands were at work, within and without, shaping the vessel with his deft touch, here widening, there leading it up into a more slender form; opening out the lip, so that from the shapeless clay there emerged a fair and beautiful vessel. When it was nearly complete, and the next step would have been to remove it, to await the kiln, through a flaw in the material it fell a shapeless ruin, some broken pieces on the wheel, and others on the floor of the house.

The prophet naturally expected that the potter would immediately take another piece of clay. Instead, the potter with scrupulous care gathered up the broken pieces of the clay and pressed them together as he had first done, and placed the clay where it had lain before, and *made it again* into another vessel.

O vision of the long-suffering patience of God! O bright anticipation of God's redemptive work! O parable of remade characters, and lives, and hopes! 'Cannot I do with you as this potter? saith the LORD. Behold, as the clay is in the potter's hand, so are ye in mine hand, O house of Israel.'

The purpose of Jeremiah's vision seems to have been to give his people hope that even though they had marred God's fair ideal, yet a glorious and blessed future was within reach; and that if only they would yield themselves to the touch of the Great Potter, he would undo the results of years of disobedience that had marred and spoiled his fair purpose, and would make the chosen people a vessel to honour, sanctified and meet for the Master's use.

The same thought may apply to us all. Who is there who is not conscious of having marred and resisted the touch of God's moulding hands? Who is there that would not like to be made again as seems good to the Potter?

## 1   The divine making of men

**a.** *The Potter has an ideal.*   Floating through his fancy there is the vessel that is to be. He already sees it hidden in the shapeless clay, waiting to evoke his call. His hands achieve so far as they may the embodiment of the fair conception of his thought.

So of God in nature. The pattern of this round world and of her sister spheres lay in his creative thought before the first beam of light streamed across the abyss. All that exists embodies with more or less exactness the divine idea – sin alone excepted. I do not know if we will ever be permitted, amid the archives of heaven, to see the transcript of God's original thought of what our life might have been had we only yielded ourselves to the hands that reach down from heaven moulding men; but it is sure that God foreordained and predestinated us, each in his own measure and degree, to be conformed to the image of his Son.

**b.** *The Potter achieves his purpose by means of the wheel.*   In the discipline of human life this surely represents the revolution of daily circumstance; often monotonous, common place, trivial enough, and yet intending to effect, if it may, ends on which God has set his heart.

Do not therefore seek to change, by some rash and wilful act, the setting and environment of your life. Stay where you are until God as evidently calls you elsewhere as he has put you where you are. Throw on him the responsibility of indicating to you a change when it is necessary for your development. In the meanwhile, look deep into the heart of every circumstance for its special message, lesson, or discipline.

You complain of the monotony of your life. Yet remember that the passive virtues are even dearer to God than the active ones. They need more courage and evince great heroism than those qualities the world admires most. But they can be acquired only in just that monotonous and narrow round of which many complain as offering so scant a chance of acquiring saintliness.

c. *The bulk of the work is done by the Potter's fingers.*   How delicate their touch! How fine their sensibility! And in the nurture of the soul, these represent the touch of the Spirit of God working in us to will and to do his good pleasure.

But we are too busy, too absorbed in many things, to heed the gentle touch. Sometimes, when we are aware of it, we resent it, or stubbornly refuse to yield to it. Hence the necessity of setting apart a portion of every day, or a season in the course of the week, in which to seclude ourselves from every other influence, and expose the entire range of our being to divine influences only.

Therefore, whenever you are in doubt as to the meaning of certain circumstances through which you are called to pass, and which are strange and inexplicable, be still; refrain from murmuring; and listen until there is borne in on your soul a persuasion of God's purpose; and let his Spirit within cooperate with the circumstance without.

## 2   God's remaking of men

'He made it again.' How often he has to make us again! He made Jacob again, when he met him at the Jabbok ford. He found him a supplanter and a cheat, but after a long wrestle he left him a prince with God. He made Simon again, on the resurrection morning, when he found him somewhere near the open grave, and left him Peter, the man of the rock, the apostle of Pentecost. He made Mark again, between his impulsive leaving of Paul and Banabas, as though frightened by the first touch of seasickness, and the times when Peter spoke of him as his son, and Paul from the Mamertine prison described him as being profitable.

Are you conscious of having marred God's early plan for you? His ideal of a life of earnest devotion to his cause has been so miserably lost sight of! Into the soul the conviction is burned: 'I had my chance, and missed it; it will never come to me again.' It is here that the gospel comes with its gentle words for the outcast and lost. The bruised reed is made again into a pillar for the temple of God. The feebly smoking flax is kindled to a flame.

### 3   Our attitude toward the Great Potter

Yield to him! Each particle in the clay seems to say 'Yes' to wheel and hand. And in proportion as this is the case the work goes merrily on. If there is rebellion and resistance, the work of the potter is marred. Let God have his way with you.

We cannot always understand his dealings, because we do not know what his purpose is. We fail to recognise the design; the position that we are being trained to fill; the ministry we are to exercise. What wonder, then, that we get puzzled and perplexed!

There is special comfort in these thoughts for the middle-aged and old. Do not look back regretfully on the wasted springtide and summer, gone beyond recall. Even though it is autumn, there is yet chance for you to bear some fruit, under the care of the great Husbandman. Only let him have a free hand. Trust in God: and according to your faith it will be done to you.

When the clay has received its final shape from the potter's hands, it must be baked in the kiln to keep it; and even then its discipline is not complete, for whatever colours are put in must be rendered permanent by fire. It is said that what is to become gold in the finished article is a smudge of dark liquid before the fire is applied; and that the first two or three applications of heat obliterate all trace of colour, which has to be renewed again and again. So in God's dealings with his people. The moulding hand has no sooner finished its work than it plunges the clay into the fiery trial of pain or temptation. But let patience have her perfect work. You shall be compensated when the Master counts you fair and meet for his use.

*5*

# The Indestructible Word

## *Jeremiah 36:23*

We are admitted to the prophet's private chamber, where he is keeping close that he may not excite the acute animosity and hatred of the people. Baruch, his trusted friend, a man of rank and learning, sits writing with laborious care at the dictation of the prophet.

When the roll was filled Jeremiah, not venturing to go into places of public assembly, entrusted it to Baruch, and urged him to read it to the assembled crowds. Jerusalem just then was unusually full. From all parts of Judah people had come to observe the great fast that had been proclaimed in view of the approach of the Babylonian army.

Choosing a position in the upper court at the entry of the new gate to the Lord's house, Baruch began to read, while the people stood densely massed around him. Amid the awestruck crowd was a young man, Micaiah, the grandson of Shaphan, who was so impressed and startled by what he heard that he hastened to inform the princes, then sitting in council in the chamber of the chief Secretary of State, in the royal palace. They in turn were so aroused by what he told them that they sent him back to the temple, and asked Baruch to come without delay and read the prophet's words to them. He came at their request, and sitting among them, began to read.

A great fear fell on them as they heard those ominous words, which were probably closely similar to those recorded in the twenty-fifth chapter of this book. It seemed their plain duty was to acquaint the king with the contents of the roll.

Before doing so, however, they counselled Baruch and

Jeremiah to conceal themselves, for they well knew the despotic and passionate temper of Jehoiakim; and the roll was left in the chamber of Elishama. It would appear that in the first instance they thought a verbal statement of the words they had heard would suffice. This, however, would not satisfy the king, who urged Jehudi to get the roll itself. It was winter, the month of December; the king was occupying the winter quarters of his palace, and a fire was burning brightly in the brazier. It is a vivid picture – the king sitting before the fire; the princes standing around him; Jehudi reading the contents of the roll; consternation and panic reigning throughout the city and darkening the faces of the prostrate crowds in the temple courts. As Jehudi began to read, the royal brow knit, and after the scribe had read three or four columns, Jehoiakim snatched the roll from his hand and, demanding the penknife he carried as symbol and implement of his calling, began to cut the manuscript in pieces, which he flung contemptuously into the fire. Nothing could stop him until the whole roll was cut to pieces, and every fragment consumed. Not content with this flagrant act of defiance, he gave orders for the immediate arrest of Jeremiah and Baruch; an order which his emissaries attempted to execute, but in vain.

The destruction of the roll did not however cancel the terrible doom to which the ship of state was hurrying. On another roll all the words of the book that he had burned were written again; and others were added foretelling the indignity and insult to which the dead body of the king would be exposed. 'His dead body shall be cast out in the day to the heat, and in the night to the frost.'

## 1   Eyes opened to see

There was a vast difference between Baruch, whose heart was in perfect sympathy with Jeremiah, and Jehudi or the princes. But there was almost as much between the faithful scribe and the heaven-illumined prophet. The one could write only as the words streamed from those burning lips; he saw nothing, he realised nothing; to him the walls of the chamber were the utmost bound of vision: while the other beheld the whole landscape of truth outspread before him. Men may be seers still.

It is very important that all Christians should be alive to and possess this power of vision. It is deeper than intellectual, since it is spiritual; it is not the result of reasoning or learning, but of intuition; it cannot be acquired in the school of earthly science, but is the gift of him who alone can open the eyes of the blind. If you lack it, seek it at the hands of Jesus; be willing to do his will, and you will know. If you have the opened eye, you will not need books of evidences to establish to your satisfaction the truth of our holy religion; the glory of the risen Lord; the world of the unseen. They who see these things are indifferent to the privations of the tent life or, as in Jeremiah's case, rise superior to the hatred of man and the terrors of a siege.

## 2   The use of the penknife

Men use the knife to the Bible in varied ways. *Teachers of error do this.* They have done it. They will do it again. They are wise to do it – I mean, wise in their own interests. For when once the Bible is in the hands of the people, the false teacher, who has deluded them for selfish purposes, must pack.

The next that follows Jehoiakim's practice is *the infidel,* who uses the sharp blade of bitter sarcasm and miscalled reason to destroy the Scriptures. The hostility that manifested itself in the winter palace among the princes of this world, has wrought in the halls of earthly learning and science, instigating similar acts to theirs. The Bible is cut up regularly once in each generation by men like these.

The next are the *higher critics* of our time, who surely have gone beyond the necessities of the case in their ruthless use of the knife. There is room for the honest examination of the fabric of sacred Scripture, its language, the evidence furnished in its texture of the successive hands that have re-edited its most ancient documents; but this is altogether different to ruthless vandalism.

We are all tempted to use Jehudi's penknife. It is probably that no one is free from the almost unconscious habit of evading or toning down certain passages that conflict with the doctrinal or ecclesiastical position in which we were reared, or which we have assumed.

In our private reading of the Scripture, we must beware of using the penknife. Whole books and tracts of truth are practically cut out of the Bible of some earnest Christians – passages referring to the Second Advent, the inevitable doom of the ungodly; those who describe the types and shadows of the ancient law; or those who build up massive systems of truth and doctrine, as in the epistles. But we can only eliminate these things at our peril. It is a golden rule to read the Bible as a whole. Of course each will have his favourite passages but, beside these, there should be the loving and devout study of all Scripture, which is given by inspiration of God.

## 3    The indestructible word

Men may destroy the words and the fabric on which they are written, but not the Word itself. It must sometimes be an uncomfortable reflection to those who refuse the testimony of the Word of God, that their attitude toward the message cannot affect the reality to which it bears witness.

Jeremiah wrote another roll. The money spent in buying up copies of the Bible to burn at St Paul's enabled Tyndale to reissue the Scriptures in a cheaper form and a better type. And perhaps the most remarkable fact in this connection is that, in spite of all that has been done to stamp out the Bible, it exists in millions of copies, and it is circulated among all the nations of the world; it is with us today in unimpaired authority.

And the facts to which Jeremiah bore witness all came to pass. Neither knife nor fire could arrest the inevitable doom of the king, city, and people. The drunken captain may cut in pieces the chart that tells of the rocks in the vessel's course, and put in irons the sailor who calls his attention to it; but neither will avert the crash that must follow unless the helm is turned. You may tamper with and destroy the record, but the stubborn facts remain.

# 6

# Jeremiah's Grandest Ode

## *Jeremiah 51*

It was a very deserted Jerusalem in which Jeremiah lived, after king Jehoiachin, his household and court, princes and mighty men of valour had been carried off to Babylon. Still, the fertility and natural resources of the land were so considerable as to give hope of its comparative prosperity, as a trailing vine dependent on Babylon (Ezek. 17).

Mattaniah, the third son of Josiah – who was now in his twenty-first year – was called to the throne by the conqueror, and required to hold it under a solemn oath of allegiance which was affirmed and sanctioned by an appeal to Jehovah himself. It was as though the heathen monarch thought to make insubordination impossible on the part of the young monarch, since his word of honour was ratified under such solemn and august conditions – conditions that under similar circumstances the heathen king would probably have felt binding and final.

At the urging of his conqueror, the young king took the name Zedekiah, 'the righteousness of Jehovah'. It was an auspicious sign; every encouragement was given him to follow in the footsteps of his illustrious father. And throughout his reign he gave evident tokens of desiring better things, but he was weak and irresolute, lacking strength of purpose. He respected Jeremiah, but did not dare to espouse his cause publicly, showing him his royal favour by stealth.

Meanwhile the kingdom was violently agitated by rumours from every side, which encouraged the hope that before long the power of Babylon would be broken and the exiles returned. These thoughts were rife among the exiles themselves, as we have seen;

they were diligently fostered by the false prophets.

About this time there was a revolt in Elam against Babylon. What if this should spread until the empire itself became disintegrated! But Jeremiah, by the voice of God, said: 'It shall not be; the bow of Elam shall be broken; her king and princes destroyed, her people scattered toward the four winds of heaven' (see 49:34–39).

Then there was the seething discontent of the neighbouring people who, though they had accompanied the invader as allies, were eager to regain their independence, and desired to draw Judah into one vast confederacy, with Egypt as its base. 'No', said Jeremiah; 'it must not be; Nebuchadnezzar is doing the behest of Jehovah; all the nations are to serve him, and his son, and his son's son' (see 27:6–7). Perhaps it was at Jeremiah's suggestion that Zedekiah at this time made a journey to Babylon to pay homage to his king, and assure him of his fidelity.

All through the troubles that followed, Jeremiah pursued the same policy; and his policy was so well known among the Chaldeans that in the final overthrow they gave him his life, and allowed him to choose where he would dwell (chap.40).

It must have seemed to his choicest friends as though his advice was often wanting in the courage of faith. Did he really favour Babylon above Jerusalem? Was he traitorous to the best interests of his people? But if they ever entertained such questions, they must have been suddenly and completely disillusioned when he summoned them to hear the tremendous indictment he had composed against Babylon in the early months of Zedekiah's reign, together with the graphic description of its fall. A copy of this prophecy was entrusted to Seraiah, the chief chamberlain, who went in the train of Zedekiah to Babylon, with instructions that he should read it privately to the exiles; and then, weighting it with a stone, cast it into the midst of the Euphrates, with the solemn words, 'Thus shall Babylon sink, and shall not rise from the evil that I will bring upon her! and they shall be weary' (51:59–64).

## 1 The prophecy of the fall of Babylon

*a. The glory of Babylon*   In glowing imagery Jeremiah depicts her glory and beauty. She had been a golden cup in the hand of

Jehovah; his battle axe and weapons of beauty. She had been a golden up in the hand of Jehovah; his battle axe and weapons of war. Her influence was carried far and wide. She dwelt by many waters, rich in treasure, and the wonder of the earth. Like a mighty tree, she stretched her branches over the surrounding lands.

**b.** *The divine controversy*   The Almighty had used her, but she had abused, for unrighteous and selfish ends, the power that God had entrusted to her. And therefore Jehovah opened his armoury and brought out the weapons of his wrath.

But God was especially against Babylon for her treatment of his people. 'As Babylon hath caused the slain of Israel to fall, so at Babylon shall fall the slain of all the earth . . . for the Lord God of recompenses shall surely requite'.

**c.** *The summons to her foes*   The standard is raised, and around it, at the sounding of the trumpet, the nations gather. 'Behold!' the prophet cries, 'a people shall come from the north; and a great nation, and many kings shall be raised up from the coasts of the earth. They shall hold the bow and the lance; they are cruel, and will show no mercy; their voice shall roar like the sea, and they shall ride upon horses, every one put in array, like a man to the battle, against thee, O daughter of Babylon' (50:41–42).

**d.** *The attack*   The archers surround the city on every side, so that none may escape. They are commanded to shoot at her, and not spare their arrows. Now the battle shout is raised, and an assault is made against her walls. Lo, the fire breaks out amid her dwelling places. The messengers, running with similar tidings from different quarters of the city, come to show the king of Babylon that the fords are in the hand of the foe, and that the city is taken.

**e.** *The overthrow of the city*   Then the captured city is given up to the savage soldiery. There is plunder enough to satisfy the most rapacious. Her granaries are ruined; her treasuries ransacked; her stores of grain blown away. All the captive peoples are set free, and especially the Jews. 'Let us forsake her', they cry, 'and let us go every one into his own country; for her judgment reacheth unto heaven, and is lifted up even to the skies'.

And now her cities become a desolation, a dry land; it lies waste from generation to generation.

Such were the predictions of Jeremiah. Seventy years were to pass before his words would be fulfilled, but history itself could hardly be more definite and precise. Those who can compare this prophecy with the story of the fall of Babylon, and with the researches of Layard, will find how exactly every detail was repeated.

'They drank wine, and praised the gods of gold, and of silver, of brass, or iron, of wood, and of stone. In the same hour came forth fingers of a man's hand, and wrote over against the candlestick upon the plaster of the wall of the king's palace . . . In that night was Belshazzar the king of the Chaldeans slain, and Darius the Mede took the kingdom' (Dan. 5:4, 30–31).

## 2  Babylon the Great

In every age of the world, Babylon has had its counterpart. Where God has built up his kingdom, the devil has always counterfeited it by some travesty of his own.

Jeremiah comforted his heart amid the desolations that fell thick and heavily on his beloved fatherland, by anticipating the inevitable doom of the oppressor. Let us strengthen our confidence in the certain prevalence of good over evil, of the church over the world, and of Christ over Satan, as we consider the precise fulfilment of Jeremiah's predictions concerning the fall of Babylon. 'So let all thine enemies perish, O Lord: but let them that love thee be as the sun when he goeth forth in his might'.

## 3  Our own Babylon

Each heart has its special form of sin, to which it is liable, and by yielding to which it has been perpetually overthrown. How bitter have been your tears and self-reproach! How you have chafed and fumed beneath the strong iron bit of your tyrant!

But there is a deliverance for you, as for those weak in misguided but suffering Jews. How exactly your life history is delineated in theirs! They were the children of God; so are you. They might have lived in an impregnable fortress of God's covenant protection; so might you. They forfeited this by their disobedience and unbelief; so have you. But as God saved them by his own right hand, so will he save you.

Accept these rules, if you would have this blessed deliverance.

# 7

# The Fall of Jerusalem

## *Jeremiah 38:39*

During the long dark months of seige, probably the only soul in all that crowded city that was in perfect peace, and free in its unrestrained liberty, was Jeremiah's. And amid the cries of assailants and defenders, unbroken by the thud of the battering rams, deep as the blue Syrian sky that looked down on him, was the peace of God that passed the understanding of those that thronged in and out, between the city and the royal palace.

### 1  The horrors of the siege

It lasted in all for about eighteen months, with the one brief respite caused by the approach of Pharaoh's army; and it is impossible for us to estimate the amount of human anguish that was crowded into that fateful space.

Imagine for a moment the overcrowded city into which the peasantry and villagers had gathered from all over the country. Who, with such of their valuables as they had been able to hastily collect and transport, had sought refuge within the grey old walls of Zion from the violence and outrage of the merciless troops. The mass of fugitives would greatly add to the difficulties of the defence by their demands on the provisions that were laid up in anticipation of the siege, by overcrowding the thoroughfares and impeding the movements of the soldiery.

So much for the earlier months of the siege; but as the days passed on darker shadows gathered. It was as though the very pit of hell added in human passion the last dread horrors of the scene. The women became cruel and refused to spare from their breast for their young the nutrition they needed for themselves. Young children asked for bread, and asked in vain. The nobles lost their portly mien, and walked the streets like animated mummies. The sword of the invader without had fewer victims than that which hunger wielded within; and, as a climax, pitiful women murdered their own children for food. Finally, pestilence began its ravages; and the foul stench of bodies that men had no time to bury, and that fell thick and fast each day in the streets of the city, caused death that mowed down those that had escaped the foe and privation. Ah, Jerusalem! who stoned the prophets, and shed the blood of the just, this was the day of the overflowing wrath and fury of Jehovah! You, O God, have slain them in the day of your anger; you have slaughtered and not pitied.

And as Jeremiah waited day after day, powerless to do anything else than listen to tidings of woe that converged to him from every side, he resembled the physician who, unable to stay the slow progress of some terrible form of paralysis in one he loves better than life, is compelled to listen to the news of its conquests, knowing surely that these are only stages in an assault that ultimately must capture the citadel of life – an assault that he can do nothing to stay.

## 2   The prophet's added sorrows

In addition to the discomfort he shared in common with the rest of the crowded populace, Jeremiah was exposed to aggravated sorrows. He lost no opportunity of asserting that Jerusalem should surely be given to the hands of the king of Babylon, and that he would take it. As these words passed from lip to lip, they carried dismay throughout the city, and the fact that Jeremiah had so often spoken as the mouthpiece of Jehovah gave an added weight to his words.

It was quite natural therefore that the princes, who knew well enough the importance of keeping up the courage of the people, should demand the death of one who was not only weakening the hands of the people generally, but especially of the men of war. The young king was weak rather than wicked, a puppet and toy in the hands of his princes and court. He therefore yielded to their demand, saying, 'Behold, he is in your hand; for the king is not he that can do anything against you'.

Without delay Jeremiah was flung into one of those rock-hewn cisterns that abound in Jerusalem, and the bottom of which, because the water was exhausted during the extremities of the siege, consisted of a deep sediment of mud, into which he sank. There was not a moment to be lost. Help was sent through a very unexpected channel. An Ethiopian eunuch – who is probably anonymous, since the name Ebed-melech simply means 'the king's servant' – with a love to God's cause, hastened to the king and urged him to take immediate steps to save the prophet from imminent death.

Always swayed by the last strong influence brought to bear on him, the king bade him take a sufficient number of men to protect him from interference, and at once release the prophet. There was great gentleness in the way this noble Ethiopian executed his purpose. He was not content with merely dragging Jeremiah from the pit's bottom, but placed on the ropes old castoff cloths and rotten rags, gathered hurriedly from the house of the king; thus the tender flesh of the prophet was neither cut nor chafed. It is not only what we do, but the way in which we do it that most quickly indicates our real selves. Many might have hurried to the pit's mouth with ropes; only one of God's own gentlemen would have thought of the rags and cloths.

From that moment until the city fell the prophet remained in safe custody; and on one memorable occasion the king sought his counsel, though in strict secrecy. Once more Zedekiah asked what the issue would be: and once more received the alternatives that appeared so foolish to the eye of sense – defeat and death by remaining in the city; liberty and life by going forth.

'Go forth?' said Zedekiah, in effect; 'Never! It would be unworthy of one in whose veins flows the blood of kings'.

'Obey, I beseech thee, the voice of the Lord', said Jeremiah, 'which I speak unto thee: so it shall be well with thee, and thy soul shall live'. Finally, in graphic words he painted the picture of the certain doom the king would incur if he stayed until the city fell into the captor's hands.

The weakness that was the ruin of Zedekiah came out in his request that Jeremiah would not inform the princes of the nature of their communications, and would hide the truth beneath the semblance of truth. It is difficult to pronounce a judgment on the way in which the prophet veiled the content of his conversation with Zedekiah from the inquisitive questions of the princes. He shielded the king with a touch of chivalrous devotion and loyalty that was probably the last act of devotion to the royal house, to save what he had poured out his heart's blood in tears and entreaties and sacrifices for nearly forty years.

## 3 The fate of the city

At last a breach was made in the old fortifications and the troops began to rush in. The terrified people fled from the lower into the upper city; and as they did so, their homes were filled with the desolating terror of the merciless army.

A hundred different forms of anguish gathered in that devoted city, like vultures to the dead camel of the desert. Woe, then, to the men who had fought for their very life! but woe more agonising to the women and girls, to the children and the little babes. 'All the princes of the king of Babylon came in, and sat in the middle gate', from which they gave directions for the immediate prosecution of their success on the terrified people, who now crowded the upper city, prepared to make the last desperate stand.

Everything had to be done to preserve the royal house. It was therefore arranged that, as soon as night fell, Zedekiah and his harem would go forth under the protection of all the men of war, through a breach to be made in the walls of the city to the south; and exactly as Ezekiel had foretold, so it came to pass.

A long line of fugitives, each carrying property of necessities, stole silently through the king's private garden, and so toward the breach; and, like shadows of the night, passed into the darkness between long lines of armed men, who held their breath. If only by dawn they could reach the plains of Jericho, they might hope to elude the fury of their pursuers. But all night Zedekiah must have remembered those last words of Jeremiah: 'Thou shalt not escape; but shalt be taken by the hand of the king of Babylon'. This was not the first time, nor the last, that man has sought to elude the close meshes of the Word of God.

Somehow the tidings of the flight reached the Chaldeans. The whole army arose to pursue. What happened the next morning in

Jerusalem, and what befell her a month later, when the upper city also fell into the hands of the conqueror, is told in the Book of Lamentations. The streets and houses were filled with the bodies of the slain, after having been outraged with nameless atrocities; but those who perished could be considered better off than the thousands who were led off into exile, or sold into slavery, to suffer in life the horrors of death. Then the wild fury of fire engulfed temple and palace, public building and dwelling-house, and blackened ruins covered the site of the holy and beautiful city that had been the joy of the whole earth; and the ear of the prophet heard the spirit of the fallen city crying,

> Is it nothing to you, all ye that pass by?
> Behold, and see if there be any sorrow like unto my sorrow, which is done unto me,
> Wherewith the Lord hath afflicted me in the day of his fierce anger!

As for Zedekiah, he was taken to Riblah where Nebuchadnezzar was at this time, perhaps not expecting so speedy a downfall of the city. With barbarous cruelty he slew the sons of Zedekiah before his eyes, so that the last scene he beheld might be of their dying agony. He was also compelled to witness the slaughter of all his nobles. Then as a *coup de grâce*, with his own hand probably, Nebuchadnezzar struck out Zedekiah's eyes with his spear.

It is indeed a subject for an artist to depict, the long march of the exiles on the way to their distant home. Delicate women and little children forced to travel day after day, irrespective of fatigue and suffering; prophets and priests mingled together in the overthrow they had done so much to bring about; rich and poor marching side by side, manacled, and urged forward by the spear-point or scourge. All along the valley of the Jordan, past Damascus, and then for thirty days through the inhospitable wilderness, retravelling the route taken in the dawn of history by Abraham, their great progenitor, the Friend of God, while all the nations around them clapped their hands. In later years the bitterest recollection of those days was the exultation of the Edomites in the fall of their rival city. 'Remember, O Lord, against the children of Edom, the day of Jerusalem!'

Thus God brought on his people the king of the Chaldeans,

who slew their young men with the sword in the house of their sanctuary, and had no compassion on young man or woman, or old person, but gave them all into his hand. And all the vessels of the house of God, great and small, and the treasures of the house of the Lord, and the treasures of the king and his princes, all these he brought to Babylon. And they burned the house of God, and broke down the wall of Jerusalem; and burned all the palaces with fire, and destroyed all the goodly vessels in them. And those who had escaped from the sword he carried away to Babylon, and they were servants to him and his sons.

# 8

# A Clouded Sunset

## *Jeremiah 40—44*

If the closing verses of the Book of Jeremiah were written by his own hand, he must have lived for twenty years after the fall of Jerusalem; but they were filled with the same infinite sadness as the forty years of his public ministry. It would appear that as far as his outward lot was concerned, the prophet Jeremiah spent a life of more unrelieved sadness than has perhaps fallen to the lot of any other, with the exception of the divine Lord.

His sufferings may be classed under three divisions – those recited in the Book of Lamentations, and connected with the fall of Jerusalem; those connected with the murder of Gedaliah, and the flight into Egypt; and those of the exile there. But amid the salt brine of these bitter experiences, there was always welling up a spring of hope and peace.

## 1 The desolate city

It is only in later years that any question has been raised as to the authorship of the Book of Lamentations. The cave in which Jeremiah is said to have written them is still shown to the western side of the city; and every Friday the Jews assemble to recite as his these plaintive words, at their wailing-place in Jerusalem where a few of the old stones still remain. There is no good reason therefore for dissociating the Book of Lamentations from the authorship of Jeremiah.

This being so, what a flood of light is cast on the desolate scene when Nebuzaradan had completed his work of destruction, and the long lines of captives were already far on their way to Babylon! How many went into exile we have no means of knowing; the number would probably amount to several thousand, principally of the wealthier classes. Only the poor of the people were left to cultivate the land that it might not revert to an absolute desert. But the population would probably be very sparse – a few peasants scattered over the sites that had teemed with crowds.

The city sat solitary, which once had been full of people. She had become as a widow. The holy fire was extinct on her altars, pilgrims no longer traversed the ways of Zion to attend the appointed feasts; her gates had sunk into the ground and her habitations were pitilessly destroyed by fire. How often would Jeremiah pass mournfully amid the blackened ruins!

## 2   Gedaliah's murder

Nebuchadnezzar and his chiefs had evidently been kept closely informed of the condition of certain people during the siege of Jerusalem; and the king gave definite instructions to his chief officers to take special precautions for the safety of Jeremiah. When the upper city fell into their hands they sent and took him out of the court of the guard; and he was brought in chains along with the other captives to Ramah, about five miles north of Jerusalem.

In a remarkable address that the captain of the guard made to Jeremiah, he acknowledged the retributive justice of Jehovah – one of the many traces of the real religion that gave a tone and bearing to these men by which they are altogether removed from the category of ordinary heathen. 'The Lord thy God hath pronounced this evil upon this place. Now the Lord hath brought it, and done according as he hath said: because ye have sinned against the Lord, and have not obeyed his voice, therefore this thing is come upon you.'

The chains were then struck from off his fettered hands, and liberty was given him either to accompany the rest of the people to Babylon, or to go where he chose throughout the land. Ultimately, as he seemed to hesitate as to which direction to take, the Chaldean general urged him to make his home with Gedaliah, to strengthen his hands, and give him the benefit of his counsel in the difficult task to which he had been appointed. Thus again he turned from rest and ease to take the rough path of duty.

Gedaliah was the grandson of Shaphan, King Josiah's secretary, and son of Ahikam, who had been sent to inquire of the prophetess Huldah concerning the newly found book of the law. On the former occasion the hand of Ahikam had rescued Jeremiah from the nobles. Evidently the whole family was bound by the strongest, tenderest ties to the servant of God, imbued with the spirit, and governed by the policy that he enunciated. These principles Gedaliah had consistently followed; and they marked him out in the judgment of Nebuchadnezzar as the fittest to be entrusted with the reins of government, and to exert some kind of authority over the scattered remnant. To him, therefore, Jeremiah came with an allowance of supplies and other marks of the esteem in which the conquerors regarded him.

For a brief interval all went well. The new governor took up his residence at Mizpah, an old fort that Asahad erected three hundred years before, to check the invasion of Baasha. The town stood on a rocky eminence, but the castle was supplied with water from a deep well. Chaldean soldiers gave the show of authority and stability to Gedaliah's rule. To Mizpah the scattered remnant of the Jews began to look with hope. The captains of the forces that were in the fields still holding out, as roving bands, against the conqueror, hastened to swear allegiance to the representative of the Jewish state, and the Jews who had fled to Moab, Edom, and other surrounding peoples returned from every place out of which they had been driven, and they came to the land of Judah to Gedaliah, to Mizpah.

How happy Jeremiah must have been to see this nucleus of order spreading its influence through the surrounding chaos and confusion; and with what eagerness he must have used all the energy he possessed to aid in the establishment of Gedaliah's authority! The fair dream, however, was rudely dissipated by the treacherous murder of Gedaliah – who seems to have been eminently fitted for his post – by Ishmael, the son of Nethaniah. In the midst of a feast given by the unsuspecting governor, he was slain with the sword, together with all the Jews who were with him and the Chaldean garrison. On the second day after that, the red-handed murderers, still thirsting for blood, slew seventy pilgrims who were on their way to weep amid the ruins of Jerusalem, and lay offerings on the site of the ruined altar. The deep well of the keep was choked with bodies, and shortly afterward Ishmael carried off the king's daughters and all the people who had gathered around Gedaliah, and started with them for the court of Baalis, the king of the children of Ammon, who was an accomplice on the plot. It was a bitter disappointment; and to none would the grief of it have been more poignant than to Jeremiah.

The people themselves appear to have lost heart, for though Johanan and other of the captains of roving bands pursued Ishmael and delivered from his hand all the captives he had taken, and recovered the women and the children, yet none of them dared to return to Mizpah; but like shepherdless sheep, harried by dogs, driven, draggled, panting, and terrified, they resolved to quit their land, and retire southward, with the intention of fleeing into the land of Egypt, with which during the later days of their national history they had maintained close relations.

They carried Jeremiah with them. They had confidence in his prayers and in his veracity, since his predictions had been verified so often by the event. They knew he stood high in the favour of the court of Babylon. They believed that his prayers prevailed with God. And, therefore, they regarded him as a shield and defence.

Halting at the inn at Chimham, the people earnestly debated whether they should go forward or return. They also came to Jeremiah and asked him to give himself to prayer. They professed their willingness to be guided entirely by the voice of God, though in this they were probably not sincere; in fact, they were determined to enter into Egypt.

For ten days Jeremiah gave himself to prayer. Then the word of the Lord came to him, and he summoned the people around him to declare it. Speaking in the name of the Most High, he said: 'If ye will still abide in this land, then will I build you, and not pull you down; and I will plant you, and not pluck you up . . . Be not afraid of the king of Babylon . . . for I am with you to save you, and to deliver you from his hand'. If, on the other hand, they persisted in going into the land of Egypt, then they would be overtaken there by the sword, the famine, and the pestilence, and they would never again see their native land. As he spoke he seems to have been sadly aware that during the ten days devoted to intercession on their behalf the prepossession in favour of Egypt had been growing, and that his words would do nothing to stop the strong current that was bearing them there.

So it befell. When he had finished speaking, the chiefs accused him of speaking falsely, and of misrepresenting the divine word. So the terrified people pursued their way to Egypt, and settled at Tahpanhes, which was ten miles across the frontier. Almost the last ingredient of bitterness in Jeremiah's cup must have been furnished by this pertinacious obstinacy.

## 3   Egypt

His life of protest was not yet complete. No sooner had the people settled in their new home than he was led to take great stones in his hand and lay them beneath the mortar in some brickwork that was being laid down at the entry of Pharaoh's palace in Tahpanhes. 'On these stones', he said, 'the king of Babylon shall set his throne, and spread out his royal pavilion upon them. He shall smite the land of Egypt, and kindle a fire in the houses of its gods, and array himself in her spoils, as easily as a shepherd throws his outer garment around his shoulders. The obelisks of Heliopolis will be also burnt with fire. To have come here, therefore, is not to escape the dreaded foe, but to throw yourselves into his arms'.

Some years must have followed of which we have no record, and during which the great king was engaged in the siege of Tyre, and therefore unable to pursue his plans against Pharaoh. During this time the Jews scattered over a wide extent of territory, so that colonies were formed in Upper as well as Lower Egypt, all of which became deeply infected with the prevailing idolatries and customs around them. Notwithstanding all the bitter experiences that had befallen them in consequence of their idol worship, they burned incense to the gods of Egypt, and repeated the abominations that had brought such disaster and suffering on their nation.

Taking advantage therefore of a great convocation at some idolatrous festival, Jeremiah warned them of the inevitable fate that would overtake them in Egypt, as it had befallen them in Jerusalem. The faithful prophet told them that God would punish Jerusalem, by 'the word, by the famine, and by the pestilence; so that none of the remnant of Judah, which are gone into the land of Egypt to sojourn there, shall escape or remain, that they should return into the land of Judah . . . to dwell there'.

A severe altercation then followed. The men indignantly protested that they would still burn incense to the queen of heaven as they had done in the streets of Jerusalem; and they even ascribed the evils that had befallen them to their discontinuance of this custom. Jeremiah, on the other hand, grey with age, his face marred with suffering, did not hesitate to insist in the name of the God he served so faithfully that the sufferings of the people were due, not to their discontinuance of idolatry, but to their persistence in its unholy rites. He went on to predict the invasion of Egypt by Nebuchadnezzar, which took place in the year 568 BC and which resulted, as Josephus tells us, in the carrying off to Babylon of the remnant of Jews who had, against Jeremiah's advice, fled there for refuge. So it was proved whose word should stand, God's or theirs.

Through all these dark and painful experiences, the soul of Jeremiah quieted itself as a weaned babe. He looked far away beyond the mist of years and saw the expiration of the sentence of captivity; the return of his people; the rebuilding of the city; the holy and blessed condition of its inhabitants; the glorious reign of the Branch, the scion of David's stock; the new Covenant, before which the old should vanish away. Therefore his days were probably not all dark; but aglow with the first rays of the Sun of Righteousness.

If these words should be read by some whose life, like Jeremiah's, has been draped with curtains of sombre hue, let them know that to none does the infinite One stoop so closely as to those that are severely broken on the wheel of affliction. It is only when we fall into the ground and die that we cease to abide alone, and begin to bear much fruit. Do not try to feel resigned. *Will* resignation. Submit yourself under the mighty hand of God. If you can say nothing else, fill your nights and days with the cry or sob of 'Father, not my will, but Thine be done.' Never doubt the love of God. Never suppose for a moment that he has forgotten or forsaken.

Scripture says nothing about the death of Jeremiah. Whether it took place, as Christian tradition affirms, by stoning in Egypt, or whether he breathed out his soul beneath the faithful care of Baruch, in some quiet chamber of death, we cannot tell.

But how gladly did the prophet close his eyes on the wreck that sin had wrought on the chosen people, and open them in the land where neither sin, nor death, nor the sight and sound of war can break the perfect rest! What a look of surprise and rapture must have settled on the worn face, the expression of the last glad vision of the soul as it passed out from the body of corruption, worn and weary with the long conflict, to hear the 'Well done!' and welcome of God.

# JOHN THE BAPTIST

# 1

# The first ministry of the Baptist

## *Luke 3*

Thirty years had left their mark on the forerunner. The story of his miraculous birth, and the expectations it had aroused, had almost died out of the memory of the countryside. For many years John had been living in the caves that indent the limestone rocks of the desolate wilderness that extends from Hebron to the western shores of the Dead Sea. By the use of the scantiest fare and roughest garb he had brought his body under complete mastery. From nature, from the inspired page, and from direct fellowship with God, he had received revelations that are bestowed on only those who can stand the strain of discipline in the school of solitude and privation. He had carefully pondered also the signs of the times, of which he received information from the Bedouin and others with whom he came in contact. Blended with all other thoughts, John's heart was filled with the advent of him, his relative who was growing up, a few months his junior, in an obscure highland home, but who was soon to be manifested to Israel.

At last the moment arrived for him to utter the mighty burden that pressed on him; and 'in the fifteenth year of the reign of Tiberius Caesar, Pontius Pilate being governor of Judaea, and Herod being tetrarch of Galilee and Annas and Caiaphas being the high priests, the word of God came unto John the son of Zacharias in the wilderness.' The word was 'Repent! the kingdom of heaven is at hand.'

It was as though a spark had fallen on dry tinder. The tidings spread with wonderful rapidity that in the wilderness of Judaea one was to be met who recalled the memory of the great prophets, and whose burning eloquence was of the same order as of Isaiah

413

of Ezekiel. People began to flock to him from all sides. The neighbourhood suddenly became black with hurrying crowds. From lip to lip the tidings sped of a great leader and preacher who had suddenly appeared.

He seems finally to have taken his stand not far from the rose-clad oasis of Jericho, on the banks of the Jordan; and men of every tribe, class, and profession, gathered there, listening eagerly, or interrupting him with the loud cries for help.

## 1   Many causes accounted for John's immense popularity

*a. The office of the prophet was almost obsolete.*   We have seen how several centuries had passed since the last great prophet had finished his testimony. It seemed unlikely that another prophet should arise in that formal, materialistic age.

*b. John gave such abundant evidence of sincerity – of reality.*
His independence of anything that this world could give made men feel that whatever he said was inspired by his direct contact with things as they literally are. It was certain that his severe and lonely life had rent the veil, and given him the knowledge of facts and realities hidden from ordinary men. When men see the professed prophet of the Eternal as eager after his own interests as any worldling, shrewd at a bargain, captivated by show, obsequious to the titled and wealthy; they are apt to reduce to a minimum their faith in his words. But there was no trace of this in the Baptist, and therefore the people came to him.

*c. Above all, he appealed to their moral convictions and, indeed, expressed them.*   The people knew that they were not as they should be. They flocked around the man who revealed themselves to themselves and indicated with unfaltering decision the course of action they should adopt. How marvellous is the fascination that *he* exerts over people who will speak to their innermost souls! Though we may shrink from the preaching of repentance, yet, if it tells the truth about us, we will be irresistibly attracted to hear the voice that harrows our soul. John rebuked Herod for many things; but still the royal offender sent for him again and again, and heard him gladly.

It is expressly said that John saw many Pharisees and Sadducees coming to his baptism (Matt. 3:7). Their advent appears to have caused him some surprise. 'O generation of vipers, who hath warned you to flee from the wrath to come?' The strong epithet he used of them suggests that they came as critics; but it is quite likely that in many cases there were deeper reasons. The Pharisees were the ritualists and formalists of their day, but the mere externals of religion will never permanently satisfy the soul made in the likeness of God. Ultimately it will turn from them with a great nausea and an insatiable desire for the living God. As for the Sadducees, they were the materialists of their time. The reaction of superstition, it had been said, is to infidelity; and the reaction from Pharisaism was to Sadduceeism. Disgusted and outraged by the trifling of the literalists of Scripture interpretation, the Sadducee denied that there was an eternal world and a spiritual state. But mere negation can never satisfy. It was hardly to be wondered at then that these two great classes were largely represented in the crowds that gathered on the banks of the Jordan.

### 2  Let us briefly enumerate the main burden of the Baptist's preaching

*a.* '*The kingdom of heaven is at hand.*'   To a Jew that phrase meant the reestablishment of the theocracy, and a return to those great days in the history of his people when God himself was Lawgiver and King. The long-expected Messiah was at hand; but some misgiving must have passed over the minds of his hearers when they heard the young prophet's description of the conditions and accompaniments of that long-looked-for reign. Instead of dilating on the material glory of the messianic period, far surpassing the magnificent splendour of Solomon, he insisted on the fulfilment of certain necessary preliminary requirements, which lifted the whole conception of the anticipated reign to a new level, in which the inward and spiritual took precedence of the outward and material. It was the old lesson, which in every age requires repetition, that unless a man is born again, and from above, he cannot see the kingdom of God.

Be sure of this, that no outward circumstances, however propitious and favourable, can bring about true blessedness. Life must be centred in Christ if it is to be concentric with all the circles of heaven's bliss. It is only when we are right with God that we are blest and at rest. When all hearts are yielded to the King; when all gates lift up their heads, and all everlasting doors are unfolded for his entrance – then the curse that has so long brooded over the world will be done away.

*b.* Alongside the proclamation of the kingdom was the uncompromising insistence on *'the wrath to come'*.    John saw that the advent of the King would bring inevitable suffering to those who were living in self-indulgence and sin.

There would be careful discrimination. He who was coming would carefully discern between the righteous and the wicked; between those who served God and those who did not serve him. There will be a very careful process of discrimination before the unquenchable fires are lighted; so that none but chaff will be consigned to the flames – a prediction that was faithfully fulfilled. At first Christ drew all men to himself; but as his ministry proceeded he revealed their quality. A few were permanently attracted to him; the majority were as definitely repelled. So it has been in every age. Jesus Christ is the touchstone of trial. Our attitude toward him reveals the true quality of the soul.

There would also be a period of probation. 'The axe laid unto the root of the trees' is familiar enough to those who know anything of forestry. The lumberjack destroys some tree that seems to him to be occupying space capable of being put to better use. But when once that word is spoken, there is no appeal. The Jewish people had become sadly unfruitful; but a definite period was to intervene – three years of Christ's ministry and thirty years beside – before the threatened judgment befell.

For all such there must be 'wrath to come'. After there has been searching scrutiny and investigation, and every reasonable chance has been given to change, and still the soul is impenitent and disobedient, there must be 'a certain fearful looking for of judgment and fiery indignation, which shall devour the adversaries' (Heb. 10:27).

The fire of John's preaching had its primary fulfilment in the awful disasters that befell the Jewish people, culminating in the siege and fall of Jerusalem. But there was a deeper meaning. The wrath of God avenges itself, not on nations but on individual sinners. 'He that believeth not the Son shall not see life; but the wrath of God abideth on him' (John 3:36). The penalty of sin is inevitable. The wages of sin is death.

Even if we grant, as of course we must, that many of the

expressions referring to the ultimate fate of the ungodly are symbolical, yet it must also be granted that they have counterparts in the realm of soul and spirit, which are as terrible to endure, as the nature of the soul is more highly organised than that of the body. Believe me that when Jesus said, 'These shall go away into eternal punishment', he contemplated a retribution so terrible, that it would be good for the sufferers if they had never been born.

All the great preachers have seen and faithfully borne witness to the fearful results of sin, as they take effect in this life and the next. On the other hand, because God is not confined to any one method, the preaching of the late D.L. Moody was especially steeped in the love of God. It is for the want of a vision of the inevitable fate of the godless and disobedient, that much of our present-day preaching is so powerless and ephemeral. And only when we modern preachers have seen sin as God sees it, and begin to apply the divine standard to the human conscience; only when we know the terror of the Lord, and begin to persuade men as though we would pluck them out of the fire by our strenuous expostulation and entreaties; only then will we see the effects that followed the preaching of the Baptist when soldiers, publicans, Pharisees, and scribes, crowded around him, saying, 'What shall we do?'

All John's preaching therefore led up to the demand for repentance. The word that was most often on his lips was 'Repent ye!' It was not enough to plead direct descent from Abraham, for God could raise up children to Abraham from the stones of the river bank. There had to be the renunciation of sin, the definite turning to God, the bringing forth of fruit meet for an amended life. In no other way could the people be prepared for the coming of the Lord.

# 2

# Baptism to Repentance

## Mark 1:4

At the time of which we are speaking, an extraordinary sect, known as the Essenes, was scattered throughout Palestine, but had its special home in the oasis of Engedi; and John must have been in frequent association with the adherents of this community. They were the recluses or hermits of their age.

The aim of the Essenes was moral and ceremonial purity. They sought after an ideal of holiness, which they thought could not be realised in this world; and therefore leaving villages and towns, they took to dens and caves and gave themselves to continence, abstinence, fastings, and prayers, supporting themselves by some odd jobs on the land. The cardinal point with them was faith in the inspired Word of God. By meditation, prayer and mortification, frequent ablutions, and strict attention to the laws of ceremonial purity, they hoped to reach the highest stage of communion with God. They agreed with the Pharisees in their extraordinary regard for the Sabbath. Their daily meal was of the simplest kind, and was partaken of in their house of religious assembly. After bathing, with prayer and exhortation, they went with veiled faces to their dining room, as to a holy temple. They abstained from oaths, despised riches, manifested the greatest abhorrence of war and slavery, faced torture and death with the utmost bravery, refused the indulgence of pleasure.

It is clear that John was not a member of this holy community, which differed widely from the Pharisaism and Sadduceeism of the time. But it cannot be doubted that he was in deep accord with much of the doctrine and practice of this sect.

John the Baptist however cannot be accounted for by any of the pre-existing conditions of his time. He stood alone in his God-given might. That he was conscious of this appears from his own declaration when he said, 'He that sent me to baptise with water, the same said unto me' (John 1:33). The distinct assertion of the Spirit of God, through the fourth evangelist, informs us: 'There was a man sent from God, whose name was John. The same came for a witness, that *all* men through him might believe' (John 1:9–10).

## 1 The summons to repent

John represents a phase of teaching and influence through which we must needs pass if we are properly to discover and appreciate the grace of Christ. In proportion to our repentance will be our glad realisation of the fullness and glory of the Lamb of God; but we must guard ourselves here, lest it be supposed that repentance is a species of good work that must be performed so that we may merit the grace of Christ. It must be made equally clear that repentance must not be viewed apart from faith in the Saviour, which is an integral part of it. It is also certain that, though 'God commandeth', Jesus is exalted 'to *give* repentance and the remission of sins'.

Repentance, according to the literal rendering of the Greek word, is 'a change of mind'. Perhaps we should rather say, it is a change in the attitude of the will. It no longer refuses the yoke of God's will, but yields to it, or is willing to yield. The habits may rebel; the inclinations and emotions may shrink back; the consciousness of peace and joy may yet be far away – but the will has made its secret decision, and has begun to turn to God.

It cannot be too strongly emphasised that repentance is an act of the *will*. In its beginning there may be no sense of gladness or reconciliation with God: it is the consciousness that certain ways of life are wrong, mistaken, hurtful, and grieving to God; and includes the desire, which becomes the determination, to turn from them.

Repentance may be accounted as the other side of faith. They are the two sides of the same coin. If the act of the soul that brings it into right relation with God is described as a turning round, then *repentance* stands for its desire and choice to turn from sin, and *faith* for its desire and choice to turn to God. We must be willing to turn from sin and our own righteousness – that is *repentance;* we must be willing to be saved by God, in his own way, and must come to him for that purpose – that is *faith.*

We need to turn from our own righteousnesses as well as from our sins. Nothing apart from the Saviour and his work can avail the soul, which must meet the scrutiny of eternal justice and purity.

Repentance is produced sometimes and especially by the presentation of the claims of Christ. We suddenly awake to realise what he is, how he loves, how much we are missing, the gross ingratitude with which we respond to his agony and bloody sweat, his cross and suffering, the beauty of his character, the strength of his claims.

At other times repentance is brought about by the preaching of John the Baptist. Then we hear of the axe laid at the root of the trees, and the heart trembles. It is at such a time that the soul sees the entire fabric of its vain confidences and hopes crumbling like a cloud palace, and turns from it all.

If John the Baptist has never brought about his work in you, be sure to open your heart to his piercing voice. Expose your soul to its searching scrutiny, and allow it to have free and uninterrupted course.

## 2   The signs and symptoms of repentance

*a. Confession*    'They were all baptised of him in the river of Jordan, confessing their sins' (Mark 1:5). On that river's brink, men not only confessed to God, but probably also to one another. Life long feuds were reconciled; old quarrels were settled; frank words of apology and forgiveness were exchanged; hands grasped hands for the first time after years of alienation and strife.

Confession is an essential sign of a genuine repentance, and without it forgiveness is impossible. 'If we confess our sins, he is faithful and just to forgive us our sins, and to cleanse us from all unrighteousness' (1 John 1:9).

Confess your sin to God, O troubled soul, from whom the vision of Christ is veiled. Excuse nothing, extenuate nothing, omit nothing. Do not speak of mistakes of judgment, but of lapses of heart and will. Do not be content with a general confession; be particular and specific. Drag each evil thing before God's judgment bar; let the secrets be exposed, and the dark, sad story told. To tell him all is to receive at once his assurance of forgiveness, for the sake of him who loved us and gave himself a propitiation for our sins. As soon as the confession leaves our heart, nay, while it is in the process, the divine voice is heard assuring us that our sins, which are many, are put away as far as the east is from the west, and cast into the depths of the sea.

But such confession should not be made to God alone when sins are in question that have injured and alienated others. If our brother has anything against us, we must find him out, while our gift is left unpresented at the altar, and first be reconciled to him. We must write the letter, or speak the word; we must make honourable reparation and amends; we must not be behind the sinners under the old law, who were instructed to add a fifth part to the loss their brother had sustained through their wrongdoing, when they made it good.

**b.** *Fruit worthy of repentance* 'Bring forth, therefore, fruit worthy of repentance', said John, as he saw many of the Pharisees and Sadducees coming to his baptism.

That demand of the Baptist probably accounted for the alteration in his life of which Zaccheus made confession to Christ, when he became his guest. The rich publican lived at Jericho, near where John was baptising, and he was probably among the publicans who were attracted to his ministry. And something touched that hardened heart. A great hope and a great resolve sprang up in it. On his arrival at Jericho he was a new man. He gave the half of his goods to feed the poor; and if he had wrongfully exacted anything of any man, he restored it fourfold. Would any ask him the reason for it all, he would answer, 'Ah, I have been down to the Jordan and heard the Baptist; I believe the kingdom is coming, and the King is at hand'.

You will never get right with God until you are right with man. It is not enough to confess wrongdoing; you must be prepared to make amends as far as lies in your power. Sin is not a light thing, and it must be dealt with, root and branch.

**c.** *The baptism of repentance* 'They were baptised . . . confessing their sins.' It was not baptism *unto remission,* but *unto repentance.* It was the expression and symbol of the soul's desire and intention, as far as it knew, to confess and renounce its sins, as the necessary condition of obtaining the divine forgiveness.

In John's hands the rite assumed altogether novel and important functions. It meant death and burial as far as the past was concerned; and resurrection to a new and better future.

It is easy to see how all this appealed to the people, and especially touched the hearts of young men. At that time, by the blue waters of the Lake of Galilee, there was a handful of ardent youths, deeply stirred by the currents of thought around them, who resented the Roman sway, and were on the tip-toe of expectation for the coming kingdom. When, one day, tidings reached them of this strange new preacher, they left all and streamed with all the world beside to the Jordan valley, and stood fascinated by the spell of his words.

One by one, or all together, they made themselves known to him, and became his loyal friends and disciples. We are familiar with the names of one or two of them, who afterward left their earlier master to follow Christ; but of the rest we know nothing, except that he taught them to fast and pray, and that they clung to their great teacher until they bore his headless body to the grave. After his death they joined themselves with him whom they had once regarded with some suspicion as John's rival and supplanter.

How much this meant to John! He had never had a friend; and to have the allegiance and love of these noble, ingenuous youths must have been very grateful to his soul. But from them all he repeatedly turned his gaze, as though he were looking for someone whose voice would give him the deepest and richest fulfilment of his joy, because it would be the voice of the Bridegroom himself.

# 3

# The Manifestation of the Messiah

### *John 1:31*

John's life, at this period, was an extraordinary one. By day he preached to the teeming crowds, or baptised them; by night he would sleep in some slight booth, or darksome cave. But the conviction grew always stronger in his soul, that the Messiah was soon to come; and this conviction became a revelation. The Holy Spirit who filled him, taught him. He began to see the outlines of his person and work.

He conceived of the coming King, as we have seen, as the Woodsman, laying his axe at the root of the trees; as the Husbandman, fan in hand to winnow the threshing floor; as the Baptist, prepared to plunge all faithful souls in his cleansing fires; as the Ancient of Days who, though coming after him in order of time, must be preferred before him in order of precedence, because he was before him in the eternal glory of his being (John 1:15–30). He insisted that he was not worthy to perform the most menial service for him whose advent he announced.

John was not only humble in his self-estimate, but also in his modest appreciation of the results of his work. It was only transient and preparatory. It was given him to do; but it would soon be done. His course was a short one, and it would soon be fulfilled (Acts 13:25). His simple mission was to bid the people to believe on him who would come after him (19:4).

## 1   Our Lord's advent to the Jordan bank

For thirty years the Son of man had been about his Father's business in the ordinary routine of a village carpenter's life. He had found scope enough there for his marvellously rich and deep nature. Often he must have felt the strong attraction of the great world of men, which he loved. But he waited still, until the time was fulfilled that had been fixed in the eternal council chamber.

As soon as the rumours of the Baptist's ministry reached him, however, he had to tear himself away from Nazareth, home, and mother, and take the road that would end at Calvary.

Tradition locates the scene of John's baptism as near Jericho, where the water is shallow and the river opens out into large lagoons. But some, inferring that Nazareth was within a day's journey of this notable spot, place it nearer the southern end of the Lake of Galilee.

It may have been in the late afternoon when Jesus arrived; a sudden and remarkable change passed over the Baptist's face as he beheld his kinsman standing there.

John said, 'I knew him not' (John 1:31); but this need not be interpreted as indicating that he had no acquaintance whatever with his blameless relative. He knew enough of him to be aware of his guileless, blameless life, as he presented himself for baptism, John felt that there was a whole heaven of difference between him and all others. These publicans and sinners, these Pharisees and scribes, these soldiers and common people – had every need to repent, confess, and be forgiven; but there was surely no such need for him. He said, 'I have need to be baptised of thee, and comest thou to me?' (Matt. 3:14).

There may have been, besides, an indescribable premonition that stole over that lofty nature. There was an indefinable majesty, a moral glory, a tender grace, an ineffable attractiveness in this man.

## 2   The significance of Christ's baptism

'Suffer it to be so now; for thus it becometh us to fulfil all righteousness' – with such words our Lord overruled the objections of his loyal and faithful forerunner. This is the first recorded utterance of Christ, after a silence of more than twenty years; the first also of his public ministry. He does not say, 'I have need to be baptised of thee'; nor does he say, 'Thou hast no need to be baptised of me'.

John's baptism was the inauguration of the kingdom of heaven. In it the material made way for the spiritual. The old system, which gave secial privileges to the children of Abraham, was in the act of passing away. It was the outward and visible sign that Judaism was unavailing for the deepest needs of that spirit of man, and that a new and more spiritual system was about to take its place.

With our race, in its sin and degradation, our Lord now formally identified himself. His baptism was his formal identification with our fallen and sinful race, though he knew no sin for himself, and could challenge the minutest inspection of his enemies: 'Which of you convinceth me of sin?'

Was he baptised because he needed to repent, or to confess his sins? No! He was as pure as the bosom of God, from which he came; but he needed to be made sin, that we might be made the righteousness of God in him.

A friend suggests that the Lord Jesus was here referring to the sublime prophecy of Daniel 9:24. That he might make an end of sin and bring in everlasting righteousness, it was essential that the

Lamb of God should confess the sins of the people as his own (see Ps. 69:5). This was his first step on his journey to the cross, every step of which was in fulfilment of all righteousness, in order that he might bring in everlasting righteousness.

'Then he suffered him'. Some things we have to *do* for Christ, and some to *bear* for him. In all our human life, there is nothing more attractive than when a strong man yields to another, and is prepared to set aside his strong convictions of propriety before the tender pleadings of a still, soft voice. Yield to Christ, dear heart. Allow him to have his way. Take his yoke, and be meek and lowly of heart – so shall you find rest.

## 3   The designation of the Messiah

It is not to be supposed that the designation of Jesus as the Christ was given to any but John. It was apparently a private sign given to him, as the Forerunner and Herald, through which he might be authoritatively informed as to the identity of the Messiah. He says, 'I knew him not' (i.e., as Son of God), 'but he that sent me to baptise with water, the same said unto me, Upon whom thou shalt see the Spirit descending, and remaining on him, the same is he which baptiseth with the Holy Ghost. And I saw, and bear record that this is the Son of God' (John 1:32–34).

What a theophany this was! As the Man of Nazareth emerged from the water, the sign for which John had been eagerly waiting and looking for was granted. He had believed he would see it, but had never thought to see it granted to a relative of his. He saw far away into the blue vault, which had opened into depth after depth of golden glory. The veil was torn to admit the coming of the divine Spirit, who seemed to descend in visible shape – as a dove might, with gentle, fluttering motion – and to alight on the head of the Holy One, who stood there fresh from his baptism.

The voice of God from heaven proclaimed that Jesus of Nazareth was his beloved Son, in whom he was well pleased; and the Baptist could have no further doubt that the Lord whom his people sought, the Messenger of the covenant, had come. 'John bare record saying, I saw the Spirit descending from heaven like a dove, and it abode upon him' (John 1:32).

The Baptist knew that his mission was nearly fulfilled, that his office was ended. The Sun had risen, and the daystar began to wane.

# 4

# 'Art thou He?'

## Matthew 11

It is very touching to notice the tenacity with which some of John's disciples clung to their great leader. The majority had dispersed: some to their homes; some to follow Jesus. Only a handful still lingered, not alienated by the storm of hate that had broken on their master, but drawn nearer, with the unfaltering loyalty of unchangeable affection. They could not forget that he had taught them to pray; that he had led them to the Christ. So they dare not desert him now, in the dark, sad days of his imprisonment and sorrow. They did not hesitate to come to his cell with tidings of the great outer world, and especially of what *he* was doing and saying, whose life was so mysteriously bound up with his own. 'The disciples of John [told] him all these things' (Luke 7:18).

It was to two of these friends that John confided the question that had long been forming in his soul, 'And John calling unto him two of his disciples sent them to Jesus, saying, Art thou he that should come? or look we for another?'

## 1   John's misgivings

Can this be he who, but a few months ago, had stood in his rock-hewn pulpit, in radiant certainty? He pointed to Christ with unfaltering certitude, saying, This is he, the Lamb of God, the Son of the Father, the Bridegroom of the soul. How great the contrast between that and this sorrowful cry, 'Art thou he?' He was for a brief spell under a cloud, involved in doubt, tempted to let go the confidence that had brought him such ecstatic joy when he first saw the dove descending and abiding.

Yes, let us believe that, for some days at least, John's mind was overcast, his faith lost its foothold, and he seemed to be falling into bottomless depths. 'He sent them to Jesus, saying, Art thou he that should come?' We can easily trace this lapse of faith to three sources.

*a. Depression*    He was the child of the desert. The winds that swept across the waste were not freer. As he found himself cribbed, cabined, and confined in the narrow limits of his cell, his spirits sank. He yearned with the hunger of a wild thing for liberty – to move without the clanking fetters; to drink of the fresh water of the Jordan, to breathe the morning air; to look on the expanse of nature. Is it hard to understand how his deprivations reacted on his mental and spiritual organisations, or that the depression of his physical life cast a shadow on his soul?

*b. Disappointment*    When first consigned to prison, he had expected every day that Jesus would in some way deliver him. Surely he would not let his faithful follower lie in the despair of that dark dungeon! In that first sermon at Nazareth, of which he had been informed, was it not expressly stated to be part of the divine programme for which he had been anointed, that he would open prison doors, and proclaim liberty to captives?

But the weeks grew to months, and still no help came. It was inexplicable to John's honest heart, and suggested the fear that he had been mistaken after all.

*c. Partial views of Christ*    'John heard in the prison the works of Jesus'. They were wholly beneficent and gentle.

'What has he done since last you were here?'

'He has laid his hands on a few sick folk, and healed them; has gathered a number of children to his arms, and blessed them; has sat on the mountain, and spoken of rest and peace and blessedness.'

'Yes; good. But what more?'

'A woman touched the hem of his garment, and trembled, and confessed, and went away healed.'

'Good! But what more?'

'Well there were some blind men, and he laid his hands on them, and they saw.'

'Is that all? Has he not used the fan to winnow the wheat, and the fire to burn up the chaff? This is what I was expecting, and what I have been taught to expect by Isaiah and the rest of the prophets. I cannot understand it. This quiet gentle life of benevolence is outside my calculations. There must be some mistake. Go and ask him whether we should expect *another,* made in a different mould, and who will be as the fire, the earthquake, the tempest, while he is as the still small voice.'

John had partial views of the Christ – he thought of him only as the Avenger of sin, the Maker of revolution, the dread Judge of all; and for want of a clearer understanding of what God by the mouth of his holy prophets had spoken since the world began, he fell into this slough of despond.

It was a grievous pity; yet let us not blame him too vehemently, lest we blame ourselves. Is not this what we do? We form a notion of God, partly from what we think he ought to be, partly from some distorted notions we have derived from others; and then because God fails to realise our conception, we begin to doubt.

## 2   The Lord's reply

'In that hour he cured many of their infirmities and plagues, and evil spirits; and unto many that were blind he gave sight'. Through the long hours of the day, the disciples stood in the crowd, while the sad train of sick and demon-possessed passed before the Saviour, coming in every stage of need, and going away cleansed and saved. Even the dead were raised. And at the close the Master turned to them, and with a deep significance in his tone, said, 'Go your way, and tell John what things ye have seen and heard; how that the blind see, the lame walk, the lepers are cleansed, the deaf hear, the dead are raised, to the poor the gospel is preached. And blessed is he, whosoever, shall not be offended in me'.

*a. It was indirect.*   He did not say, 'I am he that was to come, and there is no need to look for another'. Had he done so, he might have answered John's intellect, but not his heart. After a few hours the assurance would have waxed dim and he would have questioned again. He might have wondered whether Jesus were not himself deceived.

*b. The answer was mysterious.*   Surely, if he were able to do so much, he could do more. The power that healed the sick and lame and blind, and cast out demons, could surely deliver John. It made his heart the more wistful, to hear of these displays of power. He had to learn that the Lord healed these people so easily because the light soil of their nature could not bear the richer harvests; because their soul could not stand the cutting through which alone the brilliant facets that were possible to his could be secured. It was because John was a royal soul, the greatest born of woman, because his nature was capable of yielding the best results to the divine culture, that he was kept waiting, while others caught up the blessing and went away healed. Only three months remained of life, and in these the discipline of patience and doubt had to do their perfect work.

*c. The answer was sufficient.* The Lord strived to convince the questioner that his views were too partial and limited, and to send him back to a more comprehensive study of the old Scriptures. It was as though Jesus said, 'Go to your master, and tell him to take again the ancient prophecy and study it. He has taken the sterner predictions to the neglect of the gentler, softer ones. It is true that I am to proclaim the day of vengeance; but first I must reveal the acceptable year. It is true that I am to come as a Mighty One, and my arm shall rule for Me; but it is also true that I am to feed my flock like a Shepherd, and gather the lambs in my arm'.

We make the same mistake. We have but a partial view of Christ, and need to get back to the Bible afresh, and study anew its comprehensive words; then we will come to understand. We have not yet seen the end of the Lord: we do not have all the evidence. But our Saviour is offering us every day evidences of his divine and loving power. The world is full of evidences of his gracious and divine power. And these are sufficient, not only because of the transformations that are effected, but because of their moral quality, to show that there is one within the veil who lives in the power of an indissoluble life.

## 3 A new beatitude

'Blessed is he, whosoever shall not be offended in me.' Our Lord put within the reach of his noble forerunner the blessedness of those who have not seen and yet have believed; of those who wait the Lord's leisure; and of those who cannot understand his dealings, but rest in what they know of his heart. This is the beatitude of the unoffended, of those who do not stumble over the mystery of God's dealings with their life.

This blessedness is within our reach also. There are times when we are overpowered with the mystery of life and nature. The world is so full of pain and sorrow, the litany of its need is so sad and pitiful, strong hearts are breaking under an intolerable load.

God's children are sometimes the most bitterly tried. For them the fires are heated seven times; days of weariness and nights of pain are appointed them; they suffer, not only at the hand of man, but it seems as though God himself were turned against them, to become their enemy. The waters of a full cup are wrung out in days like these; and the cry is extorted, 'How long, O Lord, how long?'

You and I have been in this plight. We have said, 'Has God forgotten to be gracious? Has he in anger shut up his tender mercies?' We are tempted to stumbling. We are more able than ever before to appreciate the standpoint occupied by Job's wife, when she said to her husband, 'Curse God, and die.'

Then we have the chance of inheriting a new beatitude. By refusing to bend under the mighty hand of God – questioning, chafing, murmuring – we miss the door that would admit us into rich and unalloyed happiness. We fumble about the latch, but it is not lifted. But if we will quiet our souls, light will break in on us as from the eternal morning; the peace of God will keep our hearts and minds, and we will enter on the blessedness that our Lord unfolded before the gaze of his faithful forerunner.

# 5

# 'None greater than John the Baptist, yet...'

## *Matthew 11*

While John's disciples were standing there, our Lord said nothing in his praise; but as soon as they had departed, the floodgates of his heart were thrown wide open, and he began to speak to the multitudes concerning his faithful servant. It was as though he would give him no cause for pride by what he said. He desired to give his friend no additional temptation during those lonely hours.

## 1  The time chosen for the Lord's commendation of the Baptist

It was when John had fallen beneath his usual level, below high-water mark, that Jesus uttered his warmest and most generous words of appreciation – 'Among them that are born of woman there hath not risen a greater than John the Baptist.'

Heaven judges, not by a passing mood, but by the general tenor and trend of a man's life; not by the expression of a doubt, caused by accidents that may be explained, but by the soul of man within him, which is much deeper than the emotion.

Yes, the Lord judges us by that which is deepest, most perma-nent, most constant and prevalent with us; by the ideal we seek to apprehend; by the decision and choice of our soul.

There is a remarkable parallel to this incident in the Old Tes-tament. When we are first introduced to Gideon, the youngest son of Joash the Abiezrite, he is not in a very dignified position. He is threshing wheat by the wine press, to hide it from the hosts of Midian, which devoured the produce of the entire country. There was no moral wrong in trying to elude the vig-ilance of the Midian spies, but there was nothing especially heroic or inspiring in the spectacle. Yet, when the angel of the Lord appeared to him, he said, 'The Lord is with thee, thou mighty man of valour'.

'Mighty man of valour!' At first there is an apparent incon-gruity between this high-sounding salutation and the bearing of the man to whom it was addressed, yet subsequent events prove that every syllable of it was deservedly true. Gideon was a mighty man of valour, and God was with him. The heavenly messenger read beneath the outward passing incident.

Is not this, in fact, the meaning of the apostle, when he says that faith is counted to us for righteousness? Faith is counted to us for righteousness, is the seed germ from which is developed in due course the plant, the flower, the bud, the seed, and reproduction of the plant in unending succession. God counted to Abraham all that his faith was capable of producing, which it did produce, and which it would have produced had he possessed all the advantages that pertain to our own happy lot. God gives to us all that blessed flowering and fruitage of which our faith will be capable, when patience has had its perfect work and we are perfect and entire, wanting nothing.

## 2    The outstanding features of John's character and ministry to which our Lord drew attention

*a. His independence*    'What went ye out into the wilderness to see? A reed shaken with the wind?' The language of the Bible is so picturesque, so full of natural imagery, that it appeals to every age, and speaks in every language of the world. It employs natural figures and parables which the wayfaring man, though a fool, comprehends at a glance.

Thus, when our Lord asked the people whether John resembled a reed shaken by the wind, and implied their answer in the negative, could he have more clearly indicated one of the most salient characteristics of John's career – his daring singularity, his independence of mere custom and fashion, his determination to follow out the pattern of his own life as God revealed it to him? In the singularity of his dress and food; in the originality of his message and demand for baptism; in his independence of the religious teachers and schools of his time; in his refusal to countenance the flagrant sins of the various classes of the community, and especially in his uncompromising denunciation of Herod's sin – he provoked himself to be as a sturdy oak in the forest of Bashan, or a deeply-rooted cedar in Lebanon, and not as a reed shaken by the wind.

Many a saintly soul has followed him since along this difficult and lonely track. Indeed, it is the ordinary path for most of the choicest spirits of these Christian centuries.

You, my reader, admire but feel you cannot follow. When your companions and friends are speaking deprecating and ungenerous words of some public man whom you love; when unkind and scandalous stories are being passed from lip to lip; when a storm of hatred is being poured on a cause, which in your heart you favour and espouse – you find it easier to bow before the gale, with all the other reeds around you, than to enter your protest, even though you stand alone. Christ can take the most pliant and yielding natures, and make them, as he made Jeremiah, 'a defenced city, and an iron pillar, and brasen walls, against the whole land' (Jer. 1:18). You cannot; but he can. He will strengthen you; yea, he will help you.

*b. His simplicity*   A second time the Master asked the people what they went forth into the wilderness to behold; and by his question implied that John was no Sybarite clothed in soft raiment, and feasting in luxury, but a strong, pure soul, who had learned the secret of self-denial and self-control. Too many of us are inclined to put on the soft raiment of self-indulgence and luxury. The real happiness of life consists not in increasing our possessions but in limiting our wants.

So with service. It is not right to depend on others. If it is part of our lot to be surrounded by servants, let us accept their offices with grace and kindliness, but never allow ourselves to lean on them. We should know how to do everything for ourselves, and be prepared to do it whenever it is necessary. Of course, nothing would be more unfortunate than that those who are highly gifted in some special direction should fritter away their time and strength in doing trifles that others could do for them equally well. To think of a physician whose consulting room was crowded with patients needing help which he alone, of all men living, could give, spending the precious morning hours polishing his boots, or preparing his food! Let these things be left to those who cannot do the highest work to which he is called.

This is the secret of making the best of your life. Discover what you can do best. Set yourself to do this, devolving on voluntary or paid helpers all that they can do as well as, and perhaps better than, yourself. It was in this spirit that the apostles said, 'It is not reason that we should leave the word of God and serve tables. Look ye out among you seven men . . . whom we may appoint over this business. But we will give ourselves continually to prayer, and to the ministry of the Word' (Acts 6:2–4). It is good to look carefully into our life from time to time, lest almost insensibly its strong energetic spirit may not be in process of deterioration as the soldiers of Hannibal in the plains of Capua. If so, resolve to do without, not for merit's sake, but to conserve the strength and simplicity of your soul.

*c. His noble office*   'But what went ye out for to see? A prophet?

yea, I say unto you, and more than a prophet.' Subsequent ages have only confirmed our Saviour's estimate of his forerunner. We are able to locate him in the divine economy. He was a prophet, yes, and much more. He was Jehovah's messenger, the herald of that new and greater era, whose gates he opened, but into which he was not permitted to enter.

But our Lord went further, and did not hesitate to class John with the greatest of those born of woman. He was absolutely in the front rank. He may have had peers, but no superiors; equals, but no overloards. Who may be classed with him, we cannot, dare not, say. But 'there hath not risen a greater than John the Baptist'.

There was a further tribute paid by our Lord to his noble servant. Some two or three centuries before, Malachi had foretold that Elijah, the prophet, would be sent before the great and terrible day of the Lord came, and the Jews were always on the outlook for his coming. This is what was meant when they asked the Baptist, at the commencement of his ministry, if he were Elijah. He shrank, as we have seen, from assuming so great a name, and declared, 'If ye will receive it, this is Elias, which was for to come'.

## 3   The Master's reservation

Let us again quote his memorable words: 'Among them that are born of women there hath not risen a greater than John the Baptist; notwithstanding, he that is least in the kingdom of heaven is greater than he' (Matt.11:11).

The greatness of John the Baptist shone out in conspicuous beauty in his meek confession of inferiority. His greatness was revealed in the lowliness of his self-estimate.

When the Lord Jesus summarised his own character he said, 'I am meek and lowly in heart'. The greatness of John was proved in this, that like his Lord he was meek and lowly in heart. No sublimer, no more God-like utterance ever passed the lips of man than John's answer to his disciples: 'A man can receive nothing, except it be given him from heaven. He must increase, but I must decrease' (see the whole passage, John 3:27–36). The same spirit of meekness was speaking in John as acted in his Lord. There was no man, not even the apostle John or Paul, whose spirit accorded more exactly with the Master's than his faithful and self-effacing herald and forerunner, John the Baptist.

But what was in our Lord's thought when he made the reservation, '*He that is least in the kingdom of heaven is greater than he*'? It has been suggested that the Lord was speaking of John not only as a man, but as a prophet, and that this declaration applies more particularly to John as a prophet. John could say, 'Behold the Lamb of God'; but the least of those who, being scattered abroad, when everywhere proclaiming the word of the kingdom, preaching 'Jesus and the resurrection'.

But there is another way of interpreting Christ's words. John ushered in the kingdom, but was not in it. He proclaimed a condition of blessedness in which he was not permitted to have a part. And the Lord says that to be in that kingdom gives the opportunity of attaining to a greatness that the great souls outside its precincts cannot lay claim to. The least instructed in the kingdom of heaven is privileged to see and hear the things that prophets and kings longed and waited for in vain.

And may there not be even more than this? The character of John was strong, grand in its wild magnificence. He had courage, resolution, an iron will, a loftiness of soul that could hold commerce with the unseen and eternal. But is this the loftiest ideal of character? Assuredly not; there is something better, as is manifest in our Lord's own perfect manhood. The balance of quality; the power to converse with God, mated with the tenderness that enters the homes of men, wipes the tears of those who mourn, and gathers little children to its side; that has an ear for every complaint, and a balm of comfort for every heartbreak; that pities and soothes, teaches and leads; that is able not only to commune with God alone in the desert, but brings him into the lowliest deeds and commonplaces of human life – this is the type of character that is characteristic of the kingdom of heaven. It is described best in those inimitable beatitudes which canonise, not the stern and rugged, but the sweet and tender, the humble and meek; and stamp heaven's tenderest smile on virtues that had hardly found a place in the strong and gritty character of the Baptist. Truly, 'He that is least in the kingdom of heaven is greater than he'.

# 6

# Set at Liberty

## *Mark 6:27*

The evangelist Mark tells us, in the twenty-first verse of this chapter, that Herod on his birthday made a supper for his lords, and the high captains, and the chief men of Galilee. Now Galilee, over which Herod had jurisdiction, and where, for the most part, he dwelt, in the beautiful city of Tiberias, was a considerable distance from the Castle of Machaerus which, as we have seen, was situated in the desolate region on the eastern side of the Dead Sea. There would probably therefore have been a martial and noble procession from Galilee, which followed the course of the Jordan to the oasis of Jericho, and then branched off to the old, grim fortress.

The days that preceded the celebration of Herod's birthday were probably filled with merry-making and carousing. Archery, jousts, and other sports would fill the slowly-moving hours. Jests, light laughter, and buffoonery would fill the air. And all the while, in the dungeons beneath the castle, lay that mighty preacher, the confessor, forerunner, herald, and soon to be martyr.

But this contrast was more than ever accentuated on the evening of Herod's birthday, when the great banqueting chamber was especially illuminated; the tables decked with flowers and gold and silver plate; laughter and mirth echoing through the vaulted roof from the splendid company. Servants, in costly liveries, passed to and fro, bearing the rich dainties on massive platters, one of which was to be presently besprinkled with the martyr's blood.

In such a scene I would have you study the beginning of a great crime, because you must remember that in respect to sin, there is little to choose between the twentieth century and the first; between the sin of that civilisation and ours. This chapter is therefore written under more than usual solemnity, because one is so sure that, in dealing with that scene and the passions that met there in a foaming vortex, words may be penned that will help souls that are caught in the drift of the same black current, and are being swept down. Perhaps this page will utter a warning voice to arrest them, before it is too late. For there is help and grace in God by which a Herod and a Judas, a Jezebel and a Lady Macbeth, may be arrested, redeemed, and saved.

In this, as in every sin, there were three forces at work; first, the predisposition of the soul, which the Bible calls 'lust', and the 'desire of the mind'. Second, the suggestion of evil from without. Finally, the act of the will by which the suggestion was accepted and finally adopted.

It is in this latter phase that sin especially comes in. That which is of the essence of sin is in the act of the will, which allows itself to admit and entertain some foul suggestion, and ultimately sends its executioner below to carry its sentence into effect.

## 1   The predetermination toward this sin

In dealing with temptation and sin, we must always take into account the presence in the human heart of that sad relic of the Fall, which biases men toward evil. Such a bias has come to us all: first, from our ancestor Adam; and, second, by that law of heredity that has been accumulating its malign and sinister force through all the ages. God alone can compute the respective strength of these forces; but he can, and he will, as each separate soul stands before his judgment bar.

Herod was the son of the great Herod, a voluptuous, murderous tyrant; and, from some source or other, he had inherited a very weak nature. If he had perhaps come under strong, wholesome influences, he would have lived a passably good life; but it was his misfortune to fall under the influence of a beautiful fiend, who became his Lady Macbeth, his Jezebel, and brought about the ruin of his soul.

The influences that suggest and make for sin in this world are so persistent that if my readers have no other failing than that they are weak, I am bound to warn them, in God's name, that unless they succeed in some way, directly or indirectly, in linking themselves to the strength of the Son of God, they will inevitably become wicked. The men, and especially the women, who are filling our prisons as criminals, were, in most cases, only weak, but they therefore drifted before the strong, black current that flows through the world. If you are conscious of your weakness, do what the sea anemone and the limpet do, which cling to the rock when the storms darken the sky. 'Be strong in the Lord, and in the power of his might'.

Herod was reluctant to take the course of which his evil genius urged him, but she finally had her way, and dragged him to her lowest level.

Beware, then, of yourself. Take heed, to guard against anything in your life that may open the gates to a temptation that you may not be able to withstand. If you are weak in physical health, you guard against a draft and fatigue, against impure atmosphere and contagion – how much more should you guard against the scenes and company that may act prejudicially on the health of your soul? Of all our hours, none are so filled with danger as those of recreation.

If was the most perilous thing that Herod could do, to have that banquet. Lying back on his divan, lolling on his cushions, eating his rich food, quaffing the sparkling wine, exchanging conversation with his obsequious followers, it was as though the heart of his soul was open to receive the first insidious spore of evil that might float past on the sultry air.

## 2   Temptation

In the genesis of a sin we must give due weight to the power of the Tempter, whether by his direct suggestion to the soul or by the instrumentality of men and women whom he uses for his evil purpose. In this case Satan's accomplice was the beautiful Herodias – beautiful as a snake, but also as deadly. She knew the influence that John the Baptist wielded over her weak paramour, that he was accustomed to attach unmeasured importance to his words. She realised that his conscience was uneasy, and therefore the more liable to be affected by his words when he reasoned of righteousness, temperance, and judgment to come. She feared for the consequences if the Baptist and Herod's conscience should make common cause against her. She was not safe as long as John the Baptist breathed. Herod feared him, and perhaps she feared him with more abject terror, and was bent on removing him from her life.

She watched her opportunity, and it came on the occasion we have described. The ungodly revel was at its height. The strong wines of Messina and Cyprus had already done their work. Toward the end of such a feast it was the custom for immodest women to be introduced, who, by their gestures, imitated scenes in certain well-known mythologies, and still further inflamed the passions of the banqueters. But instead of the usual troupe, Salome herself came in and danced a wild gyrating dance. What must we think of a mother who could expose her daughter to such a scene? The girl, alas, was as shameless as her mother.

She pleased Herod, who was excited with the meeting of the two strong passions, which have destroyed more victims than have fallen on all the battlefields of the world; and in his frenzy, he promised to give her whatever she might ask, though it were to cost half his kingdom. She rushed back to her mother with the story of her success. 'What shall I ask?' she cried. The mother had perhaps anticipated such a moment as this, and had her answer ready. 'Ask', she replied instantly, 'for John the Baptist's head.' Back from her mother she tripped into the banqueting hall, her black eyes flashing with cruel hate, lighted from her mother's fierceness. A dead silence fell on the buzz of conversation, and every ear strained for her reply. 'And she came in straightway with haste unto the king, and asked, saying, I will that thou give me by and by in a charger the head of John the Baptist.' The imperious demand of the girl showed how eagerly she had entered into her mother's scheme.

It is thus that suggestions come to us; and as far as I can understand, we may expect them to come as long as we are in this world. There seems to be a precise analogy between temptation and the microbes of disease. These are always in the air; but when we are in good health they are absolutely innocuous, our nature offers no hold or resting place for them. So temptation would have no power over us, if our souls were filled with God. It is only when the vitality of the inward man is impaired, that we are unable to withstand the fiery darts of the wicked one.

This shows how greatly we need to be filled with the life of the Son of God. If you have the victorious nature of the living Christ in you, you must be stronger than the nature that he bruised beneath his feet.

## 3   The consent of the will

'The king was exceeding sorry.' The girl's request sobered him. His face turned pale, and he clutched convulsively at the cushion on which he reclined. On the one hand, his conscience revolted from the deed; on the other, he said to himself, 'I am bound by my oath. My words were spoken in the audience of so many of my chief men, I dare not go back, lest they lose faith in me'. 'And immediately the king sent an executioner, and commanded his head to be brought'.

Isn't it amazing that a man who did not refrain from committing incest and murder, should be so scrupulous about violating an oath that ought never to have been sworn? You have thought that you were bound to go through with your engagement, because you had pledged yourself, although you know that it would condemn you to lifelong misery and disobedience to the law of Christ. But wait a moment. Looking back, can you not see that you ought never to have bound yourself, and do you not feel that if you had your time again you would not bind yourself? Then be sure that you are not bound by that 'dead hand'. You must act in the clearer, better light, which God has communicated. You had no right to pledge half the kingdom of your nature. It is not yours to give, it is God's. And if you have pledged it, through mistake, prejudice, or passion, dare to believe that you are absolved from your vow, through repentance and faith.

'And he went and beheaded him in prison.' Had the Baptist heard anything of the unseemly revelry? Perhaps so. Those old castles are full of strang echoes. His cell was perfectly dark. Was his mind glancing back on those never-to-be-forgotten days, when the heaven was opened above him, and he saw the descending dove? Was he wondering why he was allowed to lie there month after month, silenced and suffering? Ah, he did not know how near he was to liberty!

There was a tread along the corridor. It stopped outside his cell. The light gleamed under the door; the heavy wards of the lock were turned: in a moment more he saw the gleam of the naked sword, and guessed the soldier's errand. There was no time to spare; the royal message was urgent. Perhaps one last message was sent to his disciples; then he bowed his head before the stroke; the body fell helpless here, the head there, and the spirit was free. Forerunner of the Bridegroom here, he was his forerunner there also; and the Bridegroom's friend passed homeward to await the Bridegroom's coming, where he will ever hear the voice he loves.

'And [the soldier] brought his head in a charger, and gave it to the damsel, and the damsel gave it to her mother.' There probably was not much talking while the tragedy was being consummated. When the soldier entered, carrying on the platter that ghastly burden, they beheld a sight that was to haunt some of them to their dying day. Often Herod would see it in his dreams. It would haunt him, and fill his days and nights with anguish that all the witchery of Herodias could not dispel.

Months afterward, when he heard of Jesus, the conscience-stricken monarch said: 'It is John, whom I beheaded: he is risen from the dead'. And still afterward, when Jesus himself stood before him, and refused to speak one word, he must have associated that silence and his deed together, as having a fatal and necessary connection.

So the will, which had long played around with the temptress, at last took the fatal step, and perpetrated the crime that could never be undone.

If you have taken the fatal step, and marred your life by some sad and disastrous sin, dare to believe that there is forgiveness for you with God. Men may not forgive, but God will.

But if we have not yet come to this, let us devoutly thank God, and he on the watch against any influences that may cause us to drift there. We may yet disentangle ourselves. We may yet receive into our natures the living power of the Lord Jesus. We may yet cut off the right hand and right foot, and pluck out the right eye, which is causing us to offend. Better this, and go into life maimed, than be cast, as Herod was, to the fire and worm of the unquenchable remorse.

# PETER

# 1

# A Fisher of Men

## *Luke 5:8–11*

The Master's purpose for his disciples is disclosed in the words recorded by Matthew and Mark, and which were probably addressed to them on the shore, when they had again beached their boats: 'Come ye, after me, and I will make you to become fishers of men'. We can combine this form of the summons with that especially addressed to the impulsive, vehement, warm-hearted son of Zebedee, and which is recorded in Luke 5. It should be noticed that here, as generally in the Gospels, our Lord addresses him by the more intimate name of 'Simon', as though 'Peter' was reserved until, through the months of discipline that awaited him, he was fitted to take the foremost place among his fellow apostles.

The summons came while they were engaged in their usual occupation. David was summoned from the sheepfold to shepherd the chosen race. Paul was called from making the goat's-hair tents to teach the church. The eternal springs were revealed to the woman as she rested her pitcher on the edge of Jacob's Well. It was quite befitting, therefore, that our Lord should explain to his fisher friend the momentous and glorious ministry that awaited him, through the calling in which he had been engaged from boyhood, and which had so many points of resemblance with the work of winning souls. The one difference being brought out in the Greek word translated 'catch', should be expanded to read, as in 2 Timothy 2:26, 'Thou shalt catch, *in order to keep alive'.*

In every subsequent era sincere and earnest souls have lingered wistfully over these words, longing to extract from them the precious secret of successful soul-winning.

Many a godly minister with a perfectly-appointed church, and surrounded by a devoted people – the boat, the company, and the fishing-tackle being all of the best – has watched, almost enviously, the success of some simple evangelist who, apart from all adventitious aid, has lifted netfuls of fish from the great depths of human life into his creel. The study of this narrative may bring us still further into the heart of the matter and the mind of our Lord.

## 1   Successful soul-winning is generally based on a deep consciousness of personal sin

The untiring and extraordinary labours of the great apostle of the Gentiles laid the foundations of the Gentile church, but as he reviews the past and considers his natural condition, he does not hesitate to speak of himself as the chief of sinners and the least of saints. We all once lived 'in the lusts of our flesh, fulfilling the desires of the flesh and of the mind; and were by nature the children of wrath, even as others' (Eph. 2:3).

Those who have had deep experiences of the exceeding sinfulness of sin are the better qualified to be tender and pitiful to such as are sold under sin. 'Alas, poor souls!' they cry, 'such were some of us.' The ringleaders in the devil's army make great soldiers for Christ. Their knowledge of Satan's stratagems and wiles is invaluable. The sinner knows the bitterness of the wages of sin, as an unfallen angel or an innocent child cannot. We need not be surprised, therefore, at this preparatory revelation the Lord gave of himself to Peter.

He and the rest had known the Lord for at least eighteen months, but were unaware of his true majesty and glory. For them he was the carpenter of Nazareth, the holy man, the marvellous teacher and wonder-worker. Then most suddenly and unexpectedly this shaft of his essential being struck into their ordinary commonplace, and left a trial of supernatural glory. As Peter felt the tug and pull of the bursting net, threatening to break beneath its sudden burden, he realised that his teacher and friend must have put forth a power that no mortal could resist. God was in the place, and he had not known it. At once the nakedness and sinfulness of his own heart were laid bare, and he cried: 'I am a sinful man, O Lord'. Note the significant exchange! When the boat left the shore it was *Master*, now, as this revelation has broken on him, it is *Lord*. Immediately following this Jesus said: 'From henceforth thou shalt catch men'.

There is a striking analogy between Peter's experience and Job's. The suffering analogy between Peter's experience and Job's. The suffering patriarch had persistently and successfully maintained his integrity. Then into his life God let fall visions of the Creation. He recited instance after instance of his almighty power, wisdom, and skill. As Peter's eyes were unveiled that he might behold Christ's wonders in the deep, so were Job's; and he exclaimed, as the divine glory shone on his soul, 'I have heard of thee by the hearing of the ear: but now mine eye seeth thee. Wherefore I abhor myself, and repent in dust and ashes' (Job. 42:5–6).

Whenever this experience befalls us, it may be considered as preparatory to new success in soul-winning. Expect to hear the Lord answer your confession of lowly sinfulness with a new summons to take your boat and net for a catch.

## 2    Failure and sin do not necessarily exclude from the divine partnership in soul-winning

'Depart from me,' cried the conscience-stricken disciple. We can almost see him, when the well of the boat was heaped high with the slippery silver cargo, clambering across from prow and stern on his bare feet, falling at Jesus' knees as he sat near the tiller, clasping them, with the heaving sobs of a strong man torn with conflicting emotions.

'No,' said our Lord in effect, 'that need not be. Stay with me, I will cleanse, heal, and save you, and make you the instrument of saving thousands of sinners like yourself.'

It is impossible to exaggerate the comfort that these words afforded to those who would want to serve Christ, but who are conscious of their profound unworthiness. 'I am not worthy to bear the message of salvation to others, because I am such a sinful man! How employ me, who has hosts of unfallen angels at your command? Let me stand in the outer circle and see you now and again. I cannot ask for more, for you know, and I know, that I am a sinful man.'

But Jesus has only one reply: 'Fear not; from henceforth thou shalt catch men.' 'I have blotted out your transgressions as a cloud, and will remember your sins no more. I have loved you with an everlasting love. Depart from me! It is unthinkable. You are dearer to me than all the stars in their galaxies. I have obtained from the Father that you should be with me, where I am. After you have had your Pentecost, and fulfilled your ministry and finished your course, you shall be accounted worthy to stand in my presence chamber, that you may behold my glory, and you shall share it.'

'Lord, it is too much; let me kiss your feet!'

### 3 Soul-winning, to be succesful, must be the absorbing of our lives

It cannot be one interest among many. The apostle said truly, 'One thing I do'. 'They left all and followed him.'

May we indulge our imagination here? A friendly fisherman informs his wife that the well-known boat will soon be 'in'. His food has been waiting for him since early dawn. She hastens to the shore; her husband leaps into the shallow water and lifts Jesus from boat to beach. He then approaches her wistfully, and with an unwonted tenderness that startles her, 'Can you share me for a little?' he inquires. 'The Master has asked me to go with him. He says that I am not to fear, and that he will provide for us. He has promised to teach me how to fish for men.'

And she replies: 'Husband, go with him. Mother and I will get along somehow until you get back. Stay with him as long as he needs you. Mother and I were saying only this morning that you have been a different man since you knew him.'

She came to believe also, and travelled everywhere with her husband, helping him, as Paul bears witness (1 Cor. 9:5). We cannot suppose that Peter at once entered into the Master's passion for the souls of men. At first he was content to follow him, to listen to his words, to become his companion and helper. But it could not have been long before he and his companions began to be imbued with the same passion, until it became the master motive of their existence.

So it will be with ourselves. As we walk with Christ, we shall become identified with his interests, and with no backward look on ourselves. Our life will be spent as that of Peter, who by his love for Christ was qualified to feed his sheep and lambs.

Let us ask that we may become partners with Christ in his great passion for men. Oh, to be a living flame for Jesus Christ.

# 2

# 'I give unto thee the keys'
## Matt. 16:13–20

For two years and a half our Lord had lived among his apostles. Only six months of education remained before he was taken from them – a period during which his teaching must become much more intensive; and as a preliminary it was necessary to ascertain what conclusions they had arrived at as the result of their observations and experiences. If, notwithstanding his reticence, they had discovered his intrinsic glory, 'the glory of the only begotten of the Father', it would serve as the common platform from which to ascend to higher revelations. But if not, it would be clear that he must go elsewhere for the heralds of his gospel and the foundation stones of his church.

In order to secure the necessary privacy for this all-important inquiry, our Lord journeyed to the extreme edge of the northern frontier of Palestine, where Mount Hermon lifts its mighty mass beyond the snow-line. The Jordan issues from one of the cliffs near the ancient town of Banias, known at that time as Caesarea Philippi. This was the setting of the memorable conversation which more than any of our Lord's discourses has affected the life of Christendom.

## 1  The Master's searching question

'Whom do men say that I the Son of man am?' The answers were various. It was universally acknowledged that he was no ordinary man. But their views were as various as the speakers. Some, with

Herod at their head, expressed the belief – not without a shudder – that the Baptist had risen from his lonely grave beside the Castle of Machaerus. Others said that Elijah, whom Malachi had taught them to expect, had come to them in the 'day of the Lord'. Others traced a resemblance between Jesus and one of the old prophets. But these inquiries were only intended to lead up to the second and all-important question: 'But whom say ye that I am?'

The reply came instantly, emphatically, and decisively from the lips of Peter, always the spokesman for the rest: 'Thou art the Christ, the Son of the living God'. In a most significant manner it combined the hope of the Jew for the Anointed One, with the recognition of the unique and essential nature of our Lord, as the only begotten of the eternal God. It filled the heart of Jesus with ecstasy. 'Blessed art thou, Simon Bar-Jona [son of Jonas or John]: for flesh and blood hath not revealed it unto thee, but my Father which is in heaven.'

## 2   The foundation of the church

Then for the first time our Lord spoke of his church. Notice the strong possessive pronoun 'my'. *My* church! From eternity Christ loved her. By his blood he redeemed her. Through his Spirit and by his Word he is cleansing her; and one day he will present her to himself a glorious church, 'having neither spot, nor wrinkle, nor any such thing'.

The church is the special object of hatred to the dark underworld of fallen spirits, whom our Lord refers to as 'the gates of hell'. Long and sore the conflict may be, but the issue is not doubtful. *'They shall not prevail'*. There will break on the ear of a startled world the voice of a great multitude, as they announce – first that the church has emerged victorious; and second, that the marriage of the Lamb has come, and his Bride has made herself ready. Her foundation doctrine is the deity of our Lord, as 'the Son of the everliving God'. The Greek phrasing of our Lord's reply leaves no doubt as to his meaning. Two Greek words are here. *Petros,* Simon's new name, signifying in Greek, as Cephas did in Syriac, a stone, or bit of rock, broken or hewn from its parent bed; and *petra,* the rock-bed itself. Our Lord carefully makes the distinction. If he had intended Peter to be the foundation of the church, he would naturally have shaped his sentence thus: 'Thou art

Peter, and on thee I will build my church.' But carefully selecting his words, he said: 'Thou art Peter, a stone, a fragment of rock, who under the power of God's Spirit hast spoken with strength and certainty; but I cannot build on thee, for the foundation of my church I must turn from *petros* to *petra,* from a fragment to the great truth, which for the moment has inspired thee. The truth of my eternal relationship to the Father is the only foundation, against which the waves of demon and human hatred will break in vain. No stone shall give. No bastion shall even rock'.

### 3 The gift of the keys

It must be carefully noted that our Lord used the same words that he addressed to Peter also to individual believers in Matthew 18:18, and again to his assembled apostles *and others* who were gathered with them in the Upper Room on the evening of the Resurrection Day (see Luke 24:33, and John 20:22 and 23).

In the light afforded by these references we may extend the significance of this gift of the keys to include all who live and act in the power of the Holy Spirit. If we have received that blessed gift of the Comforter, as they did on whom the Master breathed that Easter evening, we also may wield the power of the keys that will open closed doors, and emancipate prisoners from their cells.

This is the secret of the quest of the blessed life. Go through the world opening prison doors, lifting heavy burdens, giving light, and joy, and peace to the oppressed, proclaiming the Lord's Jubilee year. Close doors opening out on the dark waters of despair. Unlock and open those that face toward the sunrise, for this is a work that angels might envy. 'Receive ye the Holy Ghost'.

# 3

# 'With him on the Holy Mount'

## *Matt. 17:1–9; 2 Peter 1:16–18*

On the afternoon of the last day of our Lord's sojourn at Caesarea Philippi he proposed to his three chief apostles that they should accompany him for a season of retirement to the upper slopes of Hermon. In his last days Peter referred to it as affording the outstanding evidence of his Master's divine nature and mission. For him it was 'the Holy Mount', where he and the others had been eyewitnesses of Christ's majesty, when he received from the Father honour and glory. There could be no doubt about it. They had not followed nor promulgated cunningly devised fables!

## 1   The accessories of the transfiguration

*a. The place was clearly Mount Hermon.*   The previous days had been spent at its foot. Mount Tabor, which formerly was supposed to have been the chosen spot for this sublime spectacle, was at that time the site of a Roman fort and garrison, which would have been totally incongruous with the mystic beauty of heavenly glory. And the vivid comparison, in Peter's special Gospel of Mark, between the Master's appearance and the snow, is an additional confirmation that Mount Hermon's snow-capped heights were in his thought. Here only in Palestine is there the permanent presence of snow.

*b. The time was almost certainly the night.*   Our Lord was accustomed to spend nights on the mountains. The overpowering sleep that mastered the apostles, until the transfiguration glory was on the point of passing, also suggests the night season. The background of the night afforded additional beauty and lustre to the radiant glory that enwrapped the person and garments of the Lord.

*c. It is noticeable that the glory passed on him as he prayed.* The glory that the disciples beheld – which streamed through his garments, so that his ordinary dress became shining, exceeding white as snow – was the shining from within of the glory of the only begotten of the Father.

*d. The appearance of Moses and Elijah added greatly to the impressiveness of the spectacle.* They were the representative leaders of the Hebrew theocracy. Moses was the embodiment of the law, Elijah of the prophets. Their advent was due to the special encouragement they were able to afford the Redeemer at this great crisis.

Only a few days before our Lord had unfolded, with graphic minuteness, the scenes of his approaching death. Peter, speaking for the rest, had immediately sought to dissuade him. 'Be it far from thee, Lord,' he said; 'this shall not be unto thee.' They were not able to understand or sympathise. It was necessary, therefore, that redeemed humanity should furnish two of its strongest and noblest ambassadors to reinforce and strengthen our Lord, on the human side, before he set his face steadfastly to go up to Jerusalem to die.

## 2   The theme of the celestial visitants

'They spake of his *decease* which he should accomplish at Jerusalem' (Luke 9:31). The Greek word is 'exodus' – a term that struck Peter's imagination. Years later he used it of his own death (2 Peter 1:14).

It must have been a startling rebuke to Peter and his companions. To them the death of the cross seemed as unthinkable as it appeared unnecessary. But now, to their surprise, they discovered that heaven could speak of nothing else! It was apparently the one subject about which Moses and Elijah cared to speak. As soon as the opportunity presented intercourse with Jesus, they fell to talking on it.

*Moses* would speak of the Passover Lamb, the slaying of which preceding the Exodus by which his people passed to liberty, and would assure our Lord that his death would mean emancipation and victory, when the ransomed hosts of the redeemed would sing the song of Moses and the Lamb.

*Elijah* would remind him that the spirit of prophecy was testimony, and that it was written in the prophets and the psalms that the Christ should suffer and should enter into his glory.

*Moses* would testify that each victim that had bled on the altars of Israel had no intrinsic virtue to put away sin; and that if he were now to fail, all their suffering would be worthless, and that the redemption that the saints were already enjoying must be revoked.

*Elijah* would assure him that on the other side of the Jordan of death, the strong waters of which he would cleave as he passed, the chariot of the ascension cloud awaited him.

Clearly, the death of the Cross, which our Lord saw awaiting him on the horizon, is the theme of eternity. Can we wonder at the intense interest with which the great cloud of witnesses watched the Saviour, as (so to speak) he stepped into the stadium to run the last lap in the great race, to fight the last fight in the stupendous struggle? The battlements of the Holy City were crowded with awestruck crowds, until the ascension hour called them to follow in the glad procession of the Victor.

## 3   The enfolding cloud

Peter had made a suggestion that was as ill-considered as it was hasty. In his account of this scene, communicated through Mark, he admits that he did not know what he was saying. It was the suggestion that our Lord should disregard the claims of the lost world, and spend his remaining years in a tabernacle on the mountain top, instead of coping with such scenes as that which awaited at the foot of the mountain! Peter had much to learn.

While he was speaking he and his fellow apostles beheld a cloud descending, which enveloped the radiant vision. They feared as they saw their Master and his celestial visitors cut off from them and hidden in the brightness of that mist of glory. It was no ordinary cloud, but was probably the Shekinah cloud that led the wilderness march, that filled Solomon's temple on its dedication, and that formed the Lord's ascension chariot. From its heart the voice of the eternal God was heard, bearing sublime witness to the Saviour as the beloved Son, and demanding homage from all.

What might have been! As the sinless Man, the Second Adam need not have died. In a moment, in the twinkling of an eye, he might have passed with Moses and Elijah, through the open door of paradise. Such a translation might have been possible; but if, at any moment, it was presented to his mind, he thrust it away. For the joy that was set before him – or instead of the joy set before him – he turned his back on paradise for himself, that he might open paradise for the dying thief and for us. And when the cloud had passed, he was left alone with his apostles, and took the straight road to Calvary.

# 4

# The evening of the denial

## *Matt. 26:17–20; Mark 14:12–17; Luke 22:7–16; John 13:1–20*

The Mount of Olives, during the Passover, was covered by a large number of families, gathered from all parts of the country, and from many lands. Unable to find accommodation in the over-crowded city, they provided for themselves slight booths or tents, their cattle tethered alongside.

It would be pleasant to think that our Lord was the guest of the home at Bethany where Lazarus and his sisters loved to welcome him; but it is more than likely that, after the supper at the house of Simon on the evening of his arrival, he deliberately stayed aloof, lest his friends might become entangled in the web that was being woven about him. Already the chief priests were consulting to put Lazarus to death, because by reason of him many of the Jews believed on Jesus.

It is with Peter's share in the happenings of the last evening of

Christ's earthly life that we are now dealing. Jesus knew that the hour had come when he should depart this world to the Father. It is practically certain, therefore, that he was more concerned for 'his own', and especially for Peter, than for himself. Hence the following precautions:

## 1   He provided him with a friend

The priceless worth of friendship was a matter of daily experience with the Lord. He made no secret of the tender intimacy that knit his soul with that of the disciple whom he loved, and who, more than any other, has interpreted to the world the secret workings of his heart. He realised therefore how much a friend of the right kind would mean for Peter in his abandonment to a remorse that threatened despair.

Jesus could trust John utterly. The ultimate proof of his confidence was given when, from the cross, he committed his mother to the filial care of his beloved friend. Thus he knew what John would be to Peter in the hour of black darkness, and therefore threw them together in his last sacred commission. We are expressly told that he sent Peter and John, saying, 'Go and prepare us the Passover, that we may eat'. Thus he set his seal on their long friendship. They had been attracted to each other by an instinctive consciousness that each supplied what the other lacked. It is more than probable that each chose the other as companion when the twelve were sent out two by two. Our Lord had often noticed and rejoiced in the congenial comradeship. He therefore took special pains to cement and hallow it by this expression of confidence.

The result justified his fond anticipations. It was to John that Peter naturally turned when the storm was expending its full fury on his soul. Mary of Magdala found them together on Easter morning. Together they ran to the sepulchre. Much as John loved his friend, he could not help outrunning him, because of another love that had a prior claim, but he compensated for it shortly afterward by refusing to take advantage of the keener sight of his younger eyes that had discerned the Lord standing on the shore in the morning haze. In a whisper of reverent love he passed on the news to his friend, and was only glad to know, as he saw him plunge into the water and head swiftly to shore, that he had secured for him a moment of private fellowship and a further assurance of forgiveness from those gentle lips.

They were much together in the coming days. They went together to the temple at the hour of prayer. Peter spoke for them both when he said to the lame man, 'Look on us'. They stood side by side when arrested by the Sanhedrin, and spent a memorable night together in the prison. Together they returned to their own company, and like the diverse metals of a compensating balance, they directed the policy of the infant church. Events separated them in later years – John to Ephesus and Peter to Babylon – but that the old love remained is evident, if the slight and tender reference that John makes to the lapse of his friend is contrasted with the explicit and circumstantial account that Peter gives in the second Gospel.

## 2  He assured him of a complete cleansing

Our Lord desired to eat that Supper with the chosen band before he suffered. It would be for his own comfort and strength, and for theirs. He therefore committed the necessary preparations to his two devoted friends. They secured the lamb, brought it early to the priest for killing, purchased the bitter herbs, passover cakes, and skin of wine, and hastened back to prepare the humble meal.

The city was too preoccupied and crowded to notice the famous Teacher and his companions as they passed through the Kedron gate and made for the appointed meeting place. The sky was already darkening, and the earlier stars were beginning to appear. Apparently the embers of jealous rivalry were still smouldering, and burst into a flame as soon as the large upper room, where Peter and John had been at work all the afternoon, was reached. The walk had been hot and dusty, and all would have been thankful for the customary ablutions, common to every Jewish home. In this case, however, they were wanting. Ewer, basin, and towel were provided, but no servant could be spared from the household at that busy season. Would no apostle perform this office for the rest, and especially for the Lord? Apparently none volunteered. To undertake menial duty would be equivalent to signing a deed of abdication from the throne of power, which each was claiming. There was also the question of precedence at the table to be considered. Even if the couch on the Lord's right hand was conceded to John, who should be on his left? Ought not Peter, to whom all were indebted for his efforts to prepare the feast? But Judas insisted, as treasurer, on his superior claims. To arrest further discussion the Lord arose from the supper table, laid aside his outer garments, girded himself with the towel, poured water into the basin, and began to wash his disciples' feet, wiping them carefully with the towel. A sudden silence must have befallen them as he passed from one to another in this lowly ministry, until he came to Peter, who had been watching the process with shame and indignation. 'Dost thou wash my feet?' he exclaimed; 'thou shalt never wash my feet.' 'If I wash thee not, thou hast no part with me!' Evidently Peter caught his Master's meaning. The outward was symbolic of the inward, the physical of the spiritual; and he replied: 'Lord, not my feet only, but also my hands and my head.'

It was as though he requested that his entire being might be plunged into the fountain opened for sin and uncleanness. 'Make sure work this time, my Lord; let me begin again, as I began at the first, with Thee in my boat!'

'No,' said Jesus in effect, 'that is not necessary. He who has recently bathed does not require entire immersion, if hands or feet are dirty. It is sufficient for the soiled member to be cleansed, and the body is all clean. It is enough if the particular sin is confessed and put away. Whenever that confession is made I will show myself faithful and just to forgive the sin and cleanse from all unrighteousness.'

There was therefore a double significance in our Lord's lowly act of feet washing. He taught the royalty of service, and also that sin does not sever the regenerate soul from God. There must be confession, and there will be instant restoration.

What a wealth of comfort has been ministered by this lowly act of the Saviour to those whose feet have become soiled by the dust of earth's highways! He knew that he had come from God, was going to God, and was God; but to wash the feet of these simple men did not seem incongruous with the throne to which he went. And now that he, as the Lamb slain, is on the throne, he will turn aside from the adoration of eternity, and 'stay his ear for every sigh a contrite suppliant brings'.

# 5

# The Renewed Commission

## *John 21*

It is almost certain that the final chapter of John's Gospel – which has been described as a postscript – was appended by the beloved apostle as a tribute to the memory of his friend who, according to universal tradition, had sealed his long and glorious ministry by martyrdom – the martyrdom of the cross. In noble loyalty to Peter's memory, he desired to show how, notwithstanding his denial, the Lord had himself replaced the keys in his hand and returned his sword. The primitive church had already recognized him as one of its pillars, but the story of his actual rehabilitation had not been placed on the canvas of history.

Jesus knew that the Peter of the denial was not the real Peter, and since his future leadership depended on the concurrence of the other disciples, he skilfully contrived to bring about a revelation of Peter's innermost soul, that the effect of his denial might be neutralized, and that unquestionable proof might be given of his possession of the qualities required for the leadership of the church. The unanimity with which his leadership was agreed to proves the infinite wisdom that inspired the Lord's action when they met for the last time on the shores of the Lake of Galilee.

## 1  The scene

In obedience to their instructions, the apostles returned to Galilee and to the lake, every headland and inlet of which was fragrant with hallowed associations. Simon Peter said, 'I go a-fishing.' They immediately agreed with his suggestion, and replied, 'We also go with thee.'

Boats and nets were at hand, and with the eager alacrity with which men will respond to the call of an old-time but long-discarded habit, seven of them pushed off from shore in one of the larger fishing boats, a smaller one being attached to the stern, and made off for the familiar fishing grounds; but when the grey morning began to break – they had caught nothing.

They failed to recognize the figure standing on the white, sandy shore, enwrapped in the golden shimmer of the morning mist. Surely he was some early fish dealer; and the two inquiries addressed to them across the quiet water failed to correct their mistake. That fishermen, returning from a night of toil, should be asked by one standing on the shore, if they had fish to sell, or that they should be asked directions for catching a shoal were familiar incidents. But John, with the unerring instinct of love, discerned the presence of the Lord, and in a whisper passed his happy discovery to Peter. None of the others could, for the moment, have understood why Peter suddenly jumped up and wrapped around himself the outer coat that he had cast aside to expedite his labours, and plunged into the water, regardless of the morning chill. Those swift strokes, however, gave him a brief additional opportunity of lonely personal intercourse with Jesus.

We may not linger on the tender thoughtfulness that had kindled a fire, at which exhausted fishermen might warm their limbs and dry their clothes, and which had prepared the bread and fish. Nor may we dwell on the frugality of the miraculous, which urged the disciples to bring of the fish they had caught. It is enough if we learn from the entire incident that, from our Lord's resurrection and onward, the seine net of the gospel must be cast into the multitudinous waters of the human world, that the Master's presence and direction are absolutely essential to success, that he will welcome them as they near the heavenly shore and will feast with them and they with him.

The outstanding qualifications for religious leadership are three: passionate devotion to Christ, unfeigned humility, and indomitable courage. In each of these Peter had been proven deficient by the incidents of the betrayal night. But they were latent in his soul and only waited for favourable circumstances to call them forth.

*a. Passionate devotion to Christ*    Had it not been for the denial, none of the apostolic band would have questioned Peter's attitude toward the Master. But a shadow of grave doubt now overspread the sky, and as they spoke together they may have questioned the strength and steadfastness of his devotion. Our Lord realized this, and knew that before he entrusted to him the care of his sheep and lambs, he had to secure a very decisive and unquestionable expression of the love that he at least recognized as a dominant factor in his apostle's character.

So, when breakfast was over, Jesus repeated the same question three times: 'Lovest thou me?' and in each case addressed him as Simon Bar-Jona, i.e., Simon, son of John. Our Saviour laid this stress on his servant's earlier name because he desired to give him a fresh opportunity of acquiring the title of 'rock'.

Love to Jesus is the indispensable qualification of service. Love is needed for the fathering of tired and sick lambs to the shepherd's bosom, for the weary mothers finding the mountain path steep and difficult, and for the straying sheep, possessed by an incessant tendency to break through bars, or wander browsing on forbidden pastures. The first, second, and third qualification of the true shepherd is love. Therefore the Master asked persistently, 'Dost thou love me?' And to the thrice-repeated question Peter returned the same reply, 'Thou knowest that I love thee.'

*b. Unfeigned humility*   Two Greek words stand for love. The one expresses the reverent and adoring love with which we should regard the holy God. The other expresses love in its more human and affectional aspect. In his two first questions, Jesus asked his apostle whether he loved with the former love. This Peter modestly disclaimed. 'No,' he said, 'but I love you with the ardour of personal affection.' Finally, our Lord descended to his level and asked if indeed he loved him this way, eliciting the immediate response: 'Assuredly, and whether as Son of God or Son of man, you know it is true.'

With evident reference to Peter's boast made at the supper, that though his fellow disciples might desert the Master, yet he never would, Jesus asked him if he loved him more than the rest. But by his silence and his grief, he confessed that he dared not claim any priority in love. He was prepared to take the lowest seat, and consider himself last and least. In this also he proved that he was worthy for the foremost place, because he was willing to take the lowest. He had become as a little child; and our Lord did not hesitate, with the hearty assent of the disciples who stood by, to take him by the hand and place him in the old foremost position that he seemed to have forfeited forever.

*c. Indomitable courage*     From the beginning our Lord saw the cross standing clearly on the horizon before him. Amid all the excitement of his early appearance, he told Nicodemus that the Son of man must be lifted up. Do we sufficiently estimate his courage in treading resolutely a path that led ever deeper into the valley of death?

This was our Lord's experience. And it was to be Peter's also. 'Thou shalt stretch forth thy hands, and another shall gird thee, and carry thee whither thou wouldest not. This spake he, signifying by what death he should glorify God.' In his proud self-confidence Peter once said: 'Lord with You I am ready to go to prison and to death.' The Saviour replied: 'Thou canst not follow me *now*, but thou shalt follow me afterwards.' And the time had now dawned. The disciple was not to be above his Lord. He was to follow him to prison in Acts 12, and to death at the end of it all – the death of the cross, as tradition assures us, and this prediction suggests. In his second epistle Peter refers to these words of Jesus: 'Knowing that shortly I must put off my tabernacle, even as our Lord Jesus hath showed me' (2 Peter 1:13). Clearly for him also the cross was the ultimate goal; but he never swerved from the chosen path of service because of its menace. The courage that could stand that strain was of rare and splendid quality, and approved his fitness for leadership.

By evincing his ownership of these three qualities Peter established his right to the foremost place in the glorious company of the apostles, and he nobly fulfilled the position.

# 6

# A Witness of the Resurrection

*Acts 1:1–26; 2:1–11*

With his brethren Peter returned from the scene of the ascension to the city with great joy. Though he must have realized that the blessed intercourse of the last six weeks was now ended, and that his Master had definitely gone to the Father, yet the indubitable evidence of his great power and glory, the memory of those hands outstretched in benediction as he went, the assurance that they were to be endued with the power of the Comforter within the next few days, and the assurance that Jesus when he came again, as he certainly must, would be the same unchangeable Lord and Friend, were sufficient to lift them all into an ecstasy of joy and triumph, which exceeded and overflowed their sense of depriva-tion. It was even as he had said, their master had not left them comfortless.

Naturally they returned to *the* Upper Room, hallowed by so many precious associations. It may have been part of the house of the mother of John Mark, which afterward became the gathering place for the harried church; and probably it was filled to its utmost capacity when the entire group of apostles, disciples, holy women, and the brethren of the Lord, was assembled. Peter seemed naturally and by universal consent to become their leader; but he simply acted as chairman or moderator for the time being, because the Lord himself, though unseen, was recognized by them all as still literally present; and it was to him that the choice between the two candidates for the apostolate was referred. 'Thou, Lord, which knowest all hearts of all men, shew whether of these two thou hast chosen.' They were to be witnesses to the fact of the resurrection of their Lord. His words are very definite.

'It is necessary,' he said, 'that of the men who have been associated with us from the beginning of our Lord's ministry in the days of John the Baptist until now, one must be chosen to become *with us* a witness to his resurrection.'

## 1   The salient feature of Peter's life work

It was bearing witness to the Resurrection. The word translated witness is fraught with solemn and sacred associations. It is 'martyr'. We cannot utter the word lightly. It is significant of tears, and blood, and death agony, and the light reflected from the face of Jesus on the death pallor of upturned faces.

The resurrection of Jesus is not primarily to be argued for as a doctrine; it rests on attestation to a fact. It is indeed a gospel, a theology, and a philosophy. It was the fitting consummation of the work of Jesus. But it is primarily a historical fact, communicated and vouched for by a sufficient number of unimpeachable witnesses.

There is a vast difference therefore between the arguments on which Plato and others based their belief in the immortality of the soul and our belief in the resurrection of the Christ. But at the best, it was only a probability. In the resurrection of Jesus men were confronted with a fact, which could not be disputed, in that the resurrected body of Jesus was 'seen many days of them which came up with him from Galilee to Jerusalem, who are his witnesses to the people' (Acts 13:31). There is a clear distinction, therefore, between the Platonic philosophy which argues for immortality, and the Christian faith in the Resurrection which, as a well-attested fact, has brought life and immortality to light.

## 2   Peter's equipment for his life work

Before our Lord entered on his ministry he was anointed with the Holy Spirit, and from the wilderness he returned in the power of the Spirit into Galilee. May we not say that he also tarried until he (so far as his human nature required it) was endued with power from on high? That was our Saviour's Pentecost. How much more must his followers stoop beneath the anointing of Pentecost.

This is what he had promised. He said: 'I go to the Father, and

will ask of him, on your behalf, and he will give you another
Paraclete, that he may abide with you for ever, even the Spirit of
Truth.'

Day after day they waited, sometimes in the Upper Room, but
perhaps more often, as Luke tells us, in the temple, worshipping
Christ, blessing God with great joy, and wondering how soon,
and in what manner, the promised gift of power would be
bestowed.

It was the first day of the week, and a notable day at that, for
the priests in the special temple service would present the first
loaves of the new harvest before God. It was the early morning,
the embryo church probably was assembled in one of the courts
or precincts of the vast temple area. They were all together in one
place, when there was a sound from heaven as of the rushing of a
mighty wind, and there appeared what seemed to be tongues as of
flame that rested on each of them. Peter looked on John and saw
the expressive symbol on his bowed head, little realizing that the
same sublime event had also happened to himself. Then looking
round, and seeing each similarly crowned, he concluded that an
equal share in this fiery baptism had been imparted to him also.
The whole company was filled, and began to speak with other
tongues, as the Spirit gave them words – Peter with the rest.

Meanwhile, summoned by the extraordinary sound that evidently emanated from the temple, a vast crowd gathered. It was
composed of Jews and proselytes, religious men, gathered from
every part of the known world. As this torrent of excited and
questioning multitudes poured into the temple area, they were
accosted by the newly-anointed disciples who, with an assurance
that their new experience had given, went freely among them,
attesting the risen glory of him whom their rulers had recently
rejected and nailed to the cross. One of them accosted a Jew from
Greece, and in the purest Attic, told him that Christ had risen.
Another met a Jew who had, by residence in Rome, acquired the
right of citizenship, and told the story of Jesus in language that
Cicero or Horace could not have excelled. A third encountered a
group which, by their dress, had evidently hailed from Arabia,
and poured into their astonished ears the gospel story.

Then Peter stood up and began to speak. His sermon was little
else than the citation of long passages of Scripture, accompanied
by brief comments, showing their application to the present hour;

but the effect was extraordinary. As this Galilean fisherman began to speak, the mob suddenly became a congregation, and the crowd became as one body, swayed and inspired by a common impulse. Presently the silence was broken by the cry, and from the entire congregation the question arose: 'Men and brethren, what shall we do?'

That anointing or infilling came to Peter at least twice afterward, according to Scripture, but it probably came again and again. He was filled with the Holy Spirit on the Day of Pentecost, and a second time when he addressed the court, and was filled again on returning with John from the presence of the Sanhedrin to their own company. Why, then, should we go on without claiming our share in this Pentecostal power? Ah, why do we fail to make use of that vast spiritual dynamic of which Pentecost was the specimen! We are not held back by God, but by ourselves. We have not, because we ask not, or because we ask amiss.

The blessing, originally confined to Jews, may become the heritage of Gentiles also who believe in Christ. They also may receive the Holy Spirit through faith. There is not a single believer who reads this page who may not claim a share in the Pentecostal gift. The Spirit may be *in* us, regenerating and renewing from within, as Jesus was born of Mary through the Spirit; but it is necessary that he should be *on* us also, as he descended and remained on Jesus in his baptism, if we are to fulfil our ministry to mankind. No learning, no polished speech, no amount of evangelical teaching short of the Holy Spirit can avail. Why not acknowledge that there is a blessing here, which is yours by right, but not yours by possession? Why not confess that it is your failure and fault not to have claimed it? Why not humbly open your heart to the entrance of that blessed Spirit who changes the cowardly into courageous confessors, and makes the weakest mighty as the angel of the Lord?

### 3   The characteristics of Peter's life work of witnessing

*a. It was persistent.*   On the day of Pentecost in Acts 2; in his next great address, on the healing of the lame man in chapter 3; in his apology before the rulers, elders, priests, and scribes in 4:10; by the great power with which he gave witness to the resurrection of the Lord Jesus, in 4:33; in his second conflict with the council in

5:32; in the answer that he gave to the inquiries of Cornelius and his friends in 10:39–41 – Peter was constantly and consistently a witness to the same outstanding fact that though Jesus was crucified through weakness, yet he was living through the power of God.

*b. It was steeped in Scripture quotation.* We have already noticed this in the Pentecostal sermon, where out of twenty-two verses, twelve are taken up with quotations from the prophets and psalms. We meet with the same features in the next chapter, where Peter refers twice to the predictions of the holy prophets, that it was fitting that Christ suffer, and to rise from the dead the third day. It seemed as though a very special illumination had been given him by the Holy Spirit of inspiration, that he might understand the Scriptures and perceive the relevance to Jesus of all things written in the law of Moses, the prophets, and the psalms.

This is always the case. The Spirit bears witness to the Word. Spirit of the risen Lord, open our eyes that we may see the face of Christ reflected in every Scripture, as in a mirror, now darkly, but which one day we shall see face to face!

*c. It grew in clearness of perception* Peter begins with 'Jesus of Nazareth approved of God'. Then 'Lord and Christ'. Then 'Jesus Christ of Nazareth'. Then 'His Son Jesus'. Then the 'Holy One and the Just'. Then the extraordinary sublime phrase is piled as a climax and top stone on all the rest – 'the Prince of Life'.

Prince! He is royal, and deserves the homage of all the living. Prince of life! In the literal rendering of this great word he is the author and giver of life, so that he who believes in him, though he has died, yet shall he live; while he who lives and believes in him will never die. Prince of life! All hail!

*d. It was based on present experience.* It is remarkable that in Peter's witness to the Master's risen life he does not refer to the spectacle of the empty grave, the ordered clothes, the garden interview, the vision of his hands and side, the breakfast by the lake, or the ascension from Olivet. He says: You may judge for yourselves by *this,* 'which ye now see and hear'. In other words, he felt that not only was Jesus on the other side of the thin veil, which hides the unseen world, but that he was doing things. He had reached the Father's right hand, and was sending the Spirit, as he promised. He was empowering them with boldness, insight, and utterance. He was working with them, and confirming their words with signs following. He was making lame men walk, prison doors open, heard hearts to break. Peter said: 'He whom ye delivered up and denied in the presence of Pilate, is alive, of this we all are witnesses, and *so is also the Holy Spirit.* Thus the testimony of those early witnesses came not only in power, but also in much assurance. He stood beside them.

Similarly a holy life will corroborate our witness to the living Christ. If contrary to our former habit we seek the things that are above; if we derive from an unseen source the power that overcomes the world; if our joy abounds in pain and sorrow, if though poor, we make many rich, being hated, we love, being refused, we entreat, being crucified, we invoke forgiveness on the agents of our shame – we prove that Jesus lives.

We are not called to live always in the far-off scenes of his agony and death. We have direct and immediate fellowship with the Prince of Life. We have the mind of Christ. We speak of things that we know, and testify of things we have seen.

If only we, who profess the name of Jesus, would wait at his doors until he gave us audience, we would go to people with his accent on our tongues, and his light on our heart. Let us not abdicate from our high privilege; then we shall go forth into the world bearing such evident traces of a life that cannot be accounted for, that those who know us best will be compelled to look from us to him who lives forever.

# 7

# The Door of Faith to the Gentiles
## *Acts 6:1–7, 8:14–25, 9:31, 10:16*

We open at this point a new chapter in the history of the unfolding of the divine purpose for our race. From the first the divine objective was to include in the one church, not Jews alone, but also Gentiles who had not received the seal and sign of the Abrahamic covenant, but who had entered directly from the Gentile world by the simple act of faith. Gentiles, it was generally supposed, could enter the door of the Christian church only by first becoming Jews. When our Lord commissioned his apostles to go into all the world and make disciples from all nations, they probably supposed that the rite of circumcision would precede their administration of baptism. It was only by a very gradual process that the whole truth broke on them that in Christ Jesus there is neither Jew nor Greek, circumcision nor uncircumcision, bond nor free, male nor female, but all are one in him.

For eight years with his fellow apostles Peter had confined himself to the consolidation of the 'mother church', but he was now to learn that her children would be gathered equally from a great multitude, whom none could number, of every nation, and kindred, and people, and tongue. We have therefore to consider the steps by which he was led forth into a larger concept of the divine purpose.

Peter was a strict Jew. He was inclined to view with suspicion even the Hellenist, or Greek-speaking Jews, who were scattered throughout the Roman Empire. And he knew the Gentiles, only as he had, from boyhood, for he beheld the glitter of their cilization, that transformed the Lake of Galilee into a Roman pleasure resort. He had never entered a gentile home, had never sat at a gentile table, and had never transgressed the rigid prescriptions of the Levitical dietary. He shrank from familiar intercourse with Gentile. Hence his exclamation, when invited to eat of the heterogeneous contents of the great sheet: 'Not so, Lord; for I have never eaten any thing that is common or unclean' (Acts 10:14).

The divine Master is willing to take infinite pains with us, before he demands the ceding of our wills and the taking of an irrevocable step.

Let us watch the stages of the process in the present case.

## 1 There arose a murmuring of the Grecian, the Hellenist Jews against the Hebrews

The Hellenist always regarded Jerusalem and the temple with fond and reverent affection. He turned there as he prayed. There he came with his family, as often as the cost permitted, to the annual festivals. In the Holy City he desired to die, and in its precincts be buried. A large contingent of these Jews of the dispersion were present on the Day of Pentecost, and had then, as in the following years, identified themselves with the Christian community. Many of them, like the good Barnabas, had parted with their possessions, placing the proceeds in the common stock, and their poor were in the habit of receiving their sustenance from the common purse. But their widows complained that undue partiality was shown in the daily distribution, and that home-born women fared better at the hand of the apostolic almoners than they did.

The peril of a serious rent in the seamless robe of the church became at length so imminent that Peter and his brethren were compelled to take action. After anxious consideration, they arrived at the conclusion that their highest vocation was to prayer and the ministry of the Word, and that this service of tables should be entrusted to seven men of good report, full of the Holy Spirit and of wisdom. They advised the church, therefore, as the ultimate authority, that they should proceed to choose that number from among themselves.

It is remarkable that they were all Hellenist Jews, with the exception of the last, who was a Gentile proselyte. The unanimity of the church in this solemn act was so evidently due to the presence and direction of the Spirit, that Peter could say nothing to the contrary, however startling to his preconceptions such action must have appeared.

## 2   Then came the great arguments, apology, and martyrdom of Stephen

In the familiar intercourse that ensued, Peter would have been attracted to the eloquent young Hellenist. He often listened to the burning words with which Stephen insisted that throughout their history the chosen people had resisted the divine Spirit, when he summoned them to a new advance. As he listened, Peter may have recalled the Master's words, that it would be found impossible to put the new wine in the old bottles. Already the breath of a new age fanned his cheek, as the door was being slowly opened for the admission of the gentile world.

### 3 The mission to Samaria followed

Because of Philip's preaching vast numbers of Samaritans had been baptized in the name of Jesus. This movement needed to be regularized, and the apostles, who had dared to remain in Jerusalem, despite Saul's fiery persecution, determined to commission Peter and John to visit the scene of revival, and lead the new converts forward into the full enjoyment of the gifts of Pentecost.

Here again Peter used the keys of teaching, prayer, and the imposition of hands, with the result that the miracle of Pentecost was repeated. 'They received the Holy Ghost.' To the obvious astonishment of the apostles, the Holy Spirit, in answer to their prayer, descended on these believing Samaritans with absolute impartiality. Indeed, Peter was so impressed with what he saw that he could do no other than keep in the current of the divine purpose; and therefore he and John, in their leisurely return to Jerusalem, preached in the villages of Samaria through which they passed. Here again was a further unfolding of the horizon of God's purpose.

### 4 But the process was still further accelerated by the conversion of Saul of Tarsus

It was a startling rumour that reached Jerusalem, that the arch persecutor of the church had been arrested by the direct intervention of the Lord, and had become his humble follower. But as more news filtered in, and fuller details were furnished of this wonderful event, they learned that Saul had been compelled to flee from Damascus and had gone to Arabia. Some time elapsed, and finally, to Peter's surprise, Saul presented himself at his humble dwelling in Jerusalem, and remained as his guest for fifteen days. Suddenly the younger man came to Peter with a strange glory on his features. 'Brother,' he said, 'what do you think, as just now I was praying in the temple I seemed to lose myself, and saw the Lord, and he said to me, Get out of Jerusalem quickly because they will not receive of your testimony concerning me. Depart: for I will send you far away to the Gentiles. You see, therefore, I have no alternative, and must be gone.'

Peter must have been sorely troubled at the danger that beset his newfound friend, and took instant steps to arrange his passage out of the danger zone for Caesarea, and ultimately to Tarsus. When he was safely away, however, those parting words must have rung in his heart – 'far away to the Gentiles'. He could not challenge those words. Clearly they were spoken by the Master, but they still further prepared him for the fresh demand that would soon be made on him.

## 5   The process was completed at Joppa

After the departure of Paul the church throughout Judæa and Samaria had peace. Peter took advantage of this halcyon period to make an itinerary through the smaller congregations that were scattered throughout Judæa, and in course of time came to Lydda where, as the medium for the health giving word of Christ, he lifted Æneas from his eight-years' paralysis. Therefore he was summoned by an urgent message to Joppa, six-and-a-half miles distant on the rocky sea-coast, to the room of death, where the beloved Dorcas lay. His prayer on her behalf prevailed with God, and when he gave her his hand she arose to become once more the gentle friend of all the saints and widows in the little town. The house in which he lodged – the house of Simon the tanner – had associations with death and its accompanying ceremonial pollution, which must have been extremely distasteful to a conscientious Jew. The Jerusalem church had become so diminished by persecution, and flight, that its concerns failed to give him the wide scope and sphere to which for eight years he had been accustomed. What was to be the next step in the fulfilment of his life work? Was some new development of the divine pattern at hand that he must realize for himself and others?

At this juncture, one noon, when the blazing sunshine poured down on the burnished mirror of the sea, and on the white houses of the little town, he went up to the housetop for prayer – prayer probably for further light. While the midday meal was prepared, he fell into a trance, and through the opened heavens he caught the vision of a redeemed world, like a great white sheet. The variety of its contents – four-footed beasts, creeping things, birds clean and unclean, startled him; and still more the declaration that God had cleansed them all, that the old Levitical restrictions were removed, and that any of them were fit for food. Rise, Peter, slay and eat.

Then, while he was much perplexed in himself as to what the vision that he had seen might mean, the knocking at the gate, the voices of men that rose in the noon silence, as they called his name, together with the assurance of the Spirit that there was no need for fear or hesitation – all indicated that the hour of destiny had struck, that a new epoch was inaugurated, and that he was to lead the church into the greatest revolution she had known since the ascension of her Lord.

# 8

# 'I Will Go With Thee to Prison'

## *Acts 12:1–25*

Again it was the Passover. 'Then were the days of unleavened bread.' Fourteen years earlier Peter had been sent with John to prepare the Passover Feast for his Lord, and as the apostles were gathered around the table he had stated his willingness to go with his Master even to prison. Here he was nobly fulfilling his vow. At that Passover also he had slept, but it was the sleep of unwatchfulness, of self-confidence, of the weakness of the flesh. He failed to watch even for one hour with Christ. Here again he slept, but it was the sleep of absolute confidence in the grace of Christ, who would yet deliver him, if it were his will; but if not, would enable him to be faithful to death. Previously he had slept while Jesus prayed; now as he slept, not only did the great High Priest pray that his faith might not fail, but many were gathered together in Mary's house, and were praying for him. But he was not to die.

## 1  'The kings of the earth set themselves'

'About that time Herod the king stretched forth his hands to vex certain of the church.' He was known as Herod Agrippa, and his character bore the infamous brand of the Herod stock. By unscrupulous subservience to the caprices and crimes of Roman emperors, he had become possessed of regal power hardly inferior to that of Herod the Great. In order to ingratiate himself with the Jewish leaders he made a great show of zeal for the requirements of the Mosaic ritual. Josephus tells us that he did not allow one day to pass without its appointed sacrifice. But his further steps in the same direction were taken in the blood of Christian martyrs.

James, one of the Master's innermost circle, was the first to suffer. He had been surnamed Boanerges, and had on one occasion called fire from heaven. He proved himself able to drink of his Master's cup and be baptized with his baptism.

Agrippa saw that it pleased the Jews, and he was encouraged to strike again, but harder; and this time to arrest the leader of the hated sect, who more than once had defied the whole strength of the Sanhedrin. Peter was the strongest element in the Christian community. The precautions taken to secure him suggest that the king feared lest his arrest might lead to an attempt at rescue, and also that his advisors and supporters had a lively memory of the two previous occasions on which the prison doors had been opened for the release of this same man. A body of sixteen soldiers was set to watch and hold the prisoner. Four were on duty for three hours, and were then relieved. Two were in the cell with him, his hands fastened to one on either side. A third stood outside the bolted door, while a fourth was posted along the corridor, which led to the great iron gate. Already Herod's doom was prepared, and the angel who was to release Peter was ready to smite the tyrant oppressor in the hour of his greatest triumph. When the people were shouting in mad adulation, 'It is the voice of a god, and not of a man,' the angel of the Lord immediately smote him, because he did not give God the glory: and he was carried from the theatre to his palace, a dying man. For five long days he lay in excruciating agony, and on the sixth of August expired, unlamented.

## 2  The prayer of the church

The situation appeared desperate, so far as human judgment was concerned. If Herod succeeded in his designs against Peter, what could the rank and file look for but wholesale massacre? But there is always a weapon left to the children of God. With God all things are possible. Peter was kept in prison 'until the days of unleavened bread had passed'; but prayer was made without ceasing of the church to God for him.

Day after day passed, and the seven days of the Feast had expired. On the next day Herod would bring his prisoner to a mock trial and then a cruel death. As yet there had been no answering voice from heaven. The Passover moon was waning, the next day was climbing the sky. We are informed that Peter was not missed until it was day, i.e., sunrise, about six o'clock. Clearly then his release must have taken place between three o'clock, when a fresh quaternion had come on duty, and six o'clock when they were relieved. Some time must be allowed for the watch and their ward to become drowsy and fall into a sound sleep. Therefore it may have been about five o'clock in the April dawn that the light shone into the darkness of the cell, and the angel of the Lord stood by his servant's side.

Meanwhile he was answering prayer by the great peace that he breathed into Peter's soul. He was sleeping between two soldiers, bound with two chains, and guards before the door kept the prison. Perhaps he pillowed his heart on the never-to-be-forgotten words, which the Lord had addressed to him on the shores of the lake: '*When thou shalt be old*, thou shalt stretch forth thy hands, and another shall gird thee, and carry thee whither thou wouldest not.' But he was not old. His power was yet in its maturity; and death by crucifixion was not in Herod's power. So he rested in the Lord, and his mind was kept in perfect peace. Was not this a part at least of God's answer to the protracted intercessions of the church?

## 3  The opening of the iron gate

God's angel cast off his enshrouding veil, and instantly a mild and gentle light fell on the sleeping group, awaking none of them. He had to smite Peter on his side, and call him to arise. Naturally enough he arose, hardly aware that the fetters and chains had ceased to hold him. The apostle seems to have been dazed, and needed constant reminders of what he should do in tightening his girdle, putting on his sandals, and assuming his warm outer cloak. In answer to the angel's summons to follow him, he passed through the door of the cell as though in a dream. 'He wist not that it was true which was done by the angel; but thought he saw a vision.' The gleaming light from his form led him past the first and second sentries, but they gave no sign of awakening. 'A deep sleep from God had fallen upon them.' Did he question whether that mighty iron gate would open? But when they reached this last barrier it silently opened to them of its own accord. It was swung open and closed again by strong and invincible hands. The morning breath was in Peter's face, as in company with his angel guide he passed through one street; but that was all, and it was enough, for God is sparing of the miraculous. When our own judgment is adequate for our tasks, we are left to use it. When, therefore, they had passed through one street, the angel left him, 'and *when he had considered the thing,* he came to the house of Mary, the mother of John, where many were gathered together and were praying.' Mary was sister to Barnabas and the mother of John Mark. There had been no sleep in that home that night. Peter's coming martyrdom was on every heart; and perhaps the hope of his deliverance had faded from their thought. They were resigning themselves to what seemed to be the Lord's will, and only asking that he might be strengthened and upheld in his last hours. This may explain their incredulity when Rhoda, the servant girl, rushed into their midst with the announcement that Peter was standing at the gate. For precaution's sake she had asked who it was who sought for admittance at that unusual hour; and when she heard his voice, with which she was intimately familiar, for he was a constant visitor there, she recognized it instantly, and in her joy actually forgot to admit him, so he continued knocking.

'It is his angel,' they said, 'and thou art mad.' But her confident affirmations, and the continued knocking, at last prevailed, and they opened the door to find that it was as the girl had said. Peter did not enter the house. As soon as he was missed by his guards, search would probably be instituted in the homes of his closest friends. There must be no presumption in his part. He must use his own wit to evade his foes. Therefore, with a few hurried explanations and directions, with loving greetings to James and the others, he departed while it was yet dark and went to another place.

# 9

# Life's Afterglow

## *2 Peter 1:15*

In his epistles the apostle stored the thoughts that he was especially anxious should be associated with his memory, and we should linger a little longer to consider them; and they may be thus enumerated:

## 1 Comfort amid trial

The Lord had especially commissioned him to strengthen his brethren, and indeed they were passing through experiences that especially called for comfort and strength. They were reproached for the name of Christ. The trials to their faith, patience, and constancy were 'fiery'. They were called to be partakers of the sufferings of Christ. Arraignments before arrogant and pagan judges, the loss of property, the infliction of torture, the scattering of families, cruel scourgings, prolonged imprisonment, death in the arena or by fire – these were their experiences.

In these circumstances, what could be more exhilarating than the apostle's repeated reminder of the example and constancy of the Saviour, who had suffered for them, leaving them an example that they should follow in his steps? 'Rejoice,' he said, 'inasmuch as ye are partakers of Christ's sufferings.' Before his eyes the martyr's death was always present, as his Lord had told him; and he passed on to others the source of his own steadfastness and courage.

## 2 The sacrificial nature of the Saviour's death

That was no ordinary death before which the sun veiled his face and the rocks rent in sympathy. It was the death of the Redeemer. It was a sacrifice, as of a Lamb without blemish or spot. The Son of God had borne the sins of men in his own body on the tree. He had died, the just for the unjust, to bring them to God. The blood shed on the cross was 'precious' blood. Its sprinkling on the conscience brought peace, and severed the soul from its vain lifestyle received by tradition from the past.

## 3 The certainty of future glory

Those whom Peter addressed were reminded that they had been begotten to a living hope by the resurrection of Jesus Christ from the dead. For them an inheritance had been purchased and awaiting them, which was incorruptible, undefiled, and does not fade away. They would receive a crown of glory that could not fade away.

## 4 The urgency for a holy life

He who had called them was holy, and they had to be holy also. They were called to be a chosen generation, a royal priesthood, a holy nation, a people for Christ's own possessions.

Our space does not permit a discussion of all the exhortations to holiness that are found in these epistles, nor to indicate the qualities of Christian character on which the apostle insists; but we may specify the one grace of humility on which he lays special and repeated stress. How different are these injunctions from the old proud, boastful, and imperious spirit, which in his earlier life had so often betrayed him!

## 5 The nature of death

He thought and spoke of it as the putting off of the tent or tabernacle, which symbolized the pilgrim character of his earthly life, that he might enter the house not made with hands, his permanent dwelling place, eternal in the heavens. He said that it was a decease, or exodus. For him death was not a condition, but a passage. It was no bridge of sighs from a palace to a dungeon, but one of smiles and jubilation from a cell to the blaze of the eternal day. But all was summed up in the vision of that dear face, which he hoped to see as soon as he had crossed over. Jesus had been the daystar of his heart, and he would be the light of all his future, in the city that needs neither sun nor moon, because the Lamb is the light of it.

# PAUL

# 1

# Separated From Birth

## *Gal. 1:15*

God has a purpose in every life; and where the soul is perfectly yielded and acquiescent, he will certainly realize it. Blessed is he who has never thwarted the execution of the divine ideal.

One of the most interesting studies in human life is to see how all the circumstances and incidents of its initial stages have been shaped by a determining will, and made to serve a beneficent purpose. Every thread is needed for the completed pattern; every piece of equipment stands in good stead at the final test.

## 1   The future apostle must be deeply instructed in the Jewish law

'The law' must stand here as a convenient term, not only for the moral and Levitical code as given in the Pentateuch, but for the minute and laborious additions of the rabbis. No one could have appreciated the intolerable burden of this yoke of legalism – which even Peter said neither they nor their fathers were able to bear – unless he had been taught, as Paul was 'according to the perfect manner of the law of the fathers' (Acts 22:3).

## 2   He needed to be skilful in his quotation and application of the Hebrew Scriptures

Every question in religious and ordinary Jewish life was settled by an appeal to the Scriptures. No speaker could gain the audience, or hold the attention of a Jewish congregation for a moment, unless he could show, the more ingeniously the better, that his statements could be substantiated from the inspired Word. To the law and the testimony every assertion had to be brought. Before that venerable bar every teacher had to stand.

It was above all things necessary that Christianity should be shown to be, not the destruction but the fulfilment of the ancient law. What made Paul so 'mad' against Christianity was its apparent denial and betrayal of the obvious meaning of Old Testament prophecies and types. Neither he nor any of his co-religionists were prepared to accept a humiliated, suffering, dying Messiah, unless it could be shown without controversy that such a conception was the true reading of Moses, the Prophets, and the Law. Throughout the entire course, 'the sacred oracles' were the only textbook; and every day was spent in the careful and minute consideration of words, lines, and letters, together with the interpretations of the various rabbis.

Men might chafe at Paul's renderings of the ancient words, but they could not dispute his intimate acquaintance with them, and his profound erudition. He knew the whole ground perfectly. There was not a single argument with which he was not familiar, and for which he was not instantly ready with a reply. The field of Scripture had been repeatedly ploughed over by that keen mind, and its harvests gathered into that retentive memory. It was this power that gave him an entrance into every synagogue, and carried conviction to so many candid Jews. How richly, for instance, it was appreciated by Bible students, like those he met at Beroea!

### 3　He needed to have large and liberal views

Jewish intolerance and exclusivism had reared a high wall of partition between Jew and Gentile. The Jews had no dealings with the Samaritans; how much less with the Gentile dogs that crouched beneath the well-spread table of the children!

The majority of the apostles were largely influenced by this caste spirit. It was hard for them, though they had been moulded by the Lord himself, to break through the fence of early training. Had the shaping of the primitive church been left to them, though theoretically they might have acknowledged the equality of Jew and Gentile in God's sight, yet practically they would have drawn distinctions between the Jewish Christians and those other sheep that their Shepherd was bringing, but which were not of the Hebrew fold. The need of a trumpet voice was urgent, to proclaim that Jesus had abolished in his flesh the enmity, that he might create in himself of two one new man, so making peace.

Through the ordering of the divine providence this qualification also was communicated to the future apostle of the uncircumcision. By birth, as we have seen, he was a Hebrew: otherwise he could have influenced Jews, or obtained admission into their synagogues. But he had been brought up at the feet of the great rabbi who, while reverenced as 'the beauty of the law,' was recognized also as the most large-hearted of all the Jewish doctors. But he went so far as to permit and advocate the study of Greek literature. In his speech before the Sanhedrin, given in Acts 5, we trace the movements of a human and generous mind.

The influence of such a teacher must have been strong on the young Tarsus student, who had come to sit at his feet, and who regarded him with a boundless enthusiasm.

## 4   There was needed an especially wide knowledge of the world

The man who was to be a missionary to men had to know them. He who would be all things to all men, that by all means he might win some, had to be familiar with their methods of life and thought. A Jerusalem Jew could not possibly have adapted himself to cultured Greeks and practical Romans, to barbarians and Scythians, to bond and free; to Festus the imperial governor, and Agrippa the Hebrew king; to Onesimus the slave, and Philemon the master, as Paul did.

When his training at Jerusalem was complete he must have returned to Tarsus. In these years he probably married, or else he would not afterward have occupied a seat in the Sanhedrin; and steadily pursued his trade, or exercised his profession as a rabbi in the local synagogue, or travelled far afield on some religious mission, compassing sea and land to make proselytes.

Imagine what those seven or eight years must have meant to the young Pharisee. All the while he would be keenly observing and noting every phase of gentile heathendom. The pictures of the world of that age given in the first chapter to the Romans and the first epistle to the Corinthians, could only have been given by one who obtained his information first-hand, and by personal observation.

## 5   He needed also to be equipped with the prerequisites of a great traveller

For this there were three necessary conditions: speech, safety, sustenance. And each was forthcoming.

*a. Speech.*    Greek was the common language of the world, the medium of intercourse among educated persons, as English is in India today. And Paul was even more familiar with Greek than with the sacred Hebrew. When quoting the Scriptures he habitually employed the Septuagint (i.e., the Greek) version; and he was able to speak their tongue fluently enough to hold the attention of Athenian philosophers.

*b. Safety.*    All the world was Roman. Roman governors in every province; Roman usages in every city; Roman coins, customs, and officials. To be a Roman citizen gave a man a standing and position in any part of the empire. He might not be beaten without trail; or if he were, the magistrates were in jeopardy of losing their office, and even their life. He could demand trial at the bar of Caesar; if he appealed to Casear, to Caesar he must go. He would be permitted to plead for himself before the bar of Roman justice.

*c. Sustenance.*    This was also granted to him. On whatever shore he was cast there were always goats, and always the demand for the coarse cloth at which he had worked from his boyhood.

In all this how evidently was the divine purpose at work, shaping all things after the counsel of its own will.

# 2

# 'Thy Martyr Stephen'

## *Acts 22:20*

Sometimes God charges a man with a message, and launches him forth suddenly and irresistibly. Such a man was Elijah, with his 'Thus saith the LORD, before whom I stand'; John the Baptist, with his 'It is not lawful for thee to have thy brother's wife'; such also was Savonarola of Florence, and many others. And such was Stephen.

We know little or nothing of his antecedents. That he was a Hellenist Jew is almost certain; and that he had personally known and communicated with the Son of Man, whom he afterward recognized in his glory, is more than probable. But of father, mother, birthplace, and education, we know nothing. We have the story of one day, the record of one speech – that day his last, that speech his apology and defence for his life.

Stephen caught for a brief space the glory of the departed Lord, and reflecting it, was transformed into the same image; 'and all that sat in the council, looking steadfastly on him, saw his face as it had been the face of an angel' (Acts 6:15).

Stephen's life and death must always have attracted reverent interest; but how much more so as we trace his influence on the method, thought, and character of the great apostle.

## 1  The movement of which Stephen was the product and representative may for a moment claim our attention

It casts a suggestive sidelight on the career of 'the young man Saul'.

Three streams of thought were meeting in tumultuous eddies in Jerusalem.

There were *the Jews of the Pharisee party*, represented by Gamaliel, Saul of Tarsus, and other notable men. They were characterized by an intense religiousness that circled around their ancestry, their initial rite, their temple. Were they not Abraham's children? Had not God entered into special covenant relations with them, of which circumcision was the outward sign and seal? And as for the temple, the whole of their national life was anchored to the spot where it stood. There was the only altar, priesthood, shrine, of which their religion admitted. Narrow, casuistical, bigoted, intensely fanatical; priding themselves on their national privilege as the chosen people, but resentful against the appeals of the greatest of their prophets; counting on the efficacy of their system, but careless of personal character – such was the orthodox and conservative Jewish party of the time.

Next came the *Hebrew Christian church*, led and represented by the apostles. Of founding a new religious organization they had no plans. That they should ever live to see Judaism superseded by the teaching they were giving, or Christianity existing apart from the system in which they had been nurtured, was a thought that never occurred to them. Their Master had rigorously observed the Jewish rights and feasts; and they followed in his steps, and impressed a similar course of action on their adherents. The church lingered still in the portals of the synagogue. The disciples observed the hours of prayer, were found in devout attendance at the temple's services, had their children circumcised, and would not have dreamed of being released from the regulations that bound the ordinary Jews as with iron chains. And it seems certain that, if nothing had happened of the nature of Stephen's apology and protests, the church would have become another Jewish sect, distinguished by the piety and purity of its adherents, and by their strange belief in the Messiahship of Jesus of Nazareth, who had been crucified under Pontius Pilate.

Lastly, there were *the converts from among the Hellenist Jews*. The origin of the Hellenist or Grecian Jews must be traced back to the captivity, which God overruled to promote the dissemination of Jewish conceptions throughout the world. It was but a small contingent that returned to Jerusalem with Nehemiah and Ezra; the vast majority elected to remain in the land of their adoption for purposes of trade. They slowly spread from there throughout Asia Minor to the cities of its seaboard and the highland districts of its interior, planting everywhere the synagogue, with its protest on behalf of the unity and the spirituality of God. Egypt, and especially Alexandria; Greece, with her busy commercial seaports; Rome, with her imperial cosmopolitan influence – became familiar with the peculiar countenace and customs of this wonderful people, who always contrived to secure for themselves a large share of the wealth of any country in which they had settled. But their free contact with the populace of many lands wrought a remarkable change on them.

While the Jews of Jerusalem and Judæa shrank from the defiling touch of heathenism, and built higher the wall of separation, growing continually prouder, more bitter, more narrow, the Jews that were scattered through the world became more liberal and cosmopolitan. Compelled, as they were, to relinquish the temple with its holy rites, except on rare and great occasions, when they travelled from the ends of the earth to be present at some great festival, they magnified in its place the synagogue, with its worship, its reading of the law, its words of exhortation; and they welcomed to its precincts all who cared to avail themselves of its privileges.

After some years of absence, Paul returned to settle at Jerusalem. It is possible that its Jewish leaders, having been impressed by his remarkable talents and enthusiastic devotion to Judaism, had summoned him to take part in, or lead, that opposition to Christianity, to which events were daily more irrevocably committing them. It is almost certain, also, that to facilitate his operations he was at this time nominated to a seat in the Sanhedrin, which enabled him to give his vote against the followers of Jesus (Acts 26:10).

His first impressions about the followers of 'the Way', as the early disciples were termed, were wholly unfavourable. It seemed to him sheer madness to suppose that the crucified Nazarene could be the long-looked-for Messiah, or that he had risen from the dead. He therefore threw himself into the breach and took the lead in disputing with Stephen, who had just been raised to office in the developing church; and, not content with the conservative and timid attitude that the apostles had preserved for some five years, was now leading an aggressive and forward policy.

## 2   The burden of Stephen's testimony

It was the first attempt to read the story of God's dealings with Israel in the light of Christ; the earliest commentary on the Old Testament by the New; the fragmentary draft of the Epistle to the Hebrews. His eyes were the first that were opened to see that the old covenant was becoming old, and was almost vanishing away, because on the point of being superseded by that better hope, through which all men might draw nigh to God.

Like most who speak God's truth for the first time, Stephen was greatly misunderstood. We gather this from the charges made against him by the false witnesses, whom the Sanhedrin bribed. They accused him of uttering blasphemous words against Moses, of speaking against the temple and the law, of declaring that Jesus of Nazareth would destroy the temple, and change customs delivered by Moses. And as we attentively follow his argument, we can see how it was that these impressions had been caused.

He spoke of the God of glory; of the great ones of the past as 'our fathers'; of the angel that spoke at Sinai; and the living oracles of Scripture. And yet it is undeniable that he saw with undimmed vision that Jesus of Nazareth must change the customs that Moses delivered, and lead his church into more spiritual aspects of truth.

## 3   His martyrdom

We know little of Stephen's life. It was more than probable, as we have already said, that he knew Jesus in his earthly life, for he instantly recognized him in the heavenly vision. Surely he must have seen him die, for the traits of his dying beauty moulded his own last hours. How meekly to bear his cross; to plead for his murderers with a divine charity; to breathe his departing spirit into unseen hands; to find in death the gate of life, and amid the horror of a public execution the secret of calm and peace – all these were rays of light caught from the cross where his Master had poured out his soul to death.

This, too, powerfully affected Paul. That light on the martyr's face; that evident glimpse into the unseen Holy; those words; that patience and forgiveness; that peace which wrapped his mangled body, crushed and bleeding, as he fell asleep – he could never forget them. Not only did he mould his own great speeches on the model of that never-to-be-forgotten address; not only did those conceptions of the spiritual nature of Christ's kingdom affect his whole after teaching and ministry years later, but the very light that radiated from that strong, sweet, noble character seemed to have been absorbed by his spirit, to be radiated forth again in much pateince, in afflictions, in necessities, in distresses, in strifes, in tumults, in pureness, in knowledge, in longsuffering, in kindness, in the Holy Spirit, in love unfeigned.

The blood of the martyrs is the seed of the church.

The power of the persecutor is overcome by the patience of his victims. Saul, at whose feet witnesses lay down their clothes, is catching up and assuming the mantle of the departing prophet and saint.

# 3

# A Light From Heaven

## *Acts 26:13*

If the importance of events can be estimated by the amount of space given in Scripture to their narration, the arrest placed by the risen Lord on the career of Saul of Tarsus must take the second place in the story of the New Testament. It is described three times, with great minuteness of detail – first by Luke, and twice by himself – and the narration occupies more space than the story of any other event, except the crucifixion of our Lord.

It was one of the deepest convictions of the apostle during his life that he had veritably and certainly seen the Lord; and was therefore as really empowered to be a witness of his resurrection as any who had lived and travelled with him, beginning from the baptism of John until the day that he was received up. 'Am I not an apostle? have I not seen Jesus Christ our Lord?' he asks (1 Cor. 9:1). And after enumerating the Lord's appearances after his resurrection, he adds, placing that scene on the road to Damascus on a level with the rest, 'Last of all he was seen of me also, as of one born out of due time' (1 Cor. 15:8). Ananias said, 'The Lord, even Jesus, that appeared unto thee in the way as thou camest, hath sent me' (Acts 9:17).

Six days before, Saul had left Jerusalem with a small retinue furnished as his escort by the high priest. The journey was long and lonely, giving time for reflection, of which he had known but little during the crowding events of the previous months. It was high noon. Unlike most travellers, he forbore to spend even an hour in the retirement of his tent for shelter from the downward rays of the sun, piercing like swords, while all the air was breathless with the heat. He was too weary of his own musings, too eager to be at his work.

The goal of the long journey was well in sight. Within an hour or two he would be within the gates and traversing the street called Straight, to deliver his commission to the authorities and to ascertain the best point for commencing proceedings. But suddenly a great light shone around him; and a voice, amid the blaze, unintelligible and inarticulate to his companions, though clear enough to himself, was heard, speaking in the familiar Aramaic, and calling him by name (Acts 26:14).

In the light of that moment the apostle saw many things. It was like a sudden flashlight over an abyss, revealing secret things that had been entirely hidden, or but dimly understood.

### 1   In the glory of that light he became convinced of the truth of Christianity

There was only one thing that could convince him. He had to see this Jesus of Nazareth, whom he knew to have been crucified, living on the other side of death; he had to be able to recognize and establish his identity; he had to hear him speak. Such evidence given to himself would be conclusive; but nothing less would avail. He saw the Lord in the way, and the Lord spoke to him. He felt instantly that life henceforward had to have a new meaning and purpose, and he had to live to establish the faith of which he had made such determined havoc.

## 2   In the glory of that light he beheld the supreme revelation of God

Nature had told something of God. The heavens had told his glory, and the firmament shown his handiwork. But *this* light was above the brightness of the sun, and made all Nature's wonders pale, as stars at dawn. There is no conceivable method of divine manifestation that can excel the light that shines from the face of Jesus. He beheld the glory of God in the face of Jesus whom he had persecuted.

Would you know God? You must study him in Jesus? We need nothing beyond; there is nothing beyond. In heaven itself we will still behold the light of the glory of God in the face of Jesus. That light shone before the first ray of sunlight gleamed over the abyss; and it will shine when sun, moon, and stars are dark and cold.

## 3   In the revelation of that light Saul of Tarsus saw the real nature of the war that he had been waging against the religion of Jesus

The earliest name for the new sect was *the Way*. It was a pathetic and significant title; these simple souls had found a new and living way to the knowledge and worship of God, consecrated through the rent flesh of him whom their chief priests and rulers had delivered up to be condemned to death.

The young man Saul was exceedingly mad against the pilgrims of the Way. He made life miserable for them, and the word is that which would be used of wild boars uprooting tender vines. He was so angry against them, that when the church at Jerusalem lay desolate, and its garden was torn and trampled into a desert, he pursued the same methods in distant cities, and on the present memorable occasion had received letters to bring those of the Way that were there in bonds to Jerusalem to be punished.

This work of extermination seemed to him part of his religious duty. He owed it to God to stamp out the followers of Jesus. Might not these efforts satisfy for a falling short in respect to the demands of God's law, which now and again forced itself home on his inner consciousness? But, like the Roman soldiers who crucified the Lord, he did not know what he did. 'I was a blasphemer, and persecutor, and injurious: but I obtained mercy, because I did it ignorantly in unbelief' (1 Tim. 1:13).

However, as that light fell on his path, he suddenly awoke to discover that, instead of serving God, he was in collision with him, and was actually uprooting and ravaging that for which the Son of his love had expended tears and blood. In persecuting the sect of the Nazarenes he was persecuting the Son of God. It was a terrible and overwhelming discovery. Somehow his religion had brought him into collision with God in the persons of those who were dear to him; instead of his fanatical zeal being pleasing to God it was grievous to him, and was heaping up wrath against a day of wrath.

## 4    That light also revealed the inadequacy of his religious life

He had lived out all that he thought to be right. But of late he had been compelled to confess to a dull sense of uneasiness and dissatis-faction. He studiously fought against it by immersing himself more sedulously than ever in the work of persecution; yet there it was.

Two cases further instigated this uneasiness. First, he felt that his religion did not satisfy him; it seemed ineffective to curb the imperious demands of sin. Often the good he would do he did not do, while the evil he hated he did. Was there nothing better?

Then it seemed as though these humble disciples of Jesus of Nazareth had something better. The meekness with which they bore their suffering; the light that shone on their dying faces; the prayers for their persecutors, which they offered with their dying breath, evidenced the possession of a secret of which he knew that he was destitute. Yet how could he be the Messiah who had come to such an end! And how absurd it was to say that he had risen, when the Roman sentries had solemnly averred that his body had been stolen by his disciples while they slept.

But all these questionings were brought to a head and con-firmed when suddenly he beheld Jesus of Nazareth enthroned on the right hand of power, and shining with a light above the bright-ness of the sun.

## 5    He now discovered the source of his uneasiness of heart and conscience

He now saw that these strivings were the prickings of the great

Husbandman's goad, by which he had long been attempting to lead him to undertake that life work that had been prepared for him from the foundation of the world. From now on he was not to do his own prompting, but God's; not to be clothed in his own righteousness, but in God's; not to oppose the Nazarene, but to take his yoke to bear his burden, to do his will.

## 6   That light also revealed to him the course of his future life

He was from this day on to be a minister and a witness of those things that he had seen, and of those in which Christ would still appear to him.

It was enough. He meekly asked what he must do. And in answer, he was told to take the next step, which lay just before him, and allow himself to be led unto the city.

And then there arose before him in a flash on the high road, and in fuller development during the three days' retirement in the house of Judas, the Lord's ideal of his life – that he should be sent to Jew and Gentile; that by his simple witness he would be used to open blind eyes; that men might turn from darkness to light, from the power of Satan to God. That concept moulded his life, lingered always in his memory, and formed the basis of one of his noblest outbursts (Col. 1). He felt that he had been apprehended; he realized something of the purpose for which he had been apprehended; and with patient faith he resolved, so far as in him lay, to apprehend it.

How could he be other than obedient? As a token of his meek submission, he allowed himself to be led by the hand into the city, which he had expected to enter as an inquisitor; and bent low to receive instruction from one of those simple-hearted believers whom he had expected to drag captive to Jerusalem. Such are the triumphs of the grace of God, and in his case it was shown to be exceedingly abundant.

4

# The Emergence of the Life Purpose

*Acts 22:17–21*

At the beginning of his Christian career, the apostle felt strongly drawn to minister to his own people. He was a Hebrew, and the son of Hebrews. What was the meaning of his having been cradled and nourished in the heart of Judaism, except that he might better understand and win Jews? Did not his training in the strictest sect of their religion, and at the feet of Gamaliel, give him a special claim on those who held 'that jewel of the law' in special reverence and honour?

But he was destined to discover that his new-found Master had other purposes for his life, and that he had been especially pre-pared and called to preach *among the Gentiles* the unsearchable riches of Christ, and make *all men* see the fellowship of the mystery which from all generations had been hid in God.

## 1  Paul's cherished life

*a. During his sojourn in the Sinaitic peninsula*  we may well believe that his soul turned toward his people with ardent desire. Was he not an Israelite, of the seed of Abraham, of the tribe of Benjamin; and could he be indifferent to the needs of his brothers and sisters according to the flesh? That the law given from Sinai had been fulfilled and re-edited in the holy life of Jesus of Nazareth; that the sacrifices, offered on those sands, had pointed to the death of the cross; and that the fire which burned in the bush had also shone on his face – to teach all this, and much more, and to lead his people from the desert wastes of Pharisaism to the heavenly places of which Canaan was the type, was the hope and longing of his heart. What work could be more congenial to his tastes and attitudes than this?

*b. On his return to Damascus* he at once began his crusade in the synagogues. 'Straightway,' we are told, 'he preached Christ in the synagogues, that he is the Son of God. But all that heard him were amazed. . . But Saul increased the more in strength, and confounded the Jews which dwelt at Damascus, proving that this is very Christ' (Acts 9:20, 22). How encouraged he was by these early successes!

But the vision was soon overcast. So violent was the hatred with which he was regarded by his fellow countrymen, that he was in imminent danger of his life. The gates were watched day and night, that he might be killed if he endeavoured to escape. And finally he was lowered under cover of night by a basket over the city wall.

*c. Still, however, his purpose was unchanged.* He went up to Jerusalem with the intention of seeing Peter. But in this he would probably have failed had it not been for the intervention of Barnabas who, according to an old tradition, had been his fellow student, educated with himself at the feet of Gamaliel. Through his good offices he was brought into contact with Peter and James. A blessed time followed. He was with them, and was especially engaged in holy and loving fellowship with Peter, the acknowledged leader of the church.

It is surely an innocent use of the imagination to think of these two conversing of the great past. On one occasion their theme would be the Lord's early ministry in Galilee, so closely associated with Peter's opening manhood; on another, the discourses and scenes of the last hours before his crucifixion; on another, the precious death and burial, the glorious Resurrection and Ascension, and the appearances of the forty days. 'Tell me all you can remember of the Master,' would be the frequent inquiry of the new disciples of him who had been so specially privileged as a witness of that mystery of love.

But Saul had other business in those happy days. He again sought the synagogues. 'He spake and disputed against the Grecian Jews.' How well he could understand the passion with which his statements were received; but how skilfully would he drive home the goad, which had at last compelled his own surrender! But here also his efforts were met by rebuffs: 'They went about to slay him.'

Yet in spite of coldness and aversion, he clung tenaciously to his cherished purpose. He had great sorrow and unceasing pain in his heart; he could have wished himself anathema from Christ for his kinsmen according to the flesh.

In a similar manner we have all cherished our life purposes. Only very slowly have we yielded and accepted the inevitable. Then suddenly we have awakened to discover that while we were desiring to do one thing, God was leading us to do another.

## 2   The closing door

It began to close at Damascus; it closed still further when persecution arose at Jerusalem: but the final act was as Saul was praying in the temple.

As he knelt in prayer in some quiet spot, he saw him whom his soul loved and sought. And the risen Lord gave clear and unmistakable directions. 'I saw him saying unto me, Make haste, and get thee quickly out of Jerusalem: for they will not receive thy testimony concerning me' (Acts 22:18).

Saul, as we have seen, did not willingly accept this as the ultimatum, and still argued that Jerusalem would afford the most suitable sphere for his ministry. But all debate was at last summarily closed by the words, 'Depart: for I will send thee far hence unto the Gentiles.'

Ah, Saul! you have argued, and strived, and tried to carry your way. The Lord loves you too well to yield to you. Some day you will come to see that he was doing better for you than you knew, and was sending you into yet a wider and more productive sphere of service.

## 3   The opened door

So the disciples brought the hunted preacher down to Cæsarea, and sent him forth to Tarsus; and not improbably he resumed his tent making there, content to await the Lord's will and bidding. But the years passed slowly. Possibly four or five were spent in comparative obscurity and neglect. That he worked for Christ in the immediate vicinity of his home is almost certain, as we shall see; but the word of the Lord awaited fulfilment.

At last one day he heard a voice saying in the doorway, 'Does Saul live here?' And in another moment the familiar face of his old college friend was peering in on him, with a glad smile of recognition. Then the story was told of the marvellous outbreak of God's work in Antioch, and Barnabas pleaded with him to return to help him gather in the whitening harvest of the first great Gentile city that the gospel had moved. 'And he brought him unto Antioch. And it came to pass, that a whole year they assembled themselves with the church, and taught much people.'

# 5

# The Apostle of the Gentiles

## *Rom. 11:13*

It is probable that during his years of quiet work in Cilicia and Syria, Saul of Tarsus was being led with increasing clearness to apprehend God's purpose in his life – that he should be the apostle of the Gentiles. The vision in the temple had culminated in the words, 'Depart: for I will send thee far hence unto the Gentiles' (Acts 22:21). Until now Judaism had been the only door into Christianity; from now on the door of faith was to stand wide open to Gentiles also, without circumcision. Some suggestion of this is furnished by his own lips. But still the true direction of his life was hardly discovered until circumstances transpired that will now demand our notice.

### 1  Summoned to Antioch

Halfway through Luke's narrative the centre of interest shifts from the mother church at Jerusalem to one that had been founded shortly before the time we are describing, in the gay, frivolous, busy, and beautiful city of Antioch. It was an emporium of trade, a meeting place for the Old World and the New. It is forever famous in Christian annals because a number of unordained and unnamed disciples fleeing from Jerusalem in the face of Saul's persecution, dared to preach the gospel to Greeks, and to gather the converts into a church, in entire disregard of the initial rite of Judaism. There, also, the disciples of 'the Way' were first called Christians. From Antioch went the first missionary expedition for the evangelization of the world. In postapostolic days it was famous as the see of the great bishop, saint, and martyr, Ignatius.

It was left to a handful of fugitive, Hellenistic Jews, men of Cyprus and Cyrene, to break through the barriers of the centuries, and to begin preaching the Lord Jesus to the Greeks at Antioch. Instantly the divine Spirit honoured their word, gave testimony to the word of God's grace, and a great number believed and turned to the Lord (Acts 11:19–21).

As soon as tidings of these novel proceedings reached Jerusalem, the church sent Barnabas, who was himself a Cypriot, to make inquiries and report. His verdict was definite and reassuring. He had no hesitation in affirming that it was a definite work of God's grace; and he carried on the work that had been inaugurated with such success that 'much people was added unto the Lord'.

His success, however, only added to the perplexity and difficulty of the situation, and he found himself face to face with a great problem. The Gentiles were pressing into the church, and taking their places on an equality with Jews at the Lord's Supper and love feasts, an action that the more conservative Jews greatly resented. The single-hearted man was hardly able to cope with the problem. But he remembered that at his conversion his old friend and fellow student had been especially commissioned to preach to the Gentiles; and he departed to Tarsus to seek Saul, and brought him to Antioch. 'And it came to pass, that a whole year they assembled themselves together with the church, and taught much people' (Acts 11:26).

But this year's experience at Antioch was of the utmost consequence to Saul. He learned from Barnabas the conclusion to which the church at Jerusalem had come, on hearing Peter's recital of God's dealings with Cornelius and his household (11:18). God made no distinctions; why should he? All the while Paul's horizon was broadening, his confidence increasing, his concept of God's purposes deepening, and he was formulating the gospel that he afterward preached among them (Gal. 2:2).

We need not linger over his brief visit to Jerusalem at the end of his year's ministry at Antioch, to carry alms from the Gentile Christians to their suffering Jewish brethren. On this occasion he does not seem to have met the apostles, who probably had withdrawn from Jerusalem to avoid the murderous hate of Herod (Acts 12); and the gift of the church at Antioch was therefore left with the elders of the mother church.

## 2   Set apart by the Holy Spirit

It was a momentous hour in the history of the church when, on the return of Barnabas and Paul from Jerusalem, they met, with three others, for a season of fasting and prayer. What was the immediate reason for this special session we cannot say; but it is significant that the three prophets and two teachers represented between them five different countries. Were they yearning after their own people, and wistful to offer them the gospel, as they now saw they might offer it, apart from the trammels and restraints of Judaism? We cannot tell. That, however, was the birth of modern missions. The Holy Ghost, Christ's Vicar, the Director and Administrator of the church, bade the little group set apart two out of their number to a mission that he would unfold to them, as they dared to step out in obedience to his command.

In Cyprus, to which they were first attracted, because Barnabas was connected with it through his birth and estate, though they proclaimed the word of God from one end to the other in the synagogues of the Jews, they had no fruit until the Roman governor called them before him, and sought to hear their message, which after hearing he believed.

After landing on the mainland Paul, contrary to the judgment of John Mark, struck up from the seacoast to the far-reaching tablelands of the interior, four thousand feet above sea level, with the evident intention of establishing churches on the great trade route that ran through Asia Minor from Tarsus to Ephesus. What might not be the result for East and West, if this great mutual bridge were to become a highway for the feet of the Son of God! But there the same experience awaited him.

The Jews in Antioch and Pisidia refused, while the Gentiles welcomed them. Indeed he was compelled to turn publicly from his own countrymen, and hold up the gospel as light and salvation to those whom the prophet described as at the uttermost end of the earth. Then it was that the word of the Lord spread throughout all the region.

At Iconium, where they fled before a persecution that made it unsafe to remain in Antioch, they again found the malice of the Jews so persistent that they were driven into the Gentile cities and district of Lycaonia, where there were probably no synagogues at all. There, too, they preached the gospel, and made many disciples.

Everywhere it was the Jewish element that was obstructive and implacable; while the Gentiles, when left to themselves, received them and their message with open arms. His love was not abated. How could it be? Were they not his brethren, his kinsmen according to the flesh? But he had to follow the divine plan.

Probably Paul's greatest experience of this journey was his first visit to the warm-hearted Galatians, whose country is probably referred to in the vague allusion of Acts 14:24. In any case, his insistence in his epistle that he had preached to them the gospel as he had received it direct and undiluted from Christ, compels us to locate his first acquaintance with them at this time, and before that memorable visit to Jerusalem, to which we shall refer presently, and in which he consulted the apostles concerning the gospel he proclaimed (Acts 15; Gal. 2). It is probable that he was detained among them by a painful attack of his habitual malady, aggravated by climatic changes, or malaria. 'Ye know,' he says, 'how through infirmity of the flesh I preached the gospel unto you at the first. And my temptation which was in my flesh ye despised not, nor rejected' (Gal. 4:13–14). So far from rejecting him on this account, his sorrows and afflictions only touched them more and bound them to him. 'I bear you record,' he says, 'that, if it had been possible, ye would have plucked out your own eyes and given them to me' (v. 15).

His success among this affectionate people was remarkable,

and still further deepened the impression that he had to bend his strength to the salvation of the Gentiles, who cause had been laid on his heart at the hour of his conversion.

## 3   His apostolate recognized by the apostles

We do not propose to add anything to the discussion in which so much has been urged on either side, as to the time when the visit to Jerusalem, referred to in Galatians 2, took place. We fall back on the more generally received view that Galatians 2 refers to the visit mentioned in Acts 15, when he was sent as a deputation from Antioch to Jerusalem to obtain the view of the apostles on the admission of Gentiles into the church.

Paul sought the opinion of those in repute among the apostles on his teaching, lest by any means he should be running, or had run, in vain. In the course of several interviews it became increasingly evident to James, Peter, and John, that their former persecutor had received a divine commission to the Gentiles. They realized that he had been entrusted with the gospel of the uncircumcision. The responsible leaders of the mother church would not help perceiving the grace that was given to him; and finally they gave to him the right hand of fellowship, that he should go to the Gentiles, while they went to the circumcision.

This was the further and final confirmation of the purpose that had been forming in his heart. He never failed to begin his work in any place by an honest endeavour to save some of his own flesh; but he always realized that his supreme stewardship was to those who were called uncircumcision by that which was called circumcision in the flesh made by hands.

Surely, then, it is befitting that the church that bears his name should stand in the heart of the greatest Gentile city of the age, and bear the emblem of the death of Christ above its smoke and turmoil.

# 6

# More Than a Conqueror

*Rom. 8:36–37*

It was toward the close of Paul's third missionary journey. About three years before, he had left the Syrian Antioch for the third time, after a stay of some duration (Acts 18:23). His eager spirit could not rest amid the comparative comfort and ease of the vigorous church life that was establishing itself there, but yearned with tender solicitude for his converts throughout the region of Galatia and Phrygia. He therefore again passed the Cilician Gates, traversed the bleak tablelands of the upper or highland country, establishing all the disciples, and working toward the Roman province of Asia. This lay to the southwest, on the seaboard. He had been previously forbidden to enter it (16:6); but his steps were now as clearly led to it as they had formerly been restrained. Thus does our sovereign Lord withhold his servants from the immediate fulfilment of their dreams, that they may return to them again when the time is ripe.

It was to redeem a pledge he had solemnly made that the apostle at last came down to Ephesus. He had spent one Sabbath day there previously, on his way from Corinth to Jerusalem. On that occasion his ministry had so deeply interested the Jews, that they had urged him to stay for a longer period; but this being impossible, on account of the necessity of hastening to Jerusalem to fulfil his vow, he said, 'I will return again to you, if the Lord will.' It was in fulfilment of that promise that the apostle now visited the metropolis of Asia the Less.

A good deal had happened in the interval. Apollos, the eloquent Alexandrian, had visited the city, had met there Paul's friends, Aquila and Priscilla, who were awaiting their fellow worker's return. By them he had been led into a clear appreciation of the truth, in consequence of which his ministry had become more fruitful, both in helping those who had believed, and powerfully confuting the Jews.

But Apollos had now left for Corinth, and Paul arrived to take up and extend the work so auspiciously begun. He probably but dimly realized as he entered Ephesus how long he would remain, or the far-reaching results of his residence.

As a matter of fact it was a conflict from first to last. 'I have fought with beasts at Ephesus,' was his comment after it was all over.

## 1   The battlefield

There were several difficulties to be encountered. In the first place there was the pressure of the strange, eager mass of human beings, whose interests, aims, and methods of thought were so foreign to his own. But, besides, there was the vast system of organized idolatry that centered in the temple of Diana. Her image was said to have fallen from Jupiter (possibly a meteorite), and it was enshrined in a temple, counted to be one of the wonders of the world. The magnificence of uncalculated wealth, the masterpieces of human art, the fame of splendid ceremonials, the lavish gifts of emperors and kings, the attendance and service of thousands of priests and priestesses, combined to give it an unrivalled eminence of influence and prestige. Sooner might some humble Protestant missionary working in a back street of Rome expect to dim the magnificence of St Peter's or diminish the attendance of its vast congregations, as Paul hope that his residence in Ephesus could have any effect whatever on the worship of Diana.

In connection with the temple, a great trade in amulets and charms thrived. Each individual in the vast crowds that came up to worship at the shrine was eager to carry back some memento of his visit. What the trade in strong drink is among ourselves, that was the business in these miniature shrines manufactured by Demetrius and his fellow craftsmen. How impossible it seemed that one man, in three years, employing only moral and spiritual weapons, could make any difference to this ancient and extensive craft!

But still further, Ephesus was deeply infected with the black arts of the exorcist, the magician, and the professor of cabalistic mysteries. Even the converts to Christianity found it hard to divest themselves of their former association with these practices, and treasured their books greatly. It is no child's play to turn a nation of savages from their confidence in witchcraft and medicine men to sane views of life and divine providence.

But perhaps Paul's most inveterate foe was the Jewish synagogue, entrenched in ancient prejudices and persistent disbelief. They were hardened and disobedient, speaking evil of 'the Way'.

Such were the giant obstacles that confronted the humble tentmaker as he settled down to his trade in company with Aquila and Priscilla. But greater was he who was for him than all who there were against him.

## 2   Let us verify this assertion

Let us turn to the Acts of the Apostles, and ask if Paul was indeed more than conqueror. The answer is unmistakable. After three months' conflict with the Jews in their synagogue, the apostle was driven to the course he was wont to adopt under similar circumstances – he moved his disciples to the schoolhouse of one Tyrannus, and taught there daily, as soon as noon was past, and a break was given alike to the schoolmaster and the artisan. In consequence of this ministry, 'all they which dwelt in Asia heard the word of the Lord Jesus, both Jews and Greeks' – a very strong statement, when we bear in mind the population of that crowded province.

The trade in amulets and charms fell off so seriously that the craftsmen realized that unless they did something about it their gains would be at an end. The magicians and exorcists were utterly baffled and confounded by the much greater miracles that were wrought through Paul; so much so that the handkerchiefs he used to wipe the sweat from his brow and the aprons he wore at his trade, were made the medium of healing virtue as they were carried from his person to the sick and demon-possessed. So mighty was the impression that Christ had secrets superior to the best contained in their ancient books, that many of them who had believed came confessing and declaring their deeds. And many of those who practised magical arts brought their books together in one of the open squares and burned them in the sight of all. So mightily grew the word of the Lord, and prevailed.

The exorcist Jews also were silenced. The name of Jesus, spoken even by those who did not believe in him, had a power over evil spirits such as no other name exerted; and it had been blasphemously used by strolling Jews, who had taken on themselves to call that sweet and holy name over some who were possessed. But in one notable instance the demon himself had remonstrated, crying, 'Jesus I know, and Paul I know; but who are ye?' (Acts 19:15) and he had leaped on them, and mastered them, so that they fled from the house naked and wounded.

### 3 Let us consider the talisman of victory

If we turn from his outward life to study the diary of this wonderful man who seemed to be alone in his conflicts and victories, we find a pathetic record of his sorrows and trials. We wonder how such a man, under such drawbacks and in face of such opposing forces, could be more than a conqueror.

The only matter about which the apostle, therefore, felt any anxiety was whether anything could occur to cut him off from the living, loving Lord. 'Can anything separate me from the love of Christ?' – that was the only question worth consideration. He is like a man proving every link of the chain on which he is going to swing out over the abyss. Carefully and fervently he has tested all, and is satisfied that none of them can cut him off from the love of God; and since that is so, he is sure that nothing can ever intercept those supplies of the life and strength of God that will avail to make him more than a conqueror.

Oh, blessed love that comes down to use from the heart of Jesus, the essence of the eternal love of God. It is not our love that holds God, but God's that holds us. He will go on loving us forever, so that whatever our difficulties, we will be kept steadfast, unmovable, always abounding in the work of the Lord, and ever more conquerors through him who loved us.

# 7

# 'In a Strait, Betwixt Two'

## *Phil. 1:23*

Paul, on his arrival in Rome, was treated with great leniency. He was permitted to rent a house or apartment in the near neighbourhood of the great Prætorian barracks, and live by himself, the only sign of his captivity being the chain that fastened his wrist to a Roman legionary, the soldiers relieving each other every four or six hours.

There were many advantages in this arrangement. It kept him from the hatred of his people, and gave him a marvellous opportunity to cast the seeds of the gospel into the head of the rivers of population that poured from the metropolis throughout the known world. At the same time, it must have been very irksome. Always to be in the presence of another, and that other filled with Gentile antipathy to Jewish habits and pagan irresponsiveness to Christian fervour; to be able to make no movement without the clanking of his chain, and the consent of his custodian; to have to conduct his conferences, utter his prayers, and indite his epistles, beneath those stolid eyes, or amid brutal and blasphemous interruptions – all this must have been excessively trying to a sensitive temperament like the apostle's. But this also he could do through Christ who strengthened him. And it also helped to further the cause he loved. Many of these brawny veterans became humble, earnest disciples. With a glow of holy joy, he informs the Philippians that his bonds in Christ have become known through the whole Prætorian Guard; and we know that this was the beginning of a movement destined within three centuries to spread throughout the entire army, and compel Constantine to adopt Christianity as the religion of the State.

Three days after his arrival in Rome, Paul summoned to his temporary lodging the leaders of the Jewish synagogues, of which there are said to have been seven, for the 60,000 Jews who were the objects of the dislike and ridicule of the imperial city. At the first interview they cautiously occupied neutral ground, and expressed the wish to hear and judge for themselves concerning the sect that was only known to them as the butt of universal execration. At the second interview, after listening to Paul's explanations and appeals for an entire day, there was the usual division of opinion. 'Some believed the things which were spoken, and some believed not.' His testimony having thus been first offered, according to his invariable practice, to his own people, there was now no further obstacle to his addressing a wider audience. The message of salvation was sent to the Gentiles, and these would certainly hear (Acts 28:28). We are therefore not surprised to be told that for the next two years 'He received all that came in unto him, preaching the kingdom of God, and teaching those things which concern the Lord Jesus Christ, with all confidence, no man forbidding him.'

It might be said of the apostle, as of his Lord, that they came to him from every quarter. Timothy, his son in the faith; Mark, now 'profitable'; Luke, with his quick physician's eye and delicate sympathy; Aristarchus, who shared his imprisonment, that he might have an opportunity of ministering to his needs; Tychicus, from Ephesus, 'the beloved brother and faithful minister in the Lord'; Epaphras, from Colossæ, a 'beloved fellow servant, and faithful minister of Christ', on the behalf of the church there; Epaphroditus, from Philippi, who brought the liberal contributions of the beloved circle, that for so many years had never ceased to remember their friend and teacher; Demas, who had not yet allowed the present to turn him aside from the eternal and unseen – these, and others, are mentioned in the postscripts of his epistles as being with him. Members of the Roman church would always be welcomed, and must have poured into his humble lodging in a perpetual stream; Epænetus and Mary, Andronicus and Junia, Tryphena and Tryphosa, Persis the beloved, and Apelles the approved, must often have resorted to that apartment that was irradiated with the perpetual presence of the Lord. They had come to meet him on his first arrival as far as the Appii Forum and the Three Taverns, and would not be likely to neglect him, now that he was settled among them.

Then what interest would be aroused by the episodes of those two years! The illness of Epaphroditus, who was sick to death; the discovery and conversion of Onesimus, the runaway slave; the writing and dispatching of the epistles, which bear such evident traces of the prison cell.

It is almost certain that Paul was acquitted at his first trial, and liberated, and permitted for two or three years at least to engage again in his beloved work. He was evidently expecting this when, writing to the Philippians, he said: 'I trust in the Lord, that I also myself, too shall come shortly' (2:24). In his letter to Philemon also, he goes so far as to ask that a lodging be prepared for him as he hopes in answer to their prayers. Universal tradition affirms an interspace of liberty between his two imprisonments; and without this hypothesis, it is almost impossible to explain many of the incidental allusions of the Epistles to Timothy and Titus, which cannot refer, so far as we can see, to the period that falls within the compass of Acts.

Once more a free man, Paul would certainly fulfil his intention of visiting Philemon and the church of Colossæ. From there he would make his way to the church at Ephesus. Leaving Timothy behind him with the injunction to command some that they should preach no other gospel than that which they had heard from his lips (1 Tim. 1:3), he travelled onward to Macedonia and Philippi. What a greeting must have been given him there! Lydia and Clement, Euodias and Syntyche, Epaphroditus and the jailor, together with many other fellow workers whose names are in the Book of Life, must have gathered around the minister to that frail, worn body, to be inspired by the heroic soul.

From Philippi he must have passed to other churches in Greece, and among the rest to Corinth. Finally he set sail with Titus for Crete, where he left him to set in order the things that were wanting, and to appoint elders in every city (Titus 1:5). On his return to the mainland he wrote an epistle to Titus, from the closing messages in which we gather that he was about to winter at Nicopolis surrounded by several friends, such as Artemas, Zenas, Tychicus, and Apollos, who were inspired with his own spirit, and were gladly assisting him in strengthening the organization and purifying the teaching in these young churches.

This blessed liberty, however, was cut short. One of the most terrible events in the history of the ancient world – the burning of Rome – took place in the year AD 64; and to divert from himself the suspicion that indicated him as its author, Nero accused the Christians of being the incendiaries. As soon as the fierce flames of the first general persecution broke out, those who were resident in the metropolis, and who must have been well known and dear to the apostle, were seized and subjected to horrible tortures, while a strict search was made throughout the empire for their leaders, the Jews abetting the inquisitors. It was not likely that so eminent a Christian as the apostle would escape.

He was staying for a time at Troas, in the house of Carpus, where he had arrived from Nicopolis. His arrest was so sudden that he had not had time to gather up his precious books and parchments, which may have included copies of his epistles, a Hebrew Bible, and some early copies of the sayings of our Lord; or to wrap around him the cloak that had been his companion in many a wintry storm. From there he was hurried to Rome.

A little group of friends accompanied him, with faithful tenacity, in this little sad journey: Demas and Crescens, Titus and Tychicus, Luke and Erastus. But Erastus stayed at Corinth, through which the little band may have passed; and Trophimus fell ill at Miletus and had to be left there, as the Roman guard would brook no delay. So, for the second time, Paul reached Rome.

But the circumstances of his second imprisonment differed widely from those of the first. Then he had his own hired house; now he was left in close confinement, and tradition points to the Mamertine prison as the scene of his last weeks or months. Then he was easily accessible; now Onesiphorus had to seek him out very diligently, and it took some courage not to be ashamed of his chain. Then he was the centre of a large circle of friends and sympathizers; now the winnowing fan of trouble had greatly thinned their ranks, while others had been dispatched on distant missions. 'Only Luke is with me,' is the rather sad expression of the elderly man's loneliness. But now, as he was reviewing his career, he could say humbly and truthfully, 'I have fought the good fight, I have finished my course, I have kept the faith; henceforth there is laid up for me a crown of righteousness.'

What were the following processes of Paul's trial? How long was he kept in suspense? Did Timothy arrive in time to see him, and to be with him at the last supreme moment? What was the exact method of his martyrdom? To these questions there is no certain reply. Tradition points to a spot, about three miles from Rome, on the Ostian road where, at the stroke of the headsman's axe, he was beheaded, and his spirit leaving its frail tenement, entered the house not made with hands, eternal in the heavens. If Christ arose to receive Stephen, may he not also have stood up to welcome Paul? Again he beheld the face that had looked down on him from the opened heavens at his conversion, and heard the voice that had called him by his name. His long-cherished wish of being 'with Christ' was gratified, and he found it 'far better' than he had ever thought.

As he had kept Christ's deposit, so Christ had kept his. And as he gave in the account of his stewardship, who can doubt that the Lord greeted him with, 'Well done, good and faithful servant, enter thou into the joy of thy Lord.' What a festal welcome he must have received from thousands whom he had helped turn from darkness to light, from the power of Satan to God, and who were now to become his crown of rejoicing in the presence of the Lord! These from the highlands of Galatia, and those from the seaboard of Asia Minor. These from Judaistic prejudice, and those from the depths of Gentile depravity and sin. These from the degraded slave populations, and those from the ranks of the high-born and educated.